CIFERAE

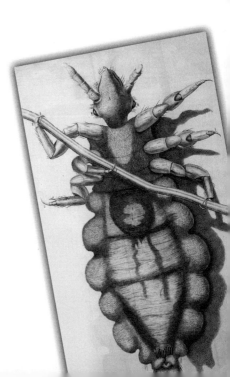

POSTHUMANITIES

Cary Wolfe, Series Editor

CIFERAE

POSTHUMANITIES 19

A Bestiary in Five Fingers

TOM TYLER

University of Minnesota Press   MINNEAPOLIS : LONDON

The ornamental capitals at the beginning of each chapter were designed in 1519 by the printer Jacques Sacon of Lyons, France.

See pages 293–95 for information on previously published material in this book.

Published by the University of Minnesota Press
111 Third Avenue South, Suite 290
Minneapolis, MN 55401-2520
http://www.upress.umn.edu

Printed in the United States of America on acid-free paper

The University of Minnesota is an equal-opportunity educator and employer.

LIBRARY OF CONGRESS CATALOGING-IN-PUBLICATION DATA
Tyler, Tom, 1968–
    Ciferae : a bestiary in five fingers / Tom Tyler.
    (Posthumanities ; 19)
    Includes bibliographical references and index.
    ISBN 978-0-8166-6543-3 (hc : alk. paper) — ISBN 978-0-8166-6544-0 (pb : alk. paper)
1. Knowledge, Theory of. 2. Animals—Miscellanea.
3. Bestiaries. I. Title.
    BD161.T95 2012
    128—dc23

                                                    2012000011

18 17 16 15 14 13 12   10 9 8 7 6 5 4 3 2 1

THE WORD "BEASTS"

should properly be used about lions, leopards, and tigers, wolves, and foxes, dogs, apes and others which rage about with tooth and claw, with the exception of snakes. Further, they are beasts because of the violence with which they rage, and are known as "wild" (FERUS) because they are accustomed to freedom by nature and are driven (FERANTUR) by their own wishes. For their wills are free, and they wander hither and thither, and where the spirit (ANIMUS) will lead them, there they roam.

T. H. WHITE

The Book of Beasts: Being a Translation from a Latin Bestiary of the Twelfth Century (translation modified)

CIFERAE

VALLATUS INDICIBUS
ATQUE SICARIIS

Surrounded by Informers and Assassins

9

RIDETO MULTUM ET DIGITUM
PORRIGITO MEDIUM

Laugh Loudly and Flip Them the Bird

77

MEDICO
TESTICULI ARIETINI

On the Ring Finger a Ram's Testicles

109

A Bestiary in Five Fingers

Acknowledgments

No work is accomplished entirely MANU PRO-PRIA, and it is my pleasure to extend gratitude and appreciation to all those who have had a hand in my own. I thank my family, especially my parents, Monica and Richard Tyler; without each of them this would have been a very different book, and without both of them it would have been altogether impossible. Many thanks go to my monkey wife, Jane Harris, who provided unvarying support and encouragement over the years. Steve Baker and Barbara Engh were instrumental in shaping the project throughout its development. Ron Broglio and Cary Wolfe gave me invaluable advice on the entire manuscript, and welcome feedback on individual chapters and sections came from Matthew Calarco, Beverley Clack, Jennifer A. Clack, David L. Clark, Henry Fisher, Derek Gatherer, Simon Glendinning, Colin Groves, Christopher Hookway, Jonathan Kingdon, Penny Lee, Jill Marsden, Robert McKay, Robert W. Mitchell, Richard Nash, Anat Pick, Constan-tine Sandis, Keith Thomson, and several anonymous readers.

Many people, too numerous to list here, were most generous in answering my often peculiar questions on their areas of expertise, from bioluminescent fish to ophidian skin shedding, from Wittgenstein's idle wheels to discourteous hand gestures. To three individuals, who especially suffered from my interminable requests, I owe particular thanks and, I fear, apologies: Danielle Kasprzak chased down endless animal images, as well as the permission to print them in this book; Jan Shirley met all my unreasonable bibliographic demands; and Ika Willis answered my unending questions about Greek and Latin translations.

I thank Kathy Delfosse for her careful copy editing, and Juliet MacDonald, who provided the elegant hand illustrations that open each chapter. To everyone who offered a helping hand, including those I have failed to mention here, I am extremely grateful.

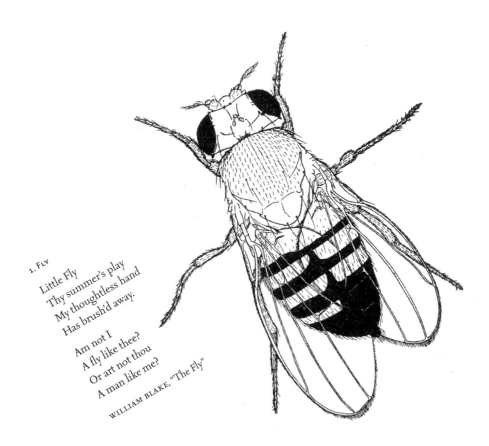

1. FLY

Little Fly
Thy summer's play
My thoughtless hand
Has brush'd away.

Am not I
A fly like thee?
Or art not thou
A man like me?

WILLIAM BLAKE, "The Fly"

Black-bellied dew-lover (*Drosophila melanogaster*), a species of
fruit fly, in T. H. Morgan, C. B. Bridges, and A. H. Sturtevant,
Contributions to the Genetics of Drosophila Melanogaster, 39.

Prelude

—What is your aim in philosophy?
—To shew the fly the way out of the fly-bottle.

LUDWIG WITTGENSTEIN, *Philosophical Investigations*

A fly-bottle is an item of laboratory equipment used in the study of fruit flies (Drosophila). It is not especially sophisticated, and in fact half-pint milk bottles were often used in the early days of research. The science writer Jonathan Weiner has suggested, nonetheless, that this humble bottle is "one of the most significant legacies that the science of the twentieth century bequeaths to the twenty-first."[1] He describes how, by studying fruit flies, early geneticists first began to fathom the complicated connections between a creature's genes and its behavior. A mutant fly, bred in one of these makeshift bottles by the biologist Thomas Hunt Morgan early in 1910, marked the first success in a lengthy experimental process that would finally discover the basic elements of inheritance. The fly-bottle is, Wiener argues, "a great gift and disturbance that human knowl-edge conveys to the night thoughts and day-to-day life of the third millennium."[2]

Ludwig Wittgenstein saw his work as a kind of therapy. Philosophy has a propensity to generalize, to draw false analogies, to misuse everyday words, and to abuse language in colorful but ultimately fruitless ways. By diagnosing the range and subtlety of this mistreatment, Wittgenstein hoped to ease the "mental cramp" that it so often engenders.[3] Only by untangling the misconceptions that lie behind seemingly intractable questions can we hope to move forward, to relieve ourselves of endless internal conflict, to free the **FLY** from the bottle. Socrates, Wittgenstein suggests, was prone to just such a generalizing weakness. In his dialogue with young Theaetetus, he sought to examine the nature of that gift and disturbance that is human knowledge. Wittgenstein's complaint is not with the stated objective of Socrates' inter-

1. Weiner, *Time, Love, Memory*, 6.
2. Ibid., 7.
3. Wittgenstein, *Blue and Brown Books*, 1.

I

rogation, but with the means by which he carries it out. "When Socrates asks the question, 'what is knowledge?' he does not even regard it as a preliminary answer to enumerate cases of knowledge."[4] Indeed, Socrates explicitly rejects Theaetetus's first attempt to provide an answer by specifying particular examples of knowledge, such as the sciences of geometry, astronomy, harmony, and arithmetic, or the practical crafts of the cobbler and carpenter.[5] Examples will never manage to convey what knowledge itself is, Socrates says, and are, moreover, "an interminable diversion."[6] He encourages Theaetetus to propose, instead, succinct definitions and considers, in turn, the suggestion that knowledge is a matter of perception, that it can be equated with true belief, and finally that it is true belief with the addition of an explanatory account. Theaetetus is persuaded that each of these possibilities is wanting and, though the exchange clarifies for him the paucity of his understanding, no conclusions are reached. Despite the older philosopher's help with his labors, we can only imagine that Theaetetus's cramps remain.

At the dialogue's close, he is left buzzing round an epistemological bottle of Socrates' making, as the latter sets out for the courthouse to answer charges of corrupting the youth and failing to worship the Athenian gods.

Socrates' own target in the early part of the *Theaetetus* is the sophist Protagoras. Only fragments of Protagoras's work survive, recounted in the writings of later commentators, but it is clear that he opposed realist accounts of knowledge, Platonic or otherwise, and subscribed to a form of relativism or, perhaps better, pragmatism. The opening words of his lost book *Truth* comprise his most famous assertion: "Man is the measure of all things."[7] Socrates takes exception to the crude phenomenal subjectivism that Protagoras seems to imply. "I don't see why he does not say . . . that a pig or a **DOG-FACED BABOON** or some still stranger creature of those that have sensations is the measure of all things."[8] Protagoras's precise meaning, presumably elaborated in the full text, has been the subject of much discussion,[9] but his basic thesis has endured, thrived even, down the centuries. The contention that humanity cannot know the world except by means of human aptitudes and abilities, that human being will inescapably, unavoidably be the measure of all things, has been formulated in a variety of captivating ways, by a good many philosophers, thinkers, and theorists. It is with this claim, regarding the nature of knowledge and of human being, that we will be concerned.

4. Ibid., 20.

5. Plato, *Theaetetus*, 146c–d.

6. Plato, *Theaetetus*, 147c, as translated in Chappell, "Plato on Knowledge," §5.

7. πάντων χρημάτων μέτρον ἐστὶν ἄνθρωπος, cited in Plato, *Theaetetus*, trans. Fowler, 152a; see also Sextus Empiricus, *Outlines of Pyrrhonism*, 131 (1.32.216). On translating ἄνθρωπος (anthrōpos), which is perhaps not quite as gender neutral as he suggests, see Schiappa, *Protagoras and Logos*, 131n4.

8. Plato, *Theaetetus*, trans. Fowler, 161c.

9. For example, Aristotle, *Metaphysics*, 1678 (11.6.1062b); Sextus Empiricus, *Outlines of Pyrrhonism*, 131–32 (1.32.216–19); Versenyi, "Protagoras' Man-Measure Fragment"; Schiappa, *Protagoras and Logos*, 117–33.

Is one obliged to assert, as has so often been suggested, that humans are stopped up, as if within a bleak, restricting container, unable to access the wider world except through the translucent but necessarily distorting sides of their prison? I wish to examine the presumed inevitability of this Protagorean perspective, this epistemological anthropocentrism, and to enquire whether it derives from elements that are intrinsic to the writings of these diverse philosophers or is, rather, an extraneous, incidental prejudice of those already inclined to hold this position.

Unlike William Blake's thoughtless hand, the fly-bottle represents a concerted effort to curtail the fly's play. Philosophy has long maintained an ambiguous relationship with animals. On the one hand, the animal frequently confronts philosophy as a problem. This is "the animal that philosophy loathes,"[10] disrupting all manner of categories and concepts, a troublesome beast that refuses to fit in.[11] On the other hand, though, philosophy never quite seems to manage without its animals. Time and again, we find a multitude of brutes and beasts crowding into the texts in which they are supposedly unwelcome. We will return in the chapters that follow to the animals who appear under both of these complementary, thoughtless hands. We will meet J. L. Austin's fish and Arthur Schopenhauer's porcupines, Augustine's eagle and Sigmund Freud's wolves, inferred swans and mice, self-absorbed lice, tautological camels,

Thomas Bewick, *Dog-Faced Baboon*, 1790, in Blanche Cirker, ed., *1800 Woodcuts by Thomas Bewick and His School*, plate 31.

2. Dog-Faced Baboon

A key to the success of the primates is superb vision. . . . Even if the primates did not evolve color vision *de novo*, it seems reasonable to believe that they at least elaborated the capacity considerably. Certainly compared to all other mammalian groups, color vision among the primates is a superior capacity, quantitatively and qualitatively. . . . Old World monkeys are likely to be routine trichromats, most having similar if not identical color vision to that of normal human trichromats.

GERALD H. JACOBS, "Color Vision Polymorphisms in New World Monkeys," 45, 64–65.

licentious gulls, and many more of philosophy's overlooked or neglected creatures. Like language, these philosophical animals often find themselves subject to casual or unwitting abuse. Wittgenstein's intention was to free his fly, however, and we will follow his example, or, better, his many concrete *examples*, by attempting to treat our own, particular, individual animals with compassion. There are many ways that we might interrogate the question of humanity's measur-

10. Krell, *Daimon Life*, 68.
11. Glendinning, "From Animal Life to City Life," 19.

ing, but it is with the help of these marginal animals, the flies and pigs and dog-faced baboons, and all manner of still stranger creatures, that we will approach it. We would do well, then, to allow them a free hand, and to indulge that play, mischievous though it often proves, for which they are known.

The first chapter is concerned with the concept of anthropocentrism and the problems raised by employing animals to address it. I examine Georges Bataille's assertion, illustrated by means of goshawk and hen, that humanity, unlike eternally immanent animality, cannot help but transcend the world, always positing distinct, durable objects. In discussing Martin Heidegger's account of disclosive demarcation, denied to the lizard and effected only by means of the unique human hand, I go on to distinguish an evaluative anthropocentrism, conceived in spatial, hierarchical terms, from the temporal, "first-and-foremost," epistemological anthropocentrism with which we will principally be concerned. Four hazards are identified for any undertaking that would put animals to philosophical work. Like Jean Buridan's hungry ass, they are often retained as mere ciphers, placefillers who sustain an argument but remain faceless and interchangeable. Alternatively, they can be found subsumed under an amorphous Animal, an abstract, generalized chimera that lays waste to rigorous thinking. On the other hand, in treating of specific, individual animals, phi-

losophy runs the risk of anthropomorphism— consider Aesop's fickle fox—an alleged disservice to both human and animal. Finally, these same individuals, as didactic exemplars, are in danger of becoming stereotypes, dulling fresh thinking by habitual repetition, as Roland Barthes's educative lion demonstrates. We must be wary, in the chapters that follow, of all these careless modes of taming the animal and attend, where possible, to the unsubstitutable singularity, and indexical import, of disruptive individuals like Jacques Derrida's indecisive but determined cat.

These potential stumbling blocks noted, the task remains to enumerate cases of knowledge, or rather cases that have been made for knowledge. How, then, might we best grasp the tangled questions of epistemology and their supposed anthropocentrism? How should we take in hand Protagoras's claim and marshal the diverse writers who have given voice to it, or, more often, have assumed or implied it, in their discussions of knowledge? Before capturing the Marathonian Bull, or venturing into Hades, the Greek hero Theseus undertook a series of six labors. Setting out from Troezen to Athens, he freed the road from the bandits and miscreants preying on those who used it. He dealt with each in the manner in which they had terrorized travelers: he hunted and slaughtered the man-eating Crommyonian Sow and the hag, Phaia, who kept her; Sciron the Corinthian he kicked into the sea, where swam a monstrous turtle; and so on.

The last of the bandits was named Procrustes, and he had a peculiar means of dispatching his victims. Having offered a night's hospitality to unsuspecting travelers, he would compel them to lay down on a special bed. Those who were too short he would stretch or hammer to fit it, and those too tall he would cut to size. Theseus saw to him as he had the others, though it is not recorded whether he had recourse to a hammer or a saw.[12] In attempting to broach the question of the measure of all things, of knowledge conceived in its broadest sense as perception, true belief, an explanatory account, or something else again, I will employ a frame or schema, perhaps a little rigid like Procrustes', of my own.

In examining the work of the varied epistemologists who populate the following chapters 2 through 4, we will fit their thoughts and theories into three paradigms, under the headings *realism*, *relativism*, and *pragmatism*. Further, these writers can be understood as conceiving their accounts and formulations according to three related qualities of knowledge that cross these paradigms: they have concerned themselves with the ontology of knowledge, which is to say with what it *is*; with the utility of knowledge, which is to say with what it *does*; and with the validity of knowledge, which is to say with what it *claims*. Thus, the works we will discuss explore or exemplify some property of knowledge, addressing it as mediated representation or as concrete practice, as explanation of the world or as the

interpretations of a worldview, as transcendental truth or as partial perspective. The schema here employed is a means of charting a course across uneven ground, of clearing a path, as did Theseus, through treacherous terrain. Any such schema or system inevitably does violence to its subject matter; *every* schema is ultimately a prescriptive, Procrustean frame. The benefits of such an approach are best measured by their effectiveness in facilitating the progress of an undertaking. The challenge, then, will be to ensure that our frame ultimately works for us, as did the bed for Theseus, lest we find ourselves in thrall to our own invention, as happened to Procrustes.

The second chapter addresses the characteristic concerns of epistemological realism. Prompted by those who would claim that "things outside of us" have no more certain an existence than the gorgons and harpies of legend, G. E. Moore was anxious to provide a proof of the external world. His personal attempt to address this scandalous assertion was carried out with his own two hands, though he ended up taking advantage of the several animals who populate his discussion. Karl Popper, meanwhile, characterized objective knowledge as a shared endeavor, produced, refined, and consumed by a busy, bustling community, like the honey of a beehive. Friedrich Nietzsche, however, in his early critique of human knowledge, denied the

---

12. My account of Procrustes' methods is based principally on that of Diodorus of Sicily, *Library of History*, 3: 4–5 (4.59.5). For alternatives, see Graves, *Greek Myths*, 1: 327–32.

very possibility of transcendental truth, whether arrived at by individual or collective means. Dissimulating and self-deceiving humans share with the lowly gnat the pathos of believing themselves to be the center of the universe, forgetting that, like the bird, the worm, and every other living thing, they create for themselves an entirely subjective structure. Human conceptions are cast forth onto the world with the same necessity as the spider spins her webs, neatly arranging it like the compartments of a dovecote. In its efforts to reach the original essences, humanity grasps after the impossible, attempting to hold fast to the back of a tiger. Given Moore's unwitting anthropocentrism and Nietzsche's critique of truth, then, I explore in this chapter the possibility that realism's conception of knowledge always entails a Protagorean perspective.

The third chapter examines epistemological relativism. The same disquiet that troubled Moore had earlier been expressed by Immanuel Kant, and it is to his transcendental idealism that we turn. Concerned to avoid mistreating a goat in his own pursuit of truth, Kant argued that a specific form of sensibility and understanding enables and determines human thought and experience. This digestive system of the mind ensures access only to phenomena, never to noumena: one encounters and can know the appearance of a dog but not the underlying "thing in itself." Kant described man, the sole being on earth in possession of reason, as the "lord of nature," and his Copernican revolution seemed to place the human subject center stage, but he discusses too the varying material and mental composition of reasoning extraterrestrials living on Mercury, Mars, Venus, and elsewhere. His representationalism exhibits an implicit, if ultimately capped, relativism. Ferdinand de Saussure's ox and his bœuf, meanwhile, as well as the dogs who bark quite differently in French and German, help demonstrate the arbitrary and immaterial nature of the linguistic sign. The reciprocal delimitation of thought and sound within diverse languages, exemplified by sheep and mouton, here moves us closer to a true relativism. Finally, an amorous raccoon and an ill-spoken sparrow permit Benjamin Whorf to argue that languages determine experience. Despite Whorf's faith in a fundamental humanism, the Hopi pohko, who may be a dog or may be an eagle, points finally toward a radical linguistic relativism. Given Kant's accounts of human and alien minds and Whorf's hope for a universal human brotherhood, then, I consider in this chapter the possibility that relativism's conception of knowledge rests always on an epistemological anthropocentrism.

The fourth chapter explores the properties of pragmatism. The Theban Sphinx challenged the truth seeker Oedipus with a deadly riddle, whose single answer accorded closely with Protagoras's concern. In contemplating her demand, however, the Sphinx taught Nietzsche to reconsider her questionable questions, and we find that there is, in fact, more than one answer both to her riddle and to the question of truth. Nietzsche pursues in his mature work an evaluative perspectivism, eschewing the lowly outlook of frogs and dusty scholars and seeking always to renew his opinions, like the snake who sheds the skin she has outgrown. During his solitary rambles in the mountains, William James is confronted with a riddle of his own, this time propounded by an elusive squirrel, and he is later shown the way out of the woods by a herd of absent cows. His interest in the practical consequences of one's explanation of the world, in the expediency of one's theories and conjectures, is echoed by Ludwig Boltzmann, whose intention in his own work is to muddy the metaphysicians' ascetic waters by slipping a pike into the complacent carp pond of philosophy. Prompted by a discourteous gesture, once employed to provoke Wittgenstein from his dogmatic slumbers, we next consider Charles Darwin's theory of evolution, but as a meme, a cultural practice shaped and impeded by environmental pressures. It was not his infamous finches but commonplace pigeons who allowed Darwin to demonstrate the malleability of species, whilst communities of enterprising passerines—thieving bluetits and voluble saddlebacks—today exchange memes of their own. Given the riddle of the Sphinx and the suggestion that human minds are composed of memes, then, I examine in this chapter the

possibility that pragmatism's conception of knowledge depends on a first-and-foremost anthropocentrism.

The writings we will consider in these three central chapters thus provide particular examples not of knowledge but of properties of knowledge as it is conceived by three epistemological paradigms. The fifth and final chapter turns to the human being on which matters of anthropocentrism ultimately rest. Heidegger complained that the question, "Who is man?"—a vital, preliminary enquiry before any investigation of "humanization"—has rarely been adequately asked, let alone answered. Michel Foucault, however, suspicious of the supple contradictions of the humanistic theme, insisted that issues of identity are never prior to the formulation of one's questions. Consistently refusing to align or ally himself, he wrote instead to excavate fresh, untraveled tunnels in a Minotaur's labyrinth of his own making, to unearth, in fact, a *new* "we." And so, we examine that distinctive, distinguishing organ, the hand, characterized in the writings of teleologist and evolutionist alike as a mark of human exceptionalism. Charles Bell dismissed the inferior analogues that are the monkey's dextrous tail and the elephant's grasping trunk, whilst Galen laughed at the ape's ludicrous hand, an inadequate, preposterous homologue. Despite the inexhaustible eulogies of Aristotle and Kant, of Anaxagoras and Frederick Engels, however, we find that the perfected human hand, the instrument of instruments, is in truth a rather primitive organ. Considerations and classifications of *anthrōpos* need, ultimately, to take account of heterogeneous, incongruous, even heteroclite modes of narcissistic identification, and we discover, in closing, a new, encompassing, more-than-human "we."

In this philosophical investigation into Protagorean presumption, we will gain no small benefit from the assistance of animals. The creatures put to work by philosophers and thinkers, though they ordinarily go unnoticed or ignored, will, in the pages that follow, nudge their way back into view, all insisting on their own distinctive, individual contributions to the task at hand. In this five-fingered bestiary, no animal will be brushed away. On the contrary, as we seek to unstop our chosen bottle and free the many prisoners from within, we will find that, as Blake suggested, we have more in common with the little fly than is oft supposed.

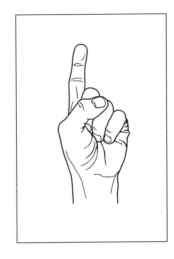

VALLATUS INDICIBUS ATQUE SICARIIS

Surrounded by Informers and Assassins

LIKE WATER IN WATER

uch ink has been spilled addressing the appropriate understanding of "animality" as it bears on the question of anthropocentrism. Georges Bataille takes this as a suitable starting point for the first chapter of his *Theory of Religion*,[2] though he admits from the outset that his account is but a means to an end: "I consider animality from a narrow viewpoint that seems questionable to me, but its value will become clear in the course of the exposition" (17). What concerns us here is the fact that this narrow viewpoint, this reflection on animality and anthropocentrism, is indeed questionable and worth exploring a little. Bataille's treatment is illustrative of a particular tendency amongst philosophers and theorists when dealing with animals' relations to their environments, and it would therefore be profitable to make that tendency clear before we approach the issue of anthropocentrism more fully. I would thus like to consider Bataille's discussion as an exemplar of this philosophical propensity, which is to say, from a narrow viewpoint that perhaps seems questionable but whose value will become clear in the course of my own exposition.

Bataille's contention is that the animal's existence in the world is immanent and immediate (17, 23). Lacking the capacity to distinguish

During the Anglo-Saxon period the forefinger was known as the scythe finger. In the time of King Canute it was the DEMONSTRATORIUS, the finger with which one points or demonstrates, and it has also been called the SAGITTATOR, the finger used to loose an arrow. Not until the fifteenth century did it become known as the forefinger, the "first" finger, perhaps following the Dutch example, voorvinger. Today it is more generally known as the index finger, from the Latin, INDICARE, meaning "to indicate." The index finger is, then, the first finger and the one used to point things out. There seems, in fact, to be a correlation between pointing and language acquisition: at about eleven or twelve months of age, when they first start pointing with their index fingers, babies will begin to use names for objects. Indeed, Ludwig Feuerbach went so far as to suggest that "the index finger shows the way from nothingness to being."[1]

1. Napier, *Hands*, 22–24; Bertelsen and Capener, "Fingers"; Isidore of Seville, *Etymologiarum sive originum*, 11.1.70; F. W. Jones, *Principles of Anatomy*, 8–9, 144–45; Hammond, *Finger Prints*, March 25, 2003; Feuerbach, *Philosophy of the Future*, 3.44.
2. Bataille, *Theory of Religion*, 17–25. Further references are in the text.

The chapter title comes from Cicero, "Pro Murena," 208–9 (24.49).

Elmer Boyd Smith, *Chicken World*.

3. HEN

Chickens, like several other species of bird, have two types of alarm calls, a series of short, narrow band whistles commonly given when they see aerial predators such as hawks, and a pulsed broad-band cackle elicited by ground predators such as dogs or foxes. . . . The cockerels gave significantly fewer aerial alarm calls when alone than when their mate or another familiar female was clearly visible and audible in an adjacent cage. . . . Cockerels also give other calls when food becomes available, and in experiments they called more when presented with preferred foods such as mealworms or peas than for peanuts or inedible nutshells. . . . Experiments certainly support the hypothesis that cockerels are appropriately selective about their use of both alarm calls and food calls according to the nature of their audience.

DONALD R. GRIFFIN, *Animal Minds*, 162–64.

objects, it is unable to discern any difference between itself and whatever surrounds it.

> There is, for the wolf, a continuity between itself and the world. Attractive or distressing phenomena arise before it; other phenomena do not correspond either to individuals of the same species, to food, or to anything attractive or repellent, so

3. Bataille passes over the fact that most animals eat not other animals but, rather, vegetable matter.

that what appears has no meaning, or is a sign of something else. (24–25)

Moreover, the animal cannot perceive an object's duration, its existence in time. It posits nothing beyond the present, and so exists in a state of immediacy. Even in eating another animal, even, presumably, in *being eaten* by another animal, there is no break in this immanent, immediate continuity. Neither predator nor prey, neither the goshawk nor the HEN he consumes, is able to distinguish the other from the self. "Animals, since they eat one another, are of unequal strength, but there is never anything between them except that quantitative difference. The lion is not the king of the beasts: in the movement of the waters he is only a higher wave overturning the other, weaker ones" (18).[3] For Bataille, "every animal is in the world like water in water" (19, 23, 25).

Humans, on the other hand, cannot even imagine this immanent world. The consciousness that allows them to comprehend distinct objects, to give meaning to the continuity, prevents them from seeing things as an animal does. In trying to imagine a world without humanity, they try to see *nothing*: "There was no landscape in a world where the eyes that opened did not apprehend what they looked at, where indeed, in our terms, the eyes did not see" (21). Worse, in pursuing that which is closed to them, in straining to see this absence of vision, humans are stupidly drawn in by the "sticky temptation" of poetry. In their confusion, they try to make positive assertions regarding the animal mind, perhaps that it is limited by terror, by suffering, and by death. They use words to describe experiences that can only be experienced *without* words, without distinctions, without consciousness. In short, they produce nonsense (21–22).

Bataille is not suggesting that animals are merely things, like stones or air. Although incautious analysts are often prone to regard them as such, for instance when they eat them, when they enslave them, or when they treat them as objects of science, animals cannot be completely reduced to this level (22). It is not entirely meaningless, Bataille begrudgingly allows, to regard the animal as a subject (although, crucially, it cannot regard itself in that way) (19). The animal is thus not *entirely* inscrutable to the human observer. Indulging in a little poetry of his own, Bataille suggests that the depth that it opens before him is familiar. But nothing, in the end, "is more closed to us than this animal life from which we are descended" (20). The depth remains unfathomable (22).

Ultimately, then, the animal is neither a man nor a thing (21). Bataille does not want to assert categorically that the animal lacks the ability to transcend itself. Humans can only know this negatively, in the sense that they cannot clearly discern in the animal any such ability. An embryo of that capacity can, perhaps, be imagined to exist in animals, but only in humans is it actually manifested (23). In reality,

Bataille suggests, transcendence is *always* embryonic, even for humans, which is to say that it is something partial, tentative, and unfinished, strategically constituted *as if* it were solid and immutable. It would be impossible to construe it otherwise, for humans could not base themselves on what are really "unstable coagulations" (24). And so, though they cannot really know for sure, human observers are bound to regard the animal, for the sake of their own transcendence, from the outside, as lacking this capacity (24).

Bataille remains true here to his own commendable prohibition: "while carrying one's elucidation to the limit of immediate possibilities, not to seek a definitive state that will never be granted" (12). But Bataille implies that the ability to transcend one's environment and posit oneself as distinct from one's surroundings is first and foremost a *human* ability when he asserts that "the animal situation does contain a component of the human situation; if need be, the animal can be regarded as a subject for which the rest of the world is an object" (19). The continuity that Bataille concedes between human and animal thus depends on a characteristic that properly belongs to the former (the capacity to transcend one's environment) displaying itself in the latter. That which in humans is fully formed appears in animals as a merely "embryonic" protomanifestation, groping toward full realization.

In his opening chapter, Bataille is principally concerned with introducing and tentatively exploring the notion of immanence. It is to this end that he embarks on a discussion of animality, and from there moves in later chapters to a study of human religious, economic, and military affairs. That Bataille has no interest in animality or animals in their own right is not, of itself, a matter for concern. But he here articulates especially clearly a pair of interrelated and frequently encountered claims regarding the relationship among humanity, animality, and knowledge. It is in an examination of these that we find the value of my own rather narrow reading of his text.

First, the perfect continuity that, according to Bataille, exists between animal and environment, the lack of transcendence, means that phenomena are not distinguished as objects. The animal has no meaning, no knowledge of the world, and exists, as we have seen, like water in water. Second, in virtue of the fact that the existence of the animal consists in this uniformity with the environment, that existence is utterly closed to human comprehension. Compelled always to impose precisely those divisions that are denied to the animal, humans cannot entertain any meaningful understanding of animal life. In short, the reason the animal is closed to the human, the reason there can be no knowledge of the animal, is that there is no meaning, no knowledge for the animal. Taken together, the

implication of these two claims is that knowledge (meaning, understanding, cognition) is always and only human. Those who do and must have knowledge are condemned to a particular perspective, to an inevitable anthropocentrism, that is entirely at odds with the animal's engagement with the world. Any attempt to step outside this limitation, to articulate an understanding or knowledge that is not constrained in this way, will unavoidably descend into poetic babbling.

It is unavoidable, Bataille says, that the human should regard the animal as lacking transcendence (23, 24). But he has here already assumed a qualitative difference between human and animal experience that he has not demonstrated. The life of the animal, he says, is closed "to us"; the animal's place in the world seems "in our eyes" to be one of complete immanence (20, 24). The first-person pronouns, here and elsewhere in the chapter, refer always and exclusively to the human. In so expressing himself, Bataille gives priority to the human perspective, "our" starting point, precluding the possibility of an alternative identification. When he asserts that "for the moment, I need to set apart from the dazzle of poetry that which, from the standpoint of experience, appears distinctly and clearly," he attempts to take stock from the standpoint of what he chooses to call human experience (23). Despite his poetic suggestion that the animal opens a depth that is familiar, Bataille assumes that "we" are, in a sense, human before we are animal.[4]

4. On Bataille's own criticism of anthropocentrism—as the denial of the universal law of expenditure, and therefore of immanence and the sacred—see Hollier, "Dualist Materialism," especially 68–70.

To proceed, we must suspend Bataille's claims that the consistency of the world of the animal is one of fluid homogeneity and that self-consciousness has erected a barrier between humans and those from whom they have "descended." This is not to claim positively that he is wrong in these assertions but, rather, to postpone judgment. It may be that on detailed examination, we would indeed want to assert a qualitative difference between human and animal being, and that the capacity to break the continuity of existence by positing durable objects can be usefully described as human. But this must remain, for the moment, an open question.

The animal, Bataille argues, opens up an unfathomable depth. His discussion of this depth focuses on that which he believes to be most distant, that which is furthest removed: the immanence of the animal itself. But to explore this characterization a little further, in order that we might bring it more precisely into question, we need to look too at what Bataille takes to be the near side of the chasm, the firm ground from which the human peers out. For this purpose I turn to Martin Heidegger and consider his own account of the animal abyss. Between them, Bataille and Heidegger will help us formulate an understanding of what it means to write from an anthropocentric perspective.

INTO YOUR HAND THEY ARE DELIVERED

In his "Letter on Humanism," Heidegger writes of "our scarcely conceivable, abysmal bodily kinship with the beast." His account of this affinity is remarkably close to Bataille's: "Of all the beings that are, presumably the most difficult to think about are living creatures, because on the one hand they are in a certain way most closely akin to us, and on the other are at the same time separated from our ek-sistent essence by an abyss."[5] For Bataille the animal itself opens up a depth, whereas for Heidegger the chasm stretches *between* human and animal. In both cases, however, the extreme difficulty, or even impossibility, of thinking about the existence of the animal is due to its radical alterity, represented by this profound and unplumbed void.[6] In light of Bataille's remarks, my objective here is thus not to discuss what Heidegger has to say about the world of animals but, rather, to examine what it is that he believes separates humanity and animality. It is not the nature of animals that now concerns us but the nature of the abyss itself.[7] On the one hand, the animal seems very close to the human, Heidegger says, whereas on

5. Heidegger, "Letter on Humanism," 230.
6. For more on this abyss and its relation to others in Heidegger's work, see Krell, *Daimon Life*, 5–13.
7. I will thus not be looking in detail at Heidegger's three infamous and much discussed heuristic theses in *The Fundamental Concepts of Metaphysics*, which compare the worlds, or particular kinds of being, of stones, animals, and humans. See Heidegger, *Fundamental Concepts of Metaphysics*, 176–78 (§42); Derrida, *Of Spirit*, 47–57; McNeill, *Heidegger*, 27–28, 34–45; Glendinning, "Heidegger and the Question of Animality," 75–80; and Calarco, "Heidegger's Zoontology."

the other hand, it resides on the far side of this abyss. And in fact the hands involved here turn out to be central to his account of the interrelation of thinking, language, and truth and therefore of what creates the distance between the human and the animal.

In *What Is Called Thinking?*, Heidegger concerns himself with the question of what it would be to learn to think. His preliminary answer is that perhaps the process is analogous to that of an apprentice cabinet builder learning the trade. The apprentice must be capable of using the appropriate tools and knowledgeable about the different things to be built, of course, but what is far more important, what will distinguish a true cabinetmaker, is that he responds to the different kinds of wood and the shapes that lie within. Similarly, in order to think, Heidegger argues, we must learn to "answer to whatever essentials address themselves to us."[8] The suggestion is that thinking, like cabinetmaking, is a particular kind of practice, a handicraft (*Handwerk*). The hand in handicraft is crucial here. The hand is commonly considered simply as part of the body, as a mere organ for grasping. This describes only the mundane physicality of the hand, however, and fails to capture its essence.

For Heidegger, the hand is intimately connected to thinking, and all the work of the hand is rooted in thinking. Thinking, in fact, is itself the hardest handicraft that can be undertaken.[9]

So what is the connection between the hand and thinking? What is the role of the hand when answering to essentials that address themselves to us? Heidegger had already taken this question in hand in an earlier lecture series, on *Parmenides*, during the course of his discussion of truth as un-concealment or dis-closure (ἀλήθεια, *alêtheia*).[10] Here he tells us that it is by means of *Handlung* (action, activity) that we engage with things. We act, he says, insofar as the things present are within reach of the hand. *Handlung* is Heidegger's translation of πρᾶγμα (*pragma*), from which we derive the English term *pragmatic*. Πρᾶγμα is customarily translated, Heidegger tells us, as "thing" or "fact," though this tends to miss the original sense, that of the process of setting this thing up as present upon arriving at it. Strictly speaking then, πρᾶγμα means both a thing and an activity, or more precisely, it designates the essentially inseparable unity of these two (80, 84). Although *Handlung* and πρᾶγμα are not literally equivalent, it is this pair of meanings that Heidegger hopes to indicate by his translation. It is in the use of things, he says, in the process of employing them as things that are ready-to-hand, that we arrive at them: "The hand reaches out for them and reaches them" (80).[11] Considered thus, in the con-

8. Heidegger, *What Is Called Thinking?*, 14.
9. Ibid., 16–17.
10. Heidegger, *Parmenides*, 79–83. Further references are in the text.
11. See also Heidegger, *Being and Time*, 95–102 (§15: 66–72). Parenthetical numbers refer to the section and pages in the German edition. For Heidegger's discussion of the closeness of things that are "ready-to-hand," see ibid., 138–44 (§23: 104–10).

text of "concernful dealings" with them, things are *equipment* (Zeug).[12]

Handlung, the manipulation of this ready-to-hand equipment, is for Heidegger the way to unconcealment, which is to say truth. In its concernful dealings, the hand indicates things and thereby discloses what was concealed. This indicating is a pointing, a marking off that brings a thing to presence. Comprehension depends on prehension, and the hand thereby manifests what was hidden. This uncovering demarcation is the true work of the hand, the job that it does, the *essence* of the hand.[13] Such demarcation can be done only with the hand, and this because the hand is essentially related to the word (*das Wort*). The marking off by the hand creates, says Heidegger, "indicating marks" (*zeigenden Zeichen*), which are called forms or signs. The sign shows; it indicates; and it is this demarcation as a *delimitation* that brings a thing to presence (82, 84). There can thus be no word without hand, but also no hand without word. The hand "sprang forth" out of the word and together with the word. Only a being that "has" the word, only a being that indicates and marks out, can (and must) have the hand in its essential sense (80).[14]

The marks and signs that are formed by the demarcating hand, the inscriptions, are called writing, and it is this handwriting that makes visible the word. The essence of the word is that it lets beings appear, or put another way, wherever beings emerge into unconcealedness, there

Being is put into words. "Being manifests itself primordially in the word" (76). Heidegger links the reading, or *lection*, of the visible, handwritten word, which is a "disclosive taking up and perceiving of the written word," to col-lection, or gathering (85). In Greek, he tells us, this gathering is called λόγος (logos), which "among the primordial thinkers, is the name for Being itself" (85). The word is humanity's relation to Being, and in handwriting this relation is inscribed in beings themselves (85). It is by means of the word, which is inextricably bound up with the hand, that it becomes possible to "disclose" beings, that is, to arrive at them as distinct things with which one can interact.[15]

Crucial to Heidegger's understanding of the correlation of hand and word is the fact that together they constitute the essential distinguishing mark of humanity (84). Only humans have the hand and the word, or more properly, it is the case that "man does not 'have' hands, but the hand holds the essence of man, because the word as the essential realm of the hand is the ground of the essence of man" (80). As the means by which Being

---

12. Heidegger, *Being and Time*, 96–97 (68–69).

13. George Herbert Mead reached similar conclusions regarding the hand, though by rather different means; see Mead, "Concerning Animal Perception," and Mead, *Mind, Self, and Society*, 184–85, 237, 248–49, 362–63.

14. In his emphasis on the essentially *indicative* nature of signs, including language, Heidegger inverts Edmund Husserl's insistence on the primacy of *expression*; see Glendinning, *In the Name of Phenomenology*, 40–47.

15. On the relation of soul, life, and logos and the tricky translation of the last (as *gathering*, as *discourse*, as *conversance*), see especially Heidegger, *Aristotle's Metaphysics*, 99–110 (chapter 2).

4. LIZARD

It was Coyote who brought it about that people die. He made it thus because our hands are not closed like his. He wanted our hands to be like his, but *kondjodji* (a lizard) said to him: "No, they must have my hand." He had five fingers and Coyote had only a fist. So now we have an open hand with five fingers. But then Coyote said: "Well, then they will have to die."

"The Origin of Death," Yokuts myth, in A. L. Kroeber, *Indian Myths of South Central California*, 231.

Illustration by T. W. Wood, engraved by G. Pearson, in J. G. Wood, *Bible Animals*, 530.

"assigns itself to man," the word is the essential characteristic of humanity (78). Heidegger outlines this fundamental and primordial relationship between Being and humanity, through language, in the opening to his "Letter on Humanism": "Language is the house of Being. In its home man dwells. Those who think and those who create with words are the guardians of this home. Their guardianship accomplishes the manifestation of Being insofar as they bring the manifestation to language and maintain it in language through their speech."[16] Humanity alone is "entrusted" with the word and thereby "assigned to the preservation of the unconcealedness of beings."[17] Only through humanity, by means of word and hand, can beings emerge from Being.[18] Beings, *as* beings, are taken in hand and there preserved as something present and ready to use.[19]

This means, of course, that animals do not have word or hand. This is where the abyss opens up, separating the essence of the human hand from what are merely "grasping organs" in animals, such as paws, claws, and fangs.[20] The human body is, for Heidegger, "something essentially other than an animal organism."[21] He does not mean to suggest, he says, that animals are lesser beings than humans, and he is uncomfortable, too, with the idea of a hierarchy composed of "higher" and "lower" animals, arguing that it would be a fundamental mistake to suppose that amoebae or infusoria are more "imperfect" or "incomplete" than elephants or apes.[22] Nonetheless, with his insistence that the hand–word nexus is distinctively and uniquely human, Heidegger does instate a fundamental, qualitative difference between human and animal.

16. Heidegger, "Letter on Humanism," 217.

17. Heidegger, *Parmenides*, 78.

18. Ibid., 76.

19. Heidegger, "Anaximander Fragment," 51–55. See also Derrida, "Geschlecht II: Heidegger's Hand," 181–82.

20. Heidegger, *What Is Called Thinking?*, 16.

21. Heidegger, "Letter on Humanism," 228.

22. Heidegger, *Fundamental Concepts of Metaphysics*, 194.

American Sparrow Hawk (*Falco sparverius*) by John James
Audubon, engraved by Robert Havell, in John James Audubon,
The Birds of America, plate 142.

5. FALCON

The belief that falcons and hawks possess extraordinary visual acuity is deeply
ingrained in language and thought. It arises in part from reports of awesome feats
of visual prowess based on casual observation under [natural] conditions. More
substantial evidence is provided by the anatomy of eye and retina, where a number
of features facilitating acuity are present. The most notable of these is a cone density
substantially greater than in the human retina. . . . Our subject was an American
kestrel (*Falco sparverius*), a small falcon . . . we named Wulst. . . . Falcon performance
was 2.6 times better than human performance. . . . What our data do provide is
behavioral evidence that falcon acuity is superior to human acuity . . . yet their
superiority is not so great as some of the more hyperbolic prior speculations have
suggested.

ROBERT FOX, STEPHEN W. LEHMKUHLE, AND DAVID H. WESTENDORF,
"Falcon Visual Acuity," 263–64.

A **LIZARD** who has sought out a warm
stone on which to bask will have, Heidegger
asserts, her own relation to those two things
that are called "stone" and "sun." This relation
is of a kind that tempts him to suggest that the
stone and sun are for the lizard simply "lizard-
things."[23] An animal can explore its environment and separate such things out in order
to stalk prey, know its dwelling places, defend
itself against predators, and so on.[24] The lizard,
then, certainly has some kind of access both to

the stone and to the sun, but the stone is not
given to her *as* a stone, nor the sun *as* the sun,
since neither stone nor sun is accessible to a
lizard *as a being at all.*[25] Like plants, Heidegger
argues, "animals are lodged in their respective
environments,"[26] environments that cannot expand or contract and to which the animals are
confined.[27] This is not quite the immersion of
Bataille's animals, existing like water in water,
who do not make distinctions at all. Heidegger
draws attention to the discriminatory capacity
of the **FALCON**'s eye and to the canine sense of
smell, both of which are *greater* than the human
equivalents.[28] The blade of grass that a beetle

23. Ibid., 196–99.
24. Heidegger, *Aristotle's Metaphysics*, 105–6.
25. On the importance of the "as," see Derrida, *Of Spirit*, 51–53, 56–57; Krell,
Daimon Life, 12–13, 116–17, 129, 276; and especially Eldred, "As."
26. Heidegger, "Letter on Humanism," 230.
27. Heidegger, *Fundamental Concepts of Metaphysics*, 198.
28. Ibid., 194.

ascends is a "beetle-path" on which he seeks "beetle-nourishment." Each different animal has a particular set of relationships with its various sources of nourishment, with its prey, its enemies, and its sexual mates.[29] But without the word, without the hand, all these animals pottering about their respective worlds do so in a radically different way from the manner in which human individuals engage with their world. Animals exist, Heidegger says, "without standing outside their Being as such and within the truth of Being." They are never placed freely "in the clearing of Being," but remain stuck— "lodged"—in their particular environments.[30]

The hand, then, denotes the essential difference between humanity and animality. Humans alone are able to point toward things, to point at things, or perhaps better, to point out things, since pointing is a matter of a disclosive assimilation of the unconcealed.[31] Man points to what is, Heidegger says, and "his essential nature lies in being such a pointer."[32] This pointing is done by the hand, and it is worth remembering that the human forefinger is called the *index* finger precisely because it is used for pointing things out: the term derives from the Latin INDICARE, meaning "to point out," "to indicate," or "to ex-

pose." For Heidegger, man is the one who indicates, and by this indicating he draws beings out from Being: "If we are to think of man not as an organism but a human being, we must first give attention to the fact that man is that being who has his being by pointing to what is, and that particular beings manifest themselves as such by such pointing."[33] Man does not *determine* what constitutes a being, does not decide "whether or how beings appear," since "the advent of beings lies in the destiny of Being" itself. But as the only being capable of this fundamental kind of disclosure, man does stand in a privileged relationship to Being, as its caretaker, the guardian of the truth of Being. It is because of this particular relationship to beings, and to Being, that Heidegger calls man the "shepherd of Being."[34] The title is apt. Heidegger's characterization of beings has them dutifully running to heel when he (Heidegger, man) points and calls them out, though they are perhaps more like the obedient sheepdog than the unruly SHEEP. Rather like Adam naming the beasts, man alone finds himself in the privileged position of being able to comprehend all God's creatures as the creatures they are, since it is in his pointing that they manifest themselves as such. Given man's special relationship with Being, as the being with the word and hand, he cannot help but get it right when he starts pointing and calling names: "Whatever the man called every living creature, that was its name."[35] Only humans can *know*

---

29. Ibid., 198.

30. Heidegger, "Letter on Humanism," 229–30.

31. Heidegger, *Parmenides*, 81.

32. Heidegger, *What is Called Thinking?*, 9.

33. Ibid., 149.

34. Heidegger, "Letter on Humanism," 234.

35. Gen. 2:19 (New Revised Standard Version [hereafter NRSV]).

things as such. Adam, the shepherd of Being, is charged with the task of preserving the uncon-cealedness of creatures, and not without reason does a fear and dread of him fall upon every beast of the earth and every fowl of the air, in-deed upon everything that moves upon the earth and all the fish in the sea, since, says Heidegger, says God, "Into your hand they are delivered."[36]

David Farrell Krell has described Hei-degger's approach to animal being(s) as "bla-tantly anthropocentric."[37] This question of the anthropocentrism or humanism unveiled by Heidegger's treatment of animals divides his commentators. On the one hand, Krell argues that Heidegger's suggestion that animal behavior is "benumbed" (benommen) works "only against the backdrop of a putatively more vigorous and vital stance toward beings as such; the animal's world reflects a deprivation only on the set of a richer, more varied and abundant openness to being."[38] Heidegger's thinking, then, is not merely humanist; rather, it displays a *hauteur* that is "hyperhumanistic."[39] Jacques Derrida, too, has questioned Heidegger's efforts to mark "an ab-solute limit between the living creature and the human *Dasein*."[40] Heidegger is at his most sig-nificantly symptomatic and seriously dogmatic, Derrida says, when he attempts to distinguish, categorically, the human and the animal.[41] Fur-ther, the words *poverty* (Armut) and *privation* (Ent-behrung), which Heidegger employs to describe the being of the animal, cannot but imply a hier-

W. F. Keyl, *Sheep Following Their Shepherd*, engraved by G. Pearson, in J. G. Wood, *Bible Animals*, 154.

6. SHEEP

The one who enters by the gate is the shepherd of the sheep. The gatekeeper opens the gate for him, and the sheep hear his voice. He calls his own sheep by name and leads them out.

John 10:2–3 (NRSV).

36. Gen. 9:2 (NRSV).

37. Krell, *Daimon Life*, 130.

38. Ibid., 130, 275. On the animal's *Benommenheit* (benumbedness, dazedness, stu-pefaction, torpidity), see Heidegger, *Fundamental Concepts of Metaphysics*, 257–61.

39. Krell, *Daimon Life*, 256.

40. Derrida, *Of Spirit*, 54.

41. Derrida, "Geschlecht II: Heidegger's Hand," 173–74.

archy and evaluation.[42] This conception, Derrida argues, promotes "a certain anthropocentric or even humanist teleology."[43] Simon Glendinning has further suggested that Heidegger's essential contrast of humanity and animality requires us to make too sharp a distinction between human and animal being.[44] Glendinning argues that the analysis ignores "the possibility that different animals can be, in different respects, 'another like myself.'"[45] As such, Heidegger's analytic remains "stubbornly and problematically humanist."[46]

On the other hand, Michael Eldred has argued that quite the reverse is the case. Heidegger's analysis, he suggests, carefully and deliberately resists the charge of anthropocentrism by recognizing "the insuperable difficulties of gaining access to animal being." By respecting the difference between human and animal, Heidegger thus avoids assimilating "all openness to the openness of human being" and refrains from "anthropomorphically transferring the scheme of human understanding to animals."[47] This theme of difference, of otherness, is, Will McNeill argues, crucial to Heidegger's understanding of beings. On this account, man is not just one being amongst others, privileged by his "having" a language that enables him to make interpretations: "It is interpretation or logos itself, and not anthrōpos, which is the centre and measure of all things."[48] As such, it actually makes possible an understanding that "opens our access to other things and to otherness in general."[49] Heidegger is trying to understand not the essence of the animal "in itself," which would be a misguided and metaphysical endeavor, but in its otherness. Finally, Steve Baker argues that Heidegger's concern is not just to understand the animal in its otherness but to "let that otherness be."[50] Only by recognizing and accepting the otherness of the animal is there any possibility of our "going-along-with" it in order to understand "how it is" with the animal.[51]

Is Heidegger anthropocentric? His writings, and those of his commentators, point toward two modes of anthropocentric thought that we might usefully distinguish. First, there is the bald belief or supposition that the human species is, in some sense, of greater importance and value than all else. This is a spatial characterization, perhaps, illustrative of the term anthropocentric's Greek roots in ἄνθρωπος (anthrōpos), meaning "human," and κέντρον (kentron), meaning "center," in that humanity is presumed to

---

42. Derrida, *Of Spirit*, 55–56.

43. Ibid., 55.

44. Glendinning, "Heidegger and the Question of Animality," 78–79.

45. Ibid., 78.

46. Ibid., 70. See also the critique of Heidegger's "metaphysical anthropocentrism" in Calarco, *Zoographies*, 15–54 (chapter 1).

47. Eldred, "As," Part 3. Jill Marsden makes an identical point regarding Bataille's "refusal to commute his meditation on animality to humanist paradigms of thought"; Marsden, "Poetic Fallacy," 43.

48. McNeill, *Heidegger*, 25.

49. Ibid., 26.

50. S. Baker, "Sloughing the Human," 160.

51. Ibid., 160. On "going-along-with" the animal, see Heidegger, *Fundamental Concepts of Metaphysics*, 201–9.

take center stage. This spatial anthropocentrism implies a hierarchy, or chain of being, from the summit of which humanity gazes down on lesser creatures. It is an *evaluative* anthropocentrism, judgmental and disparaging, and it is exemplified by the prejudice that Derrida detects in Heidegger's words, despite the latter's protestations to the contrary.

Second, there is the contention, already articulated by Protagoras, that "man is the measure of all things."[52] This is the *epistemological* claim that all knowledge will inevitably be determined by the human nature of the knower and that any attempt to explain experience, understanding, or knowledge—of the world, of Being, of others—must inevitably start from a human perspective. Bataille demonstrated precisely this epistemological anthropocentrism when he argued that humans, unlike animals, are compelled to comprehend the world as distinct, durable objects. Any account that attempts to do otherwise, he suggested, indulges and abuses a poetic capacity that conjures senselessly with "the absurdity of things envisaged without man's gaze."[53] Epistemological anthropocentrism is thus characterized by a *temporal* preoccupation, whereby the human being arrives or appears before all else. It suggests not that humanity must occupy center stage but that one's entrance onto the stage, from whatever quarter, will be, first and foremost, as a human. Heidegger was wary of any claim that "human beings are cornered in the blind alley of their

own humanity."[54] But in his account of the means by which human beings alone are entrusted with the word and are thus uniquely placed to preserve the unconcealedness of beings, he presupposes an absolute distinction between human and animal.[55] He offers no argument for the claim that "an abyss of essence" separates that vital human hand from the many paws, claws, and fangs of other creatures, asserting only that these latter are all mere "grasping organs." There are undeniable differences amongst the organs and appendages he mentions, but that there is a single, fundamental division between human hand and animal paw or maw, that the hand is always and only human, is assumed rather than demonstrated. Heidegger begins with the presumption that the being with the hand is human.[56]

These two modes of anthropocentrism, the evaluative and the epistemological, need not go together. It is entirely possible to envisage an evaluative anthropocentrism that does not commit humanity to the stricture of its own blind

52. Plato, *Theaetetus*, 152a; see the prelude above.

53. Bataille, *Theory of Religion*, 22.

54. Heidegger, *Nietzsche*, 99.

55. In his *Introduction to Metaphysics*, Heidegger describes this as "their distinction and also their predicament," though he would there divorce speaking from biology: "Even if we had a thousand eyes and a thousand ears, a thousand hands and many other senses and organs, if our essence did not stand within the power of language, then all beings would remain closed off to us"; Heidegger, *Introduction to Metaphysics*, 86.

56. Derrida points out that persistent reference to "the hand" in the singular marks Heidegger's insistence that "*the* hand of man" is, in essence, something other than the prehensile organs of other creatures; Derrida, "Geschlecht II: Heidegger's Hand," 182. But see also McNeill, "Spirit's Living Hand," 113–14.

alley, or an epistemological anthropocentrism that does not subscribe to notions of human superiority.[57] But Heidegger combines them. The means of apprehension made possible by the hand confers on humanity a singular dispensation. Indeed, Heidegger's objection to traditional humanism is, in part, that it does not sufficiently emphasize this unique and privileged relationship that "*Homo humanus*" has to Being: "The highest determinations of the essence of man in humanism still do not realize the proper dignity of man."[58] Only once we recognize the special role of human beings as guardians over the truth of Being is humanity restored to its proper place. This done, Heidegger is prepared to contemplate the possibility of reclaiming the term *humanism*.[59] The hand, then, is Heidegger's humanistic, or hyperhumanistic, starting point, and it betrays an anthropocentrism in which human being is characterized as both spatially and temporally preeminent.

The hand, which Heidegger takes as the mark of the *human*, will help us in the chapters that follow to lay our hands on the *humanist*. It recurs with remarkable frequency in the writings of those who subscribe, explicitly or otherwise, to a Protagorean perspective that would start from the human. We might designate this outlook, in which humanity is taken to be the measure of all things, as *first-and-foremost* anthropocentrism. Bataille and Heidegger certainly both pursue investigative strategies that begin with the human, the former as he reflects, by way of the inconceivable alterity of "animality," on immanence, the latter as he considers the means by which Being "assigns itself to man." And just as hands will frequently appear at work amongst the theses of anthropocentric philosophers, so too do animals. Bataille and Heidegger each employ a number of beasts in the service of their anthropocentric assertions, though the creatures themselves are rarely the focus or object of attention. More often than not, these animals are of only passing interest to the philosophers, who take no interest in the hawk and the hen, or the lizard and the sheep, in their own rights. As we shall see, however, like those indicative hands, these creatures can be instructive. It is with these casually employed, marginal animals, and the mischief they can wreak in a philosopher's text, that the next sections are concerned.

DECIPHERING DECIPHERING

The term *cipher* derives from the Sanskrit *śūnya*, which literally means "empty." Translated into Arabic, it became the adjective *çifr*, also employed as a substantive to designate the arithmetic symbol for "zero" or "nought." The concept was adopted by Europeans in this latter sense during

57. Corliss Lamont, for example, takes human welfare as his overriding concern, whilst adhering to principles of scientific reason in the pursuit of truth; Mary Midgley, on the other hand, deplores hierarchical anthropocentrism, whilst maintaining the utility and inevitability of a degree of human centering. See Lamont, *Philosophy of Humanism*; and Midgley, "End of Anthropocentrism?"
58. Heidegger, "Letter on Humanism," 245, 233–34.
59. Ibid., 245, 247–48.

the Middle Ages and became the Latin CIFRA or CIFERA.[60] Acceptance of "Arabic" numeric notation (really Indian) was slow and in many quarters reluctant, but the addition of the symbol for zero was revolutionary, and the whole system came to be known by its name, "cipher." The process of calculating by means of the new system was, by extension, "ciphering."[61] By the sixteenth century the term *cipher* was being used figuratively of a person or thing "who fills a place, but is of no importance or worth" in its own right. The real power residing elsewhere, the cipher remains "a nonentity, a 'mere nothing.'" Further, the term *cipher* also came to designate codes in which either specially invented characters or conventional letters and characters employed "in other than their ordinary sense" produced a "secret or disguised manner of writing . . . intelligible only to those possessing the key." Finally, the word was used of symbolic characters, such as Egyptian hieroglyphs, that frequently took the forms of animals. Here the creatures, of no consequence in their own rights, filled a place in the script so that a meaning might be conveyed.

Although all manner of entities are fair game for cipherous appropriation, philosophers have been especially keen on animals. A good many appear in J. L. Austin's *Sense and Sensibilia*, his reconstructed lectures on perception and knowledge. Austin believed that the first step toward relieving a significant number of philosophical perplexities is to enumerate at least

some of the diverse uses to which contentious words are actually put. Without such elementary ground laying, philosophers embark on speculative analyses and semantic tampering at their peril. The seventh lecture in this volume concerns the complex set of concepts denoted by the word *real*.[62] Austin's chief interest in this entertaining essay is to show how all manner of metaphysical pseudoproblems are resolved, or dissolved, if we attend to the ways in which the word *real* is ordinarily used: "real cream" (as opposed to a synthetic substitute), "a real hiding" (as opposed to just a light beating), and so on. Several different animals put in appearances, including a horse, a number of ducks, a chameleon, a goose, and even a talking cat or two. Most, though not all, do little more in the text than fill a place, as his pigs well demonstrate.

Austin points out that one of the many uses to which the word *real* is actually put is as an "adjuster-word." The demands of the world upon language are innumerable and largely unforeseeable, and no matter how wide-ranging our vocabulary, there will inevitably be occasions when we do not have ready to hand words that are entirely adequate to our new experiences.

> We have the word "pig," for instance, and a
> pretty clear idea which animals, among those we

---

60. All quotations in this paragraph are from the *Oxford English Dictionary*, 2nd ed., s.v. "cipher."

61. On the history of zero, see D. E. Smith and Karpinski, *Hindu-Arabic Numerals*, 51–62; Menninger, *Number Words and Number Symbols*, 396–403, 422–24; Reid, *From Zero to Infinity*, 1–15.

62. Austin, *Sense and Sensibilia*, 62–77.

Winifred Austen, *American Tapirs*, in Frank Finn, *The Wild Beasts of the World*, 2:16.

7. TAPIR

There is something curiously old-world and unfinished about the appearance of the [Tapir], as if it had failed to complete its evolution—something recalling both a Pig and a Pony, while the short trunk suggests an abortive attempt at an Elephant. This little trunk is freely movable, and is used to grasp the herbage on which the creature feeds. . . . The limbs have four hoofs on the fore feet and three on the hind; the animal, however, like the Rhinoceros, does not rest entirely on these hoofs, but also on a pad under the base of the toes. The tail is almost as short and insignificant as a Bear's.

FRANK FINN, *The Wild Beasts of the World*, 2:17.

fairly commonly encounter, are and are not to be so called. But one day we come across a new kind of animal, which looks and behaves very much as pigs do, but not *quite* as pigs do; it is somehow different.[63]

About these new creatures we may remain silent, or we may immediately invent an entirely new word with which to refer to them. More probably, though, we would initially say that such animals were *like* pigs, but, if pressed, that they were not *true* pigs, or perhaps that they were not *real* pigs. We would thus be able to talk about these creatures even without their having a specific name of their own. A similar advantage would be gained, Austin suggests, if we talked about the members of the new species as "piggish" or as "pig-type" animals, or perhaps referred to them as "quasi-pigs."

Austin's point is to demonstrate that our uses of the word *real* are many and varied and that frequently the creature or object to which the term is applied is not a real something as opposed to an *unreal* (illusory, insubstantial, merely phenomenal) something but, rather, a *genuine* something (a real pig) as opposed to a similar something else (a real quasi pig). His concern is with the everyday discourses involving the word *real* and with the light they can throw on the half-baked theories so often invented by philosophers. To this end, *any* animal could have filled the place of the pigs (and quasi pigs) quite adequately. There is nothing about the pig, qua pig, that lends itself to the discussion; any other creature would have done. In fact, any object, animate or otherwise, might be substituted here. Cats (and their catlike kin), dogs (and their doggy relatives), tables or chairs (and examples of quasi furniture)—indeed any entity amongst those we commonly encounter—would have made Aus-

63. Ibid., 74.

tin's point just as clearly. The pig fills a place but is of no importance or worth in his or her own right *as a pig*. The pig, in short, is a cipher.

A second example further illustrates the frequently neglected and unhappy lot of the philosophers' cipherous animals. The paradox of "Buridan's ass" has recurred within philosophical circles for donkey's years. A hungry **ASS**, we are told, stands between two bales of hay. The bales are identical in every respect, or at least as regards their size and succulence, and the ass stands exactly equidistant from each. The ass looks longingly from one to the other but, due to their equal merit, is unable to choose between them and consequently starves to death. This poor beast, it turns out, has the dubious honor of functioning as a cipher on two distinct levels.

First, as with Austin's pigs, it is not necessary that the indecisive creature be an ass: any animal placed between identical food sources would do. And, in fact, Jean Buridan's beast was not a donkey. The first of many confusions regarding this tale arises from the fact that Buridan's ass is never actually mentioned in Buridan's writings.[64] As Nicholas Rescher notes in his meticulously researched essay on the history and employment of Buridan's ass, the philosopher does discuss a dog, similarly paralyzed by indecision between two equal portions of food, in his commentary on Aristotle's *On the Heavens*.[65] And, further, in Aristotle's own example, it is not even a hungry dog. Ar-

8. Ass

The ass and the little ass [ASINUS ET ASELLUS] are so called from sitting (SEDENDO) as if [the word were] (ASSEDUS). . . . Whenever he wishes, man tames the animal, which is naturally slow and obstinate for no reason. He tames Arcadian asses, so called because they came first from Arcadia; they are big and tall. The little ass, although smaller than the wild ass, is more indispensable, because he both tolerates work and almost never protests neglect.

WILLENE B. CLARK, *A Medieval Book of Beasts*, 155 (translation modified).

Medieval bestiary, c. 1240–50. Bodleian Library, University of Oxford, MS Bodley 764, fol. 44.

64. Schopenhauer complains bitterly that "one has now been searching [Buridan's] writings for some hundred years. . . . I myself own an edition of his *Sophismata* . . . , in which I have repeatedly searched for it in vain, although asses occur as examples on virtually every page"; quoted in Rescher, "Choice without Preference," 110n29. Other writers have encountered the same difficulty, including, it has to be said, the present author.

65. Rescher, "Choice without Preference," 87. Further citations from Rescher are in the text.

Bill Waterson, *Calvin and Hobbes.*

9. TIGER

istotle discussed, rather, "the analogy of the hair which, stretched strongly but evenly at every point, will not break, or the man who is violently, but equally, hungry and thirsty, and stands at an equal distance from food and drink, and who therefore must remain where he is."[66] In fact, Rescher observes, as the example was taken up with alacrity by commentators, the role of the cipher was filled variously by the place of the earth in the heavens, by a man between equally appetizing food and water (or between two dates, or different parts of a loaf, or wine and gammon), by a lamb between two fierce wolves, a hound between two does, a student between two books, a man between two knives, a courtier between two ladies, and even an accused between two identical doors that are

to decide his fate, behind which are secreted a ferocious **TIGER** and a fair maiden (79–99).

Second, the cipherous nature of the ass is demonstrated especially clearly by the fact that the function of the story, the philosophical point that is intended, has changed over time. This is one ass who has indeed had to tolerate a good deal of work without protesting his neglect. Rescher identifies several distinct roles for which the example has been appropriated (103 and passim), but for the sake of brevity we will here confine ourselves to just two. We find that the story has been deployed as a means of addressing the problem of the *freedom of the will.* This is the role that it is generally believed to have played in Buridan's own teachings (see, however, 87–88). In his questions on Aristotle's *Nichomachean Ethics,* Buridan asks, "Would the will, having been put between two opposites, with all being wholly alike on both sides, be able to determine itself

66. Aristotle, *On the Heavens,* 237 (2.13.295b).

rather to one opposed alternative than to the other?"[67] His answer is no. Buridan provides the examples of a traveler presented with two routes to the same destination (from Paris to Avignon via Lyon or via Dun-le-roy), and of a sailor caught in a storm, trying to decide whether to dump his cargo or risk holding on to it. In a formulation that David Hume will later turn precisely on its head, Buridan argues that the will is not capable, in itself, of making choices but is subject to the dictates of reason. Should the latter discern an advantage in a particular course of action, the will can only follow, and conversely, if reason can find no advantage, the will remains dormant. The ass, and for that matter the human, unfortunate enough to find him- or herself between equally pressing alternatives, be they bales of hay or paths to Avignon, will be unable to pursue either.

Thus it is clear, to Buridan at least, that the ass must starve. However, an alternative interpretation of the paradox is possible, which allows us to save our ass. Rescher has suggested that the tale of the starving ass was told not by Buridan but by his opponents (88, 110–111n34). On this reading, the patent absurdity of the outcome—that an ass would starve to death whilst standing before not just one but two perfectly good meals—lays bare the error of Buridan's theory of the will. The tale, far from demonstrating the "intellectual determination of the will" (88), reaffirms instead the (fourteenth-century) commonsense belief in the freedom of the will.

Buridan himself, we are now being told, was a bit of an ass. Unless further textual evidence comes to light that would allow us to decide definitively whether the ass belongs to Buridan or to his naysayers, a choice between these equally appetizing alternatives seems impossible. But either way, the very fact that this ass has been used to argue for diametrically opposing accounts of the will serves further to reveal the cipherous role that the poor creature has been required to play.

In addition to the question of the freedom of the will, Buridan's ass has also been used to illustrate the apparent paradox of making a *reasonable choice without preference*. The object of discussion shifts from a contentious human or animal capacity—free will—to the allegedly paradoxical limitations of pure reason. Presented with two alternatives, between which, by definition, one has no preference, it seems on first sight to be obvious that there can be no reason to choose between them. We are driven to conclude that there can be no reasonable choice without preference. But on the other hand, Buridan's ass, being a reasonable creature, would certainly prefer the outcome of a full stomach to that of starvation. The ass, therefore, must choose one of the bales of hay, but without having any reason for preferring one bale to the other (78–79). How to resolve this paradox? Entering enthusiastically into the spirit of the debate, Rescher provides an ingenious, and only seemingly paradoxical, solution, which dictates that the reasonable course

67. Buridan, quoted in Rescher, "Choice without Preference," 87.

of action is in fact to choose a bale at random (99–103). Whether this solution, or indeed the very paradox it is designed to resolve, is convincing need not concern us here. What is of import is that our ass has once again succumbed to the cipherous requirements of the philosophers, uncomplainingly undertaking duties wholly different from those previously proposed.

Both Austin's pigs and Buridan's ass operate, in their respective texts, in the first of our three senses of cipher: they are nonentities, of no importance or worth in their own rights, designated to "fill a place." We can also understand each of them in terms of the second definition, as codes awaiting interpretation. The didactic fables, in which pigs and ass are employed "in other than the usual sense," convey esoteric, philosophical arguments that are intelligible to the initiated. As such, these animals become ciphers in the third and final sense, as symbolic characters in animal form, hieroglyphs utilized by philosophy that a meaning might be conveyed. This casual use of animal ciphers by philosophers has been extensive. Disputants have frequently conversed by *means* of animals, in ways that are not at all *about* animals. They remain invisible, figurative phantoms, installed purely as examples of epistemological problems or metaphysical speculations. When ciphers are involved, the focus is not on the animal but on the argument or the problem to be solved.

This elision is an example of the animal made "absent referent," a process described by Carol J. Adams that "permits us to forget about the animal as an independent entity. . . . The absent referent is both there and not there. . . . We fail to accord this absent referent its own existence."[68] Although the animals are there, they are not there as *animals*, that is, as particular pigs or asses in their own rights. The cipherous absent referent is not accorded its own existence but derives its meaning from its application or reference to some entirely unrelated endeavor. In addition, it is not uncommon, and perhaps not entirely coincidental, that these ciphers, these philosophical beasts of burden, dutifully carrying out their delegated tasks without protesting neglect, find themselves on the receiving end of a little offhand animal abuse or even, as with our unfortunate ass, meet an untimely end. More often than not, the place that needs filling is a less-than-happy one. We will encounter a number of these unfortunate souls, as they suffer at the hands of a diverse range of thinkers and philosophers.

If we are to avoid this careless textual abuse, then it is important, our duty perhaps, to decipher the ciphers. This should not be a matter of decoding them, of interrogating the tales so that we might uncover the truth of the philosophical problem that lies beneath: did the ass belong to Buridan or to his opponents? Still less

68. Adams, *Sexual Politics of Meat*, 51–53. Adams discusses three methods by which animals are made absent referents: through the eating of meat, through linguistic definition, and through metaphorical appropriation for human experiences.

Lowly Worm, from *Richard Scarry's What Do People Do All Day?*, 35.

10. WORM

To whom do lions cast their gentle looks?
Not to the beast that would usurp their den.
Whose hand is that the forest bear doth lick?
Not his that spoils her young before her face.
Who scapes the lurking serpent's mortal sting?
Not he that sets his foot upon her back.
The smallest worm will turn being trodden on,
And doves will peck in safeguard of their brood.

WILLIAM SHAKESPEARE, *The Third Part of King Henry VI*, 2.2.11–18.

is it a matter of providing a preferred explanation, one favored interpretation amongst others: how might Buridan's ass be best understood in light of more recent debates concerning reasonable choice without preference? This is not an exegetical or hermeneutic matter at all. In our dealings with the animals of philosophy, we must cease to understand them as arbitrarily chosen placeholders, unwittingly serving some higher pedagogic purpose. We must *de-cipher* the ciphers, that is, stop treating them as ciphers altogether. And, far from requiring assistance in this, it turns out that many have already begun the good work themselves.

PRICKLY PORCUPINES AND DOCILE DOGS

There is hope for the workhorses of the philosophers, for those who are made to carry out all manner of onerous donkey work. As we saw earlier, ciphers entered the English language as CIFERAE, an imported consignment of docile placeholders. Hidden within, we now discover a multitude of FERAE, wild animals straining at the leash. This wild side endures in even the most domesticated beasts, and we will find that whenever we meet a cipher, there is every chance that all the careful work undertaken for their master has already begun to come undone. These animals are not content to remain mere ciphers and demand to be treated otherwise. As the philosophers discover to their cost, it is often the case (though, alas, not always) that the **WORM** turns, and these beasts prove to be the downfall of their incautious employers. Like Balaam before him,[69] Buridan is made to look an ass by his donkey, and more philosophers are destined to suffer a similar fate in the pages that follow.

A French writer of the fifteenth century, distrustful of the cipherous new numeral, suggested that "just as the rag doll wanted to be an eagle, the donkey a lion, and the monkey a queen, the CIFRA put on airs and pretended to be a digit."[70] The ciphers with whom we are

69. Num. 22:21–39 (NRSV).

70. Quoted in Menninger, *Number Words and Number Symbols*, 422. The animal references are to Aesop's fables, some of which we will examine shortly; see "An ABC of Animals," below.

A Mother's Love: A Study of Domestic Rats. Photograph by Noah McConnell.

11. RAT

In a series of classic experiments on rats, researchers put baby rats on cage floors, and mother rats (and in some cases females who were not mothers) proved zealous at retrieving the babies and bringing them into their nests. They would cross an electrified grid to get to the babies, and would retrieve unrelated babies as quickly as their own. . . . The experimenters offered one rat fifty-eight babies, each of whom she picked up and crammed into her nest. . . . The experimenters . . . went on to offer mother rats odder babies. The rats readily adopted baby mice. If they were strong enough to drag a baby rabbit to their nest, they did so. They also retrieved young kittens and tried to keep experimenters from taking them out of the nest again.

JEFFREY MASSON AND SUSAN MCCARTHY, *When Elephants Weep*, 101, 117.

concerned, the placeholding zeroes, do indeed become digits, and not just any old digit. The animal cipher becomes an INDEX, both in the sense that Heidegger helped point out to us, as that which indicates or discloses, but also in

the more specific, original Latin sense of one who informs or betrays. The overworked cipher finally **RATS** on his or her employer. Animal indices, disgruntled with the ill-treatment suffered at the hands of hard-hearted taskmasters, thus do not merely give their philosophers the finger, though this is a start. Nor do they stop at simply fingering the abuser by betraying them to interested parties, though this is certainly a step forward. More important than each of these, the obliging animal index can disclose the direction we must take next, and this is a pointing, or pointing out, that is far from the single-minded concern of Heidegger's shepherd of Being. Indices are like finger-posts, helpfully indicating avenues of thought that might prove productive. The surest way of letting these coded creatures de-cipher themselves, then, is both to attend to the ways in which they betray their users and abusers, and to permit them to point us in the right direction.

The best-known discussion of the index is surely that of Charles Peirce. He describes an index as a sign that has an "actual" or "real" association with its object,[71] as one that has a "dynamical (including spatial) connection both with the individual object, on the one hand, and with the senses or memory of the person for whom it serves as a sign, on the other."[72] This "association by contiguity" has the effect of "forcing the attention upon its object."[73] More generally, then, the index is "anything which focuses the atten-

71. Peirce, *Collected Papers*, §2.286, §5.75.
72. Ibid., §2.305.
73. Ibid., §2.306, §2.357.

12. WEATHERCOCK

I am puff-breasted, proud-crested,
a head I have, and a high tail,
eyes and ears and one foot,
both my sides, a back that's hollow,
a very stout beak, a steeple neck
and a home above men.
                        Harsh are my sufferings
when that which makes the forest tremble takes and shakes me.

Here I stand under streaming rain
and blinding sleet, stoned by hail;
freezes the frost and falls the snow
on me stuck-bellied. And I stick it all out
for I cannot change the chance that made me.

Anglo Saxon riddle, in Michael Alexander,
The Earliest English Poems, 81.

Erecting a weathercock on the newly completed Westminster Abbey; Bayeux Tapestry, eleventh century.

tion."[74] Throughout his writings, Peirce provides examples of a great number of indices: a photograph,[75] a person's rolling gait or bow legs, a sundial, a rap on the door,[76] the pole star, a spirit level,[77] a variety of different kinds of pronoun,[78] and a bullet hole,[79] amongst many others. By far his favorite example, however, which recurs several times in his work, is the **WEATHERCOCK**:

> A weathercock is an index of the direction of the wind; because in the first place it really takes the self-same direction as the wind, so that there is a real connection between them, and in the second place we are so constituted that when we see a weathercock pointing in a certain direction it draws our attention to that direction, and when we see the weathercock veering with the wind, we are forced by the law of mind to think that direction is connected with the wind.[80]

74. Ibid., §2.285. Peirce discusses indices on several occasions, but his clearest exposition is probably that to be found at §2.283–291.

75. Ibid., §2.281.

76. Ibid., §2.285.

77. Ibid., §2.286.

78. Ibid., §2.287, §2.289, §2.305.

79. Ibid., §2.304.

80. Ibid., §2.286. See also §2.257, §2.265, §2.357. In using the phrase "we are so constituted," Peirce does not mean to suggest that there is anything *biologically* necessary in the action of a particular sign on those for whom it operates as an index. Anyone who is not already familiar with weathervanes would not *necessarily* realize that a particular weathercock was indicating the direction of the wind. Even a pointing forefinger, the original index, is a sign that must be learned. In his discussion of games and rule following, Wittgenstein points out that there might be doubt as to how we should follow even a finger-post; Wittgenstein, *Philosophical Investigations,* 39–40 (§85). For Peirce's own pointing fingers, see *Collected Papers,* §2.286, §2.305, §2.357, §5.75.

13. CHAMELEON

The feet are modified by the fusion of the five toes into two groups—two toes in one group and three in the other—which can oppose one another like the thumb and fingers of primates. . . . Color change in chameleons . . . is not so pronounced as is often thought. . . . Although chameleons can often match themselves to their surroundings so perfectly as to bewilder the onlooker, their coloration is not necessarily related to that of the background. The motivational state of the animal determines its color to a considerably greater extent. For example, an animal that is annoyed or attacking a rival displays a different color and patterning than one which is ill or submissive. Sometimes females about to lay eggs are especially strikingly colored. Furthermore, chameleons change their color according to the time of day; during the daylight hours they often display intense shades, whereas at night they become quite light in color.

    BERNHARD GRZIMEK, *Grzimek's Animal Life Encyclopedia*, 227–28.

Chameleons, in Jim Harter, *Animals*, 171.

Our own weathercock is, in fact, a triple index. First, as Peirce explains, it is an index of the wind direction. Second, for the medieval audience of the Bayeux Tapestry, it represented the placing of the very final piece in the building of Westminster Abbey, thereby indicating that the structure was complete: the Hand of God above the nave signals the consecration of the Abbey shortly thereafter.[81] Finally, the weathercock helps point out how indices function. As an index of an index, the weathercock's particular qualities and roles—as a weathervane, as a finishing touch—demonstrate the operation of indices in general.

As we saw, the animal used as a cipher is employed to *make a point*, and there is no obvious or necessary reason for choosing this particular animal. Austin's pigs and Buridan's ass were, for all philosophical intents and purposes, interchangeable, faceless placeholders. An index, on the other hand, points out what is of interest, using a quality or behavior peculiar to the animal, and is therefore intrinsic to the philosophical argument. What creature could better demonstrate the operation of an index than Peirce's eternally indicative weathercock? The cipherous use, in which the choice of creature is entirely arbitrary, stands in direct contrast to the indexical use, in which specific traits are especially

81. D. M. Wilson, *Bayeux Tapestry*, 182.

Deep Sea Angler Fish (*Melanocetus*).
NOC/imagequestmarine.com.

14. BIOLUMINESCENT FISH

In deeper waters (say 100–1000m) very little light penetrates, so everything is mostly just a very dull "grey," barely visible against an even darker background. Here, in fact, the fish may be "colored" to maximize its darkness in its natural setting so as to not be seen by predators. Since red is one of the first colors to be absorbed, anything that is red at depth actually looks very black—but bring it to the surface, and it will be brightly colored red. Most fish, however, take the black route. Now one possible exception for color at depth might be when the organism is "bioluminescent," i.e., it creates its own light. Generally, this light is a greenish color, but the rest of the fish is black or dull brown. When brought to the surface, the "light" would not be on (the fish is usually dead by then), so its color would still just be the dark brown/black.

ROBERT K. COWEN, personal communication.

selected. Both means of employment retain the services of animals, but whereas the cipherous use denies significant attributes to the animal, the indexical use relies on them.

Austin himself employs an enlightening index in the same lecture in which his cipherous pigs appear. He is discussing yet another way in which we use the word *real*:

> Suppose . . . that there is a species of fish which looks vividly multi-coloured, slightly glowing perhaps, at a depth of a thousand feet. I ask you what its real colour is. So you catch a specimen and lay it out on deck, making sure the condition of the light is just about normal, and you find that it looks a muddy sort of greyish white. Well, is *that* its real colour?[82]

Austin's point here is to demonstrate that the "real colour" of something cannot be defined, as some have been inclined to say, simply as the color that it appears to be "to a normal observer in conditions of normal or standard illumination."[83] If we observe of someone, "That isn't the real color of her hair," we are not suggesting that, stretched or otherwise, once she moved her hair into normal light we would find that it is in fact a different color.[84] The word *real*, as we have seen, has many varied applications that cannot be reduced to some core element. And in contrast to his cipherous pigs, Austin's deep-sea fish has here been carefully chosen to help illuminate this point. His **CHAMELEON** aside, there are relatively few creatures whose coloration can change so drastically with their environment, and substituting asses, wolves, or even quasi pigs for the **BIOLUMINESCENT FISH** would render Austin's lesson meaningless.

The final parable of Arthur Schopenhauer's *Parerga and Paralipomena* provides us with a third example of the animal index:

82. Austin, *Sense and Sensibilia*, 65–66.
83. Ibid., 65.
84. Ibid.

Louis A. Sargent, *Common Porcupine*, in Frank Finn, *The Wild Beasts of the World*, 204.

15. PORCUPINE

A porcupine leads a solitary existence throughout much of its life. . . . Why are porcupines solitary? . . . One of the proposed benefits of group living is defense against predators. A group has more eyes and ears to detect a predator and possibly more muscle to repel an attack. But the porcupine defense is so powerful against all but a handful of predators that an early warning is not necessary, and a single porcupine can be as effective as a herd.

ULDIS ROZE, *The North American Porcupine*, 167, 182.

One cold winter's day, a number of **PORCUPINES** huddled together quite closely in order through their mutual warmth to prevent themselves from being frozen. But they soon felt the effect of their quills on one another, which made them again move apart. Now when the need for warmth once more brought them together, the drawback of the quills was repeated so that they were tossed between two evils, until they had discovered the proper distance from which they could best tolerate one another.[85]

In like manner, Schopenhauer goes on to tell us, with characteristic misanthropy, that human society is the result of a compromise between the emptiness and monotony of people's individual lives, which draw them together, and their many unpleasant and repulsive qualities, which drive them apart. Whether this adequately accounts for humans' capacity to endure living together is less interesting, for us, than the fact that this apologue would not work were the protagonists any other creatures than porcupines. Perhaps another species with some antisocial disposition could be imagined, but none, surely, as evocative and appropriate as a porcupine. The porcupine and the point, both of the quill and of the story, are intrinsic to Schopenhauer's fable. These porcupines are not interchangeable ciphers, then, but carefully selected indices.

Like Peirce's weathercock and Austin's fish, Schopenhauer's porcupines are indices from the outset. But what of those creatures who begin their labors as incommunicative ciphers before transmuting into indices who are not just indicative but informative too? What of the ciphers who turn? We will find no better illustration of CIFERAE who unleash the FERAE within, and indeed of the dangers of dealing with informants, than in the work of Sigmund Freud, who endeavored always to transform the ciphers of

85. Schopenhauer, *Parerga and Paralipomena*, 2: 651–52 (chapter 31, parable 396).

his patients' dreams and phobias into instructive indices.

Freud's "From the History of an Infantile Neurosis," better known as the case of the Wolf Man, includes a vast number of different animals—snakes, horses, flies, beetles, foxes, sheep, a lion, caterpillars, a butterfly, and a giant snail—but one species in particular predominates. Freud tells us that when he was first approached by his twenty-three-year-old Russian patient, who remains nameless throughout the account, the young man was suffering from poor health, was completely dependent on others, and had found himself obliged to spend time in sanatoriums, diagnosed with "manic-depressive insanity."[86] The true causes of his suffering, we learn, were brought to light only after a lengthy analysis, many of the details of which were so extraordinary that Freud initially hesitated to report the case lest it place too great a strain on the credulity of his readers (12). Happily for us, the demands of medical science won out.

The key to the analysis lay concealed, Freud believed, in a singular childhood dream dating from around the time of the patient's fourth birthday, which had been related early in the analysis but whose correct interpretation took several years (33):

> I dreamt that it was night and that I was lying in my bed. (My bed stood with its foot towards the window; in front of the window there was a row of old walnut trees. I know it was winter when I had the dream, and night-time.) Suddenly the window opened of its own accord, and I was terrified to see that some white **WOLVES** were sitting on the big walnut tree in front of the window. There were six or seven of them. The wolves were quite white, and looked more like foxes or sheep-dogs, for they had big tails like foxes, and they had their ears pricked like dogs when they pay attention to something. In great terror, evidently of being eaten up by the wolves, I screamed and woke up. (29)

Delving into the childhood of his patient, Freud uncovers several encounters with wolves. We hear, as did the young patient, of the wolf in "Reynard the Fox" who used his tail as fishing bait and thereby broke it off in the ice (25). We are reminded of the wolves in the fairy tales "Little Red Riding Hood" and "The Seven Little Goats," both of whom were eventually cut open in order that their victims might be rescued (25, 31). Freud speculates that his patient's father may well have played with him by pretending to be a dog or a wolf (32, 44, 106); in addition, his elder sister used to torment him with a terrifying picture-book illustration in which a wolf walked upright (29–30). And finally, the element that Freud believes instigated the dream, the young patient was told a tale by his grandfather in which a wolf who attacked a tailor had his tail pulled off (30–31, 102). Using these clues and more, Freud begins to construct an analysis of the dream.

---

86. Freud, "From the History of an Infantile Neurosis," 7–8. Further references are in the text. The Wolf Man's name was, in fact, Sergei Pankejeff.

Medieval bestiary, c. 1200. Aberdeen University Library, MS 24, fol. 16v.

16. Wolf

A Wolf's eyes shine at night like lamps, and his nature is that, if he sees a man first, he strikes him dumb and triumphs over him like a victor over the voiceless. But, also, if he feels himself to have been seen first, he loses his own ferocity and cannot run.

T. H. WHITE, *The Book of Beasts*, 58 (translation modified).

Freud divines that the wolf who so terrifies the patient is in fact a surrogate, used by the patient as a placeholder, and that his real fear is of his father (32, 34, 40). Why does he fear his father? His anxiety is the result of the patient repudiating his own desire for sexual satisfaction from his father. The repression that causes this anxiety results from a conflict between the patient's realization that castration is the necessary precondition for satisfaction of his desire, and a narcissistic genital libido concerned for his male organ (46). What, then, were the origins of his desire for sexual satisfaction with his father and thus of his castration anxiety? Having long admired his father, the patient began to desire him sexually following an unfortunate seduction by his slightly older sister and the later rejection of his own attempted seduction of his nanny, all of which resulted in a passive sexual attitude (20, 24, 27). Most significantly, Freud deduces that at the age of a year and a half, in a malarial haze, the patient witnessed the primal scene of his parents' enthusiastic copulation A TERGO (from behind), a fascinating and edifying spectacle that, Freud informs us, subsequently confirmed his patient's suspicions regarding castration due to the particularly clear view of both sets of genitalia that this union afforded (36–38). But still, why did his fear and anxiety manifest as a terror of being eaten by a wolf? Why were his prior experiences of wolves, in fairy tales and picture books, now activated? What could this seemingly unconnected animal cipher tell us?

The answer lies, in part, in the particular method of copulation chosen by his parents, a bonding, Freud helpfully points out, that was MORE FERARUM (in the manner of wild animals). This required his father to be upright, just like the wolf in the picture book that was to so terrify the young patient later in life, and his mother to be bent over like an animal (39, 41). Similarly, the wolves who lost their tails, in "Reynard the Fox" and in his grandfather's story, will have naturally associated themselves with his fears of castration. With the wolf theme established, further elements of the dream now fall into place: the violent action of his parents is transposed into the immobility of the wolves, the patient's own intense attention to the primal scene becomes that of the wolves, their color is a reflection of his parents' bedclothes and undergarments, their prominent tails are an attempt to deny the confirmation of castration, and so on (34–35).[87] The patient's fear of "being eaten by a wolf" derives not from the content of the dream itself but from the fairy tales in which ravenous wolves were featured. The anxiety prompted by his conflicting desires causes his relation to his father to be displaced onto a father surrogate, the wolf, whom he fears will eat him (64). Here, then, the animal cipher, the wolf, becomes in Freud's expert hands an index, helpfully pointing us circuitously but inevitably back to the cause of the patient's debilitating neurosis.

As the wolves take on this new role within the narrative, Freud reveals that they have a new form too. The wolves in the dream, it turns out, were not in fact wolves at all; they were sheepdogs. Up to this point, Freud has been cautious in his explanation of the primal scene. Afraid that it might be the point at which the reader abandons him, he asks that we adopt only a provisional belief in its reality: it may well have been a primal *fantasy*, the elements of which were drawn from elsewhere (36, 39). It is entirely possible, Freud tells us, that it was not his parents that the patient observed copulating, but animals. Shortly before the dream, he had been taken repeatedly to visit the flocks of sheep on the family estate. There, Freud speculates, he would have been able to see large white sheepdogs "and probably also observe them copulating" (58). Remember that in the dream, by the patient's own admission, the wolves "looked more like foxes or sheep-dogs, for they had big tails like foxes, and they had their ears pricked like dogs." The patient subsequently conflated this observation with a perfectly innocent scene of his two parents together. The creatures of the dream, then, were in fact sheepdogs in wolves' clothing. This alternative explanation of the primal scene, and of the wolves, certainly reduces the demands on our credulity (57–60, 120),[88] but the transformation from wolf to dog has a curious side effect on Freud's analysis.

Freud's determination to demonstrate the precise entities to which the various elements of the dream refer can be understood as a psychoanalytic variant of the error that Gilbert Ryle has called the "'Fido'–Fido Principle."[89] The blunder to which Ryle takes exception is the assumption that the significance or meaning of an

---

87. A concise and comprehensive account of the significant features of the dream can be found at ibid., 42–44n2.

88. Ultimately, Freud admits, the evidence is inconclusive as to whether the child observed a primal *scene* or imagined a primal *fantasy*, but for the purposes of the role it plays in his neurosis and in its subsequent analysis, the distinction is a "matter of indifference."

89. Ryle, "Discussion." Faithful Fido returned in 1957; Ryle, "Theory of Meaning."

expression is the process or object that it designates, just as the appellation "Fido" names the particular dog who answers to that name. This equation of words with names is, Ryle argues, "a monstrous howler."[90] We might similarly reason from the model expression "he took a stick" that the phrases "he took a walk," "a nap," "a job," "a liking," "the opportunity," or "time" also refer to a selection of rather odd entities.[91] Freud is resolved to provide an exhaustive account of the component parts of the dream. He assumes that every term must designate *something*, even if it is not immediately apparent what that something should or could be. Keen to demonstrate that *wolf* means "father," he neglects not only the possibility that it might not mean anything at all but also, more seriously, the specificity of the particular animal in question. Freud does not draw our attention to any characteristic of wolves, qua wolves, that leads him to his discovery. Unlike Schopenhauer's porcupines,[92] there is nothing about wolves in themselves that facilitates this unveiling. In fact, it is only by means of a transformation (from wolves into sheepdogs) and then a speculation (that the young patient saw these sheepdogs copulating) that Freud is able definitively to discern the wolf as a father substitute at all. So why does he feel compelled to turn wolves into dogs? We can hazard two separate

answers, one AD HOMINEM, and the other, in a sense, AD CANEM.

First, Freud's determination to make this equation between wolf and dog is an overdetermination. Just as dreams can tell us about the dreamer, so analyses can be revealing of the analyst, and the introduction of dogs perhaps tells us more about Freud than about his patient. In his "Going to the Dogs: Freudian Caninophilia," Gary Genosko explores what he calls "the rich textual and extra-textual caninophilia" within the history of psychoanalysis and catalogs Freud's great fondness for dogs in both his life and his work.[93] We learn, for instance, not only of the routine presence of dogs during psychoanalytic sessions (48) and of their frequent occurrence in Freud's letters, diary, snapshots, and home movies (51), but also how Freud was inclined to feed the family dogs from the table (50), how his daughter Anna's Alsatian, named Wolf, once bit Freud's disciple Ernest Jones (49–50), and especially how Freud came to provide a German translation of his friend Marie Bonaparte's tale *Topsy: The Story of a Golden-Haired Chow* (57–58, 65–72). Genosko's account of Freud's history as a dog lover might suggest to us that the transformation with which we are concerned is in fact a *displacement*, the pack of wolves nudged aside by their canine kin. These latter creatures slink into the manifest content of the analysis from some unacknowledged cache of Freud's own latent concerns. Or perhaps, rather than a case of

90. Ryle, "Theory of Meaning," 243.

91. Ryle, "Discussion," 70.

92. Freud would go on to employ these same porcupines himself; see Freud, *Group Psychology*, 101.

93. In Genosko, *Undisciplined Theory*, 71. Further references are in the text.

metonymic transposition, this is an example of metaphoric identification. Freud combines wolf and dog into a single composite structure, drawing on recognized and entirely innocent shared features—their general form and disposition—that in fact mask some concealed, displaced common element, perhaps even a commonality that is wished for by Freud. What could such a common element be, that wolf and dog jointly identify and conceal? We will come to this in a moment. It almost seems as if Freud were modeling the dream wolves on the only Wolf he knew personally: his daughter Anna's pet, who though named Wolf, *was* in fact a dog. Wolf was certainly in the house at the times of the young Russian's analysis and may even have been present during the analytic hour (50–51). Or perhaps Freud was thinking of one Dr. Wulff, with whose work he was familiar, who had psychoanalyzed a nine-year-old boy with a dog phobia.[94] Whatever the specific psychic mechanisms at work here, Genosko notes, Freud seems to have been "blinkered by his puppy love" (7) and to have been made silent on the matter of wolves.

Derrida was similarly puzzled by Ryle's canine preoccupation. Was his choice of exemplar entirely arbitrary?

> Why did "Ryle" choose this name, Fido? . . . Because a dog is the figure of fidelity and that better than anyone else answers to his name, especially if it is Fido? . . . Fido answers without answering, because he is a dog, he recognizes his name but he never says anything about it. . . . If he is there, Fido, he cannot make the reference lie, without saying anything he answers to his name. . . . Why did Ryle choose a dog's name, Fido? . . . "so that the example will be obedient."[95]

Here, perhaps, is the second reason that Freud settles on dogs in his narrative. Faithful Fido is chosen by Freud, as he is by Ryle, because he is docile. More accommodating even than the bestiarist's ass, he represents for Ryle the placid, brute referent, unprotesting, proving an argument without ever uttering a premise or conclusion, "answering without answering." For Freud, he bounds enthusiastically forward, ready to take his place within the analysis, uttering never a yap nor yowl of complaint. The dutiful house dog is altogether more suited than the wild wolf to the family setting in which Freud wants his analysis to play out.

Genosko argues that Freud's predilection for dogs ends up skewing the psychoanalytic endeavor. This weakness manifests in two related guises, which Genosko calls "pillars of the psychoanalytic bestiary" (58). First, it causes Freud to domesticate the animals that appear in the analysis. Freud suggests that the anxiety-animal, the wolf, was not easily accessible to observation by the young patient, as a horse or dog might have been, and was known only from stories and picture books.[96] But, in fact, Genosko notes

---

94. Freud, "Return of Totemism," 128.

95. Derrida, *Post Card*, 243–44.

96. Freud, "From the History of an Infantile Neurosis," 32; "Return of Totemism," 127.

that, as a Russian living in "wolf-country," where wolves were part and parcel of "popular culture and aristocratic sport," Freud's patient is likely to have had plenty of exposure to large white wolves (60–61).[97] He may well have encountered them outside the orderly structures of childhood fairy tales. Thus, the wolves of the dream could well have been wolves and not dogs. Whether or not this detail of personal history seriously affects Freud's explanation becomes immaterial, however, when we consider the second pillar.

The transformation from wolf to dog demonstrates that it does not really matter which animal operates as father surrogate in this, or indeed any other psychoanalytic narrative involving the animal phobias of young boys. Turning to *Totem and Taboo*, Genosko shows that for Freud all animals play this same role, whether we consider Little Árpád slaughtering and caressing his toy chickens or Little Hans donning his horse's nose bag and biting his father. "It was the same in every case: where the children concerned were boys, their fear related at bottom to their father and had merely been displaced

on to the animal."[98] Just like the boy who cried wolf, Freud is in danger of straining credibility. The Wolf Man's father is even represented by a lion at one point.[99] Genosko argues that Freud's "zoological vision was blinkered by his approach to animals as phobic objects," causing him to see them as no more than "sign vehicles" (60). There is nothing especially significant about dogs or wolves, or indeed about chickens or horses, that indicates a father substitute; as B. F. Skinner would famously put it, "Pigeon, rat, monkey, which is which? It doesn't matter."[100] They are all really just Daddy. This is the displaced common element that Freud's latent analysis-thoughts willfully wish into existence between dogs and wolves: that both represent the father. In short, Genosko reveals Freud's indices as the interchangeable placeholders they always were. The animals seem to point toward the father, but, their individual characteristics having been effaced, they remain mere ciphers. In his bid to decipher the dream, Freud fails to de-cipher the wolves.

Freud's faithful dogs, silently lying doggo, were perhaps a little too quiet. Like the faithful hound in the Sherlock Holmes mystery "The Adventure of Silver Blaze," by submitting to their master, by failing to give voice in loud and distinctively doglike tones, they denounce him. Their submissive, cipherous silence speaks volumes. Freud sets out to domesticate the wolves by transforming them into indexical dogs, but

97. For the Wolf Man's own account of his childhood, which features wolves, dogs, horses, and a good many sheep, see Gardiner, *Wolf-Man*, 17–36. On Freud's domestication of the wolves, see Deleuze and Guattari, *Thousand Plateaus*, 26–38.
98. Genosko, *Undisciplined Theory*, 59. Freud points out that no detailed examination had been made of children's animal phobias and that their general meaning may not turn out to be uniform: the widespread phobias of rats and mice may well result from different mechanisms. Those cases at which he does look, however, which all involve large animals, all submit to the guiding thesis that he here proposes; see Freud, "Return of Totemism," 127–28.
99. Freud, "From the History of an Infantile Neurosis," 39.
100. Skinner, "Case History," 230.

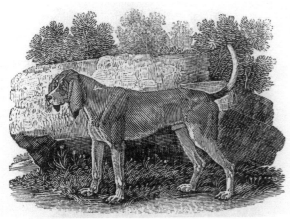

Thomas Bewick, *Old English Hound*, 1807, in Blanche Cirker, ed., *1800 Woodcuts by Thomas Bewick and His School*, plate 1.

17. Dog

"Is there any point to which you would wish to draw my attention?"
"To the curious incident of the dog in the night-time."
"The dog did nothing in the night-time."
"That was the curious incident," remarked Sherlock Holmes.

ARTHUR CONAN DOYLE, "The Adventure of Silver Blaze," 244.

paw) not at the preoccupations of the so-called Wolf Man (the Dog Man? the Lion Man?) but at those of Freud himself. The ciphers that were indices that were ciphers become, one final time, indices once more, and in so doing they betray their inattentive employer.

despite his best attempts to show the necessity of the connection, they remain obstinately cipherous within the narrative, contributing nothing in their own right as **DOGS**. Inside any CIFERAE, however, we find untamed FERAE, just as within every *Canis familiaris* there remains an ancestral *Canis lupus*.[101] These are not quite the docile doggies that the psychoanalyst had wished for. In treating his patient, Freud thought that he had espied the wolves first and thereby deprived them of all their ferocity. In reality, however, they had been keeping their eye on him long before he had adjusted to the twilight gloom,[102] and his own obmutescence is the result. At the precise moment that Freud inadvertently makes his patient's animals into ciphers, dutifully filling their places, they reveal themselves as indices once more, this time pointing an accusing finger (or

AN ABC OF ANIMALS

We have seen how Bataille concerned himself with the question of "animality," whilst Heidegger addressed the impoverished lot of "the animal." In both accounts there was an implicit leveling at work. In deploying the notion of animality, or the animal, an inconceivable variety of living beings is flattened into a more manageable philosophical form. This compression of diversity, this indifference to difference, is described by David Wood as a "deadening

---

101. The designation *Canis lupus familiaris* for the domestic dog has been proposed as a replacement for *Canis familiaris* precisely in order to acknowledge this wolfish ancestry; see Wang and Tedford, *Dogs*, 65–67.

102. "For centuries everyone feared the hunting packs [of wolves] who appeared at dusk to ravage their flocks and herds. Sheep and cattle could not be left unguarded. During the daytime, the flocks could be looked after by a shepherd boy and his dog, but at night their protection was men's work. In English, Latin and French there is the same expression for dusk, the changeover period: 'between dog and wolf,' 'INTER CANEM ET LUPUM,' '*entre chien et loup*'"; Watkins and Hughes, *Book of Animals*, 48.

shorthand."[103] This shorthand—a short, grasping, human hand, of course—holds us back. It presupposes, as Derrida argues, "one thing, one domain, one homogeneous type of entity, which is called animality in *general*, for which any example would do the job," a hypothesis that is, he says, "irreducible" and "dogmatic."[104] It constitutes, he contends, an *asinanity* (*une bêtise*).[105] To be sure, both Bataille and Heidegger mention specific animals—the goshawk and the hen, the lizard and the beetle—but insofar as these creatures serve only as exemplars from the larger set of which they are a part, they remain entirely interchangeable.

The Animal: this strange creature remains enclosed, Derrida says, as if within a "space of domestication," perhaps a paddock or a zoo, by a definite article that strictly separates "Man with a capital M and Animal with a capital A" (34, 29). From Plato to Heidegger, he complains, no philosopher who has dealt with the question of the animal has protested against the general singular of the Animal (40). This Animal is "a sin against rigorous thinking, vigilance, lucidity, or empirical authority" (48). It subsumes a multiplicity of animals (*animaux*) under a single word (*mot*), blends the plural and the singular, takes animals to be *l'animot* (41). The creatures that make up this *animot* are like the sad subjects of a circus trainer, bent low, filing past, "domesticated, bro-

ken in, trained, docile, disciplined, tamed" (39). This singular, generalized Animal constitutes a second potential stumbling block for any philosophical endeavor that would attend to what animals have to offer. In addition to acknowledging the neglected ciphers, if we are to make headway in our enquiry into Protagorean prejudices, it is vital that we free ourselves from the influence of this confusing animal amalgam. This Animal is a dubious, dangerous compendium of all possible animals and none, "a monstrous hybrid, a CHIMERA waiting to be put to death by its Bellerophon" (41). We must take up Derrida's call, therefore, and seek the death of the Animal. As Bellerophon found before us, the slaying of mythical monsters with the form of multiple beasts is no easy task, and we will need to enlist the aid of a good number of collaborators, a small army of assassins in fact, before we are done. The first step in dealing with this deadly or deadening creature, however, given the function that it plays within both philosophical and everyday discourse, will be to ask the question, "What is an animal?"

An animal, we are told, is

1. A living being, endowed with sensation and voluntary motion, but in the lowest forms distinguishable from vegetable forms only by evident relationship to other animal forms.

2. One of the lower animals; a brute or beast, as distinguished from man.

---

103. D. Wood, "Deconstruction and Humanism," 29.

104. Derrida, *Of Spirit*, 57.

105. Derrida, *Animal That Therefore I Am*, 31. Further references are in the text.

Walter Crane, *Bellerophon Slays the Chimaera*, in Nathaniel Hawthorne, *A Wonder Book for Girls and Boys*, 200.

18. CHIMERA

Iobates ordered [Bellerophon] to kill the Chimera, believing that he would be destroyed by the beast, for it was more than a match for many, let alone one; it had the fore part of a lion, the tail of a dragon, and its third head, the middle one, was that of a goat, through which it belched fire. And it devastated the country and harried the cattle; for it was a single creature with the power of three beasts. It is said, too, that this Chimera was bred by Amisodarus, as Homer also affirms, and that it was begotten by Typhon on Echidna, as Hesiod relates. So Bellerophon mounted his winged steed Pegasus, offspring of Medusa and Poseidon, and soaring on high shot down the Chimera from the height.

APOLLODORUS, The Library, I: 151–53 (2.3.1–2).

Hence animals, as moving, breathing, living beings, included moving, breathing, living humans. However, the Latin ANIMA also referred to the *rational* soul or spirit, that is, to mind, and so to that which was considered unique or proper to "Man." As the only ANIMAL that partakes of reason and reflection, Man is thus also to be distinguished from those beings that are *merely* animal in nature.[108] Finally, and precisely because he maintains this duplicitous relationship with the Animal, when Man's deficiencies, his brutish stupidity or irrationality, are brought to the fore, he is said to resemble an animal in his "want of intelligence, cruelty, coarseness, etc."[109] Those humans who are less than they can be, less than they should be, are considered animals. Animals comprise, then, a peculiar set of beings, a set that, at one and the same time, manages both to include and exclude Man. This ambiguity

3. A human being in whom the animal nature has the ascendancy. Cf. *creature*.[106]

The English noun *animal* was inherited, with identical form and meaning, from the Latin ANIMAL. This in turn derived from ANIMA, meaning "air," "a breeze," or "breath," but also, metonymically, both life in general and individual living beings in particular (as in "the breath of life").[107]

106. *Shorter Oxford English Dictionary*, 3rd ed., s.v. "animal."
107. Lewis and Short, *Latin Dictionary*, s.v. "ANIMA."
108. Cicero, *De re publica*, 321 (1.22).
109. *Shorter Oxford English Dictionary*, 3rd ed., s.v. "brute."

extends both to the older but virtually synony-mous terms *brute* and *beast* and to the ancient and more encompassing term *creature*.[110] Humans are animals, of course, but they are not really *animals*, except on those regrettable, anomalous occasions when, according to Socrates, the reasoning, rul-ing, *human* power is asleep.

> Then the wild beast within us, gorged with meat or drink, starts up and having shaken off sleep, goes forth to satisfy his desires; and there is no conceivable folly or crime—not excepting incest or any other unnatural union, or parricide, or the eating of forbidden food—which at such a time, when he has parted company with all shame and sense, a man may not be ready to commit.[111]

These are the obvious, ambiguous, everyday meanings of the Animal, a prefatory ABC of ani-mals, beasts, and creatures.

Do such definitions tell us what an animal is? Like Austin, Wittgenstein believed that in order to understand a term it is vital to attend to the concrete cases in which it is employed. In-deed, as we saw in the prelude, he took issue with Socrates for his failure to do precisely this. Dis-missing specific instances as irrelevant, Socrates' discourse was characterized instead by an attempt to *define* knowledge, that is, to discover its key, identifying characteristic. This craving for gener-ality, which is so common to philosophy, betrays,

Wittgenstein says, a "contemptuous attitude towards the particular case," is the true source of metaphysics, "and leads the philosopher into complete darkness."[112] We must resist the asinan-ity of the general term, the deadening shorthand that draws in a confusing cloud of darkness. If we wish to understand what an animal is, if we want to kill off the Animal, we must refrain from seek-ing a definition of "the animal" or of "animality" and look instead to the *animals*.

Our text has been, and will continue to be, accompanied by a succession of animals, concrete creatures running alongside our philosophical investigations. Each is a particular, tangible indi-vidual in his or her own right, not an instance of animality or of the Animal. These animal com-panions are FERAE, wild and unruly enough to escape cipherous substitution by means of their spirited heterogeneity. We could never hope, of course, to indicate the true diversity of what Wood has called "the animal alphabet," the vast and dizzying variety of animal life from aardvark to zebra.[113] Wood can do no more than recount the first few members of this alphabet: "ants, apes, arachnids, antelopes, aardvarks, anchovies, alligators, Americans, Australians."[114] And Der-rida's own attempt to disclose the "infinite space" that separates one animal from another—"the lizard from the dog, the protozoon from the dolphin, the shark from the lamb, the parrot from the chimpanzee, the camel from the eagle, the squirrel from the tiger, the elephant from the

110. Ibid., s.vv. "brute," "beast," "creature."
111. Plato, "Republic," 280 (9.571c–d).
112. Wittgenstein, *Blue and Brown Books*, 18.
113. D. Wood, "Deconstruction and Humanism," 29.
114. Ibid.

cat, the ant from the silkworm, or the hedgehog from the echidna"—ends when he is forced to invoke Noah's help, to "insure that no-one gets left on the ark."[115] We must settle instead for a tiny selection, a mere 101 chosen creatures, who are neither exhaustive nor representative, though munificently instructive. From each we can learn much, so long as care is taken that they are not diminished to characterless, domesticated space fillers. These 101 are easily distinguished: it should prove unproblematic to spot the difference. As moving, breathing, living beings, they retain their distinctive, individual qualities, so that they cannot be exchanged, one for the other, like Buridan's ass, his dog, his traveler, his sailor. Every last one of the 101 must be given space to be wild animals, not ciphers. They must be CI FERAE, not CIFERAE.[116]

These beasts and brutes are indices, aiding our enquiry by pointing things out. Some are informers, ciphers turned indices, like Freud's domesticated wolves, pointing the finger and betraying the arguments of their insensitive taskmasters. Others have always been indices, like Schopenhauer's chilly porcupines, generously illustrating their companion-philosopher's conjectures by means of their own distinctive characteristics. By their instruction, then, these CI FERAE will begin to show us the way. It is only with their assistance that we will be able to eradicate both the vacantly obfuscating ciphers and the monstrously misleading Animal that have plagued philosophy. It is the

Clyde Geronimi, Hamilton S. Luske, and Wolfgang Reitherman, directors, *One Hundred and One Dalmatians* (movie, Disney, 1961).

19. DALMATIAN

particularity of the index, or rather, the particularities of a host of indices, that will undo both the cipher and the Animal. The undertaking of these indices, the elementary education required by Animals 101, is the groundwork necessary in order both to bring about the death of the Animal and to reanimate the lifeless ciphers.

The medieval bestiary relied on the peda-

115. Derrida, *Animal That Therefore I Am*, 34.
116. The texts of late antiquity were written in SCRIPTIO CONTINUA, that is, without separating words, their interpretation and the imposition of interpuncts (points between words) being left to the reader. The practice of inserting spaces between written words was not common in the West until the ninth century; see Parkes, *Pause and Effect*, 10–11; Fischer, *History of Writing*, 260–61. The distinction between CIFERAE and CI FERAE is thus not quite so clear (see below).

20. EAGLE

AQUILA the Eagle is called so from the acuteness (ACUMINE) of her eyes, for she is said to have such wonderful eyesight that, when she is poised above the seas on motionless plume—not even visible to the human gaze—yet from such a height she can see the little fishes swimming, and, coming down like a thunderbolt, she can carry off her captured prey to the shore, on the wing. And it is a true fact that when the eagle grows old and her wings become heavy and her eyes become darkened with a mist, then she goes in search of a fountain, and, over against it, she flies up to the height of heaven, even unto the circle of the sun; and there she singes her wings and at the same time evaporates the fog of her eyes, in a ray of the sun. Then at length, descending into the fountain, she dips herself three times in it, and instantly she is renewed with a great vigour of plumage and splendour of vision.

T. H. WHITE, *The Book of Beasts*, 105 (translation modified).

Medieval bestiary, c. 1200. Aberdeen University Library, MS 24, fol. 61v.

gogic potential of individual animals. This compendium of observation and time-honored anecdote derived from sources stretching back to the ancients and before, drawing on the works of Aristotle, Pliny, the anonymous "Physiologus," and many others.[117] The medieval scholar appreciated that the animals that the bestiary contained could be edifying. Thus the beaver, knowing himself to be pursued for his medicinal testicles, would remove them with a bite and cast them before the huntsman. In like manner, the bestiarist asserted, "Every man who inclines toward the commandment of God and who wants to live chastely, must cut off from himself all vices, all motions of lewdness, and must cast them from him in the Devil's face."[118] The weasel, meanwhile, who conceives through the ear and gives birth through the mouth, signifies those "who willingly accept by ear the seed of God's word, but who, shackled by the love of earthly things, put it away in the wrong place and ignore what they hear."[119] The principal role of the bestiary, then, was didactic. It was recognized that all its beasts could teach the reader something different, and this by virtue of their distinctive ways of life. There is no place for a cipher in a bestiary.

Our CI FERAE comprise, then, a bestiary for today, 101 indexical instructors charitably and patiently waiting to point things out to us. Two

117. T. H. White, *Book of Beasts*, 230–47.

118. Ibid., 28–29.

119. Ibid., 92–93 (translation modified).

observations regarding the nature of these tutors and their lessons are in order, the first concerning their very existence. Around the turn of the fourth century, long before the first true bestiaries were compiled, St. Augustine of Hippo asserted:

> Whether those things be true, brethren, which are said of the serpent, or those which are said of the **EAGLE**, or whether it be rather a tale of men than truth, truth is nevertheless in the Scriptures, and not without reason the Scriptures have spoken of this: let us do whatever it signifieth, and not toil to discover how far that is true.[120]

Whether those things be true that are said of our sundry CI FERAE, whether, indeed, every one of our CI FERAE actually exists, are questions less important than the lessons we might learn from them. Whether AQUILA really renews her eyesight by flying from sun to fountain is less important than the indexical example that she sets, which points us in two complementary directions. On the one hand, as the bestiarist explains, the eagle's efforts are undertaken, at least in part, in order to improve the acuity of her vision. On the other, as Augustine has shown, the veracity of these efforts is of less importance than the fact that they impart a lesson. The eagle, as is fitting for so perspicacious a bird, is a double index, but the two points, the two pointings, are related: it is by ignoring the question of the truthfulness of the account that we will ourselves gain greater insight. Whether the remarkable reports of

aquiline behavior are true or entirely a matter of imaginative invention ("a tale of men") is doubtless an important question in other contexts, but it is not one that need concern us here. We must attend, rather, to what the individual animals, factual or fictional, can show us.

The terms *cipher* and *index* do not exhaust the ways in which animals can appear in philosophical texts, and doubtless there are many more functions that the birds and the beasts are required to fulfill. But it is the cipher that we must guard against and the index on whom we must rely, and this brings us to the second qualification we need to make regarding the nature of these creatures. Neither the CIFERAE nor the CI FERAE are intrinsically or exclusively one thing or the other. As we have seen, many a cipher will metamorphose into an index, but in fact plenty of philosophical beasts will demonstrate, simultaneously, qualities of both. Consider Aesop's fables, more ancient even than the bestiaries but similarly recounted in order to convey a moral lesson. On the one hand, each animal is carefully selected for the qualities they exemplify. As George Fyler Townsend says of the fables:

> The introduction of the animals or fictitious characters should be marked with an unexceptionable care and attention to their natural attributes, and to the qualities attributed to them by universal popular consent. The Fox should be always cunning, the Hare timid, the Lion bold,

---

120. Augustine, *Exposition on the Book of Psalms*, 510 (67.10); see T. H. White, *Book of Beasts*, 245.

Illustration by Thomas and John Bewick, in Blanche Cirker, ed., *1800 Woodcuts by Thomas Bewick and His School*, plate 212.

21. Fox

A Fox, running before the hounds, came across a Woodcutter felling an oak and begged him to show him a safe hiding-place. The Woodcutter advised him to take shelter in his own hut, so the Fox crept in and hid himself in a corner. The huntsman soon came up with his hounds and inquired of the Woodcutter if he had seen the Fox. He declared that he had not seen him, and yet pointed, all the time he was speaking, to the hut where the Fox lay hidden. The huntsman took no notice of the signs, but believing his word, hastened forward in the chase. As soon as they were well away, the Fox departed without taking any notice of the Woodcutter: whereon he called to him and reproached him, saying, "You ungrateful fellow, you owe your life to me, and yet you leave me without a word of thanks." The Fox replied, "Indeed, I should have thanked you fervently if your deeds had been as good as your words, and if your hands had not been traitors to your speech."

"The Fox and the Wood-Cutter," in Aesop, *Three Hundred Æsop's Fables, Literally Translated from the Greek*, 93–94.

121. Townsend, in Aesop, *Three Hundred Æsop's Fables*, vi.

122. Chesterton, in Aesop, *Æsop's Fables*, trans. Jones, vii–viii.

123. Aesop, *Æsop's Fables*, trans. Jones, 6–7.

124. Ibid., 26–27, 205.

125. Ibid., 15–16, 42.

126. Chesterton, in ibid., vii.

the Wolf cruel, the Bull strong, the Horse proud, and the Ass patient.[121]

Similarly, G. K. Chesterton reiterates that "the lion must always be stronger than the wolf, just as four is always double of two. The fox in a fable must move crooked, as the knight in chess must move crooked."[122] So, if a **FOX** meets a crow, he will flatter her into dropping her cheese;[123] if he disputes with a monkey or a leopard, we know that he will best them;[124] and if he befriends an ass or a goat, he is more than likely to betray them.[125] Throughout his many appearances in the fables, the fox is deceptive, cunning, and treacherous. Without a doubt he is, like his fabulous colleagues, an index.

On the other hand, however, we know that the animals in the fables are present only as impersonal instances of the qualities they represent. They are, as Chesterton puts it, "like abstractions in algebra, or like pieces in chess," chosen over human characters the better to communicate the truths, or moral truisms, of the tales.[126] Chesterton argues that it is only by stripping the tales' protagonists of individual traits that the virtues or vices they exemplify can be made incontestably clear. Human persons would not do, and the animals that take their places must be of emblematic, even heraldic types: "In this language, like a large animal alphabet, are written some of the first philosophic certainties of men. As the child learns A for Ass or B for Bull or C for Cow, so man has learnt here to

Winifred Austen, *Black-Backed Jackals*, in Frank Finn, *The Wild Beasts of the World*, 105.

22. JACKAL

The Lion went once a-hunting along with the Fox, the Jackal, and the Wolf. They hunted and they hunted till at last they surprised a Stag, and soon took its life. Then came the question how the spoil should be divided. "Quarter me this Stag," roared the Lion; so the other animals skinned it and cut it into four parts. Then the Lion took his stand in front of the carcass and pronounced judgment: "The first quarter is for me in my capacity as King of Beasts; the second is mine as arbiter; another share comes to me for my part in the chase; and as for the fourth quarter, well, as for that, I should like to see which of you will dare to lay a paw upon it."

"Humph," grumbled the Fox as he walked away with his tail between his legs; but he spoke in a low growl.

"The Lion's Share," in Aesop, *The Fables of Æsop, Selected, Told Anew, and Their History Traced*, 8–9.

connect the simpler and stronger creatures with the simpler and stronger truths."[127] In fact, this impersonalization belies the claims made by both Townsend and Chesterton regarding the consistency of association between creature and quality. First, the different beasts do not unvaryingly exemplify a particular virtue or vice. When the fox is betrayed by the woodcutter, he is neither cunning nor crooked but simply wronged. During the frequent appearances that he, and occasionally she, makes in the fables, the fox is not only cunning, but also cheeky, inquisitive, perceptive, foolish, indecisive, proud, and very often straightforwardly wise.[128] Second, the vari-

ous virtues and vices are not unvaryingly exemplified by a single beast. Like Buridan's ass, who was sometimes a dog, Aesop's foolish ass, who in one fable is tricked by the fox into the lion's den, is in many tellings a stag.[129] The creatures are subordinate to the lesson, and since their selection is frequently arbitrary, "natural" or universally acknowledged attributes are not always apparent. When the lion, king of the beasts, goes hunting with the fox, the **JACKAL**, and the wolf, he certainly behaves like some medieval sovereign, throwing his weight about and claiming his titular share. The jackal and the wolf, however, do and say nothing at all, and our fox is simply chastened by his misfortune. As in a number

127. Chesterton, in ibid., x.

128. Aesop, *Æsop's Fables*, trans. Jones, 105 (cheeky), 70 (inquisitive); Aesop, *Three Hundred Æsop's Fables*, 132; Aesop, *Æsop's Fables*, trans. Jones, 53 and 56 (perceptive), 202 and 212 (foolish); Aesop, *Fables of Æsop*, 90–92 (indecisive); Aesop, *Æsop's Fables*, trans. Jones, 91 (proud), 78–79, 187, 205–6; Aesop, *Three Hundred Æsop's Fables*, 126, 157 (wise).

129. Aesop, *Fables of Æsop*, 176–77; Aesop, *Æsop's Fables*, trans. Jones, 212–14.

of the fables, he is no more than a bit player, an arbitrarily chosen foil to the central character.[130] He is, in short, a cipher.

Aesop's animal alphabet is composed, then, of both ciphers and indices. The creatures may or may not be chosen for their peculiar characteristics, but they always serve as media for the time-honored moral at the heart of the fable. Similarly, in Freud's case study, the function of the wolves alternated between cipher and index. Even Buridan's cipherous ass betrayed an indexical aspect if we attribute to his critics the metamorphosis of a faithful dog into a revealingly dumb ass. In the fables, as with philosophical and theoretical texts, animals *are* neither ciphers nor indices. Aesop's fox is not intrinsically one or the other but, rather, *functions* in a more or less cipherous or indexical manner, often exhibiting elements of both. With the introduction of a heterogeneous array of different animals, we are better placed to achieve the death of the Animal, but in its place we are left instead with an *animal function*. With no natural or absolute distinction between CIFERAE and CI FERAE, our de-ciphering will depend, as Wittgenstein would urge us, on paying close attention to the concrete cases, to the particular roles, both cipherous or indexical, that individual animals play within their philosophical texts.

In contributing to the death of the Animal, our manifold animal assassins tell us far more than any attempt to ask what so singular (and yet so general) a creature might be. We are left with no answer or definition, to be sure, and we attain no stable body of knowledge that can tell us what an animal is. Such a body would be an inflexible corpus, a rigidifying *corpse* of knowledge, no better than the inanimate ciphers. The death of the Animal leaves no such carcass or cadaver. There remains instead a new set of questions concerning the functions of our animal indices, and it is Aesop, we now find, who prompts the first of these fresh queries. Even for those creatures who resist cipherous substitution and escape the fatal breath of the chimerical Animal, Aesop's exemplary animals highlight a third potential danger. To the extent that the qualities associated with an animal index are attributed by universal popular consent, to the extent, that is, that the fox has the temerity to be wily or the ass stupid, these creatures may be taken to be trespassing on properly human concerns. It is with this suspected transgression that we must now deal.

IF A LION HAD HANDS

Both Bataille and Heidegger, in their respective treatments of animality and the Animal, were at pains to avoid a particular, pernicious pitfall. The sticky temptation to attribute to animality experiences such as terror or suffering or to confer on the Animal an openness that is in truth unique to human *Dasein* is the temptation to cast the Animal in the image of Man. Such an error would, it seems, be a disservice to both

---

130. Aesop, *Æsop's Fables*, trans. Jones, 92–95, 160.

human and animal and an affront to genuine philosophical thought. To this temptation, it might be argued, both Aesop and the bestiarists have fully, indeed willfully, succumbed. Though their indexical tales purport to use the exemplary qualities of animals in order to provide moralistic observations on the behavior of humankind, in fact they have managed to invert the order of attribution. These animals, such an argument would continue, do not in reality display these traits, which are part only of human being, of human beings. Assigning them to the brutes could only ever be a reckless projection, a kind of misattribution known as *anthropomorphism*.

The term *anthropomorphism*, from ἄνθρωπος (*anthrōpos*), meaning "man," and μορφή (*morphē*), meaning "form," initially referred to the practice of attributing human shape or traits to the deities. Xenophanes was dismissive:

> But if horses or oxen or lions had hands
> or could draw with their hands and accomplish
>   such works as men,
> horses would draw the figures of the gods as
>   similar to horses, and the oxen as similar to
>   oxen,
> and they would make the bodies
> of the sort which each of them had.[131]

Xenophanes's fragment is usually taken to be a wry criticism, aimed principally at Homer perhaps, of this fanciful tradition. Characterizing the divine as an assortment of capricious and petulant individuals is, Xenophanes seems to be suggesting, risible. His contention that horses or oxen or lions, given the opportunity, would reproduce their likenesses in a similarly parochial fashion demonstrates, like Socrates's critique of Protagoras, the absurdity of the idea when taken to its logical, inhuman conclusion.[132] The Christian anthropomorphite heresies of the fourth and tenth centuries were similarly condemned for their overly literal reading of passages in the Old Testament—"His all-seeing Eye," "His everlasting Arms," and so on[133]—and for their ensuing attribution to God of a human bodily form.[134] It was not until the mid-nineteenth century that the term *anthropomorphism* moved closer to its contemporary meaning and began to refer to the practice of attributing human characteristics to entities other than deities, such as abstractions or "anything impersonal or irrational."[135] This came to include animals, and it was in this sense, for instance, that George Henry

---

131. Xenophanes, *Fragments*, 25. Compare Bertrand Russell on the subjects of animal psychologists: "Animals studied by Americans rush about frantically, with an incredible display of hustle and pep, and at last achieve the desired result by chance. Animals observed by Germans sit still and think, and at last evolve the solution out of their inner consciousness"; Russell, *Outline of Philosophy*, 33.

132. See Holtsmark, "Precursor to Plato," 6b. Hume has Philo, in a similar spirit of gentle mockery, imagine a parallel scenario in which, on "a planet wholly inhabited by spiders (which is very possible)," the idea that the world is spun from the bowels of an "infinite spider" is taken seriously; Hume, *Dialogues Concerning Natural Religion*, 51 (part 7). For a more cautious reading of Xenophanes's fragment, see Lesher in Xenophanes, *Fragments*, 24–25, 89–94.

133. Sir. 14:22 (Douay-Rheims), Deut. 33:27 (NRSV).

134. Herbermann et al., *Catholic Encyclopedia*, s.v. "anthropomorphism."

135. *Oxford English Dictionary*, 2nd ed., s.v. "anthropomorphism."

Nathan R. Howe and Younus M. Sheikh, "Anthopleurine," 386–87.

23. Sea Anemone

The sea anemone *Anthopleura elegantissima* responds with characteristic contraction to a pheromone released by wounded conspecifics. . . . We now report the discovery, isolation, and chemical structure of an alarm pheromone in . . . *Anthopleura elegantissima.* . . . When an anemone was mechanically damaged, first the other anemones in that bowl, and subsequently the anemones downstream in that tier, responded with a characteristic contraction, elicited by no other stimuli. This "alarm response" consists of a series of one to four rapid (about 0.3-second duration), convulsive, radially symmetrical flexures of the tentacles toward the base of the column.

NATHAN R. HOWE AND YOUNUS M. SHEIKH, "Anthopleurine," 386–87.

Lewes, in his *Sea-Side Studies* of 1858, warned against attributing alarm to **SEA ANEMONES** or vision to simple species of mollusk.[136] "As we are just now looking with scientific seriousness at our animals," he asserted, "we will discard all anthropomorphic interpretations."[137] Lewes's caution and his corresponding use of the term *anthropomorphic* exemplify a particular vigilance that has endured, and indeed flourished, in both scientific and philosophical discourse.

Today the term *anthropomorphism* tends to be used in any of three distinct ways. With decreasing regularity, it is employed in its very literal sense to refer to the practice of attributing physical human form to some nonhuman being, as did the Christian anthropomorphite heretics. Second, it refers to the overenthusiastic ascription of distinctively human activities and attitudes to real or imaginary creatures, a practice frequently encountered, for instance, in children's stories. Rupert **BEAR** and his chums, anthropoid one and all, invariably dress in carefully pressed jerseys and blazers and, in addition to unlatching gates, enjoy traditional childhood pursuits such as flying kites and sledging, as well as exotic adventures in faraway places.[138] The third use is most frequently encountered in scientific and philosophical literature and refers to the practice of attributing intentionality, purpose, or some other mental state to a creature or abstraction that (allegedly) does not possess these things. This particular charge of anthropomorphism is most often directed at doting animal behaviorists or sloppy evolutionary theorists who are careless in the terminology they employ. The suggestions that a particular aspect of a species has been "designed" by nature or that evolu-

136. Ibid.; Lewes, *Sea-Side Studies,* 255, 341; see Midgley, "What Is Anthropomorphism?" 129.
137. Lewes, *Sea-Side Studies,* 255.
138. On the use of latches, see Heidegger, *Being and Time,* 96 (67).

tion has been teleologically "working toward" some ideal type fall under this heading.

It has tended to be those intent on what Lewes called "scientific seriousness" who have most objected to anthropomorphic language in the discussion of animals. The entomologist John Kennedy, a vocal critic of anthropomorphism, has objected to it precisely because it is, he says, unscientific.[139] Amounting to a kind of modern-day animism, or vitalism (3–4, 9, 13–14, 157, 159), anthropomorphism assumes more than it explains by unthinkingly attributing all manner of mental states to animals (self-awareness, thought, purpose, mental images) without demonstrating that these states exist (157–60). In short, Kennedy argues, when looking at animal behavior, anthropomorphism confuses function with cause (166). As such, it is a fatal mistake for any enquiry (31) and a drag on the study of the true mechanisms behind animal activities (5). Even beyond any narrowly defined scientific endeavor, there is a sense in which anthropomorphism is always seen as a mistaken approach. Implicit within the very concept is the idea that uniquely human traits are being attributed to creatures or beings to whom (or to which) they do not belong. Indeed, if it were believed that the traits in question might possibly be shared, if God or sea anemones might have that particular quality or characteristic in common with humanity, there would be no need to draw attention to this state of affairs with such a unique

and highly specific term: the inquiry would instead be an open question concerning degrees of commonality. The very suggestion that a theory or approach is "anthropomorphic" is, implicitly, always an accusation.

This accusation might be leveled, in some instances at least, at our use of animal indices. By highlighting instructive qualities that a creature exhibits, we are in danger, it could be argued, of drawing parallels where none exist. Aesop's fox furnishes an appealing apologue, but just how

---

24. BEAR
The little bear looks up and blinks,
"I wish I'd seen it too," he thinks.

ALFRED E. BESTALL, "Rupert and the Sky-Boat," 87.

Alfred E. Bestall, "Rupert and the Sky-Boat," 87.

---

139. Kennedy, *New Anthropomorphism*. Further references are in the text. Kennedy seems unsure whether anthropomorphism is best characterized as a virus in need of a cure (160, 167) or vermin that should be driven underground (157), but his antipathy is unequivocal.

25. PANDA

I was amazed by their dexterity and wondered how the scion of a stock adapted for running could use its hands so adroitly. They held the stalks of bamboo in their paws and stripped off the leaves by passing the stalks between an apparently flexible thumb and the remaining fingers. . . . The panda's "thumb" is not, anatomically, a finger at all. It is constructed from a bone called the radial sesamoid, normally a small component of the wrist. In pandas, the radial sesamoid is greatly enlarged and elongated until it almost equals the metapodial bones of the true digits in length.

STEPHEN JAY GOULD, "The Panda's Thumb," 21–22.

Photograph by Maarja Vigorito.

140. Gaylin, *Adam and Eve*, 11. Gaylin's book styles itself as a "necessary corrective" to the lack of confidence that the human species currently has in itself and as an attempt to "reacquaint ourselves with our nature" (inside cover, 10). See especially the prologue, "What's So Special about Being Human," which, one should notice immediately, is not a question but a declaration (3–19). The penchant for ignoring the specific concerns of animal rights activists by focusing instead on the purported effects for humans or on the alleged motives of the activists themselves is common amongst those unsympathetic to their views. For an instructive discussion of this "denial of the animal," see S. Baker, *Picturing the Beast*, 211–17.

141. Derrida, *The Animal That Therefore I Am*, 37.

far should parallels be drawn between *Homo* and *Vulpes*? No real-world relatives of Rupert Bear, even the manually dextrous **PANDA**, have yet been sighted flying kites in the wild. There appear to be two distinct hazards here. On the one hand, such anthropomorphism is in danger of demeaning humans by failing to appreciate their unique traits. The psychiatrist and psychotherapist Willard Gaylin detects just this tendency in the animal rights movement:

> The purpose of the people in this movement is not to diminish *Homo sapiens* but to protect the beast. They do so by elevating animals, often endowing them anthropomorphically with features the animals do not possess. Their purpose is noble—to protect helpless creatures from unnecessary suffering—but one untoward consequence of this decent enterprise is a reduction of the distance between the nature of people and that of animals. Animal rights advocates constantly emphasize the similarity between the human and the subhuman in a worthy attempt to mitigate our abuses of the subhuman. But in so doing they seriously undermine the special nature of being human.[140]

Leaving aside the question of Gaylin's incautious use of the term *subhuman*, do we not risk, when we gather together our carefully selected posse of educational animals, ignoring the "special nature" of human being? Do we misrepresent what is distinctive and perhaps even superior in humanity? The flying of kites or the wearing of blazers are hardly the only areas in which humans have excelled over their animal kin, after all.

On the other hand, it might be argued that we do these animals no favors either. By drawing about him the cloak of human habits and foibles, we fail to recognize Master Reynard's own impressive and idiosyncratic qualities as a fox. Fables, indexical or otherwise, are, as Derrida has suggested, an "anthropomorphic taming, a moralizing subjection, a domestication. Always a discourse of man, on man, indeed on the animality of man, but for and as man."[141] By focusing on that which the animal shares with the human, we are in danger of missing all that is peculiar and proper to the fox or to the bear or to the eagle. "We try so hard to show that chimpanzees, or monkeys, or dogs, or cats, or rats, or chickens, or fish are like us in their thoughts and feelings," says Stephen Budiansky, that "in so doing we do nothing but denigrate what they really are."[142] An oft-recounted equine example furnishes a good illustration. At the beginning of the twentieth century, in Berlin, one Wilhelm von Osten, an elderly schoolmaster, presented to the public and scientific community a **HORSE** who, he claimed, possessed extraordinary mental abilities approaching those of a human being. Clever Hans, as this horse was known, communicated with von Osten and with anyone else who cared to make his acquaintance by tapping his right forehoof an appropriate number of times or by nodding or shaking his head to indicate yes and

no. Amongst his many feats were the ability to pick out colored cloths, tell the time, solve complex mathematical equations, identify musical intervals and scores, read and spell (though admittedly in German only), and even answer questions about European politics.[143] Hans was certainly no one-trick pony. A hoax was suspected, of course, but a committee of thirteen respected professionals—including a psychologist, a physiologist, a veterinarian, a director of the Berlin zoo, and a circus manager—certified that Hans was not responding to cues, intentional or otherwise, from von Osten or any other person.[144] Incredible though it seemed, Hans appeared to possess a power of abstract thought uncannily close to that of humans, and pretty well-educated humans at that.[145]

After extensive and meticulous experimentation by Oscar Pfungst, the psychologist charged with the task of undertaking a serious scientific inquiry into Hans's abilities, it was eventually found that questioners were, by means of their body language, unconsciously providing subtle, almost undetectable cues, to

142. Budiansky, *If a Lion Could Talk*, 194. Note that this objection to anthropomorphism on the grounds that it demeans animals is not quite the same as those directed at chimps' tea parties or similarly degrading instances of performing animals. Such protests, necessary and well-founded though they are, do not constitute an argument against anthropomorphism per se, since they fail to apply to performances that do not so obviously demean an animal (cinematic representations of faithful collie dogs adept at child rescue, for example).
143. Pfungst, *Clever Hans*, 18–24.
144. Rosenthal in Pfungst, *Clever Hans*, x.
145. "Experienced educators" declared his development to be equivalent to that of a human child aged about thirteen or fourteen; Pfungst, *Clever Hans*, 24.

Oskar Pfungst, *Clever Hans*, frontispiece.

26. Horse

Upon request he would count objects of all sorts, the persons present, even to distinctions of sex. Then hats, umbrellas, and eyeglasses. Even the mechanical activity of tapping seemed to reveal a measure of intelligence. Small numbers were given with a slow tapping of the right foot. With large numbers he would increase his speed, and would often tap very rapidly from the start, so that one might have gained the impression that knowing that he had a large number to tap, he desired to hasten the monotonous activity.... "Zero" was expressed by a shake of the head.

OSKAR PFUNGST, *Clever Hans*, 20.

which Hans was responding. As Hans tapped his hoof, observers tended to tense up very slightly in anticipation of the correct answer, and then, when he reached the right number of taps, they relaxed or provided other inadvertent cues that he noticed.[146] This finding was taken to indicate that Hans was exhibiting none of the complex cognitive faculties that had been claimed for him, and the case has been considered a cautionary tale for animal behaviorists ever since. This rather perverse conclusion ignores the fact, however, that Hans was actually demonstrating a fantastically keen ability to read the attitudes and behaviors of those around him, an ability far exceeding that of the trained human scientists conducting the experiments. In fact, Hans was so good at this that even when Pfungst had discovered his secret and intentionally tried to suppress his own cues, Hans was still able to ascertain the correct answers.[147] The anthropomorphic attitude shared by Hans's enthusiasts and detractors alike blinded them to his truly impressive talents. Hans may not have had hands, may not have been engaging in any of Heidegger's disclosive demarcation, but that did not stop him from being clever after his own fashion, nor from pointing out, for us, the dangers of characterizing his abilities, real or imagined, in terms of human faculties. The objections to anthropomorphism that argue that it demeans either human or animal suggest, then, that significant differences between the two are being ignored.

There have been two main responses to these attacks on anthropomorphism. First, it has been argued that discussion of animals will inevitably involve anthropomorphism and that it is therefore not something about which we should

146. Pfungst constructed an elaborate instrument to amplify the questioner's head movements and measure their respiration; Rosenthal in Pfungst, *Clever Hans*, xii.

147. Ibid. For a detailed discussion of Clever Hans, von Osten, and Pfungst, see Candland, *Feral Children*, 111–33, 134–55 (chapters 5 and 6).

complain too loudly. Interestingly, Kennedy himself has emphasized this point. He suggests that anthropomorphic thinking is "built into us," and is impossible to abandon. "It is dinned into us culturally from earliest childhood. It has presumably also been 'pre-programmed' into our hereditary make-up by natural selection, perhaps because it proved to be useful for predicting and controlling the behaviour of animals."[148] Budiansky, too, suggests that anthropomorphism is a hardwired, evolved trait, arguing that

> natural selection may have favoured our tendency to anthropomorphize: . . . Being good at thinking "what would I do in his position" can help us calculate what our rivals may be up to and outsmart them. . . . Our tendency to anthropomorphize the animals we hunt may have given us a huge advantage in anticipating their habits and their evasions.[149]

This explanation of the inevitability of anthropomorphism and of the evolutionary advantage that it bestows suggests a second potential defense of the practice.

The psychologist Gordon Burghardt has suggested that "anthropomorphism can be a pragmatic strategy" that "aids in formulating testable hypotheses."[150] Excessive rigor in avoiding potentially misleading terminology produces, he suggests, rigor mortis in attempts to devise pertinent research questions, and so investigators should feel perfectly free to ask, for instance, "'Well, if I were a rat faced with

this problem what would I do?' or 'Does that monkey want his rival to think there is a leopard in that tree?'" (916).[151] The data used in formulating working hypotheses should arise, he argues, from all manner of sources, including one's own prior experience, anecdotes, imagining being the animal, insight from observing one's maiden aunt, and so on (163). Burghardt calls this "critical anthropomorphism," and he suggests that it is both useful and healthy for the purpose of speculative enquiry just so long as we remember that we are not seeking to verify postulated characteristics or attributes but are, rather, using this strategy as an exploratory, investigative tool (916–18). Variations on this pragmatic approach are recommended by the primatologist Frans de Waal, who calls it "heuristic anthropomorphism,"[152] and by the philosopher Daniel Den-

148. Kennedy, *New Anthropomorphism*, 5; see also 28–32.
149. Budiansky, *If a Lion Could Talk*, xviii. Kennedy and Budiansky get themselves into something of a pickle here. On the one hand, they are both inclined to suggest that the predisposition to anthropomorphize is "hardwired" (genetically determined); Kennedy even calls it "human nature" (155). On the other, they are of the opinion that one should try one's damnedest to transcend this decidedly unscientific inclination (Kennedy, 160–68, and especially Budiansky, 192–94). Neither writer is clear as to how we might engage in this literally superhuman overcoming, however, a point that the primatologist Frans de Waal delights in pointing out (de Waal, *Ape and the Sushi Master*, 68). Kennedy encapsulates the tension when he suggests that the anthropomorphic disease "cannot be cured completely" but, with the right treatment, "need not be fatal" (167, 160).
150. Burghardt, "Animal Awareness," 916, 905. Further citations are in the text.
151. Burghardt's rigor mortis quip (908) is borrowed from Griffin, *Question of Animal Awareness*.
152. De Waal identifies three types of anthropomorphism: animalcentric, anthropocentric, and heuristic; de Waal, *Ape and the Sushi Master*, 74–78; see also 37–42 and 320–21.

nett, who calls it "the intentional stance."[153] Even Kennedy and Budiansky, who call it "mock anthropomorphism,"[154] consider it a useful "metaphorical" mode of thinking about the development of particular species or the processes of evolution. All these writers issue stern warnings concerning the danger of conflating anthropomorphic language with anthropomorphic thinking, however.[155]

Both the objections to anthropomorphism (that it denigrates human and animal) and the responses they have elicited (that it is inevitable and informative) are superseded, or rather preceded, by a more fundamental question. This concern, which renders problematic the very notion of anthropomorphism, is articulated most clearly by Heidegger. During his second lecture course on Nietzsche, Heidegger points out that in order even to raise "suspicions" concerning anthropomorphism, one must assume that one knows "ahead of time" what human beings are.[156] To be able to claim that a characterization or representation of some being assigns to it a quality or state that is actually distinctively human, one would need to know just what it is about human beings, in themselves, that makes them the kind of being that they are. But this question concerning the nature of human beings, the question "Wer ist der Mensch?" ("Who is man?"), is one that, according to Heidegger, is rarely even properly asked and has certainly not been answered satisfactorily. Without posing and answering this question, any suspicions concerning "humanization," as well as all refutations tendered, do not even make sense. They amount, says Heidegger, to mere "idle talk" (Gerede), to "superficial and specious discussion."[157] Heidegger is right to argue that the very claim that anthropomorphism is a potential danger for philosophical enquiry depends on far more than has been adequately established. This is true of anthropomorphism both as a term and as a concept, if we can separate the two for a moment.

There can be no doubt that there are certainly cases when behavior that might usefully be described as distinctively human is attributed to animals. Rupert Bear has already helped estab-

153. Dennett, *Intentional Stance*; Dennett, *Kinds of Minds*, 35–54.

154. Kennedy, *New Anthropomorphism*, 9, 158–59; Budiansky, *If a Lion Could Talk*, 33–36.

155. The psychologist Randall Lockwood has also discussed this constructive method, which he calls "applied anthropomorphism," as well as the important safeguards that he believes must be set in place in order to prevent it from becoming an anthropomorphism of a less benign kind (Lockwood, "Anthropomorphism"). Kant himself takes a similarly pragmatic approach, suggesting that it is beneficial to study nature (or the Author of the world) *as if* it had systematic and purposive unity (desires, volitions, understanding, etc.). This "subtler anthropomorphism" (*subtilerer Anthropomorphismus*), is a useful regulative principle of speculative reason, provided we remember that we are only applying an idea of such a being, not establishing knowledge of it; Kant, *Critique of Pure Reason*, 568–69 (A700–701/B728–29). See also his discussion of "symbolic anthropomorphism" (*symbolischer Anthropomorphismus*); Kant, *Prolegomena*, 123–28 (§§57–58). On the varied uses to which self-consciously constructive anthropomorphism has been put, see Mitchell, Thompson, and Miles, *Anthropomorphism, Anecdotes, and Animals*; and Daston and Mitman, *Thinking with Animals*.

156. Heidegger, *Nietzsche*, 98–105 (chapter 13). Heidegger uses the terms *Vermenschung* and *Vermenschlichung*, translated by Krell as "humanization" and "anthropomorphism," respectively.

157. Ibid., 102.

Winifred Austen, *Indian Flying Foxes* (Pteropus giganteus), in
Frank Finn, *The Wild Beasts of the World*, 176.

27. BAT

The scientific name for bats is *Chiroptera* (pronounced "Kirop-tera"), which means
hand-wing. . . . There are about 950 species of bats in the world, in 18 families. . . . The
evolution of flight has required comprehensive modifications of the whole body. The
wings are made from the elongated arm and hand. The fingers have been lengthened
to form the ribs of the wing. . . . The thumb has been left free of the wing and has a
claw on the end that is used for grooming and clinging to roosts.

SUE CHURCHILL, *Australian Bats*, 1: 1–2.

lish this much for us. It is unfortunate, however,
that a special term, *anthropomorphism*, has been
appropriated to describe this practice. There
is an asymmetry in place here that renders the
expression prejudicial. What of those occasions
when behavior characteristic of bears is erroneously attributed to humans? Or to wolves? Or
fish? How often does one encounter accusations
of "arktomorphism"?[158] The very fact that there
are no equivalent terms for other species seems
to imply that there is something rather special
about humans, bursting as they are with a host

of unique qualities that unwary writers cannot
resist attributing to other beings. If occasion
arises when it seems important to point out
that bears do not really indulge in the kinds of
activities practiced by Rupert, it would perhaps
be more informative to draw attention to these
errors in their specificity ("Hold on, real bears
don't wear clothes!") rather than unnecessarily
entangling the revelation in loaded terminology.
Simply by employing the term *anthropomorphism*
one has already adopted a set of unexamined assumptions about human beings and has begun
to engage in Heidegger's idle talk.[159]

The objection here is to more than just the
terminology, however. We can, in fact, go further
than Heidegger's claim that we have not yet adequately answered (or even asked) the question,
"Who is man?" The designation of any quality or
attribute as distinctively human, a designation
required by the concept of anthropomorphism,

158. The *Oxford English Dictionary* includes an entry for *zoomorphic*, a general term
that covers any and all cases in which "the form or nature of an animal" is attributed to something, though even this is principally used only of "a deity or
superhuman being"; 2nd ed., s.v. "zoomorphic."

159. See Plumwood, *Feminism*, 57.

is unwarranted, even were we able, by means as yet unknown, to identify a characteristic or attribute as being uniquely human. It is dangerous and misleading to suppose that attributes or behaviors belong to the creatures who display them, even in those cases where these creatures seem to be the only ones who exhibit a particular quality. This point is perhaps best demonstrated by an example of convergent evolution, in which the same adaptation is evident in unrelated species. **BATS** (order Chiroptera) are well-known for their distinctive means of navigation: sonar, also known as echolocation.[160] This remarkable ability is so different from anything experienced by humans that it has even prompted the philosopher Thomas Nagel to claim, notoriously, that it is literally impossible to imagine what it is like to be a bat, a supposition with which Bataille would doubtless concur.[161] But as Richard Dawkins has pointed out, sonar is by no means unique to bats. It has evolved, independently, in two different genera of birds, in **DOLPHINS** and whales, and, to a lesser extent, in shrews, rats,

and seals. Even in bats it has (probably) evolved on two quite separate occasions, in two distinct groups.[162] It was first suspected that bats could "see with their ears" in the eighteenth century and was confirmed in the 1930s, whilst it was not verified in dolphins until the 1950s.[163] This contingent historical fact, concerning the order in which different instances of sonar were discovered, gave scientists no reason to suggest, thankfully, that dolphins are "chiropteromorphic." That a trait has been identified in only one class of creatures thus far is no guarantee that it is unique to that class of creatures, be they bears, bats, or life forms more alien still.[164]

Philosophers love to hate those creatures who disrupt the carefully organized categories and arguments in which they refuse to be contained. The **BLACK SWAN** is often invoked in debates over the validity of induction as a method of reasoning: spy a single black swan, we are urged, and your confidence in the previously reliable but entirely inferred conclusion that "all swans are white" is suddenly shown to be misplaced.[165] Understood more broadly, this **BLACK SHEEP** of the Cygnus genus has something to tell us about anthropomorphism. The fact that, to date, human beings are the only creatures to have been observed exhibiting a particular trait does not justify the claim that this trait is fundamentally or uniquely human, no matter how clever or intellectually advanced it is. It is not, in the literal sense, inconceivable that

---

160. On bat sonar, see Dawkins, *Blind Watchmaker*, 21–37; Fenton, *Bat*, 27–32.

161. Nagel, "What Is It Like?" For refutations, see Dennett, *Consciousness Explained*, 441–48; Dawkins, *Blind Watchmaker*, 33–36.

162. Dawkins, *Blind Watchmaker*, 94–97. Dawkins also points out that, *pace* Nagel, even (blind) humans make some use of echoes in order to find their way about (23).

163. Fenton, *Bat*, 24–27.

164. On convergent evolution, see Gould, "Double Trouble"; Dawkins, *Blind Watchmaker*, 94–109.

165. This argument is most closely associated with Karl Popper, who used it on more than one occasion; see Popper, *Logic of Scientific Discovery*, 27; Popper, *Realism*, xx, 54, 60, 235, 256; Popper, *Philosophy of Karl Popper*, 2: 982–83, 1020–21.

Jacob Knight, *Liberatus* (detail), 1988. Painting in oils; privately owned.

28. DOLPHIN

An Atlantic bottlenose dolphin can discriminate circles, squares and triangles (all of the same standardized area), using only its sonar. It can tell which of two targets is the nearer, when the difference is only 1¼ inches at an overall distance of about 7 yards. It can detect a steel sphere half the size of a golf ball, at a range of 70 yards. This performance is not quite as good as human vision in a good light, but probably better than human vision in moonlight.

    RICHARD DAWKINS, *The Blind Watchmaker*, 96.

29. BLACK SWAN

On July 5, 1636, Antonie Caen, skipper of the Dutch ship *Banda*, came in sight of an island, apparently Bernier Island, off the north-west coast of Western Australia. In his log he recorded having seen on the sea two stately black birds as large as swans, which had orange yellow bills and were almost "half a yard" long. Here, almost certainly, is the first record of the Australian Black Swan.

    HUBERT MASSEY WHITTELL, *The Literature of Australian Birds*, 5.

Black Swan (*Cygnus atratus*) by the anonymous Port Jackson Painter, between 1788 and 1792, Watling Drawing no. 351, Natural History Museum, London.

30. BLACK SHEEP

Coloured Welsh wool was called "cochddu" in the Middle Ages or "cochddu'r ddafad" (undyed wool of black sheep, the second word apparently being a form of "defaid" the word for sheep). It is tempting to detect in this the forerunner of the modern Black Welsh Mountain breed, which has a dominant black gene. There is no word for brown in Welsh and "cochddu" can be translated as "red-black."

M. L. RYDER, *Sheep and Man*, 500.

Hand-colored lithograph by Fairland, after a drawing by William Nicholson, after a painting by William Shiels, *Breed of the Higher Welsh Mountains*, in David Low, *The Breeds of the Domestic Animals of the British Islands*.

extraterrestrial visitors might land tomorrow, visitors who engage in all kinds of activities and behaviors that had, up until that point, only appeared on earth when practiced by humans. This would not entitle anyone to claim that these aliens were presumptively "anthropomorphic" in their behavior, especially if it subsequently transpired that they had evolved those same advanced traits and abilities long before *Homo sapiens* did.[166] Better, then, to recognize and identify the quality in its own right and to leave as an open or empirical question its manifestation, or not, in diverse beings.[167]

The danger of anthropomorphism, according to its opponents and its followers alike, is a kind of narcissism, an excessive love of self. Those who succumb to its temptations cannot stop themselves from dwelling on their own image, reflected always back at them. It is important to remember, however, that Narcissus himself did not realize that the image with which he had fallen in love was his own.[168] Whilst hunting in the forest, the conceited hero chances upon a perfectly clear, untouched pool.

> There stands a fountain in a darksom wood,
> Nor stain'd with falling leaves nor rising mud;
> Untroubled by the breath of winds it rests,
> Unsully'd by the touch of men or beasts;[169]

As he gazes into the fateful water, he believes his reflection to be a mysterious, beautiful youth who

166. Gould has argued that the existence of convergent evolution on earth makes extraterrestrial intelligence a real possibility; Gould, "SETI." We will return to intelligent aliens and the question of their existence in chapters 2 and 3.
167. Midgley develops this point more fully when she discusses the possibility of understanding moods and feelings in both human and nonhuman creatures; Midgley, "What Is Anthropomorphism?" 129–33.
168. See McLuhan, *Understanding Media*, 41–42.
169. Ovid, *Metamorphoses*, 3.407–10.

seems to reciprocate his protestations of love, but remains, tantalizingly, just beyond his grasp.

> For as his own bright image he survey'd,
> He fell in love with the fantastick shade;
> And o'er the fair resemblance hung unmov'd,
> Nor knew, fond youth! it was himself he lov'd.[170]

Narcissus's appearance is delicate (TENERA) and he has an excess of pride (SUPERBIA), but he is not, it turns out, narcissistic.[171] It is not those who yield to the appeal of anthropomorphism who reproduce the sad story of Narcissus but, rather, those who believe in its very existence. Those who see anthropomorphism about them in the discourses of science and culture, whether they would eliminate it or extol its utility, believe, at heart, in a distinct and recognizable human form. Both parties see animals transformed, recast with human features. They see animals given hands: Rupert is no mere forest bear, inclined to lick someone else's hand, but rather one who uses his own hand to manipulate equipment. Those who recognize the anthropomorphite heresy, whether they condemn or commend it, assume that these hands belong originally and exclusively to humans. Those who believe in the possibility of this species of narcissism fail to appreciate that what they see is of their own making, and they practice, thereby, a true form of species narcissism. Like Narcissus, they fail to realize that they themselves are captivated by their own image,

whilst remaining ignorant regarding the very thing on which they have set eyes. If we suspend this assumption, this implicit and uncritical prior belief in uniquely human capabilities, then the very notion of anthropomorphism fails to make sense. Budiansky suggests that anthropomorphism betrays a "lack of imagination" in those struggling to conceive what it could be like to be something else.[172] Truer to say, perhaps, that the very belief in anthropomorphism betrays a lack of foresight or self-reflection on the part of those so thoroughly wedded to the idea that they are, before all else, human.

Anthropomorphism, both term and concept, starts with the human, then, even whilst the nature of that tricky category remains underdetermined. Anthropomorphism as a notion is, in short, anthropocentric. Those inclined to this first-and-foremost anthropocentrism, having started with the human, become preoccupied with the human form, even though, as Heidegger argues, they do not know quite what form the human takes. The belief in anthropomorphism is the corollary and consequence of the anthropocentrism articulated so clearly by Bataille. Supposing themselves to be human first and foremost, anthropocentrists find the world of the animal, the being of animality, incomprehensible, unfathomable, absolutely other. The epistemological anthropocentrists are thus disposed to draw one of two now-familiar conclu-

170. Ibid, 3.416–20.
171. Ibid, 3.354.
172. Budiansky, *If a Lion Could Talk*, xvii.

sions. They assert either that one must endeavor always to abstain from the sticky temptation that leads to poetic babbling and adhere instead to the limited but reliable methods of scientific seriousness, or that one must accept the inevitability and pragmatic utility of this constructive dissimulation and indulge the temptation to speak of animals "as if" it were possible to understand inhuman beings. Both conclusions hinge, ultimately, on a belief in anthropomorphism that is generated by epistemological anthropocentrism. Horses and oxen and lions, and even bats and bears, need not be considered victims of anthropomorphism even when they are discovered accomplishing such works as men, even when caught inscribing idolatrous figures. This alleged danger to our indices is of the anthropocentrist's own making.

QUIA EGO NOMINOR LEO

The charge of anthropomorphism poses no immediate threat for our animal indices, then, begging as it does the very question of anthropocentrism, which we have yet properly to address. There is, however, a more pressing potential problem for the indices. As instructors, educators who are more than mere ciphers, indices draw on that which is distinctive or characteristic in order to inform. The danger here is that animal indices are reduced to mere exemplars of their species characteristics. Chesterton pointed

out that, for the sake of the fable and its moral, it is vital that any individual traits of the animal are suppressed. Is this also the fate of our indices? There is the risk, for instance, when the dolphin shows us that bats are not the only echolocating species, that he becomes no more than a demonstration that this is the case. The danger is that the indexical use will define and delimit the animal, specifying that the dolphin or the falcon or the rat is always and only like this. The effect of this PIGEONholing is that the potential elucidation that the animal undertakes for us as an index is likely to fall back into a hackneyed, clichéd, or stale mode of thinking. In short, though carefully selected for some distinctive quality, indeed because this is the case, the index is still a sign, and as Roland Barthes pointed out, "in each sign sleeps that monster: the stereotype."[173]

It was Barthes's semiological project, he said, to understand "how a society produces stereotypes, i.e., triumphs of artifice, which it then consumes as innate meanings, i.e., triumphs of Nature."[174] His analyses of this process of naturalization, this "mythical speech," are well known from his Mythologies. The most famous, perhaps, and certainly the most frequently quoted, is his discussion in "Myth Today" of the colonial ideologies represented and affirmed by the saluting black soldier on a particular cover of the weekly magazine Paris-Match.[175] But there is another example, usually passed over, which immediately precedes this one, an example that

173. Barthes, "Inaugural Lecture," 461.
174. Ibid., 471.
175. Barthes, "Myth Today," 116. Further references in the text.

31. Pigeon

The traditional view . . . is that dovecotes were introduced
[to Britain] by the Normans. The earliest known examples
of dove-keeping occur in Norman castles of the 12th century.
. . . Dovecotes have been found on top of granaries, above
piggeries, hen houses, . . . wells, bee holes, game larders, ice-
houses, mortuaries, even privies. . . . Dovecotes had to be
protected from human, airborne and animal predators. They
also had to be sealed in order that the birds could be trapped
by their legitimate owners. Features to look out for include
shuttered louvre windows, small flight holes which enabled
the doves to enter but not their larger predators, and reinforced
doors to keep out intruders. . . . The best preserved dovecotes
retain their nest boxes or nest holes, which had to be dark,
private and dry.

  KLARA SPANDL, "Exploring the Round Houses of
  Doves," 6–7.

Wild and domesticated pigeons (woodcut). Jean Hansell, *The Pigeon in History; or, The Dove's Tale,* 154.

involves an animal. Imagining himself a pupil
in a French lycée (secondary school) once more,
Barthes opens his Latin grammar and reads a
phrase taken from none other than that mythic
author, Aesop himself: QUIA EGO NOMINOR LEO
("because I am named Lion") (115). At the level
of the linguistic system, Barthes points out, this
short phrase has "a fullness, a richness, a history" drawn from the fable and beyond: "I am an
animal, a lion, I live in a certain country. I have
just been hunting, they would have me share my
prey with a heifer, a cow and a goat; but being the
stronger, I award myself all the shares for various
reasons, the last of which is quite simply that my
name is lion" (117–18).[176]

   As part of a mythical system, however, this
rich set of values and meanings is put aside.

When it is used as a grammatical example,
concerning the agreement of the predicate, the
phrase has a new function. The old values make
way for a whole new set of ideas and assumptions, this time concerning the importance of
Aesop, of Latin, of grammar itself. We focus
no longer on the intriguing details of Aesop's
tale and are required, instead, to concentrate

176. Barthes here describes one of the fables we encountered earlier, and the
cipherous nature of Aesop's animals is demonstrated once more: the fox, jackal,
and wolf who then accompanied the lion on his hunting expedition have here
transformed, rather improbably, into a heifer, a cow, and a goat. In alternative
versions of the fable, the lion takes with him a buffalo and a wolf, a chicken and
a goat, and even a single wild ass. Following Paul Valéry, Barthes's discussion is
most probably based, as he says, on Phaedrus; see Barthes, "Myth Today," 115;
Valéry, *Tel Quel,* 191; Phaedrus, *Fabvlae Aesopiae,* 3–4. On different versions of
the fable, see *Babrius and Phaedrus,* 82–85 (§67), 198–99 (§5), 449–50 (§149);
Adrados, *Graeco-Latin Fable,* 3: 204–6 (H. 154), 673–74 (M. 218b), 678 (M. 225),
680 (M. 228), 683 (M. 232b), 792 (M. 464); Aesop, *Æsop's Fables,* trans. Jones, 66;
Aesop, *Aesop's Fables,* trans. Gibbs, 10.

on the "grammatical exemplarity" of the phrase (118–19). The rich detail of the lion's story is not entirely suppressed, however. By keeping it close to hand, "an instantaneous reserve of history" on which it can draw, the myth lends itself an air of the natural (118). This is how the myth, the stereotype, works, by invoking a "natural history" that is not its own but that shores up its legitimacy. The lion, so ferocious, so regal, so wild in Aesop, is tamed in the grammatical example, the better to naturalize the assumptions and values that accrue, at a particular time and place, around the student learning Latin in the second form of a French lycée. How obvious that one should learn Latin, that one should ensure that the predicate always agrees with the subject, that Aesop is a worthy pedagogical text for pursuing these worthy scholarly goals.

In fact, the lion functions not as an index here but as a cipher, and doubly so. First, as Barthes demonstrates, the grammatical example "tries very little to tell me something about the lion and what sort of name he has" (116). The lion is an arbitrary placeholder, used only in order to illustrate the agreement of the predicate: any predicate and any subject would have done as well. Second, Barthes's own analysis uses the lion merely in order to illustrate the technical details of the operation of mythical speech. As his second and very different example (the *Paris-Match* cover) demonstrates, more or less any sign would have done. In examining how "speech enters the service of power," how language is "worked on by power,"[177] Barthes is interested not in lions per se—nor in black French soldiers, for that matter—but in the largely unconnected stereotypes that they are made to perpetuate. Our own use of indices is not cipherous in this way: we attend immediately, necessarily even, to the rich history that we find in Aesop, in the bestiary, and elsewhere. But in doing so we still risk succumbing to the danger that Barthes has pointed out, the danger of the stereotype. Just as the lion is impoverished by his employment in the service of myths concerning education and pedagogy, so he is likely to be similarly deprived should we invoke him for some indexical purpose of our own. The vibrant detail and wealth of his history is retained, to be sure, since it is his characteristic qualities qua LEO that attracted us in the first place. But in focusing on *these* details, perhaps on his stately nobility, or on his royal cupidity, all else that he might be is pushed aside. The majestic lion is reduced to no more than a highly motivated metonym. An altogether different myth from that of Barthes is here in play, but it is a mythical stereotype that impoverishes and diminishes nonetheless. Barthes calls the stereotype a monster. Our wayward indices can certainly be wild, feral, perhaps even ferocious, but what is monstrous about the stereotype, as Barthes shows, is that, as a mode of speech, as a mode of thinking, it is reserved, curtailed, *tame*.

Are the CI FERAE destined to be domesti-

177. Barthes, "Inaugural Lecture," 461, 471.

cated, like CIFERAE? Richard Dyer has argued, following Walter Lippmann, that there is an inevitability to stereotyping. In order to make any kind of sense of what William James called the "great, blooming, buzzing confusion" of reality,[178] in order to get a hold on the "mass of complex and inchoate data that we receive from the world,"[179] it is necessary, inescapable even, that we employ generalities, patternings, typifications. Stereotypes are simply a form of this "ordering" and in themselves need not be considered a force for evil: the stereotype sleeps within *every* sign, after all. The risk lies in allowing stereotypes to hide their limitations and partiality, in failing to appreciate that it is an incomplete picture that they paint.[180] Given the potential instruction that indices offer, the possibilities for thought that they open up, this must be a risk worth taking. Aware, then, of this monstrous, slumbering menace, we must strive to prevent indices from becoming *merely* stereotypes. There are two precautions we can take.

It is the unreflective iteration of signs that lends them their stereotypic character, resulting in increasingly rigid, sharply defined categories.[181] Homi Bhabha has argued, in fact, that stereotypes achieve their fixity by means of an *anxious repetition*, vacillating as they do between that which is always "in place," obvious, known, and that which can never in fact be proven.[182] There is, it seems, an ambivalence at the heart of the stereotype. Similarly, Dyer suggests that

the rigidity and shrillness of a stereotype is inversely proportional to the internal fluidity that threatens its coherence.[183] The first strategy for preventing the stereotyping of our animal indices, then, is to indulge this ambivalence. Whatever boundaries the index sets up must remain fluid rather than fixed. What we need, in fact, are disruptive and unruly indices who question and contradict the stereotypes into which they might otherwise be fitted.[184] They need to be drawn not from the pool of received wisdom—no one learns much by being told that lions are bold—but from altogether different sources. Our indices must come from histories or contexts that are unfamiliar or that deploy characters in other than their ordinary sense. They must either teach us new lessons or present old lessons in a fresh light. The medieval bestiary, both temporally and conceptually distant, will prove an especially fruitful source for such instruction, but the origins of our indices will be various. William Shakespeare, writing from within another historical and literary context, has already shown us that even a lowly worm can turn. Rupert Bear, drawing on a rich tradition of children's fiction, took an adventurous hands-on approach. The

178. Dyer, "Role of Stereotypes," 11–12; Lippmann, *Public Opinion*, 54–55; James, *Principles of Psychology*, 1: 488.
179. Dyer, "Role of Stereotypes," 12.
180. Ibid.
181. Ibid., 16.
182. Bhabha, "Other Question . . . ," 18.
183. Dyer, "Role of Stereotypes," 16.
184. Dyer alludes very briefly to this subversive potential; ibid., 15.

rat, far from any sinking ships and now subject to the worst excesses of scientific seriousness, proved to be a devoted mother. And our chameleon, famous for her camouflage, showed that there is more to her inconstant appearance than first meets the eye. Our indices may not all seek to betray (they are not all employed as ciphers, after all), but they should all tend toward the troublesome and the disorderly, the striking or the surprising. One way or another they should all, in their individual ways, interrupt the stereotype's overeasy iteration.

A second means by which we might curtail the stereotypic appropriation of our indices is to remember that they are made up of individuals, resolutely resistant to cipherous exchange; to keep in mind, in fact, what Derrida has called the "unsubstitutable singularity" of irreplaceable living beings.[185] Even were we able to identify the precise kind of bear that Rupert is, we could not consider him a *mere* exemplar of that species.[186] He is not like any other bear; rather, he is a unique character in his own right, unremittingly polite and unaccountably attached to red jumpers and yellow trousers. He is *this* Rupert, a little bear like you've never seen before. Similarly, Clever Hans was not just any old horse. In contrast to the cipherous nags who appear in Austin, Freud, and Xenophanes, it was as a particular, extraordinary individual that he became the talk of Berlin. The same is true of the other named individuals we have met: the sparrow hawk Wulst, the Alsatian called Wolf, Calvin's friend Hobbes, Lowly Worm, Reynard the Fox. A name is no guarantee of individuality, to be sure. Fido, who simply filled a space for Ryle, was employed indexically by Derrida, who showed how only a dependable dog, only one named Fido who answered to his name, could take this place. But at precisely that moment, when Derrida demonstrated that Fido was no cipher but the epitome of the devoted hound, he became, like all those dogs of myth and fable before him, just one more man's best friend. He was now Faithful Fido, the embodiment of canine companionship. Fido, whose name was, after all, his chief claim to indexical status, became a stereotype.

Our other indices, even those who remain unnamed, all have names, of course. Aesop's lion declared EGO NOMINOR LEO, but this did not make him, as Chesterton emphasized, a particular, idiosyncratic individual. Our sheep and porcupines and dalmatians are named as such, though not as individuals. Less, even, than a personal name, does a collective designation make an individual, but these groups of sheep and porcupines and dalmatians are, nonetheless, made up of separate individuals. Our swan, chosen for his characteristic color, is intended to be taken as paradigmatic of his kind. But he was, we should remember, a single swan, disrupting induction by means of his solitary appearance. "The black swan" is a species, *Cygnus atratus*, but

---

185. Derrida, *Animal That Therefore I Am*, 9.
186. On Rupert's "ambiguous identity," see S. Baker, *Picturing the Beast*, 127–31.

each individual black swan is also, simultaneously and necessarily, a member of a genus (Cygnus), a family (Anatidae), an order (Anseriformes), a class (Aves), a phylum (Chordata), and other taxa. In fact, many of our animal indices have been drawn from higher-level taxonomic categories: "the panda" is a single species (Ailuropoda melanoleuca), but "the chameleon" is the common name for a family (Chamaeleonidae), and "the bat" for an entire order (Chiroptera). Any individual animal, every individual animal, will belong to taxa at each of these taxonomic ranks and more.[187] This does not stop them being irreducible, irreplaceable individuals. We must understand that all our indices, whilst sharing characteristics and faculties with their conspecifics (and confamilials, and symphyletai), perhaps even characteristics and faculties that lend them their indexical import, remain individuals. As individuals, singular and unsubstitutable, they will always retain the capacity, whether it is exercised or not, to disrupt the repetition on which stereotypes depend.[188]

Derrida has insisted on the importance of a singular, concrete, individual animal. In The Animal That Therefore I Am, he talks at length about a particular CAT. He first mentions, briefly, some of the other individual cats, named or not, who have appeared in philosophy and literature.[189] He refers to Franz Kafka's "vast zoopoetics," thinking especially, presumably, of the ominous tale of the kitten–lamb hybrid. He mentions The

Life and Opinions of the Tomcat Murr by E. T. A. Hoffmann, as well as Sarah Kofman's own "magnificent and inexhaustible" text about the same feline. Montaigne's cat, from "Apology for Raymond Sebond," also appears, as do the poetic cats of Charles Baudelaire and Rainer Rilke, and a watchful feline from the philosophy of Martin Buber. Even Lewis Carroll's cats and kittens, including, of course, the Cheshire Cat (le Chat du comté de Chester), are brought into the picture. None of these are the particular cat that Derrida wants to talk about, however, and he certainly does not wish here to concern himself with any cat who is a figure or allegory, who appears as an ambassador or representative of the "immense symbolic responsibility" with which cats have always been charged (9). He wants to discuss a real, actual cat, the unsubstitutable singularity of a particular cat, sitting now, gazing at him.

This cat is the one who lives with Derrida, the one insisting that she be fed or let outside. She is the one who follows him every morning from the bedroom into the bathroom and there sees him naked, before instantly changing her mind and demanding to be let out again (5–6,

187. On different scales of individual—organism, deme, species, genera, and so on—see DeLanda, Intensive Science and Virtual Philosophy, 45–58. We will return to biological systematics in "Four Hands Good, Two Hands Bad" in chapter 5.
188. It is instructive to compare here the "unsubstitutable singularity" to which Derrida appeals with the "attenuated individuality" that Raimond Gaita, assuring us that humans are "unique and irreplaceable . . . in a way that nothing else in nature is," would extend only to some few nonhuman animals; see Gaita, Philosopher's Dog, 83, 78.
189. Derrida, Animal That Therefore I Am, 6–9. Further references are in the text.

Darby Conley, *Get Fuzzy*

32. CAT

9, 13). This cat is the one who sits, now, gazing at him as he writes. This cat is, without question, an individual, though for us she remains unnamed within Derrida's amiable discourse: "Nothing can ever rob me of the certainty that what we have here is an existence that refuses to be conceptualized. And a mortal existence, for from the moment that it has a name, its name survives it" (9). Derrida does not actually say that "it has a name," of course: the reifying pronoun is an unfortunate consequence of the translation into English. Derrida has pointed out to us, indeed it is relevant to the embarrassment that he feels, that his cat is a female cat, "*une chatte*" (6 and passim). But having made this specification, having drawn our attention to her gender, Der-

rida persists in using the "generic masculine" (*un chat*) that he had formerly confined to the cats of figure and allegory: he says "il a un nom." Derrida's cat, who has a name, though she remains unnamed, is both *une chatte* and *un chat* (9–11). Her existence both as a female cat and as an individual cat seems, by this curious conflation, temporarily to be neglected.[190] These oversights, if such they are, take nothing from Derrida's important point that it is individual animals who can discourage us from tame, routinized, stereotyped modes of thought. They point, rather, to the persistence with which forms of discourse, philosophical and otherwise, can work against the attempt to use words that are genuinely naked.

Derrida is embarrassed before the gaze of this cat. He is embarrassed because, he tells us, he is naked. He wants to choose words that are naked, "words from the heart" (1). He wants to

---

190. On the prevalence of this elision, made by substituting or withholding genders, see Adams, *Sexual Politics of Meat*, 74–77, 81–85; Dunayer, *Animal Equality*, 149–56 (chapter 10).

avoid unreflective iteration, wants to resist a habit or convention that, like a repetitive training (*dressage*), would program the very act of thinking. He wants, in fact, to be naked before *an* animal in order to avoid stereotyped ways of thinking about animals. He has in mind here all those philosophers who discuss, as we have seen, that strange creature that they call "the Animal" without ever calling into question this "general singular" (34, 40–41), or those who would gaze *at* the animal, who turn it into something that is seen, without ever considering the possibility that an individual animal might gaze back, might see them, might address them (13–14). These are stale, formulaic, easy modes of thinking that are repeated far too often by philosophers and theoreticians, when they think about "the Animal." Derrida wants, by contrast, to allow himself to feel uncomfortable, naked even, before the gaze of an individual animal. The animal he chooses, or perhaps the animal who chooses him, is his cat, the cat who lives with him, the cat who looks at him in his bedroom or bathroom, the cat who, like all other cats, is an irreplaceable living being, an individual.

TAKING ANIMALS IN HAND

Philosophy has sought to tame its animals. On the one hand, they have been marginalized, neglected, underdetermined. They have been ciphers, faceless placeholders of no consequence in their own rights, turned to meaningless drudgery and donkey work; or else they have been subsumed under an amorphous Animal, that curious *animot*, a monstrous, chimerical hybrid who was confined to a strictly enclosed paddock, awaiting death. On the other hand, they have been driven too hard, overtaxed, overdetermined. They have been cast in the image of Man, subjected to an anthropomorphic domestication, put to work that they can manage, it seems, only by exercising vulpine wile; or else they have been bold stereotypes, clearly defined and delimited clichés, conventionally trained by means of relentless repetition. In explaining the origins of animal husbandry, Varro suggested that on moving from a state of nature to a pastoral way of life, men "caught, confined, and tamed [MANSUESCERENT] such wild animals as they could, for their advantage."[191] MANSUESCERE literally means "to accustom to the hand." In the texts of philosophy, that human hand has taken advantage of animals by taking them in hand. It has disciplined and domesticated them, has required them to submit, has accustomed them to the hand. This attempt to catch, confine, and tame wild animals has been, however, only partially successful.

At the close of this first, indicative chapter, there is one more animal to whom we should attend and for whom such taming seems particularly ill-advised. This regal creature has already appeared several times: he has been a powerful wave for Bataille, a role model for a donkey, a

191. Varro, *On Agriculture*, 2.1.3–4 (translation modified).

33. LION

The Lion, mightiest of beasts, fears nothing he meets. . . . Now LEO in Greek is translated "king" (REX) in Latin, because he is the ruler of all beasts. His species is said to have three types, of which the small ones and the ones with curly mane are peaceful, the tall ones with straight hair are fierce; it is the brow and tail that indicate their characters [ANIMI]. . . . The nature of lions is such that they cannot become angry toward men, unless they are hurt. Rational men should reflect upon their example, men who become angry when not hurt, and who oppress the innocent, because Christian law requires that even the guilty be set free. For the mercy of the lion is apparent in continuous examples, for they spare the prostrate, and allow captives they encounter to return home. They rage against men rather than against women. They do not kill children unless they are very hungry. Likewise, they all eat food moderately. First, they drink on some days, and take food on others. But frequently, if digestion has not occurred, they skip a day of their usual eating. Consequently, because having eaten an excess of meat they feel burdened, they voluntarily draw out the excess by sticking their claws in their mouths.

WILLENE B. CLARK, *A Medieval Book of Beasts*, 119–21 (translation modified).

Medieval bestiary, c. 1200–1210. British Library Royal, MS 12 C. xix, fol. 6r.

gentle guardian for Shakespeare, a substitute for the Wolf Man's father, the forepart of a chimera, an image carver for Xenophanes, a regular protagonist in the fables of Aesop, and a grammatical and mythological paradigm for Barthes. He is, of course, the **LION**, and it is fitting that he should conclude the chapter. Traditionally, LEO, ruler of the beasts, first among animals, appeared always at the beginning of the bestiary. Having been usurped from his rightful place, it is only proper that he be saved till last, that we may pay him due tribute. The lion will be, for us, an exemplary, authoritative instructor, pointing out and summarizing the chapter's two key themes.

First, the lion demonstrates the vital role of animal indices amongst the brutes and beasts who appear in the texts of philosophy and critical theory. He has functioned, at different points in the chapter, according to all three of the principal characteristics of the index. In the first place, he has appeared as a worthless cipher, the menial part assigned to so many of those who subsequently become something more. Freud and Xenophanes both used him this way as they pursued their own projects. Second, indices can inform on and betray their employers, indicating oversights, ellipses, or limitations in their work. The lion helped show how, in demonstrating the nefarious workings of mythic speech, Barthes overlooked the cipherous nature of his own example. Finally, and most importantly, indices can draw things to our attention, can educate us, can remind us of forgotten lessons or point out new avenues of thought. The lions of the bestiary illustrate how we can learn not just *about* specific animals—how we can determine the nature of an individual lion from his mane, brow, and tail, for instance—but also *from* animals, in this case the valuable lessons of temperance, mercy, and abstinence.

The lion is the king of the beasts, the index of the indices. These 101 wild animals resist the varied attempts to trap and tame them. The vast animal alphabet of heterogeneous species gives the lie to the myth of undifferentiated animal life, the surging but homogeneous mass of "animality" with which we started. The goshawk and the hen, the sea anemone and the chameleon, along with all the other untrained but enthusiastic SICARII, help bring about the death of the Animal in the general singular. The Animal is dead: long live LEO. At the same time, pursuing this bid to debunk philosophy's propensity to generalize, to ignore the concrete case, a number of educative indices helped invigorate the listless ciphers fated to a life of unfulfilling toil. An illuminating fish, a herd of spiny porcupine, a perspicacious eagle, and others all required due acknowledgment of their specificity. The indeterminate CIFERAE became precisely CI FERAE. Those creatures destined for anthropomorphic domestication, to the playing of roles that are not, according to the scientifically serious, their

own, were saved by the sharp senses of their fellows. The bats and the dolphins, aided by a single black swan, pointed out the ill-formed traps of their would-be captors. Finally, the precisely programmed stereotypes, ceaselessly repeating their thoughtless training, were released both by disruptive indices and by irreplaceable individuals. A lowly, turning worm, a devoted mother rat, and a betrayed fox all resisted typecasting, whilst Wulst and Wolf, Rupert and Hans, and their unnamed associates were not insistent stereotypes but unsubstitutable singularities.

Second, the lion reminds us of the anthropocentrism that our animal indices will help us investigate in the chapters to come. "If lions had hands," Xenophanes began, "then they would also have the word," Heidegger would be required to conclude. But "if a lion could talk," Wittgenstein famously suggested, "we could not understand him."[192] There are three assumptions at work in these theses, which the discussion of anthropocentrism thus far has sought to highlight and to bring into question. In proposing the fanciful possibility that lions might have hands, Xenophanes reaffirms that, in reality, they do not. That is, he reiterates the supposition that there is a distinctive trait or attribute—"the hand"—that should be considered unique and proper to "Man." This unique trait, Heidegger proposes, gives humanity privileged access to the world: only because they have "the hand" do humans have "the word" and are thereby able

---

192. Wittgenstein, *Philosophical Investigations*, 223 (2.11).

to partake in the unconcealedness of beings. Man is the measure of all things. Finally, Wittgenstein's enigmatic aphorism has been taken to articulate the complementary thesis that the animal will always be absolutely other.[193] Even if, by some fabulous means, certain animals did have the word, their worldviews would be so alien that the uncrossable abyss would open up once more. These three assumptions—that there is some characteristic or trait that should properly be called "human," that it provides human beings with a privileged and determining means of apprehending the world, and that "the animal" thereby remains obstinately and absolutely other—articulate a form of epistemological anthropocentrism. This true species narcissism, which places the human first and foremost, precludes the investigation of the three theses themselves. There may be some trait proper to humanity that makes possible an exceptional epistemology and that in turn renders the animal forever unknowable, but these are questions that have yet to be adequately formulated, let alone resolved. This first-and-foremost anthropocentrism, this Protagorean presumption, forecloses both what "the animal" is permitted to be and what "the human" can think.

This foreclosing is a form of domestication that depends on capturing and confining, which simultaneously regulates both "the animal" and the very thinking that addresses it. It is a matter of MANSUESCERE, a taming that relies on the authority of the hand. It does not merely brush the fly away with a casual, thoughtless hand but entraps and imprisons, as within a fly bottle. Animality and the Animal, philosophy's ciphers and its stereotypes: all begin by restricting and delimiting the possibilities of both what animals can be and what philosophy itself can know. In order to hold back this taming hand, in order to maintain an openness toward animals and toward thought, we must permit the animals to be wild. This wildness is not of the frenzied, reckless kind described by Socrates, which brutishly pursues its rapacious desires unhindered by reason or restraint. Rather, like the animals of the medieval bestiary, the CI FERAE are wild in the sense that they wander hither and thither, roving wherever the spirit (ANIMUS) leads them. They are wild in the sense that they will not be pinned down. They retain a deliberate air of ambivalence or ambiguity, wending an unhurried course through life. They are itinerant, unmanageable, and just a little unruly: pests rather than pets.[194] They are FERA like Derrida's cat, accustomed to freedom by nature and driven (FERANTUR) by their own wishes. She does not rage about with tooth and claw but, rather, wanders from one room to the next, insistently roaming first this way, then that, an amiably unruly, indexical individual. Can animals remain wild and untamed? Are animals not always

193. Wittgenstein's precise meaning has been a matter of debate. See, for instance, Luckhardt, "Lion Talk"; Sandis, "Lion for Real"; and Wolfe, "In the Shadow of Wittgenstein's Lion."

194. See Glendinning, "From Animal Life to City Life."

already tamed by thought? Is it not *inevitable* that thinking, both about animals and about thought itself, will always, unavoidably, take the human as its starting point? Is Man the measure of all things? In short, are not thought and knowledge always, inherently, anthropocentric? The CI FERAE, the 101 wild animals, will help us investigate these questions. In the next three chapters we will explore whether or to what extent it is meaningful or productive to suggest that philosophy, and especially the philosophy of knowledge, is implicitly or intrinsically anthropocentric, before returning, in the final chapter, to the question of the nature of *anthrōpos* itself.

Arctognathus curvimola, digital art by Nobumichi Tamura.

34. GORGON

Gorgonopsids were the largest predators of the late Paleozoic, the era just before dinosaurs. They grew as large as 10 feet long and were among the most ferocious predators ever. . . . Their heads appeared somewhat dog-like, with large saber-tooth upper canine teeth up to 4 inches long. Though they had a somewhat mammalian appearance, their eyes were set at the sides of the head like those of a lizard, and the body was probably covered with scales rather than hair. The gorgons would have resembled a cross between a lion and a large monitor lizard—leading to the name science has given them. "Gorgons" are mythical monsters with such a horrible appearance that gazing upon them turns an observer to stone.

VINCE STRICHERZ, "First Complete Fossil of Fierce Prehistoric Predator Found in South Africa."

The chapter title comes from Martial, *Epigrams*, 1: 152–53 (2.28). The full text of this fantastically filthy poem is as follows:

RIDETO MULTUM QUI TE, SEXTILLE, CINAEDUM
    DIXERIT ET DIGITUM PORRIGITO MEDIUM.
SED NEC PEDICO ES NEC TU, SEXTILLE, FUTUTOR,
    CALDA VETUSTINAE NEC TIBI BUCCA PLACET.
EX ISTIS NIHIL ES FATEOR, SEXTILLE: QUID ERGO ES?
    NESCIO, SED TU SCIS RES SUPERESSE DUAS.

"Laugh loudly, Sextillus, at whoever calls you a queen and put your middle finger out. But you are no sodomite nor fornicator either, Sextillus, nor is Vetustina's hot mouth your fancy. You are none of these, I admit, Sextillus. What are you then? I don't know. But *you* know that two possibilities remain" (translation modified). On the sexual taxonomy on which this insult depends, see H. N. Parker, "Teratogenic Grid," 51.

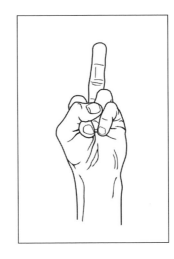

RIDETO MULTUM ET DIGITUM PORRIGITO MEDIUM

Laugh Loudly and Flip Them the Bird

TWO HANDS ARE BETTER THAN ONE

t the British Academy Annual Philosophical Lecture in November 1939, G. E. Moore delivered a paper boldly entitled "Proof of an External World." Moore took his cue directly from Immanuel Kant, who had suggested that

it still remains a scandal to philosophy and to human reason in general that the existence of things outside us (from which we derive the whole material of knowledge, even for our inner sense) must be accepted merely on faith, and that if anyone thinks good to doubt their existence, we are unable to counter his doubts by any satisfactory proof.[2]

Unconvinced by Kant's own refutation of what he had called "material idealism,"[3] Moore sought in his lecture to provide, once and for all, a sound proof that there exist "things outside of us," that is, a proof that there are "things external to our minds" that do not depend on someone experiencing them.[4] Moore took this scandal to philosophy seriously, and that the existence of the external world could be doubted was for him a genuinely pressing philosophical problem. By the time of the lecture, he had been a long-standing critic of idealism and had indeed been described as "the spearhead of the attack and one of the major leaders of the modern move-

The middle finger, the MEDIUS, is the vulgar, obscene finger. The "one finger salute," also known as "flipping the bird," is widely recognized in many countries around the world, and the gesture was employed at least as far back as Roman times. Speculation regarding the origin of the finger's profane association has been extensive and of varying plausibility. John Napier points out that as the longest digit, it is "ideally disposed to carry out sexual caresses of the female genitals or indelicate scratching operations," and it has also been suggested that it is the finger used most when going to the toilet. The Romans had several colorful names for this finger: the DIGITUS IMPUDICUS (the shameless or immodest finger), the DIGITUS FAMOSUS or INFAMIS (the defamatory or infamous finger) and the DIGITUS OBSCENUS (the repulsive or lewd finger). One tale, perhaps apocryphal, recounts that when offering his hand to be kissed, the emperor Caligula would sometimes extend only his IMPUDICUS, a truly obscene and insulting gesture.[1]

1. Napier, *Hands*, 22–24; Hammond, *Finger Prints*, April 1, 2003; D. Morris et al., *Gestures*, 79–92; Isidore of Seville, *Etymologiarum sive originum*, 11.1.71; F. W. Jones, *Principles of Anatomy*, 8–9, 145.
2. Kant, *Critique of Pure Reason*, 34 (Bxxxix).
3. Ibid., 244–47 (B274–79).
4. Moore, "Proof of an External World," 129 and passim.

35. HARPY

The most powerful bird of prey on Earth, the harpy eagle, weighs up to 20 pounds (nine kilograms), has a seven-foot (2.1-meter) wing span, and is armed with talons as big as grizzly bear claws. Those deadly talons can exert several hundred pounds (over 50 kilograms) of pressure, crushing the bones of the sloths, monkeys, and other prey the eagle snatches from the rain forest canopy, often killing its victims instantly. It's no wonder that early South American explorers named harpy eagles after the predatory half-woman, half-bird monster of Greek mythology.

SHARON GUYNUP, "Conservationists Fight to Save Harpy Eagles."

Photograph by Carlos Henrique Reinesch.

ment known as philosophical realism."[5] When the philosopher John Wisdom suggested to him that those thinkers who denied the existence of matter were not doing so in quite the literal manner Moore had supposed,

> he reached down from his shelves MacTaggart's [sic] *Some Dogmas of Religion* and pointed to the words "The result is that matter is in the same position as the **GORGONS** and the **HARPIES**. Its existence is a bare possibility to which it would be foolish to attach the least importance, since there is nothing to make it at all preferable to any other hypothesis however wild."[6]

As a "commonsense" philosopher, however, Moore believed that the difference between John McTaggart's mythical monsters and real, material objects was significant. Contrary to Augustine's contention, it mattered a good deal whether gorgons and harpies roam the world at large or are creatures only of the imagination.

Moore's lecture begins with an extended explanation of precisely what he intends by the phrase "external to our minds."[7] Following Kant, we might usefully consider it more or less equivalent, he suggests, to the words "things which are

5. Schilpp, *Philosophy of G. E. Moore*, xiii. See, for instance, Moore's influential early essay "Refutation of Idealism."

6. Wisdom, *Paradox and Discovery*, 83.

7. The phrase is Moore's, not Kant's, and he takes it from "a long philosophical tradition" that goes back at least as far as René Descartes; Moore, "Proof of an External World," 129. In fact, Moore reproaches Kant for rather imprecisely using a range of similar expressions that he takes to be equivalent but that in fact are not (129–39). Kant states his objective variously to be to prove the existence of (1) things outside us (*Critique of Pure Reason*, 34/Bxxxix note), (2) the objective reality of outer intuition (ibid.), (3) things to be met with in space (348/A373), and (4) things presented in space (ibid.). We will return to Kant's own discussion of things outside us in chapter 3.

to be met with in space," which would include "my body, the bodies of other men, the bodies of animals, plants of all sorts, stones, mountains, the sun, the moon, stars, and planets, houses and other buildings, manufactured articles of all sorts—chairs, tables, pieces of paper, etc."[8] These we should distinguish, Moore argues, from those things that might be described as "in my mind" (140). As it has been appropriated by philosophers, however, this latter phrase has gained employment, Moore concedes, that is "not quite in accordance with any usage common in ordinary speech" (141). In everyday parlance, those who use a phrase such as "I had you in mind" mean simply, of course, that they were thinking of you (140). You will be external to a philosopher's mind, however, even at the moment when they have you in mind. Examples of things that should, philosophically, be considered under the heading "in my mind" are remembering, thinking, and imagining; feeling "mental pains" like disappointment; "mental occurrences or processes" such as seeing, hearing, smelling, and tasting; bodily pains, including headaches and smarting fingers; visual afterimages seen with closed eyes; and any images "seen" whilst asleep or dreaming (140–41). In short, they are those things that entail us "having an experience" or of which we could say that they "furnish data for psychology" (141–42). Things that are wholly external to my mind, such as stars or stones, will not necessarily furnish such data or automatically involve anyone in having an experience: they may very well remain unobserved throughout their existence.

What then was Moore's proof of the existence of such external things? He told his audience, "I can prove now, for instance, that two human hands exist. How? By holding up my two hands, and saying as I make a certain gesture with the right hand, 'Here is one hand,' and adding, as I make a certain gesture with the left, 'and here is another'" (145–46). How does this prove the existence of external things? Moore maintains that his demonstration fulfills the three key conditions necessary for a rigorous proof. First, the conclusion that he draws is different from the premise on which it is based. The conclusion "two human hands exist" is certainly different from the premise "here is one hand and here is another" (with accompanying gestures), since the former could be true even if the latter were false (a pair of human hands could exist *somewhere*, whether or not Moore's were currently employed as a philosophical proof). Second, the premise is known to be true, rather than merely believed. How absurd it would be, Moore argues, to suggest that he did not *know* there was a hand in

8. Moore, "Proof of an External World," 130. Further references are in the text. In a discussion of A. J. Ayer's rather similar collection of "material things," J. L. Austin later captured the spirit if not the entirety of Moore's list with his much-cited phrase "moderate-sized specimens of dry goods"; Austin, *Sense and Sensibilia*, 8. Karl Popper once supposed that "the most central usage of the term 'real' is its use to characterize material things of ordinary size—things which a baby can handle and (preferably) put into his mouth"; Popper and Eccles, *Self and Its Brain*, 9.

the place indicated by his gesture and utterance and that he only *believed* something that might actually turn out to be false. Third, the conclusion follows from the premise. It is quite certain, Moore says, that the conclusion (there are two hands in existence) follows from the premise (there is one hand *here* and another *here*) (146–47).[9]

For those who remain doubtful, Moore points out that people happily employ proofs of exactly this kind on a regular basis. Imagine, he says, a disagreement over the number of misprints on a certain page of a book. The individual arguing that there were three such misprints might prove that this was the case by pointing at the offending typography and saying, "Here is one misprint, here is another, and here is another" (147). Provided there were indeed missprints in evidence, their existence would thereby have been proven. And what applies to newspaper misprints, Moore argues, also applies to his hands. He is aware that many might find these arguments unsatisfying, but he maintains that his proof is sound and, further, that it is (perhaps) impossible to give a better or more rigorous proof of anything whatever (146).

Moore's proof is indeed unlikely to convince skeptics or those whose faith in the existence of things outside us has not been shaken, but my objective here is not to prove or disprove his argument.[10] Rather, I wish to employ his lecture as an exemplar of that philosophical

position known as *realism*, to which this chapter is devoted. We will examine the distinguishing properties of this position shortly, but for the moment it is enough to note that Moore's confidence in external objects that exist outside personal and potentially idiosyncratic experiences of them is characteristic of realism. I want to suggest that Moore's realist proof, his demonstration that there really are "things outside of us," exhibits a certain anthropocentrism and that his anthropocentric presuppositions, accompanied by signifying human hands once more, are pointed out to us by the cipherous animals employed during the course of his exposition.

It is whilst clarifying the subtle difference between "external to our minds" and "to be met with in space," which Kant took to be synonymous, that Moore introduces the question of animal minds. "If by our minds be meant, as is, I think, usually meant, the minds of human beings living on the earth, then it will follow that any pains which animals may feel, any afterimages they may see, any experiences they may have, though not external to *their* minds, yet are external to *ours*" (143). Thus, Moore argues, we can see that many things, for instance animal pains or afterimages or experiences, will be "external to our minds" but clearly not "met with in space," a distinction that his proof proceeds to utilize. What is interesting here, however, is that Moore takes the trouble to mention that "our minds" should be taken to mean—"as is usu-

9. Moore had employed human hands in similar fashion in his earlier essay "A Defence of Common Sense."

10. The most famous critique of Moore's argument is Wittgenstein's *On Certainty*.

ally meant"—human minds. He acknowledges, by the very fact that he allows the possibility, at least in principle, of animals feeling pains, seeing afterimages, or having experiences, that "minds" can be attributed to creatures other than human beings.[11] We can certainly imagine, for instance, that each of the two dogs (137–39), the cat (141–42), the **UNICORN** (145), and perhaps even the spider (140), who appear during the course of the lecture, might experience bodily pains such as headaches or might partake of mental occurrences and processes such as seeing, hearing, smelling, and tasting. And there is, in fact, no requirement for Moore to introduce this clarification to his argument. That the phrase our minds is or should be taken to mean the minds of human beings living on earth (or presumably anywhere else) is quite unnecessary for this or any other part of his proof. To demonstrate the difference between the phrases "external to our minds" and "to be met with in space," Moore might just as easily have discussed the minds of two human beings, each of whose experience of a smarting finger would have been external to the mind of the other, though both fingers could themselves be met with in space.

Moore undoubtedly wants the external things he has in mind, such as bodies and buildings and miscellaneous manufactured articles, to be external to all minds, including those of other animals. He says of his perception of a soap bubble, for instance, that "if, when I say that

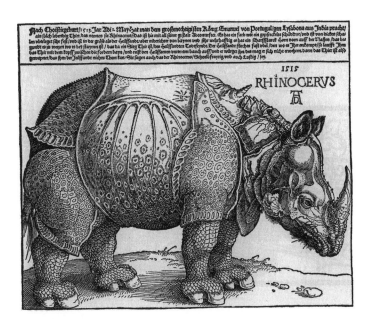

Albrecht Dürer, "Rhinoceros"; woodcut, 1515.

36. UNICORN

[In the kingdom of Basman] they have wild elephants, and great numbers of unicorns, hardly smaller than elephants in size. Their hair is like that of a buffalo, and their feet like those of an elephant. In the middle of the forehead they have a very large black horn. You must know that they do not wound with their horn, but only with their tongue and their knees. For on the tongue they have very long, sharp spines, so that when they become furious against someone, they throw him down, and crush him under their knees, wounding him with their tongue. Their head is like that of a wild boar, and is always carried bent to the ground. They delight in living in mire and in mud. It is a hideous beast to look at, and in no way like what we think and say in our countries, namely a beast that lets itself be taken in the lap of a virgin. Indeed, I assure you that it is quite the opposite of what we say it is.

MARCO POLO, The Travels of Marco Polo, 283.

11. In his use of a modal verb—"any pains which animals *may* feel, any after-images they *may* see, any experiences they *may* have" (my emphasis)—Moore might conceivably be taken to be implying that there is some doubt as to whether animals do in fact feel pain, see afterimages, or have experiences or minds at all, though this is certainly not necessary for the point he is here making.

anything which I perceive is a soap-bubble, I am implying that it is external to my mind, I am, I think, certainly also implying that it is also external to all other minds" (145). But he chooses to confine himself, for the purpose of his proof, to the human minds that he takes to be intended, ordinarily, by the phrase "our minds." Moore is perhaps right to observe that "our minds" is usually taken to mean the minds of human beings, at least amongst the philosophers who made up his British Academy audience, and perhaps beyond. He is under no obligation to follow this usage himself, however. There appears to be an unacknowledged and unwarranted anthropocentrism at work here, an assumption that, when considering the "us" of "things outside of us," or the "our" of "things external to our minds," he is dealing only, or at least first and foremost, with humans. This anthropocentric inclination seems quite unnecessary to the particular realist argument that Moore pursues. Is this the case? Are anthropocentric or Protagorean prejudices entirely extrinsic to realism? Or is there perhaps, as Nietzsche claims, an inevitable anthropocentrism always at work within the philosophies of those who have "felt a deep distrust against any idealism"?[12] Is realism, perhaps, inherently

and unavoidably anthropocentric? An examination of Nietzsche's infamous essay "On Truth and Lies in an Extra-Moral Sense" will provide a valuable means of exploring the interrelation between the philosophical impulse to establish unassailable knowledge of the external world and the allegedly determining constitution of human knowers. Before turning to Nietzsche's critique, however, it is important that we clarify what might be meant by the term *realism*.

THE TRUTH ABOUT MICE AND DUCKS

There are almost as many varieties of realism as there are thinkers who claim the term as their own, and so a certain caution is required when approaching realist conceptions of the nature of knowledge and the world it would capture.[13] For the purposes of our Procrustean schema, we will here take *realism* to designate the philosophical position holding that a reality exists independently of the beliefs and ideas of those who come into contact with it and that true knowledge consists in the correspondence of one's beliefs and ideas with that independent reality. Bas van Fraassen characterizes *scientific realism*, for instance, as "the position that scientific theory construction aims to give us a literally true story of what the world is like, and that acceptance of a scientific theory involves the belief that it is true."[14] Brian Fay, considering *social scientific* knowledge, uses the alternative term *objectivism*, which

---

12. Nietzsche, "On Truth and Falsity," 185.

13. There are almost as many texts again that attempt to summarize the key claims and components of the various realist positions, often according to quite varied criteria. See, for instance, the opening chapters of van Fraassen, *Scientific Image*; Fay, *Contemporary Philosophy of Social Science*, 199–222 (chapter 10); and Hacking, *Representing and Intervening*.

14. Van Fraassen, *Scientific Image*, 9.

claims that the structure of reality exists separately from the mind and thus that objective truth exists whether cognizers know about it or not, or value it or not, or wish it were the way it is or prefer some alternative. States of the world already exist in the world itself, and knowledge consists of discovering the nature of these states. So reality must be pre-ordered in the sense that its states are there waiting for knowers to find them. On an objectivist view the basic structures of reality are uncovered, not made by human knowers; they exist already preformed in reality itself.[15]

What is most important from a realist perspective—scientific, social scientific, or otherwise—is that reality, the entirety of "things outside of us," exists independently of the mind and that true knowledge of that mind-independent reality is possible, at least in principle, whether anyone currently holds such knowledge or not. When a knower's beliefs correspond exactly with the mind-independent entities of the world, they have not beliefs but true knowledge.[16]

We will here discuss, far too briefly, the work of three writers who, considered in turn, illustrate what I shall take to be three key properties of a realist epistemology.[17] Richard Dawkins is a firm believer in the advances and benefits of modern science. He has been outspoken, and occasionally perhaps even a little rude, about those who would question its unique significance:

There is a fashionable salon philosophy called cultural relativism which holds, in its extreme form, that science has no more claim to truth than tribal myth: science is just the mythology favored by our modern Western tribe. . . . Show me a cultural relativist at thirty thousand feet and I will show you a hypocrite. Airplanes built according to scientific principles work.[18]

Dawkins believes in truth, the first and most important property of a realist epistemology. In considering the validity of knowledge, which is to say what it claims or posits, realism measures its worth according to its veracity. The pursuit of knowledge, properly so called, is about attaining truth. During the course of his critique of relativism, Dawkins recounts a myth of his own invention, which tells of an imaginary tribe who believe that the moon is an old calabash, tossed into the sky and hovering now just above the tree tops.[19] This account of the world, Dawkins asserts, is simply not true, in contrast to the ac-

15. Fay, *Contemporary Philosophy of Social Science*, 202–3.
16. As Ian Hacking explains, though realism will often contain both an ontological and an epistemological component, it is possible to distinguish realism about entities (for example, "My hands exist") and realism about theories (for example, "My theory about my hands is true"); see Hacking, *Representing and Intervening*, 26–29.
17. Whether these three writers should themselves be called "realists" is less interesting than the philosophical position they here represent. As has been pointed out many times, laying one's hands on a "classic" realist is not always a straightforward matter.
18. Dawkins, *River out of Eden*, 31–32. Christopher Norris relishes this quotation so much that he reproduces it twice; see *Against Relativism*, vii and 314. In a similar vein, Dawkins once advised Prince Charles that "of course we must be open-minded, but not so open-minded that our brains drop out"; Dawkins, "Don't Turn Your Back on Science."
19. Dawkins, *River out of Eden*, 31. A calabash is a kind of gourd whose hollow shell can be used as a water bottle or cooking utensil.

cepted scientific explanation that the moon is a rocky body about a quarter of a million miles away and a quarter the diameter of the earth. Any tribe subscribing to the calabash myth would, in fact, be just plain wrong, and what Dawkins calls their "tribal science" fundamentally at fault.[20]

In his lecture "Science, Delusion, and the Appetite for Wonder," Dawkins makes a similarly forthright attempt to jolt relativists from their open-minded complacency, this time regarding their skepticism of *enduring* truths:

> Let's keep a sense of proportion about this! Yes, there's much that we still don't know. But surely our belief that the earth is round and not flat, and that it orbits the sun, will never be superseded. That alone is enough to confound those, endowed with a little philosophical learning, who deny the very possibility of objective truth: those so-called relativists who see no reason to prefer scientific views over aboriginal myths about the world.[21]

In fact, realism need not go quite this far. Van Fraassen characterizes the belief that "today's theories are correct" as "naïve" realism.[22] A more cautious realism might accept that the theories currently held as true may well turn out in the future not to be so. Brian Ellis, for instance, takes scientific realism to be the view that "the theoretical statements of science are, or *purport to be*, true generalized descriptions of reality."[23] But the

idea that theories *can* be true, that it is possible at least in principle to capture the "states of the world," is a cornerstone of the realist position. A significant portion of the literature concerning the merits and demerits of realism takes "knowledge" to be all but synonymous with "science." This is a prudent approach if science is indeed realism's best-case scenario, but it is worth stressing that regardless of the form they take, it is the fact that there *are* or *could be* truths that is important here. In principle it is not inconceivable that we might arrive at certain knowledge by other means. Moore's ARGUMENTUM AD DUAS MANUS is certainly not, whatever its merits, a scientific demonstration.

Daniel Dennett shares both Dawkins's commitment to universal truths and his suspicion of relativism. He reserves his own most withering comments for misguided social scientists and those notorious, INFAMIS "deconstructionists and rhetoricians":

> It is worth bearing in mind that mathematics and physics are the same throughout the entire universe, discoverable in principle by aliens (if such there be) no matter what their social class, political predilections, gender (if they have genders!), or peccadilloes. I mention this to ward off the recent nonsense you may have heard emanating from some schools of thought—I speak loosely—in the sociology of science. . . . It is not "scientism" to concede the objectivity and precision of good science, any more than it is history worship to concede that Napoleon did

20. Ibid., 32.
21. Dawkins, "Science, Delusion."
22. Van Fraassen, *Scientific Image*, 6–7.
23. Quoted in van Fraassen, *Scientific Image*, 7, my emphasis.

once rule in France and the Holocaust actually happened.[24]

We should remember, Dennett suggests, that the structures and organizing principles that govern matter are the same throughout the universe. Mathematics and physics have, to some degree, been mastered here on earth, but this does not preclude the possibility that those same underlying structures might also be uncovered, understood, and represented by extraterrestrials.[25] The second key property of realism to which I would like to draw attention is its understanding of what knowledge is, its conception of what we might call the ontology of knowledge. Realism has traditionally characterized knowledge as *representation*. True knowledge will represent things perfectly, of course, but even partially true or downright untrue knowledge—the "tribal science" of Dawkins's calabash mythologists, for instance—is considered by realism to be a representation of reality (it just happens to be wrong). The objective of any good theory, scientific or otherwise, is thus to "carve nature at the joints."[26]

Fay argues that this notion of the correspondence of knowledge with reality is a vital element of objectivism:

> When the pre-existing order of reality is discovered one's beliefs replicate this pre-existing order. That is, what one claims to be the case corresponds to what is actually the case. This is what makes them true: true beliefs are copies of

mind-independent entities. . . . Indeed, such correspondence is precisely what truth is.[27]

Knowledge, as a representation, attempts to "mirror" the entities and structures of reality.[28] Theories that turn out to be true are discoveries that accurately describe those preexisting states of the world. Van Fraassen identifies these two related themes, representation and discovery, as the central components of the realist position: "[Realism] answers two main questions: it characterizes a scientific theory as a story about what there really is, and scientific activity as an enterprise of discovery, as opposed to invention."[29] It matters not whether it is Dawkins himself, his imaginary tribe, or Dennett's postulated extraterrestrials who tell the story, so long as it is the right (true) story. That it is a story, however, a representation corresponding to the structures that lie beneath, is characteristic of the traditional realist account of knowledge.

---

24. Dennett, *Darwin's Dangerous Idea*, 275n2, 494n2.

25. On the problematic equivalence of "Alien Science," see Hacking, *Social Construction of What?* 74–78.

26. This gruesomely telling phrase was originally Plato's. It has been taken up by a good many philosophers since, including Dennett. See Plato, *Gorgias and Phaedrus*, 265e; Dennett, *Darwin's Dangerous Idea*, 39. Realists are not obliged to be representationalists, though they have most often tended to be so. Manuel DeLanda argues, for instance, that Deleuze is best understood as a nonrepresentationalist realist philosopher; see DeLanda, *Intensive Science and Virtual Philosophy*.

27. Fay, *Contemporary Philosophy of Social Science*, 203.

28. See, for instance, van Fraassen's discussion of Michael Dummett's desire for a "kind of mirroring of the structure of things by the structure of ideas"; *Scientific Image*, 38–39.

29. Van Fraassen, *Scientific Image*, 7.

37. Mouse

OncoMouse™ [was] the first patented animal in the world. . . . OncoMouse™ contains a cancer-causing bit of DNA, called an oncogene, derived from the genome of another creature and implanted by means of genetic engineering techniques. A model for breast cancer research, the redesigned rodent is like a machine tool in the workshops for the production of knowledge. OncoMouse™ is a transgenic animal whose scene of evolution is the laboratory. . . . Defined by a spliced genome, identified with a spliced name, patented, and trademarked, OncoMouse™ is paradigmatic of nature enterprised up.

DONNA HARAWAY, Modest_Witness@Second_Millenium. FemaleMan©_Meets_OncoMouse™, 253–55.

Photograph courtesy of Philip Leder.

30. C. Norris, *Against Relativism*, vii.

31. Van Fraassen credits the rule itself to C. S. Peirce, who called it "the method of hypothesis" or abduction, but he also discusses Wilfred Sellars, J. J. C. Smart, and Gilbert Harman; van Fraassen, *Scientific Image*, 19–23. Hacking tells us that it was first used as an argument for realism by the nineteenth-century scientist H. Helmholtz; Hacking, *Representing and Intervening*, 52–53.

32. Quoted in van Fraassen, *Scientific Image*, 19.

33. Van Fraassen, *Scientific Image*, 19–20.

Christopher Norris is himself unquestionably one of those "deconstructionists" of whom Dennett is wary, but the two share more than might be supposed. In his forcefully argued collection of essays *Against Relativism*, Norris asserts, unequivocally, his commitment to realism: "My own position is that of a causal realist who believes—as a matter of inference to the best explanation—that science has achieved genuine advances in our knowledge of a (largely) mind-independent and language-independent reality."[30] The explanatory power of knowledge is the third and final property of the realist position, and it is this notion of inference to the best explanation that is often employed in order to argue that such a position is the only rationally tenable one.[31] Put simply, the claim is that, of all the hypotheses that might be tendered as accounts of a given phenomenon, we should infer the one that provides the best explanation. Further, as Wilfred Sellars argues, "to have good reason for holding a theory is *ipso facto* to have good reason for holding that the entities postulated by the theory exist."[32] The logical outcome of inference to the best explanation is thus, it is suggested, realism.

Van Fraassen enlists the help of a neighborly mouse in order to present the argument in the best possible light:

> I hear scratching in the wall, the patter of little feet at midnight, my cheese disappears—and I infer that a **MOUSE** has come to live with me.

Not merely that these apparent signs of mousely presence will continue, not merely that all the observable phenomena will be as if there is a mouse: but that there really is a mouse.[33]

These indexical scratchings and patterings are in fact a cipherous variant on the common wisdom that "when I see a bird that walks like a duck and swims like a duck and quacks like a duck, I call that bird a **DUCK**": induction entails a duck.[34] A still stronger formulation of the argument by explanation is that if scientific realism were not true, we would have to believe that the explanatory power of science to date has been no more than a stupendous cosmic coincidence, on a scale fast approaching the miraculous. If there is really no mouse, what could possibly have been causing the scratching, pattering, and persistent cheese theft? Or, mice aside, it would be a literally incredible stroke of luck that scientists had managed to put people on the moon, rather than on a calabash, if the innumerable, complex laws and theoretical entities employed in the endeavor had no corollary in the external world.

Norris's appeal to explanatory power recurs throughout his chapter "Metaphor, Concept, and Theory Change: Deconstruction as Critical Ontology." Here he argues that, contrary to crude versions of relativistic deconstruction, we cannot simply reduce all linguistic utterances to mere metaphor. Those who believe that Derrida sets out to demonstrate the internal inadequacy of concepts like "scientific truth" are woefully

"Mallard Drake RoboDuk, Model RD303," RoboDuk Decoys.

38. Duck

Add unmatched realism and lifelike detail to your decoy spread with the newest generation of the Ultimate Duck Attractor. This highly effective decoy boasts a full body design simulating a duck in the landing position. RoboDuk is a state of the art decoy that runs on an extremely quiet direct drive motor and is powered by a rechargeable battery that will give you 10–12 hours of run time.... Decoy comes field ready—everything you need is included in the box, battery, charger, two piece pole and carry bag.

RoboDuk Decoys

misguided.[35] Scientific terms certainly begin life as metaphors, when scientists first grope for appropriate labels with which to christen their new discoveries. Having uncovered the basic building blocks of living organisms, for instance, the biologist borrowed from the zoologist by designat-

34. Attributed to the poet James Whitcomb Riley, probably erroneously. On the question as to whether a decoy duck can be considered a *real* duck, see Austin, *Sense and Sensibilia*, 67–70.

35. The key text here is Derrida's "White Mythology: Metaphor in the Text of Philosophy," which Norris believes to have been almost universally misunderstood; see Derrida, *Margins of Philosophy*, 207–71.

36. C. Norris, *Against Relativism*, 16. The example is drawn from Georges Canguilhem and discussed by Derrida. See Derrida, *Margins of Philosophy*, 261–63.

39. BEE

Bees (APES) are so called either because they cling to things with their feet (A PEDIBUS) or else because they are born without feet, for they only receive their feet and wings later on. They are skilled in the art of making honey. They live in assigned dwellings. They build their homes with evident craft, making them out of various flowers and filling innumerable cells with woven wax.... Alone among every species of living thing, the bees have children which are common to all. All inhabit the same dwelling, all are enclosed within the threshold of one fatherland. Work is common to all, food is in common, labour and the habit and enjoyment of flight are all in common.... What indeed is a honeycomb except a sort of stronghold? For these enclosures the bee-wax of the bees is laid up. What four-walled stronghold can show so much skill and beauty as the frame-work of their combs shows, in which small round cells are supported by sticking one to the other? What architect taught them to fit together hexagonal chambers with their sides undistinguishably equal? To suspend thin wax cells inside the walls of their tenements? To compress honey-dew and make the flower-granaries to swell with a kind of nectar?

T. H. WHITE, *The Book of Beasts*, 153–56 (translation modified).

Medieval bestiary, c. 1200. Aberdeen University Library, MS 24, fol. 63r.

ing them "cells," like the component parts of a **BEE**hive. All manner of additional connotations were thereby carried over with this metaphorical application, such as the notion of cooperative endeavor vital to the manufacture of the honey-comb.[36] An element of creativity is unavoidable within this "context of discovery."

Following this early, embryonic stage of a theory's development, however, comes the "context of justification," when the metaphor is thoroughly tested and assessed by the wider scientific community. The distinction between these two contexts is a venerable one within the philosophy of science, but it was given its

contemporary character by Karl Popper,[37] who argues that knowledge is objective in the sense that it is "exosomatic": it exists and evolves outside any particular individuals, in books, librar-ies, universities, and so on. Knowledge, he says, is like honey:

> The honey is made by bees, stored by bees, and consumed by bees; and the individual bee which consumes honey will not, in general, consume only the bit it has produced itself: honey is also consumed by the drones which have not produced any at all. . . . It is also in-teresting to note that, in order to keep up its powers to produce more honey, each working bee has to consume honey, some of it usually produced by other bees.[38]

37. Popper, *Logic of Scientific Discovery*. On earlier forms of the distinction, see Hoyningen-Huene, "Context of Discovery," 502–3.

38. Popper, *Objective Knowledge*, 286.

Popper's point is that "we have to consume other people's theories, and sometimes perhaps our own, if we are to go on producing."[39] That is, we must digest, criticize, and change theories, refining or demolishing them, in order to arrive at better ones. Objective knowledge is, in short, a collective endeavor.

Subjected to this communal interrogation, the value-laden appropriation that is the metaphor must prove itself a sufficient explanation or be replaced by another. If it is what Norris calls theoretically "adequate" it will be retained and move across the "epistemological break" that separates mere metaphor from true scientific concept.[40] Thus, rather like deconstruction itself and the best kinds of philosophy,

> [scientific standards involve] a process of conceptual exegesis and critique, one that starts out from images, naturalized metaphors, intuitive sense-certainty and the like, but which then—through successive refinements and elaborations—achieves a more adequate theoretical grasp of the phenomena it seeks to describe or explain.[41]

Derrida successfully demonstrates that the theories and concepts will remain metaphors of a sort, but, argues Norris, they are now scientific metaphors, of a qualitatively different kind from their progenitors: "In the case of scientific metaphor[s] . . . knowledge comes about through a more exact grasp of their explanatory powers and limits, along with a variety of relevant procedures—experimental, theoretical, hypothetico-

deductive and so forth—for determining their validity conditions in any given case."[42] Scientific theories explain things. For Norris, this explanatory power derives from theories' ability to represent accurately the objects and entities of the external world, that is, from their conceptual adequacy.[43] This explanatory power is crucial to the realist position, and in fact Norris's account exhibits each of the three key properties that we would expect to find in a realist epistemology: knowledge attempts to provide a representation of reality that is true and that will therefore explain things to us. Nietzsche engages with each of these properties during his early attack on the pretensions of human knowledge, and it is to this essay that we now turn.

THE PHILOSOPHER AND THE GNAT

Nietzsche wrote "On Truth and Lies in an Extra-Moral Sense" in 1873, just a year after the publication of The Birth of Tragedy.[44] The text com-

39. Ibid.
40. The notion of an "epistemological break" between prescientific and scientific modes of knowledge is taken from Gaston Bachelard; C. Norris, *Against Relativism*, 23.
41. C. Norris, *Against Relativism*, 17.
42. Ibid., 25.
43. Hacking, a committed realist who is especially interested in the explanatory power of scientific theories, explicitly argues that inference to the best explanation does *not* entail realism; see Hacking, *Representing and Intervening*, 52–57. We will return to this issue in "A Tale of Three Fish" in chapter 4.
44. Nietzsche, "Über Wahrheit und Lüge im aussermoralischen Sinne." There have been many translations into English of this essay (for example, by M. A. Mügge, Walter Kaufmann, Daniel Breazeale, and Ronald Speirs). My quotations, cited in the text, are taken from Mügge's translation, "On Truth and Falsity in Their Ultramoral Sense."

Illustration by Harry Rountree, in Lewis Carroll, *Through the Looking Glass*, 201.

40. GNAT

"What sort of insects do you rejoice in, where you come from?" the Gnat inquired.

"I don't rejoice in insects at all," Alice explained, "because I'm rather afraid of them—at least the large kinds. But I can tell you the names of some of them."

"Of course they answer to their names?" the Gnat remarked carelessly.

"I never knew them to do it."

"What's the use of their having names," the Gnat said, "if they won't answer to them?"

"No use to *them*," said Alice; "but it's useful to the people that name them, I suppose. If not, why do things have names at all?"

"I can't say," the Gnat replied. "Farther on in the wood down there, they've got no names."

LEWIS CARROLL, *Through the Looking Glass*, 199.

prises a wide-ranging and strongly worded attack on the naivety of truth seekers, alongside an especially disparaging assessment of humanity's self-knowledge and significance.[45] Nietzsche opens with a typically humbling sketch of the importance of human beings:

> In some remote corner of the universe, effused into innumerable solar-systems, there was once a star upon which clever animals invented cognition. It was the haughtiest, most mendacious moment in the history of this world, but yet only a moment. After Nature had taken breath awhile the star congealed and the clever animals had to die. (173)

Nietzsche goes on to describe cognition (*das Erkennen*), the quality that sets these clever animals apart from all others, as wretched, shadowlike, transitory, purposeless, and fanciful.[46] Humans themselves, and Nietzsche is thinking particularly of philosophers, mistakenly believe that the world revolves around this intellect. If,

45. Nietzsche does not employ the term *realism* in this essay, his attacks being largely confined to the notion of truth alone, but the utility of employing his essay to explore all three properties of realist epistemology will, I hope, become apparent.

46. *Das Erkennen* has been translated as either "cognition" (Mügge, Spiers), "knowledge" (Kaufmann), or "intellect" (Breazeale). None of these rather substantial contemporary nouns adequately conveys the *process* Nietzsche describes in this essay, by which objects are perceived, identified, or recognized. Closer, perhaps, would be the archaic English verbal noun *kenning*, meaning "mental cognition; knowledge, cognisance; recognition." *Kenning* and *das Erkennen* derive from a common Germanic root, though the former survives today only in Scottish and northern English dialects; *Oxford English Dictionary*, 2nd ed., s.v. "kenning."

however, they were only able to see things as does the **GNAT**, they would realize that she too "swims through the air with the same pathos, and feels within herself the flying centre of the world" (173; translation modified).[47]

In this short, passionately argued essay, the philologist turned philosopher gives vent to his impatience with the self-satisfied complacency of philosophers and scientists who assume that the human intellect is the pinnacle of nature's achievement. He detests that element of anthropocentric thinking that would set human beings above all other life. He rejects too the implicit realism at work in conceited philosophical attempts to understand the world, as it truly is, by means of this great intellect. Nietzsche's invocation of the lowly gnat is intended to demonstrate that humanity does not occupy any such privileged position. It is natural enough, perhaps, to believe that one's own understanding is to be preferred, but the very fact that everyone does this, whether philosopher, porter, or mere gnat, and each in a unique way, begins to suggest that there is no single, absolutely correct way of comprehending reality.

At this stage in Nietzsche's thinking there are thus two interconnected, mutually reinforcing components: his antirealism and his antihumanism. Select passages from this essay are often quoted to lend the weight of Nietzsche's authority to antirealist or relativist arguments, but equally important is his simultaneous attack

on what he considers to be realist philosophers' unacknowledged anthropocentric presuppositions. Throughout the essay, Nietzsche employs a host of animal allies to promote his antirealist thesis and to demonstrate the implicit anthropocentrism within any attempt at a realist account of knowledge. The remaining sections of this chapter will examine the detail of Nietzsche's several attacks on realism, the role that diverse species of animal play in that critique, and, in closing, the foundations that his essay lays for our discussion of relativist epistemologies in the following chapter.

According to Nietzsche, the true purpose of the human intellect is the preservation of the individual, and the principle way in which it does this is by means of deception (174). Given that humans, he argues, are the most unfortunate, the most delicate, the most transient of beings, lacking horns, sharp teeth, or any of the means of self-preservation possessed by the beasts of prey, it is only by dissembling and dissimulating that humanity has endured at all. Only by perfecting deception, flattery, falsehood, fraud, slander, display, pretentiousness, disguise, and acting (both to others and to oneself), has humanity been able to thrive (175). The question that naturally presents itself, then, is quite how the "impulse to truth" (*Trieb zur Wahrheit*), so lauded by traditional philosophers, ever arose in the first place. Nietzsche suggests both that

47. Nietzsche would later recast this cipherous gnat as a self-absorbed ant, trudging through the forest; see Nietzsche, *Human, All-Too-Human*, 194 (2.14).

the basic state of nature is a "BELLUM OMNIUM CONTRA OMNES" (war of all against all) and that people, as Schopenhauer's porcupines illustrated earlier, desire a social existence "both from necessity and boredom" (176). Humans are, at base, gregarious liars (181). It follows that conventions must arise that will allow a tentative peace to endure. Individuals, who are fundamentally selfish and deceitful, cannot be permitted to threaten this precarious social state by lying and falsification; those who are seen to do so must be excluded. It thus seems to all right-thinking members of civil society, then, that they love truth and hate deception. In fact, Nietzsche argues, humans deceive themselves even in this: what they hate is not dissimulation per se, but the adverse consequences of socially disruptive deception, and what they love is not truth but the agreeable consequences of advantageous truths. Beneficial lies are actually tolerated and encouraged, and those truths that might prove harmful or destructive are actively discouraged. Thus do humans deceive themselves into thinking that they love truth.

The origin of the impulse to truth, which at first seemed so unlikely, is now explained. At an early stage in societal development, humans mistakenly believed that truth is vital to self-preservation. That one should pursue truth becomes self-evident, and that one can achieve it, a necessary assumption. Liars are dangerous, and therefore despised, because they say things that

are not true: "He says, 'I am rich,' whereas the right designation for his state would be 'poor'" (176). The words of liars do not correspond to reality as they should, but Nietzsche is not convinced that words and things *ever* coincide. Is language, he asks, "the adequate expression of all realities?" (177). Does it, or even can it, provide a sufficient, commensurate representation of the way the world really is? Do creatures, insects or otherwise, "answer to their names" as Alice's Heideggerian gnat seems to think? Nietzsche believes not. He argues that we can convince ourselves that language is a means of obtaining truth about reality only by forgetting that words are both arbitrary and metaphorical and that there is never any necessary, causal connection between a word and its object.

For instance, Nietzsche notes, we (which is to say, speakers of German) allocate genders to different objects, so that the tree is "masculine" (*der Baum*) and the plant "feminine" (*die Pflanze*) (177). It is unclear why a tree or plant should have a gender at all, let alone the particular one arbitrarily assigned to it. Further, the very fact that there are so many different languages suggests that the terms of any given language can hardly be an *adequate* expression of reality (178). Even a descriptive name like the **SERPENT**'s (*die Schlange*, which derives from *schlingen*, meaning "to wind" or "to twist"), might as easily be applied to another creature, such as the worm (177–78). The creator and user of language cannot

41. Serpent

The Chinese character for "other" or "it"—它—was probably originally the pictographic character for "snake." Pictographic characters are the simplest and oldest of the five main forms of character formation, as they are a representation of the thing they refer to. However, another method of character formation was "borrowing": this occurred when there was a spoken word for something, but no character for it. They would then use a character with the same or similar pronunciation but a different meaning for the word which had no character; over time the original meaning was often forgotten. A variation of this borrowing process may well have occurred here: the 它, "snake," was borrowed to mean "other." Later, the "insect" radical—虫—was added, possibly to help distinguish the two. Words with the "insect" radical are usually some kind of insect, small reptile, or creepy-crawly such as scorpions, bugs, and worms.

DAVID PATTINSON, personal communication.

reach the "thing in itself"; the words we employ are arbitrary designations that do not correspond to the essence of things. Further, our understanding of the "external" world passes through several successive spheres before it ever filters through into the medium of language. An object is experienced first, at the basest physiological level, simply as a nerve stimulus in our sensory organs. This nerve stimulus is then transformed into a percept, an image (Bild), the mental phenomenon prompted by that object. This percept is then converted into a sound, a word, a linguistic designation. At each stage we move from one sphere into another, entirely different in kind. The relationship among the different spheres is at best an aesthetic one, "a suggestive metamorphosis, a stammering translation into quite a distinct foreign language" (184).

Metaphor, Nietzsche says, is heaped upon metaphor, and all our talk of trees and flowers, of snow and colors, fails to correspond to the original entities (178). In using the term *metaphor* here, Nietzsche does not just attack the inadequacy of the ways in which we try to describe these objects and qualities. His concern is not simply with inappropriate connotations carried from one use to another. He means, rather, to draw attention to the changes taking place between the distinct spheres involved in the process of knowing. The translation of the nerve stimulus into a percept, for instance, is a halting, inaccurate transmission, an "artistic metamorphosis" of a physiological process into something altogether different (182). This hap-

48. Breazeale, in Nietzsche, *Philosophy and Truth*, xxxiii–xxxiv. On this metaphorical transformation, see also Nietzsche's unpublished notes in the same volume, 50–51 (§147–49). On the distinction between intuited metaphors (*Anschauungsmetaphern*), which express the "singular truths" of animal existence, and metaphors (*Metaphern*), which separate the human from the animal, see Lemm, *Nietzsche's Animal Philosophy*, 115–19.

pens involuntarily in the human subject, long before we reach the level of language. As David Breazeale suggests, Nietzsche here uses the term *metaphor* in a sense close to that of its Greek source word, indicating a transfer, or carrying over, and this transposition between dissimilar spheres inevitably involves a transformation.[48] Language is metaphorical not just in the sense that nonliteral relations pertain between words but also in the sense that it is able to represent the world only after it has been radically "aesthetically transformed" several times over.[49]

Nietzsche seeks to demonstrate that language does not correspond directly to things themselves. It can only ever be metaphorical and remains several places removed from the objects it represents. The very medium with which the truth seeker works is of a different kind from the objects that are to be known (179). In fact, words do not even correspond to *particular* experiences or objects. No single leaf, Nietzsche points out, is

identical to any other. This is true even of leaves from the same tree, let alone those from different species. The word *leaf*, however, is required at different times to refer to any one of these particular leaves. Whenever we employ the word, we must ignore all the differences between individual leaves and allude instead to some vague, generalized "leaf." The word corresponds to nothing but a metonymic abstraction, an archetype, a supposed "primal form" (Urform) (179).[50] Similarly, after observing numerous honest actions in a variety of individuals, we extrapolate the virtue "honesty." We are even tempted retrospectively to attribute someone's virtuous actions to this peculiar quality.[51] But we can equate these various acts under the term *honesty* only by ignoring their differences, and in fact we know nothing about this mysterious QUALITAS OCCULTA (hidden quality) itself.

Nature, the real world existing beyond our description of it, contains no such abstractions or ideas. Things exist in their specific, varying, nonuniform ways. Nature sees no forms, no types, no species (180). These are all "anthropomorphic" inventions, says Nietzsche, imposed on reality by humans at the expense of variety and particularity. We carve out unities not at nature's joints but according to human conceptions.[52] This charge of anthropomorphism is of a kind with the epistemological anthropocentrism of Protagoras (see my prelude). Nietzsche is convinced that all attempts to understand the

49. Nietzsche thus uses the term *metaphor* in the sense that Jonathan Culler dubs the VIA PHILOSOPHICA, which "locates metaphor in the gap between sense and reference, in the process of thinking of an object *as* something." Culler contrasts this with the VIA RHETORICA, which situates metaphor "in the space between one meaning and another, between the literal or 'proper' verbal expression and its periphrastic substitute." The distinction, as Culler goes on to show, does not hold, and each definition slips unhappily but inevitably into the other; see Culler, "Commentary," 219.
50. Compare Wittgenstein's discussion of the word *leaf* considered as a general term; Wittgenstein, *Blue and Brown Books*, 17–18.
51. Nietzsche would return to this theme of "backwards reasoning" many times. For his discussion of the tendency to impute a causative role to imaginary, abstracted psychological "entities," see, for instance, "The Four Great Errors" in *Twilight of the Idols*, 33–34.
52. Nietzsche, *Unpublished Writings*, 74 (19.236).

world, to gain true knowledge of the world, will inevitably be determined by the human nature of the knower. An anthropomorphic fiction is thus, for Nietzsche, one that has been invented by humans and imbued with their own small-minded, self-centered values.[53] And so Nietzsche is forced, famously, to ask:

> What therefore is truth? A mobile army of metaphors, metonymies, anthropomorphisms: in short a sum of human relations which became poetically and rhetorically intensified, metamorphosed, adorned, and after long usage seem to a nation fixed, canonic and binding; truths are illusions of which one has forgotten that they are illusions; worn-out metaphors which have become powerless to affect the senses; coins which have their obverse effaced and now are no longer of account as coins but merely as metal. (180)[54]

The real world remains utterly inaccessible in its true immediacy, and language necessarily lies far removed from its referents. It is, Nietzsche says, not quite a product of *Nephelococcygia* (Νεφελοκοκκυγία), the cloud-**CUCKOO**-land first proposed to the **HOOPOE** of Aristophanes's *Birds*, but it certainly does not express the essence of things (179). Admittedly, there is that "stammering translation" that implies, however remotely, *some* connection between sign and referent, but ultimately humanity is constrained by linguistic forms, leashed at the end of a tortuous metaphorical chain. The real objects at the far end of that chain remain forever out of reach.

A. W. Seaby, *Cuckoo Uttering Its Note*, in F. B. Kirkman, ed., *The British Bird Book*, 464.

42. CUCKOO
When a nest parasite lays an egg in another bird's nest, it exploits the likelihood that the foster parents will raise it as one of their own. . . . Because the nestling cuckoo evicts all host young from the nest and then grows to several times their size, it has a double problem. It not only has to elicit feeding by the host, but requires as much provisioning as an entire brood of the foster parents' nestlings. Remarkably, it accomplishes this by mimicking one aspect of the host's begging behavior, the rate of calling. A cuckoo chick calls very rapidly, with what appears to be a chorus of rapid "si-si-si" calls, sounding like an entire brood of host chicks.

PETER MARLER, "Bird Calls," 132–77.

53. Nietzsche, then, uses the term *anthropomorphic* to designate what I have been calling "epistemological anthropocentrism." The shapes and capabilities of adventurous bears and mathematically inclined horses are not here at issue. For Nietzsche's uses of the term, see "On Truth and Falsity," 180, 183, and 187.
54. For a valuable discussion of Nietzsche's epistemology in this essay, see M. Clark, *Nietzsche on Truth*, 63–93 (chapter 3), especially 69–77 on Nietzsche's objections, on the basis of language, to what Clark calls "transcendental truth."

43. Hoopoe

HOOPOE: But what should we do?

PEISTHETAERUS: Stay in one place and found a city.

HOOPOE: What kind of a city could birds found, I ask you.

PEISTHETAERUS: That's a stupid question if ever there was one: look down there!

HOOPOE [looking down]: Well?

PEISTHETAERUS: Now look up there.

HOOPOE [looking up]: Well?

PEISTHETAERUS: Turn your head, look around you, that way, this way, behind you . . .

HOOPOE [doing his best]: All I'm getting out of this is a crick in the neck.

PEISTHETAERUS: And what do you see?

HOOPOE: Only the clouds and the sky.

PEISTHETAERUS: The sky, exactly: the great vault of heaven. Revolving on its axis—to which only the birds have access. Build a wall around it, turn this vast immensity into a vast, immense city, and then—you'll rule over man as you now rule over the insects; and as for the gods, they'll starve to death, like the Melians.

ARISTOPHANES, *The Birds*, lines 171–88 (trans. Barrett and Sommerstein).

This is not to say, of course, that language has no use. As Alice wisely points out to the gnat, the fact that creatures do not answer to their names, the fact that their names are imposed arbitrarily, does not render those names useless. On the contrary, they can still be of great utility to those doing the naming, as Nietzsche goes on to concede.

THE BIRDS AND THE BEES

This army of abstracted anthropomorphisms comes to dominate human thought. Nietzsche notes, "Everything which makes man stand out in bold relief against the animal depends on this faculty of volatilising the concrete metaphors into a schema, and therefore resolving a perception into an idea" (181). The unrefined, immediate sense impressions that suffice for the brutes are left far behind. Man, the "'rational' being," relies instead on a growing schema of ideas and forms, arranged into an ever-more-complicated and transcendent hierarchy. Humanity builds a huge pyramidal structure of logic and order, supported by great laws, suborders, castes, and grades. Against the seemingly intangible world of first impressions and unreflective perception is constructed a regular, generalized edifice of reliable knowledge (181). Popper argued that

Winifred Austen, *Hoopoes at Their Nest-Hole*, in F. B. Kirkman, ed., *The British Bird Book*, 440.

objective knowledge, like honey, is something that is refined, stored, and consumed by individuals beyond those who initially produced it. Nietzsche too believes knowledge to be analogous to honey, but in a rather different way. Just like the worker bees filling up the cells of their marvelous hive, humans stuff the whole of the empirical world into regular, carefully prepared, architecturally perfect cavities (187).[55]

The problem with this great tower of truth is that its basic building block is the idea, which, as we saw, is no more than the "residuum of a metaphor" (182). Originally it was just language that worked at constructing ideas, whereas nowadays, Nietzsche says, it is science (187). Either way, like Aristophanes's Peisthetaerus ("Trustyfriend") and Euelpides ("Goodhope"), building their ideal city in the clouds, humanity erects its well-meant edifice of ideas on rather slight foundations: not rock but running water lies beneath this dome. In order to rest on such a base, this structure must be like a thing made from **SPIDERS**' webs, delicate enough to be carried along by the waves, yet strong enough to resist the winds (182). Whichever metaphor we choose to convey the materials of this wobbly architectural feat, and Nietzsche does not confine himself to just web and water,[56] the fast moving and varied flux that is nature is only crudely modeled by the stilted artifice of human words and concepts. That humanity managed to construct this building in the first place is perhaps to be admired: "Man as

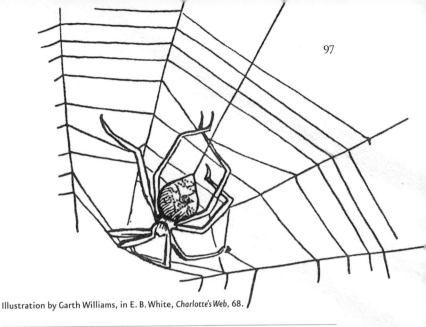

Illustration by Garth Williams, in E. B. White, *Charlotte's Web*, 68.

44. SPIDER

Spider silk is not a single, unique material—different species produce various kinds of silk. Some possess as many as seven distinct kinds of glands, each of which produces a different silk. Why so many kinds of silk? Each kind plays particular roles. All spiders make so-called dragline silk that functions in part as a lifeline, enabling the creatures to hang from ceilings. . . . Dragline silk also forms the radial spokes of the web; bridgeline silk is the first strand, by which the web hangs from its support; yet another silk forms the great spiral. . . . A dragline strand is several times stronger than steel, on a weight-for-weight basis, but a spider's dragline is only about one-tenth the diameter of a human hair.

WILLIAM K. PURVES, "Why Is Spider Silk So Strong?"

55. Nietzsche later returned to this analogy, with a formulation closer to Popper's: "Rightly has it been said: 'Where your treasure is, there will your heart be also.' *Our* treasure is there, where stand the hives of our knowledge. It is to those hives that we are always striving; as born creatures of flight, and as the honey-gatherers of the spirit, we care really in our hearts only for one thing—to bring something "home to the hive!"; Nietzsche, *Genealogy of Morals*, 1 (Preface, §1).

56. On Nietzsche's varied architectural metaphors, or "Metaphorical Architectures," including the beehive and the spider's web, see Kofman, *Nietzsche and Metaphor*, 59–80 (chapter 4).

an architectural genius rises high above the bee: she builds with wax, which she brings together out of nature; he with the much more delicate material of ideas, which he must first manufacture within himself" (182–83).

Nietzsche's words seem ironic, even mocking, but Norris would have us believe otherwise. He argues that Nietzsche is not, as postmodernist or quasi-deconstructive readings take him to be doing, "denouncing 'truth' as a species of rhetorical imposture."[57] In fact, his intention is to demonstrate his *respect* for science as a "genuinely truth-seeking mode of enquiry."[58] Nietzsche, Norris argues, has changed his mind. He has moved "from what looks at the outset like a wholesale sceptical position to one that acknowledges precisely this distinction between truths arrived at through disciplined (scientific) labour of thought and truths which merely pass themselves off as such owing to their suasive or rhetorical power."[59] Norris cites the opening passage from the second section of Nietzsche's essay in order to press his point:

> Science works irresistibly at that great columbarium of ideas, the cemetery of perceptions,

builds ever newer and higher storeys: supports, purifies, renews the old cells, and endeavours above all to fill that gigantic framework and to arrange within it the whole of the empiric world, i.e., the anthropomorphic world. And as the man of action binds his life to reason and its ideas, in order to avoid being swept away and losing himself, so the seeker after truth builds his hut close to the towering edifice of science in order to collaborate with it and to find protection. And he needs protection. For there are awful powers which press continually upon him, and which hold out against the "truth" of science, "truths" fashioned in quite another way, bearing devices of the most heterogeneous character.[60]

Nietzsche does not here change his mind. He has already established, at length, that the very idea of truth as some kind of transcendental knowing is one more instance of self-deception on the part of humankind. Having done so, he now *elaborates* his thesis in order to demonstrate that not only are conventional notions of truth and reality illusory, but so too are those scientific ideas by which people nowadays put such store. Nietzsche's distrustful quotation marks nestle up against the idea of scientific "truth" just as readily as they do against "truths" of other kinds. All such human pretensions are here held up for ridicule, not respect. In fact, on consulting his notebooks from this period, we find that Nietzsche positively detests what he calls the "barbarizing influence of knowledge."[61] Science pursues an "immoderate, indiscriminate drive

---

57. C. Norris, *Against Relativism*, 21.

58. Ibid.

59. Ibid.

60. Nietzsche, "On Truth and Falsity," 187–88, quoted in C. Norris, *Against Relativism*, 21. COLUMBARIUM is the Latin name for a dovecote, deriving from COLUMBA (a dove or pigeon). These structures are composed, as we saw in chapter 1, of numerous regular pigeonholes, which led to the term being used of catacombs; hence Nietzsche's "cemetery" of perceptions.

61. Nietzsche, *Unpublished Writings*, 20–21 (19.51).

for knowledge," attempting to gobble up any knowledge that it considers certain, no matter how trivial.[62] This results in, or is perhaps the consequence of, an impoverished life, a declining culture, and, all too often, a petty and malicious scientist.[63] We should admire and respect the earnest architectural genius, fashioning his tower from within himself, in the same way that we should take seriously the porter and the philosopher who suppose that the world revolves around themselves.

What are those other, mysterious "truths," at which Norris's quotation stops tantalizingly short? They are, like science, more fabrication. Humanity's inborn impulse to invent, to construct metaphors, to dissimulate, cannot be easily quashed by the imposition of a geometric order by science. Humanity cannot resist its desire "for shaping the existing world of waking man as motley, irregular, inconsequentially incoherent, attractive, and eternally new as the world of dreams is" (188). This impulse finds for itself a new riverbed and realm of action, in myth and art. Man is to be admired, "but not on account of his impulse for truth" (183). Humans love both to deceive and to be deceived, and so long as these inventions are not actually injurious, they will happily believe, as did the "mystically excitable" earlier Greeks, that a god can disguise himself as a **BULL** in order to carry away virgins, or that Athena herself might suddenly appear, driving a team of heavenly horses through the markets

45. BULL

A Gnat alighted on one of the horns of a Bull, and remained sitting there for a considerable time. When he had rested sufficiently and was about to fly away, he said to the Bull, "Do you mind if I go now?" The Bull merely raised his eyes and remarked, without interest, "It's all one to me; I didn't notice when you came, and I shan't know when you go away."

"The Gnat and the Bull," in Aesop, *Æsop's Fables*, trans. Jones, 30.

Arthur Rackham, "The Gnat and the Bull," in Aesop, *Æsop's Fables*, trans. Jones, 30.

of Athens (189). Nietzsche is interested less in forms of "truth" than in the creative lies that always underpin them.

There are, as Nietzsche argues, distinctions to be drawn among different forms of invention, but to do so is by no means the same as positing a single demarcation between merely metaphorical "truths" and genuine scientific truth.

62. Ibid., 8 (19.21), 14–15 (19.37), 32 (19.86).
63. Ibid., 8 (19.21), 54 (19.171), 61 (19.198), 63 (19.206).

Nietzsche acknowledges that many scientific metaphors are productive, and perhaps that they provide useful explanations, but he rejects the notion that this makes them true in any special or absolute sense. It is by means of a framework of ideas that "needy man saves himself through life" and knows "how to meet the most important needs with foresight, prudence, regularity" (190). Science is indeed a wonderful means by which to ward off misfortune and pain, but this does not make it transcendentally true. Those who wish to avoid getting wet do well to build their huts within the shelter of the tower of science, but that is certainly not the only place they might be built.[64] Norris misses Nietzsche's irony, his passion for dissimulating to rhetorical or humorous effect, which leads to an understanding of the essay at odds with Nietzsche's central thesis. Deleuze has underlined the importance of irony in Nietzsche's work, suggesting provocatively that "those who read Nietzsche without laughing, without laughing often and a lot, and at times doubling up with laughter, might as well not be reading Nietzsche."[65] Despite the enormous breadth of readings that Nietzsche's work

invites, we must reject, Deleuze says, illegitimate interpretations that are characterized by "a spirit of seriousness, of heaviness, by the ape of Zarathustra."[66] These readings come from imprudent "Hegelian commentators";[67] like Nietzsche himself, Deleuze happily RIDET MULTUM ET DIGITUM PORRIGIT MEDIUM.

Norris's reluctance to accept that Nietzsche is no scientifically inclined stoic persistently seeking, as Nietzsche puts it, "uprightness, truth, freedom from deceptions and shelter from ensnaring and sudden attack" (191) recalls Dawkins's exasperation at the very idea that anyone would doubt the permanence of scientific truths. Nietzsche anticipates them both:

> Surely every human being who is at home with such contemplations has felt a deep distrust against any idealism of that kind, as often as he has distinctly convinced himself of the eternal rigidity, omnipresence, and infallibility of nature's laws: he has arrived at the conclusion that as far as we can penetrate the heights of the telescopic and the depths of the microscopic world, everything is quite secure, complete, infinite, determined, and continuous. (185)

That self-deceiving "impulse to truth," which derives from the expedient impulse to lie that Nietzsche locates at the heart of human endeavors, manifests in traditional realists' faith that science can uncover the eternal, omnipresent, and infallible laws of nature.

Given, then, that human ideas have only

64. Drawing on themes developed in *The Birth of Tragedy*, Nietzsche contrasts the stoical and scientifically inclined "man of reason" with the spontaneous and artistic "man of intuition." The former will manage only to cope with calamities and will find no happiness in life, whereas the latter will attain "a continuous in-pouring of enlightenment, enlivenment and redemption." The price that this "exuberant hero" pays is that, when he suffers, he does so more severely, having failed to learn from experience; Nietzsche, *Birth of Tragedy*, 190–92.

65. Deleuze, "Nomad Thought," 18.

66. Ibid., 19.

67. Ibid.

the most tenuous, metaphorical connection with reality, in what sense *can* they be said to be true? To what do they most properly relate? The answer, Nietzsche says, is to more ideas. The great schema of interconnected ideas is little more than a complex tautology. The successive metaphorical refinements of the original nerve stimuli into generalized ideas have made those ideas all but autonomous: they now refer only to one another. Having hidden something behind a bush, there is no great virtue in seeking and then "finding" it again, but this, Nietzsche argues, is exactly analogous to our search for truth within the realm of reason (183). Having created a definition for the term *mammal*, no great truths are revealed when, upon inspection, we discover that a **CAMEL** is a mammal:[68]

> A truth is brought to light thereby, but it is of a very limited value, I mean it is anthropomorphic through and through, and does not contain one single point which is "true in itself," real and universally valid, apart from man. The seeker after such truths seeks at the bottom only the metamorphosis of the world in man, he strives for an understanding of the world as a human-like thing and by his battling gains at best the feeling of an assimilation. (183)[69]

Looking back, toward the objects that language purports to represent, the scientific endeavor manages only to understand the world in human terms, and "discoveries" are a matter of making those objects conform to specifically human classifications. Dennett's aliens, gazing over at earth from some remote corner of the universe, will not necessarily categorize a camel as a mammal. The history of their own predilections and peccadilloes will have furnished them with their own productive and conceptually adequate set of terms and categories. Their "truths," according to Nietzsche's conception of knowledge, will be no more "real and universally valid" than those of human beings. Just as the astrologer discerns human affairs in the stars, so the human scientist unwittingly applies "man as the measure of all things" (183).[70] Nietzsche's critique here invokes the necessary limitations and distortions of unacknowledged anthropocentric presuppositions. Further, extraterrestrials are not the only beings who understand the world in different ways.

For his final assault on the pretensions of those clever animals who invented cognition, Nietzsche calls to his aid an impressive army of animals. As the pathetic gnat has already shown, it is not only pathetic humans who perceive the world. "If each of us had for himself a different sensibility, if we ourselves were only able to perceive sometimes as a bird, sometimes as a worm, sometimes as a plant . . . then nobody

---

68. For the problems that Aristotle faced in defining camels, see Eco, "Horns, Hooves, Insteps." Alec Issigonis, the inventor of the Mini, reportedly suggested that "a camel is a horse designed by committee," a sentiment Aristotle seems almost to share; Partington, *Oxford Dictionary of Quotations*, 360.
69. Clark describes this as Nietzsche's "Humean" understanding of concepts as merely providing a priori analytical truths; see M. Clark, *Nietzsche on Truth*, 84.
70. See also Nietzsche, *Unpublished Writings*, 75 (19.237).

46. & 47. Bactrian Camel and Arabian Camel

Camels have an exceptional part wherein they differ from all other quadrupeds, and that is the so-called hump on their back. The Bactrian camel differs from the Arabian; for the former has two humps and the latter only one, though it has a kind of hump below like the one above, on which, when it kneels, the weight of the whole body rests. The camel has four teats like the cow, a tail like that of an ass, and the privy parts of the male are directed backwards. It has one knee in each leg, and not, as some say, several joints, although they appear to have several because of the constricted shape of the region of the belly. It has a huckle-bone like that of the ox, but meagre and small in proportion to its bulk. It is cloven-footed, and has not got teeth in both jaws; and it is cloven-footed in the following way: at the back there is a slight cleft extending as far up as the second joint of the toes; and in front there is a long cleft, extending as far as the first joint of the toes, but superficial; and there is something actually between the clefts, as in geese. The foot is fleshy underneath, like that of the bear; so that, when the animal goes to war, they protect its feet, when they get sore, with sandals.

ARISTOTLE, *The History of Animals*, 794 (2.1.499a).

Thomas Bewick, *Camel and Arabian Camel or Dromedary*, 1785, in Blanche Cirker, ed., *1800 Woodcuts by Thomas Bewick and His School*, plate 10.

would talk of such an orderliness of nature, but would conceive of her only as an extremely subjective structure" (186). Other species need to understand nature, and they do so in a multitude of vastly different ways (184). Humanity conveniently forgets that the world is a subjectively constructed place. Only by choosing to ignore the diversity of David Wood's animal alphabet (see "An ABC of Animals" in chapter 1), the members of which perceive the world in wildly varying ways, is it possible to assume or assert that *human* understanding arrives at something that is "true in itself" or "universally valid." To mention just those few beasts whom Nietzsche deploys in this essay, there are, in addition to human perceptions, the sensibilities of the gnat, of the various beasts of prey, of tigers, serpents, worms, bees, camels, insects, birds, spiders, bulls, and horses. In fact, there is no way of choosing between these different forms of perception. There is no standard or criterion that would make it possible to decree that humans, or for that matter gnats or extraterrestrials, see things in a more correct manner:

> Already it costs [man] some trouble to admit to himself that the insect and the bird perceive a world different from his own, and that the question, which of the two world-perceptions is more accurate, is quite a senseless one, since to decide this question it would be necessary to apply the standard of *right* perception, i.e., to apply a standard which does not exist. (184)

We might take a little trouble to consider some few of these diverse perceptual worlds. With Heidegger and the bestiarist, we have already noted the superior visual abilities of two birds of prey, the falcon and the eagle. Nietzsche's insects, meanwhile, demonstrate a huge range of visual capacities among them. The gnat, swimming through the air, has compound eyes that perceive an extensive, wide-angled picture of the world.[71] However, as a bloodsucker, the female gnat will tend to rely not just on sight but also on her keen sense of smell, by which she detects tiny variations in the body odors secreted by potential victims.[72] Those busy bees, tirelessly filling their precisely fashioned cells with honey, are trichromats whose vision extends into the ultraviolet range and who navigate by the polarization of light,[73] whilst Nietzsche's six- or eight-eyed spiders, spinning their vast geometric webs, have no lens accommodation and can see only a foot or so beyond their own bodies.[74] The lowly, sinuous worm, meanwhile, has no eyes at all but, rather, photosensitive cells, primitive "eyespots" scattered over the whole of the body and capable of detecting only the difference between light and dark.[75] Finally, the majority of serpents de-

71. On compound eyes, see Sinclair, *How Animals See*, 22–28; Land and Nilsson, *Animal Eyes*, 125–77 (chapters 7 and 8).

72. Syed and Leal, "Acute Olfactory Response."

73. Sinclair, *How Animals See*, 32–33; Land and Nilsson, *Animal Eyes*, 24–31; A. Parker, *Seven Deadly Colours*, 238.

74. Sinclair, *How Animals See*, 14–20 (chapter 3); Land and Nilsson, *Animal Eyes*, 95–99.

75. Sinclair, *How Animals See*, 9–10; Land and Nilsson, *Animal Eyes*, 4–5.

pend on their fantastically keen sense of smell rather than on their poor eyesight. The characteristic flicking of the snake's forked tongue is in fact the means by which she "tastes the air."[76]

Moore's objective was to demonstrate the existence of "things outside of us." His argument was an explicit attempt to refute idealism, that is, the claim that objects are not external to our minds but, rather, depend on someone's experiencing them. Norris's and Dawkins's own inclinations were as much away from such subjectivism as they were toward scientific realism. As a critic of truth-obsessed realism, however, Nietzsche subscribed, in 1873, to a form of idealism. He employs the term twice as a direct counter to the naive realism with which he takes issue (185, 186). To be sure, his earlier critique of "the leaf" and "honesty" as enduring, essential forms ensures that he could not be accused of Platonism, but we have seen how, for Nietzsche, humans comprehend the world only through an assemblage of mediating ideas. Additionally, in his brief discussion of the "laws of nature," Nietzsche suggests that the primal forms (Urformen) of time and space are innate conceptions (Vorstellungen) through which humans are compelled to perceive the world:

> Everything wonderful . . . that we marvel at in the laws of nature, everything that demands an explanation and might seduce us into distrusting idealism, lies really and solely in the mathematical rigour and inviolability of the conceptions of time and space. These however we produce within ourselves and throw them forth with that necessity with which the spider spins. (186)[77]

These conceptions, he argues, necessarily condition experience of what Moore called "things outside of us." When humans discern laws of nature regarding chemical processes or the orbits of the stars—when they discern with Dennett, perhaps, the supposedly universal workings of mathematics and physics—they see only qualities that they themselves attach to natural events. All that is really known is what is added, which is to say, relations of sequence and number. There can be no truth beyond the empty husks of tautology, Nietzsche says, no grasp of the eternal essentials that make up reality, due to the forms and ideas that humanity cannot help but impose. Like every other animal, humans are condemned to a particular, contingent understanding of the world.

THE BACK OF A TIGER

We have examined, in the previous sections, the conflicting arguments of a number of philosophers. Some, like those of Moore, were models of respectful disputation. Others proved, on occasion, to be somewhat less courteous: Dawkins, Dennett, and Norris all felt no qualms at being rude about relativism. Nietzsche, infamously, made generous use of reproach and ridicule.

76. Halliday and Adler, *New Encyclopedia of Reptiles*, 181–82.

77. On Nietzsche's spiders, both creative and predatory, see Schrift, "Arachnophobe or Arachnophile?"

Michel Foucault approvingly suggested that Nietzsche's claims in "On Truth and Lies" were "insolent," and even before he philosophized with a hammer, Nietzsche employed, where he felt it necessary, a particular, forthright finger.[78] We will return to his outspoken ways in later chapters, but where have our rude philosophers left us for the moment? How do things stand with realism? Nietzsche's critiques of "truth" and of foolish, cloudy-eyed truth seekers take several forms in this essay: he points to the many metamorphoses, or metaphorical transformations, through which nerve stimuli must pass before they become meaningful, to the number and variety of always arbitrary languages, to the analogous diversity of different species' world perceptions, and to the Urformen that determine the ways in which human beings conceive all things. His several attacks do not constitute a unified campaign, and there are perhaps even conflicts between them.[79] What is of greatest import for present purposes, however, is Nietzsche's allegation that nesting within any realist epistemology is an unacknowledged anthropocentrism, a failure to appreciate the humanist measuring on which it depends. Is realism guilty as charged? Do the component properties of a realist epistemology necessarily involve a form of anthropocentrism?

Nietzsche is disdainful of the status accorded the utility of knowledge by those sobered by science (189) and of their small-minded fixation on warding off misfortune and freeing themselves from pain (191). Nonetheless, he certainly accepts that it is with foresight, prudence, and regularity that the rational man meets the most important needs (190), and thus, with Norris, that scientific knowledge fulfills a useful explanatory function. But Nietzsche is also concerned to emphasize that humans are not the only animals abroad in the world, finding their way about and indeed flourishing as they do so. Bees, perceiving polarization and ultraviolet wavelengths that remain invisible to humans, excel in the construction of their perfect waxy cells, and the solemn, self-assured gnat more than copes with compound eyes and her highly developed sense of smell. To isolate just one of the infinitely many understandings of the world and accord it transcendental status, simply because it is a human invention, is precisely what Nietzsche calls "anthropomorphism." Although he would reject Norris's argument that effective explanation makes knowledge true in any kind of absolute sense, he nonetheless acknowledges that varied metaphors, lies, and world perceptions, whether they be had by humans or other creatures, allow us to get things done. The ques-

78. Foucault, "Truth and Juridical Forms," 6. On rudeness as a virtue, see Nietzsche, *Ecce Homo*, 19.

79. It is not entirely clear, for instance, how the conceptions of time and space persist through successive metamorphoses and ultimately furnish human beings with a perfect, tautological structure of ideas. And having claimed that nature knows no forms or species (180), Nietzsche then seems to base his idealism on the fundamental *Urformen* shared by all (and only?) members of the human species. On the internal contradictions within "On Truth and Lies," see M. Clark, *Nietzsche on Truth*, 90–93.

tion of conceptual or perceptual "adequacy" need not distract us from matters of practical utility. The "explanatory" aspect of epistemological realism, in and of itself, need not be considered anthropocentric (we will return to the question of explanation in "A Tale of Three Fish" in chapter 4.).

The pursuit of *truth*, with which Dawkins was concerned, is central to realism. Nietzsche argues that truth seekers fail to appreciate that all the marvelous laws and structures they discern are nothing but human laws and structures, necessarily thrown forth by those clever animals who invented cognition. It costs them some trouble, he says, to admit that other creatures perceive other worlds. To do so would require them to concede that there is no criterion for deciding which of these world perceptions provides the "right perception" and thus that the very question of which is the more accurate, the closer to the truth, is entirely meaningless. Truth-seeking realists, then, anxious to attain definitive truths and reluctant to consider anything but a human worldview, are, by Nietzsche's account, inevitably anthropocentric in their assumptions. But we need not confine ourselves to such a rudimentary realism and can extend to the realist a more inclusive conception of the

subject of knowledge. Even should the realist baulk at competing animal world perceptions, there are still Dennett's extraterrestrials, if such there be. As he argued, the principles of mathematics and physics are for the realist, in principle at least, as accessible to aliens as they are to humans. What Fay called the "basic structures of reality" pertain across the entire universe, after all, and there remains the possibility that aliens might share in a collective exosomatic production, refinement, and consumption of knowledge.[80] Humans need not be the only ones equal to the task of discovering the "states of the world," and the realist commitment to truth can avoid the charge of anthropocentrism.

Finally, it is significant that whilst Nietzsche explicitly takes truth as his principal target, and, en passant, knocks explanation from the prime position that Norris accords it, his approach to the question of *representation*, the third property of a realist epistemology, is altogether different. In fact, Nietzsche implicitly endorses the realists' representational conception of knowledge. Lurking beneath the vast edifice of ideas lies the unattainable real world, "an x, to us inaccessible and indefinable" (180). But for Nietzsche, knowledge is still a reflection or representation of that world, even if it has been metaphorically transformed and artistically metamorphosed during the course of its passage through the different spheres of cognition, held at arm's length by "an epistemological process that does not capture

80. Dawkins has suggested, for instance, that, should aliens ever visit the earth, they will doubtless judge human intelligence on the basis of the speed with which they discovered the theory of evolution. For his own speculations on the alienness of alien life, see Dawkins, *River out of Eden*, 145, 151–61; and Dawkins, "What's Wrong with the Paranormal?" We will return to the question of extraterrestrial knowledge in the next chapter.

the essence of things."[81] Further, by invoking varied animal sensibilities to counter anthropocentric myopia, he conceives the different world perceptions of the birds and the beasts as similarly representative. Each species perception emulates its environment in the same manner as does human knowledge, even if it is skewed by a different sensibility or lacks the later stages of metaphoric transformation provided by word and idea.[82] The representational aspect of realism is by no means anthropocentric.

Moore held fast both to realism and to an anthropocentric assumption in his attempt to provide a proof of the external world. The things whose existence he wanted to establish—his body and those of other people and animals, the sun and the stars, mountains and buildings, tables and chairs, and so on—were to be "external to our minds," that is, demonstrably, objectively real things. Nietzsche would lambaste him heartily for this, since

> only by forgetting that primitive world of metaphors, only by the congelation and coagulation of an original mass of similes and percepts pouring forth as a fiery liquid out of the primal faculty of human fancy, only by the invincible faith, that this sun, this window, this table is a truth in itself: in short, only by the fact that man forgets himself as subject, and what is more as an *artistically creating* subject: only by all this does he live with some repose, safety and consequence. (184)

Moore falls foul of this forgetful trap. He argues that his proof—"here is one hand and here is another"—compels us to accept the existence of external objects, but in so doing, Nietzsche would argue, he forgets that those hands, like the window and the table, are themselves no more than "manufactured articles," constructed according to distinctively human perceptual and conceptual capacities. They are lies, in the extramoral sense, and Moore, or man, "indifferent to his own ignorance, is resting on the pitiless, the greedy, the insatiable, the murderous, and, as it were, hanging in dreams on the back of a tiger" (176). As Nietzsche argues, there is no clear reason for preferring human percepts ("this sun, this window, this table") to those of other species. Human beings are subjects, artistically constructing the world, just as birds, insects, and worms do. Moore's grasping after reality, his persistent grip on the tiger's back, betrays his unacknowledged anthropocentrism. When he announces, "I can prove now . . . that two *human* hands exist" (146, my emphasis), those clutching hands gesture toward the fact that, for Moore, only humans have minds of the sort that can arrive at truth. Those hands are indices both of his commitment to realism and of his anthropocentric bias, which Nietzsche would point out.

Although in many respects Moore represents precisely the philosophical target at which

---

81. Nietzsche, *Unpublished Writings*, 74 (19.236).
82. Lemm, on the other hand, emphasizes what she calls the singular, "silent truth of the animal" in Nietzsche's essay; see Lemm, *Nietzsche's Animal Philosophy*, 114–19.

Nietzsche was aiming—the self-assured philosopher keen to demonstrate and demarcate the bounds of certain knowledge—we should remember that the former's enthusiasm for minds as they are "usually" conceived, which is to say *human* minds, was a rather late addition to his argument and is in fact quite unnecessary for his proof. Not only were his dogs, spider, cat, and unicorn cipherous, but so too were his hands. Though Moore uses the word *hand* nearly fifty times in the course of his short essay, on none of those occasions does he discuss these hands in and of themselves. They remain either, on the one hand, mere figures of speech, or, on the other, arbitrarily chosen exemplars of "things external to our minds." Like the animals, they serve entirely as media for his arguments, useful to us now as indices of his assumptions but unnecessary in their own right. Moore was anthropocentric, but, with regard at least to the logic of his realist argument, he need not have been.

Moore and Nietzsche between them help demonstrate that there is no inherent anthropocentric bias to the component properties of epistemological realism. Moore, whose anthropocentrism seems incidental, and Nietzsche, who explicitly takes up Protagoras's saw, both advocate a form of *ontological* realism that posits a realm of objects existing beyond any partial or erroneous knowledge of it. For Nietzsche our knowledge of the world, like that of the birds and the bees, is mediated through metamorphosing representations, but the existence of that which prompts those representations remains intact. For all his attacks on truth and the limits of explanation, the early, idealist Nietzsche sustains the realist's commitment to representation. His retention of a representationalist conception of knowledge highlights a significant conjunction between realism and the relativism from which it recoils. The scandal that spurred Moore to action, concerning the uncertain existence of objects outside us, was articulated by Kant. Nietzsche likewise concerned himself with the troublesome passage between Kant's *Ding an sich* (thing in itself), the "enigmatic *x*" (178–79), and a mendacious *Erkennen* (knowing). In the next chapter we will examine Kant's own representationalist account of knowledge. Both the realists, who permit the possibility of extraterrestrial cognition, and Nietzsche, who sought out animal sensibilities, suggest that such an account need not be anthropocentric. But what is the nature of representation, that humans might share with other beings, alien or animal, celestial or terrestrial? The forms of human representation are, in fact, one of Kant's chief epistemological concerns. We turn to his *Critique of Pure Reason*, and especially to those elements that Nietzsche draws from it, as the starting point for an examination of relativism, our second epistemological paradigm.

On the Ring Finger a Ram's Testicles

THE DIGESTIVE SYSTEM OF OUR MIND
ietzsche, in his early essay "On Truth and Lies," owes a debt to Kant. We saw in the previous chapter that, toward the close of his Protagorean critique of truth and corresponding account of the essentially inventive nature of perception and knowing, Nietzsche invokes a set of primal forms (Urformen), innate elements of the human mind that structure and determine the way in which all things are conceived. In contrast to metaphor and animal perception, which he discusses in detail, these Urformen seem curiously underdeveloped. Whence did they come, and how do they contribute to his analysis? As we shall see, in order to question truth, in order to bring truth into question, Nietzsche took these forms from Kant's own

The chapter title comes from [Cicero], *Ad C. Herennium*, 214–15 (3.33) (translation modified). This text, traditionally but erroneously attributed to Cicero, is the oldest extant Latin treatise on the art of rhetoric. The final sections of book 3, from which this quotation derives, deal with memory and mnemonics. The author recommends that we might better remember the details of a court case if we were to form a picture of it in our minds. In his example, a man lies ill in bed. The cup that he holds in his right hand indicates the poison used to kill him, whilst the writing tablets in his left represent the inheritance that was the murderer's motive. The ram's testicles on his ring finger indicate the witnesses to the crime, for two reasons: first, the word TESTICULI (testicles) is the diminutive of TESTIS (testicle), whose homonym TESTIS means "witness"; second, since it was a common practice to fashion purses from the scrotums of rams, the money used to bribe the witnesses may also be suggested; ibid., note b.

The third finger has traditionally been associated both with rings and with medicine. The common practice of wearing a ring on this finger dates back at least to Roman times and probably earlier. It was reported that the ancient Egyptians believed that a nerve or vein led directly from this finger to the heart, making it particularly worthy of adornment. More practically minded authors have suggested that, as the finger best protected by its fellows, it is the one most appropriate for valuable rings. To the Romans it was known as the DIGITUS MEDICUS or DIGITUS MEDICINALIS, the medical finger. In Anglo-Saxon times it was the goldfinger, and later the ANNULARIS, from the Latin ANULUS meaning "ring." Alchemists and medics would come to call it the leech finger or physic finger, and used it to stir their concoctions and apply remedies. Following Galen's description of ancient practices, the prominent seventeenth-century medical scholar Isbrand de Diemerbræck tells us that "persons formerly admitted doctors of physic were wont to wear a gold ring upon that finger."[1]

1. Magyar, "Digitus Medicinalis"; Gellius, *Attic Nights*, 2:236–37 (10.10); Macrobius, *Saturnalia*, 498–500 (7.13.7–16); T. Browne, *Pseudodoxia Epidemica*, 4.4; Napier, *Hands*, 22–24; Knowlson, *Origins of Popular Superstitions*, 98–100 (2.3); Isidore of Seville, *Etymologiarum sive originum*, 11.1.71; F. W. Jones, *Principles of Anatomy*, 8–9; Hammond, *Finger Prints*, April 8, 2003.

48. RAM

The wether (VERVEX) [a castrated ram] is so called either from his might (A VIRIBUS) because he is stronger than the other sheep; or else it is because he is a man (VIR), i.e. masculine; or else it is because he has maggots (VERMES) in his head. It is from the itch occasioned by the worms that these creatures mutually rush together and collide with a great impetus, butting.

T. H. WHITE, *The Book of Beasts*, 73 (translation modified).

Medieval bestiary, c. 1200. Aberdeen University Library, MS 24, fol. 21r.

pursuit of this great question of truth. But Kant himself had previously cautioned that

> to know what questions may reasonably be asked is already a great and necessary proof of sagacity and insight. For if a question is absurd in itself and calls for an answer where none is required, it not only brings shame on the propounder of the question, but may betray an incautious listener into absurd answers, thus presenting, as the ancients said, the ludicrous spectacle of one man milking a he-**GOAT** and the other holding a sieve underneath.[2]

Some brave soul has indeed been milking a he-goat. Worse, they have enlisted an assistant in this unwitting animal abuse, who has dutifully held the dry sieve beneath. This chapter is concerned with epistemological relativism, often conceived as realism's polar opposite. Whereas the latter has predominated as the preferred epistemology of the natural sciences, the former, in a variety of guises, has become ensconced in the humanities with the stubbornness of the proverbial **MULE**. This willful obstinacy, in fact, was precisely what got the goat of our three outspoken realists (see "The Truth about Mice and Ducks" in chapter 2). Knowingly or otherwise, a good many contemporary theorists inherit and perpetuate a Kantian epistemology, along with the anthropocentric presuppositions that appear to go with it. More than just a pair of Teutonic philosophers can be found interfering with farmyard animals these days.[3]

2. Kant, *Critique of Pure Reason*, 97 (A57/B82–83). The ancients in question are Virgil and Lucian of Samosata, both of whom make use of this cautionary fable; see Genosko, *Undisciplined Theory*, 65.

3. Indeed, in order that no single writer be cast as scapegoat, we will examine the work of two such successors later in the chapter.

Illustration by W. F. Keyl, engraved by G. Pearson, in J. G. Wood, *Bible Animals*, 206.

Illustration by W. F. Keyl, engraved by G. Pearson, in J. G. Wood, *Bible Animals*, 286.

49. GOAT

Country people used to think that keeping a goat maintained their other farm animals in good condition; any disease would settle on the poor goat, leaving the cattle healthy. . . . We call anyone who is made to suffer for, or answer for, another person's crime, a "scape-goat." "Scape" is a shortened form of "escape." There was an ancient belief that evil, disease and sin were pollutions which could be removed by various means, including transferring them to an animal which was then driven out into the wilderness. The goat was traditionally a "sin-carrier."

PETER WATKINS AND ERICA HUGHES, A Book of Animals, 42.

50. MULE

Mules are not stubborn. One reason they survived war conditions with a ratio of 5:1 over horses is because of their cautiousness and good judgment. If a mule is confronted with a strange or fearful situation, he stops and thinks it over. We call him stubborn for his wisdom. If we try to hurry him through or by the objects of his fear, he may not budge until he understands that they are harmless. . . . From the mule's point of view those activities in which we humans ask him to engage may be unfamiliar to his past experiences, contrary to his nature, or downright unreasonable in the amount of pain or trauma inflicted on him. . . . A horse can be goaded into jumping from a cliff but not a mule!

MELVIN BRADLEY, The Missouri Mule, 2: 331–34.

It is well known that Kant attributed the interruption of what he called his "dogmatic slumber" to David Hume.[4] In turn, as we saw in the previous chapter, it was a particular "scandal to philosophy," highlighted by Kant, that roused Moore to action (see "Two Hands Are Better Than One" in chapter 2). Further, as we shall see, Kant's work was one of the goads that prompted Nietzsche's unwavering attack on truth. Hume's prodding provoked Kant to embark on his *Critique of Pure Reason*, a treatise concerned with the nature of human reason and the possibility of necessary truths and objective knowledge. This work laid a modern philosophical foundation on which realist and relativist thinkers alike have subsequently built. Whether that foundation should ultimately be considered a dependable or a dubious substrate, a thing of substance or of waterlogged cobwebs, is not our concern here. Rather, Kant will help illuminate that which realist and relativist epistemologies have in common. Moreover, Kant was an undeniably anthropocentric writer. In his *Critique of Judgment*, he suggested, "Man is indeed the only being on earth that has understanding and hence an ability to set himself purposes of his own choice, and in this respect he holds the title of lord of nature."[5] The *Critique of Pure Reason* sets out to demonstrate exactly how the knowledge possessed by this lord of nature inevitably and unavoidably depends on human faculties. Determining whether Kant's epistemology and his anthropocentrism are, as is often supposed, codependent will be our first step in exploring whether relativism should be considered intrinsically anthropocentric. The chapter as a whole will address three characteristic properties of relativist epistemology, and we begin here with the first, which it shares with realism: a concern with representation.

There are for Kant two basic powers or capacities of the mind, two "fundamental sources" from which all knowledge springs. The first concerns one's immediate impressions of the objects one experiences, and the other what can be thought about those impressions. The former he calls the *sensibility* and the latter the *understanding*.[6] These two faculties are of equal importance and depend on one another: "Without sensibility no object would be given to us, without understanding no object would be thought. Thoughts without content are empty, intuitions without concepts are blind."[7] The study of the rules of sensibility, that is, the science of its a priori principles, Kant names *transcendental aesthetic*, whilst the study of the rules of understanding, the science of the principles of pure thought, is *transcendental logic*.[8] We will look briefly at both.

---

4. Kant, *Prolegomena*, 9 (preface, §2). On the correct translation of Kant's comment to this effect, see Scarpitti and Möller, "Verschlimmbesserung," 60–65.

5. Kant, *Critique of Judgment*, 318 (§83). For a similar sentiment, see also the preface to Kant's *Anthropology*, 3 (119), and the section "On Self-Consciousness," 9–10 (127–28; parenthetical numbers refer to pages in the German edition).

6. Kant, *Critique of Pure Reason*, 92–93 (A50–51/B74–75).

7. Ibid., 93 (A51/B75).

8. Ibid., 93 (A52/B76), 66–67 (A21/B35–36). Kant explains that his use of the term *aesthetic* thus more or less corresponds to that of the ancients, rather than

The sensibility is that capacity in us that permits our most immediate relationship to the things around us: it is our passive "receptivity" for receiving impressions and representations.[9] It does this by yielding in us what Kant calls intuitions. When we come into contact with an object, we experience *sensation*, the content or "matter" of the intuition.[10] We can call this intuition empirical, since it is an *appearance*, given to us a posteriori, but there is another aspect to these intuitions. Though the content of intuitions is presented empirically, the specific form they take is determined a priori by the mind. This nonempirical *form* of sensibility, the innate structure of the mind that makes sensation possible, Kant calls *pure intuition*. The objective of transcendental aesthetic is thus to determine the nature of this pure intuition. Ordinarily, intuition will of course always be empirical, but by "theoretically" removing all sensation from intuition, Kant is able to reveal the fundamental principles of sensibility.[11]

There are, it turns out, two such pure forms of intuition: space and time. Space, purely a subjective property of the mind, is the means by which we represent to ourselves objects as outside us, and it is for this reason that Kant calls the "outer sense." Space determines for us the shape and magnitude of objects, as well as their relation to one another. Kant is keen to emphasize that space is not a *concept* that we have derived empirically from our experiences

of objects. Indeed, on Kant's account, it would be impossible even to *have* experiences of objects outside us, if we did not already (a priori) have the capacity (the pure form of intuition) to experience them *as* outside us. In short, space is the very *condition of possibility* within the subject of experiencing outer appearances.[12]

Time, meanwhile, is the "inner sense" by means of which we inwardly intuit ourselves and our inner states. Time determines the relation of representations within us as either simultaneous or successive. Like space, it is not an empirically derived concept but a pure, a priori intuition: it is the very means by which we are able to experience ourselves. In fact, time goes beyond this and is even more fundamental than space, since, whilst space makes possible the experience of just outer objects, the pure form of time underlies *all* intuitions. All representations, whether they are prompted by an outer object or not, are ultimately determinations of the mind, so whilst time is the immediate condition of inner appearances, it is also the "mediate" condition of outer appearances. Without it we would not be able to experience *any* appearances, inner or outer.[13]

to the contemporary, idiosyncratic German usage signifying a critique of taste and beauty; ibid., 66–67 (A21/B35–36).

9. Kant calls the sensibility the capacity, power, or receptivity for receiving representations, ibid., 65 (A19/B33), 93 (A51/B75), 92 (A50/B74); the receptivity for impressions, 92 (A50/B74); and the faculty of representation, 65 (A19/B34). See also Kant, *Prolegomena*, 38 (§9).
10. Kant, *Critique of Pure Reason*, 65–66 (A19–20/B33–34), 92 (A50/B74).
11. Ibid., 65–67 (A19–22/B33–36); *Prolegomena*, 38–40 (§§9–11).
12. Kant, *Critique of Pure Reason*, 67–70 (A22–25/B37–40).
13. Ibid., 74–82 (A30–41/B46–58).

The understanding,[14] the second capacity of the mind from which knowledge springs, allows us to think and make judgments. Whereas the sensibility is our capacity to receive representations, Kant describes the understanding as our ability to spontaneously produce concepts. Concepts result when we actively unify various representations and arrive at a "higher," more general representation.[15] Thought is simply knowledge arrived at by means of these concepts: it is the process of making judgments. And just as we can consider intuitions in both their empirical and pure forms, so too with concepts. Like the pure intuitions of space and time, the pure concepts, or "categories,"[16] are a priori, innate elements of the mind. The objective of transcendental logic is thus to determine the number and nature of these pure concepts. In the same way that he removed the empirical element from intuitions in order to discover the nature of pure intuition, Kant now abstracts the content from our ordinary judgments in order to determine the nature of the pure concepts of the understanding.[17]

The key, underlying action that the understanding performs is to judge,[18] and all acts of the understanding are judgments in some form or other. The understanding makes use of concepts in order to perform these judgments. Kant deduces that whilst the sensibility has just two pure forms, the understanding has twelve.[19] These include, for instance, the concepts of cause (a means of relating things), of necessity (a mode of existence of things), and of plurality (regarding quantity of things), amongst others.[20] These twelve (the predicaments) have further "derivative concepts" (predicables) that, when sketched out, would provide a complete family tree of pure concepts of the understanding.[21] Pure concepts are simply empty logical functions by means of which we can make judgments.[22] To employ them, intuitions must be provided by the sensibility. Each concept thus has a corresponding schema, a kind of rule, by means of which its application to sensibility is determined.[23] This done, we can arrive at empiri-

14. Kant calls the understanding the faculty of understanding, ibid., 103 (B90); a faculty of thought, 106 (B94), 114 (B106); a faculty of judgment, 106 (B94), 114 (B106); and a faculty of knowledge, 105 (B92).

15. Ibid., 105–6 (A67–69/B92–94).

16. Kant mostly uses the terms *categories* (*Kategorien*) and *pure concepts of the understanding* (*reine Verstandesbegriffe*) interchangeably, though sometimes the latter includes the predicables as well as the predicaments (see below).

17. Kant, *Critique of Pure Reason*, 92–93 (A50–51/B74–77), 104–6 (A66–69/B91–94).

18. Kant, *Prolegomena*, 86 (§39).

19. Kant is most insistent that his list of categories, unlike that of Aristotle for instance, is both complete and, crucially, logically coherent; ibid., 84–86 (§39); *Critique of Pure Reason*, 114 (A80–81/B106–7).

20. The complete list of predicaments is as follows: unity (whose corresponding judgment is *universal*), plurality (*particular*), totality (*singular*), reality (*affirmative*), negation (*negative*), limitation (*infinite*), substance (*categorical*), cause (*hypothetical*), community (*disjunctive*), possibility (*problematic*), existence (*assertoric*), and necessity (*singular*); *Prolegomena*, 62 (§21); *Critique of Pure Reason*, 106–18 (A70–83/B95–113).

21. Kant postpones this "useful and not unpleasant task" until another occasion; *Critique of Pure Reason*, 114–15 (A82/B108).

22. Kant, *Prolegomena*, 87 (§39).

23. Kant, *Critique of Pure Reason*, 263 (A245). Umberto Eco characterizes the schema as a kind of "figure," suggesting that it is rather like a computer flow-

cal concepts (of things) and thus make empirical judgments (about actual objects).[24]

The seemingly complex process of making judgments of experience, of knowing about something that exists in the world, can be best understood by means of a concrete example. In his discussion of the schemata of the understanding,[25] Kant engages the services of a dog, and this cipherous canine can help us again here. When I encounter a dog, my senses yield in me a range of sensations such as colors, sounds, and perhaps smells.[26] Prompted by these stimuli, I begin to experience something,[27] thanks to the pure forms of intuition, space and time, which are the very condition of possibility of such experience.[28] The sensibility, my receptivity for impressions, thus arrives at empirical intuitions. Meanwhile, the understanding, my faculty for thought, brings to bear the enabling authority of the categories, without which no entity could be understood *as* a substantial entity, affecting and relating to others.[29] It thus takes from its repertoire the appropriate empirical concept ("dog") and, by means of its corresponding schema (the rule of the concept's application) determines that it is indeed a dog that I am experiencing.[30] This done, I am now in a position to think (make further judgments) about this particular dog (that he looks friendly, for instance) or about dogs in general (perhaps that they are four-footed animals).[31] In effect, the sensibility provides sensations and the understanding makes them

intelligible; only through their combination can knowledge arise.[32]

Thus does Kant describe the inseparable processes of perceiving and knowing. All the various elements of sensibility and understanding are in effect the "digestive system of our mind," to employ Popper's evocative description of this mechanism.[33] The actual procedure by which the schemata are applied to appearances, a process Kant calls the "schematism" of the understanding, he finds to be "an art concealed in the depths of the human soul, whose real modes of activity nature is hardly likely ever to allow us to discover, and to have open to our gaze."[34] Umberto Eco enlists Kant's own dog, who thereby reveals himself to be rather less dependable than Ryle's faithful Fido, to demonstrate the difficulties that this

chart, a spatial representation of the (nonlinear) temporal stages through which a computer runs in order to perform an operation; see Eco, *Kant and the Platypus*, 80–84.

24. Kant, *Prolegomena*, 87 (§39); *Critique of Pure Reason*, 263 (A244). Eco is especially clear on the difference between pure and empirical concepts; Eco, *Kant and the Platypus*, 74.

25. Kant, *Critique of Pure Reason*, 180–87 (A137–47/B176–87).

26. Ibid., 73–74 (A28–30/B44–45).

27. Ibid., 121 (A86/B118–19).

28. Ibid., 123 (A89/B121–22).

29. For more detailed accounts of this process, see Eco, *Kant and the Platypus*, 71–73; Deleuze, *Kant's Critical Philosophy*, 16.

30. Kant, *Critique of Pure Reason*, 182–83 (A141–42/B180–81).

31. Ibid., 183 (A141/B180).

32. Ibid., 93 (A51/B75). Eco provides a detailed account of an alternative example, a stone heating up under the sun's rays, drawn initially from the *Prolegomena*, 63–64 (§22); Eco, *Kant and the Platypus*, 71–74. Sections 21, 21a, and 22 of the *Prolegomena* (61–64) succinctly summarize this whole cognitive process.

33. Popper, "Kant's Critique and Cosmology," 180.

34. Kant, *Critique of Pure Reason*, 183 (A141/B180–81).

Louis A. Sargent, *Duck-Billed Platypus*, in Frank Finn, *The Wild Beasts of the World*, 2: 180.

51. PLATYPUS

The platypus is a strange animal. It seems to have been conceived to foil all classification, be it scientific or popular. On the average about fifty centimetres long and roughly two kilos in weight, its flat body is covered with a dark-brown coat; it has no neck and a tail like a beaver's; it has a duck's beak, bluish on top and pink or variegated beneath; it has no outer ears, and the four feet have five webbed toes, but with claws; it stays underwater (and eats there) enough to be considered a fish or an amphibian. The female lays eggs but "breast-feeds" her young, even though no nipples can be seen (the male's testicles cannot be seen either, as they are internal).

UMBERTO ECO, *Kant and the Platypus*, 58.

omission produces for his account of the process of perception. Where, exactly, does the schema come from? How *does* the mind apply it?[35] And if faithful Fido presented such difficulties, how much more so would certain other creatures, especially those "as yet unknown" (89)? Eco returns

35. Eco, *Kant and the Platypus*, 84–89. Further citations in this paragraph are in the text.

several times to the question, What would Kant have made of a **PLATYPUS**? This shy creature, stranger still than Aristotle's composite-looking camel, was first introduced to the Western world only after Kant had published his last work. How would he have arrived at a schema for such an implausible looking beast (89–98)? As Eco points out, however, Kant was less concerned with how we know the objects of everyday experience than with how he could provide an irrefutable explanation of a propositional knowledge modeled on Newtonian laws. His interest was not so much in explaining knowledge of dogs and hands, or of manufactured goods such as chairs and tables and windows, as in establishing the a priori necessity of pure mathematics and physics (69). To this end he issued stern warnings to those who would attempt to extend the use of the digestive system he described beyond the bounds to which it should be confined, as we shall now see.

AN UNKNOWN SOMETHING

The distinction Kant draws, between that which can be safely assimilated and that which is epistemologically indigestible, lies at the heart of the representationalist understanding of knowledge common to both realism and relativism, but it is here too that Kant's anthropocentric prejudices begin to impinge on his project:

> The territory of pure understanding . . . is an island, enclosed by nature itself within unalterable limits. It is the land of truth—enchanting

Medieval bestiary, c. 1230–40. British Library, MS Harley 4751, f. 69.

name!—surrounded by a wide and stormy ocean, the native home of illusion, where many a fog bank and many a swiftly melting iceberg give the deceptive appearance of farther shores, deluding the adventurous seafarer ever anew with empty hopes, and engaging him in enterprises which he can never abandon and yet is unable to carry to completion.[36]

The adventurous seafarers, also referred to as extravagant "young thinkers,"[37] are those who attempt to employ the pure understanding without the input of intuition provided by the sensibility. These attempts to apply the categories beyond the limits of actual experience lead always, according to Kant, to failure and worse, and in the past such attempts have been the ruin of many a good brain, exhausted in "obscure and vain subtleties."[38] Having taken its principles (the a priori categories) from within itself, the understanding moves enthusiastically from their legitimate, limited application to experience, to their illegitimate use in speculating about wholly new forces and beings.[39] These forces and beings that the understanding strives to know suprasensibly are "things in themselves," objects as they really are, unadulterated by their particular presentation to the human subject in the form of sensible intuitions. The farther shores that adventurous seafarers attempt to reach are not *phenomena* but *noumena*.

52. WHALE

There is an ocean monster which is called . . . a whale (CETUS) because of the frightfulness of his body and because it was this animal which snatched (EXCEPIT) Jonah, and his belly was so great that people took it to be Hell. . . . This animal lifts his back out of the open sea above the watery waves, and then he anchors himself in the one place; and on his back the shingle of the ocean is drawn there by gales, and bushes begin to grow there. Sailing ships take him to be an island, and land on him. Then they make themselves a fireplace. But the Whale, feeling the heat of the fire, suddenly plunges down into the depths of the deep, and pulls down the anchored ship with him into the profound.

T. H. WHITE, *The Book of Beasts*, 197 (translation modified).

36. Kant, *Critique of Pure Reason*, 257 (A235–36/B294–95).
37. Kant, *Prolegomena*, 78–79 (§35).
38. Ibid., 87 (§39).
39. Ibid., 78–79 (§35).

Phenomena are appearances, the objects of empirical intuitions, thought according to the categories.[40] They are what we experience. The dog I see, hear, and smell is a phenomenon. So what of the actual dog, the *real* dog who exists "external to my mind," quite apart from his representation in me? What lies behind the phenomenon? Noumena are the "real objects" or "bodies outside us," the "thinghood" or "reality" behind the appearance.[41] Corresponding to the phenomenal dog whom I experience is a noumenal "thing in itself."[42] To clarify the distinction, Kant considers the rainbow produced by a sunny shower. The rainbow is, of course, an appearance, a phenomenon, but so too are the drops of rain and even their round shape. The noumena in this case would be whatever realities lie behind these empirical objects that we experience.[43]

Caution must be exercised regarding what we say about noumena. Since we can only know objects by means of the sensibility and the understanding, which jointly yield phenomena in us, to assert anything about that which lies outside these faculties is to embark on an ill-fated voyage. To suggest that there is a "dog in itself" or a "raindrop in itself" is already to have taken a step too far. The term *noumenon* is best understood as a "limiting concept"[44] that reminds us of the boundary of our knowledge. This boundary lies precisely at the limits of our sensibility. The term *noumenon* should have only a "negative" employment,[45] and it is a reminder to the understanding not to overreach itself. Kant has no doubt that there is *something* that is the ground for phenomena,[46] but about that something we can know absolutely nothing:

> Thus beings of the understanding are admitted, but under inculcation of this rule which suffers no exception: that we know and can know nothing determinate whatever about these pure beings of the understanding, because both our pure concepts of the understanding and our pure intuitions bear on nothing but objects of possible experience, which are mere beings of the sense, and as soon as we depart from these not the slightest meaning is left to those concepts.[47]

40. Kant, *Critique of Pure Reason*, 265 (A248–49). In fact, the term *appearance* (*Erscheinungen*) is used by Kant both for the "undetermined" object of an empirical intuition (65 [A19/B34]) and for the object of an empirical intuition that has had the categories applied to it. It is not entirely clear whether the term *phenomenon* refers to just the latter or to both of these possibilities. Most secondary texts take *appearance* and *phenomenon* to be synonymous: see, for instance, Peter Lucas's introduction to his translation of Kant's *Prolegomena*, xxiv; but also Roger Scruton's discussion in his *Kant*, 42–46.

41. Kant, *Critique of Pure Reason*, 265–75 (A248–60/B305–315), 184 (A143/B182); Kant, *Prolegomena*, 45 (note II).

42. Whether Kant's term *noumena* should be taken as entirely synonymous with *things in themselves* has been a matter of much debate; see, for instance, Palmquist, *Kant's System of Perspectives*, 161–93 (chapter 6) and 385–94 (appendix 6).

43. Kant, *Critique of Pure Reason*, 84–85 (A45–46/B62–63).

44. Ibid., 271–73 (A254–56/B310–12).

45. Ibid., 268–70 (B307–9); 272 (A255/B311).

46. Kant, *Prolegomena*, 45–46 (note II), 75–76 (§32), 79 (§36); *Critique of Pure Reason*, 269 (A251–52).

47. Kant, *Prolegomena*, 76 (§32).

and

> All our representations are, it is true, referred by
> the understanding to some object; and since ap-
> pearances are nothing but representations, the
> understanding refers them to a something, as
> the object of sensible intuition. But this some-
> thing, thus conceived, is only the transcendental
> object; and by that is meant a something = X, of
> which we know, and with the present constitu-
> tion of our understanding can know, nothing
> whatsoever.[48]

Noumena must remain, then, in Kant's rather
charming phrase, "an unknown something."[49]
They represent a problem that is intelligible but
that, given the composition of the understanding, we cannot solve.[50] Phenomena are "sensible
entities," whereas noumena are, strictly speaking,
merely "intelligible entities,"[51] a variety of placeholding cipher in Kant's philosophical system.[52]

To be sure, the temptation to employ the
concepts of the understanding in a "hyperphysi-
cal" manner is great.[53] It seems that, freed of the
appearances of the senses, they must therefore
refer to things in themselves; and containing
a true "necessity of determination" (the effect
always follows its cause, for instance) that mere
experience lacks, they seem so much more reliable.[54] The mistake that adventurous seafarers
make here is to think that they can know things
in themselves simply by stripping away the empirical content supplied by the sensibility. The
partial input from the senses would be thereby

removed, and by employing the understanding
alone, they hope to reason their way to things in
themselves. But as Kant demonstrates, dispens-
ing with the sensibility is not so easy, since it
does more than simply provide empirical input.
As we saw, the two pure forms of sensibility,
time and space, are what make possible our very
experience of objects. Without them, we cannot
know anything.

In the *Prolegomena*, Kant provides a thought
experiment to help his readers appreciate the
import of the sensibility in this regard.[55] He asks
us to imagine his right hand, held before a mirror. Looking into the glass we see its exact image,
except that, of course, in the reflection it appears
as a left hand. Comparing the two, there are no
differences between them that the understanding could think. They are absolutely identical
with regard to their composition and structure,
"in all determinations belonging to quantity
and quality," as Kant puts it, and yet the senses
tell us that the two *are* different: "The left hand
cannot be enclosed in the same boundaries as
the right . . . the glove of the one hand cannot be
used on the other." We know this because "these

---

48. Kant, *Critique of Pure Reason*, 268 (A250).

49. Ibid., 273 (A256/B312).

50. Kant, *Prolegomena*, 78 (§34).

51. Kant, *Critique of Pure Reason*, 266–67 (B306).

52. Scruton suggests that the *thing in itself* is, for Kant, a term standing "proxy"
for the ideal of perspectiveless knowledge; Scruton, *Kant*, 42.

53. Kant, *Critique of Pure Reason*, 101 (A63/B88).

54. Kant, *Prolegomena*, 76–77 (§33).

55. Ibid., 41–43 (§13).

objects are not representations of the things as they are in themselves and as a pure understanding would know them, but sensible intuitions, i.e. appearances, the possibility of which rests on the relation of certain things, unknown in themselves, to something else, namely our sensibility."[56] The pure form of space, the form of outer intuition, is the means by which we experience objects as outside us. We can only know anything about Kant's hand, a part of space, by determining its relation to space as a whole. The relation of his right hand to the whole of space is different from the relation of his left hand to the whole of space, as either one of his gloves demonstrates, but this is only something we could know with the benefit of outer intuition. The role of the pure form of sensibility is indispensable, and without it we can know nothing of objects. We certainly cannot employ the pure concepts of the understanding alone to gain knowledge of things in themselves. This would be what Kant calls a *transcendental* employment of the understanding, a metaphysical juggling of concepts with no real meaning. Without the sensibility, the concepts of the understanding are mere empty forms. Like G. E. Moore, Kant chooses that mark, or marker of the human, the hand, in order to make his point, but where Moore's two hands served together as a realist proof of the external world (see "Two Hands Are Better Than One" in chapter 2), Kant's comparison of one with the other provides an idealist demonstration of the primacy of the mind in our knowledge of that world.

Given that Kant believes in "bodies outside us" and is categorically opposed to any transcendental discussion of those bodies, it might seem a little odd that he should take the name "transcendental idealism" for his philosophy. In fact, Kant points out that, in certain senses at least, his philosophy is neither transcendental nor idealist. As we have seen, his is not an idealism that would deny the existence of objects outside thinking beings.[57] That would be the idealism of George Berkeley, a "chimera of the brain" that Kant calls *visionary* or *mystical* idealism,[58] or even *dogmatic* idealism.[59] Nor is Kant's idealism the same as what he calls René Descartes's *empirical*[60] or *skeptical*[61] or *problematic*[62] idealism, which is a kind of default doubt regarding the corporeal world, prompted by our incapacity to prove its existence through experience.[63] Kant is an idealist, he explains, insofar as he is concerned not with the existence of things but only with the *sensible representation* of things.[64] To the so-called

56. Ibid., 42 (§13).

57. Kant, *Prolegomena*, 45 (note II); *Critique of Pure Reason*, 244 (B274).

58. Kant, *Prolegomena*, 50 (note III).

59. Ibid., 146 (appendix); *Critique of Pure Reason*, 244 (B274), 350 (A377).

60. Kant, *Prolegomena*, 50 (note III).

61. Ibid., 146 (appendix); *Critique of Pure Reason*, 350–51 (A377–78).

62. Kant, *Critique of Pure Reason*, 244 (B274).

63. For Kant's full discussions of the problems with traditional idealism, see *Prolegomena*, 45–51 (notes II and III), 143–46 (appendix); and *Critique of Pure Reason*, 244–47 (B274–79). It was the inadequacy of the last that prompted Moore's own realist gesticulations; see "Two Hands Are Better Than One" in chapter 2.

64. Kant, *Prolegomena*, 50 (note III).

secondary qualities of objects—heat, color, taste, and so on—Kant adds the "primary qualities" of extension, place, and space and thus argues that all the qualities that make up our intuition of an object belong only to its appearance.[65] It is thus in his assertion of the ideality of space and time, of their a priori existence in the knowing subject, that Kant can properly be called idealist.[66]

Similarly, Kant is anxious to distance himself from the transcendentalism of his forebears. Their error was to confuse the logical possibility of a concept, the fact that it does not contradict itself, with the supposition that something corresponds to it without there also being required intuition. It is the necessity of reference to intuition in addition to conceptual possibility that is the transcendental possibility of concepts referring to objects.[67] In their disregard for experience, these "metaphysical jugglers"[68] blithely employed the categories transcendentally rather than reserving for them only transcendental meaning.[69] It is in this sense that Kant's philosophy is transcendental. He is absolutely opposed to any purported "higher" knowledge of things "beyond all experience," and he concentrates exclusively on the a priori means by which empirical knowledge is possible. "Not on your life the higher," says Kant.[70] The term transcendental refers, then, only to our faculty of knowing, never to our knowledge of things.[71]

The term transcendental idealism, coined in the first edition of the Critique,[72] generated what

Kant saw as a good deal of confusion and misunderstanding amongst his critics, who proceeded not by concentrating "on the spirit of philosophical nomenclature" but instead by "clinging to the letter."[73] For this reason he proposed, in the Prolegomena, the alternative names formal idealism or critical idealism for his own "quite peculiar" kind of idealism,[74] though he did not in fact go on to adopt either term in the second edition of the Critique. In his keen focus on empirical intuition and on the reality of objects "outside us"[75]—those very things that are met with in space, presented in space, or outside of us, whose external existence Moore was so keen to prove—there is a clear commitment to empirical realism in Kant's philosophy, as he himself points out.[76] This is possible due to the key role that representations play in his thinking.

The concept of phenomena requires the concept of noumena. As Kant points out, the very notion of the phenomenon demands a

---

65. Ibid., 45–46 (note II).

66. Ibid., 45–46 (note II), 145–46 (appendix).

67. Kant, *Critique of Pure Reason*, 259–65 (A238–49/B297–305).

68. Ibid., 100 (A63/B88).

69. Ibid., 265 (A248/B305).

70. "*Bei Leibe nicht der höhere*"; *Prolegomena*, 144 (appendix).

71. Kant, *Critique of Pure Reason*, 59 (A11/B25); *Prolegomena*, 50–51 (note III).

72. Kant, *Critique of Pure Reason*, 345–47 (A369–71), 359 (A392).

73. Kant, *Prolegomena*, 50 (note III).

74. Ibid., 51 (note III), 146 (appendix).

75. Kant, *Critique of Pure Reason*, 348 (A373), 349 (A374–75).

76. Ibid., 72 (A28/B44), 78 (A36/B52), 347–49 (A371–75). See also Scruton, *Kant*, 44; Deleuze, *Kant's Critical Philosophy*, 13; Popper, "What Is Dialectic?" 324–25.

ground to that phenomenon.[77] But as we saw, in positing the existence of noumena, Kant is forced to concede the existence of something about which he can say precisely nothing. We must not submit to the sticky temptation of attempting to characterize noumena, the "unknown somethings." "All bodies," says Kant, "together with the space in which they are, must be held to be nothing but mere representations in us, and exist nowhere else than merely in our thoughts."[78] That which corresponds to, and is distinct from, our knowledge must remain an "object in general," an unknowable x.[79] Kant describes it as the nonempirical "transcendental object = x."[80] In putting aside this necessarily elusive x, all that we are left with, all that we can know about, all that we can actually discuss, are the representations:

> We must give full credence to this paradoxical but correct proposition, that there is nothing in space save what is represented in it. For space is itself nothing but representation, and whatever is in it must therefore be contained in the representation. Nothing whatsoever is in space, save

in so far as it is actually represented in it. It is a proposition which must indeed sound strange, that a thing can exist only in the representation of it, but in this case the objection falls, inasmuch as the things with which we are here concerned are not things in themselves, but appearances only, that is, representations.[81]

In short, Kant's philosophy is one of "representationalism."[82] As Richard Aquila points out, the standard English translation of *Vorstellung* as "representation" is not without its dangers, but "it expresses an important part of what Kant was after . . . [namely,] the notion that we, as cognitively active beings, represent the world to ourselves as being of a certain sort (whether or not in every case it really is of that sort)."[83] The German term might as easily be translated as "presentation," "mental representation," or even "idea,"[84] and Kant provides the Latin REPRAESENTATIO, meaning "a making present," as equivalent.[85] The key drawback with the English term *representation*, Aquila believes, is that, in a philosophical context at least, it seems to imply that the representations are "mental objects" (like the "ideas" of Berkeley and Hume), which goes too far, perhaps, in attributing to the representations a distinct ontological status that Kant never intended.[86] The precise nature of these representations need not concern us, so long as we retain the notion of some variety of mental mediation and keep in mind that this mediation is, by Kant's account, all

77. Kant, *Critique of Pure Reason*, 269–70 (A251–52).
78. Kant, *Prolegomena*, 45 (note II).
79. Kant, *Critique of Pure Reason*, 134–38 (A104–10).
80. Ibid., 137 (A109).
81. Ibid., 349 (A374–75, note a).
82. See Aquila, *Representational Mind*, x.
83. Ibid.
84. Ibid., x, 1.
85. Kant, *Critique of Pure Reason*, 314 (A320/B376).
86. Aquila, *Representational Mind*, x–xi.

that we can properly discuss.[87] We will return to the question of representationalism shortly, but we need first to clarify Kant's views on the veracity of his *Vorstellungen* and to look briefly at his aliens.

It is important to remember that for Kant the inaccessibility of noumena does not mean that appearances are merely erroneous representations or illusions. The necessity of dealing only with phenomena does not preclude the possibility of objective knowledge. On the contrary, Kant's explicit goal in the *Critique of Pure Reason* is to provide a solid metaphysical foundation for the objective knowledge that he believes already to exist in mathematics and the natural sciences.[88] Appearances *cannot* be merely illusions, because the sensibility does not represent things as they are, erroneously or otherwise; rather, it presents them only as they affect the senses. Truth and error do not lie in the intuited object but instead are a function of the understanding as it *judges* intuited objects: "It is therefore correct to say that the senses do not err—not because they always judge rightly but because they do not judge at all. Truth and error, therefore, and consequently also illusion as leading to error, are only to be found in the judgment, i.e. only in the relation of the object to our understanding."[89] There is not a difference of "clarity" between the representations provided by the sensibility and things as they are in themselves, as if the former were merely poor imitations of

the latter. Rather, there is a "genetic" difference, a difference in kind, between noumena, whose existence is known only by means of the conjecture of the understanding, and the wholly empirical representations provided by the sensibility on which the understanding can go to work to produce knowledge.[90]

Properly speaking then, the illusions that might beset the understanding are of two kinds, neither of which, Kant would argue, present a problem for his epistemology. The first are of the "empirical" variety, where the employment of the understanding IN CONCRETO leads to "accidental" errors, caused by one's wandering attention, doubts, hesitations, and so on,[91] or perhaps by the influence of the imagination producing dreams and delusions.[92] Errors of this sort are a matter for the study of "applied" logic and are not at all the sort of thing with which Kant is dealing.[93] Additionally, there are the illusions of the "transcendental" variety at which we have already looked, produced by philosophasters with

---

87. Aquila outlines five different ways in which we might understand Kant's representations. They might be seen as cognitive relations to a thing, quasi relations to a possible thing, states or properties in a subject, mental objects in a mind, or sensations contributing to internal states. Aquila himself is keen to demonstrate that representations are certainly not objects but are, rather, states that make relations possible; ibid., xi, 3–4, 33–35.

88. Kant, *Prolegomena*, 15–35 (§§1–5), and see also Lucas's preface, vii.

89. Kant, *Critique of Pure Reason*, 297 (A293/B350).

90. Kant, *Prolegomena*, 47 (note III); *Critique of Pure Reason*, 88–89 (B69–71).

91. Kant, *Critique of Pure Reason*, 95 (A54–55/B78–79), 350 (A376).

92. Ibid., 247 (B278), 298 (A295/B351–52), 350 (A376).

93. Ibid., 95 (A54–55/B78–79).

overactive understandings.[94] Here, appearances are taken for things in themselves, a situation described by Kant as the childish effort by metaphysics to snatch at soap bubbles.[95] Far from turning representations into mere illusions, then, Kant believes that he has provided the only way to ensure that appearances are something of which we can have true, objective knowledge.[96]

We know nature (the world) as the totality of appearances, that is, as representations within us. How then can our knowledge of nature be described as true and objective? The answer Kant gives is ingenious and follows directly from his explanation of sensibility and understanding. Nature, he argues, is only possible for us, "materially," due to the particular quality of our sensibility. The peculiar way in which it is affected, by those unknown somethings, is what presents nature before us as intuitions. Similarly, nature

is simultaneously only possible "formally" due to the particular quality of our understanding. The peculiar way in which it governs our thinking by means of rules is what organizes those appearances and makes nature appear the way it does. The universal or "pure" laws of nature[97] thus do not come from experience. Experience itself *needs* those laws, because they provide for the very possibility of experience. The laws of nature are provided a priori by the sensibility and understanding. In short, "the possibility of experience in general is thus at the same time the universal law of nature, and the principles of the former are themselves the laws of the latter."[98]

Thus, the propositions of geometry, for instance, hold *necessarily* of space and everything in it because space is the very form of outer appearances in us. Only by means of this form of intuition can objects of the senses be given to us, and only by means of the rules of the understanding can we arrive at judgments about those objects' precise length, their relationships to one another, and so on. The outer objects of the world *must* agree with the propositions of geometry because it is sensibility that makes these objects possible and understanding that enables us to think about them. The reality of geometry is objective *because* it deals with the "objects of the senses" and not with things in themselves.[99]

The "universal law of nature" thus contains the conditions of the unification of perceptions in experience. "Nature" and "possible experi-

94. Kant also discusses the inevitability of the illusions of transcendent (as opposed to transcendental) judgments of reason. Deleuze emphasizes the deep torment of the understanding and of reason as they struggle to resist their joint ambition to overreach themselves; see Kant, *Critique of Pure Reason*, 298–300 (A295–98/B351–55); Deleuze, *Kant's Critical Philosophy*, 24–26.

95. Moore, as we saw, deliberately chooses to play with these notoriously impermanent structures in his bid to prove the existence of "things external to our minds," and his efforts come dangerously close to just this ill-advised snatching against which Kant cautions; see "Two Hands Are Better Than One" in chapter 2.

96. Kant, *Critique of Pure Reason*, 349–50 (A375–77); *Prolegomena*, 49 (note III).

97. As opposed to the empirical laws of nature that depend on particular perceptions and that we learn simply through experience.

98. Kant, *Prolegomena*, 80 (§36). On phenomena as objective knowledge and the relation of the "object in general" to the unity of consciousness, see Deleuze, *Kant's Critical Philosophy*, 12–17.

99. Kant, *Critique of Pure Reason*, 349–50 (A375–76); *Prolegomena*, 43 (note I), 80 (§36).

ence" are one and the same. As Kant says, "The understanding does not draw its laws (a priori) from nature, but prescribes them to nature,"[100] as one might in fact have expected from its lord. This is Kant's famous "Copernican Revolution,"[101] summarized by Ilya Prigogine and Isabelle Stengers thus: "The subject no longer 'revolves' around its object, seeking to discover the laws by which it is governed or the language by which it may be deciphered. Now the subject itself is at the center, imposing its laws, and the world perceived speaks the language of that subject."[102] This effects what Prigogine and Stengers call Kant's "critical ratification." Kant, they argue, allows only one, unique set of a priori principles and denies the possibility of diverse scientific viewpoints. "Transcendental philosophy thus ratified the physicist's claim to have found the definitive form of all positive knowledge," they say, or, as Feyerabend would have it, Kant "consecrated" the absolute space-time frame of classical physics.[103] Objective knowledge is possible, then, for those whose appearances benefit from the inner sense of time and the outer sense of space (the two forms of intuition) and, at the same time, employ the twelve categories (the forms of understanding). Foucault called this "transcendental narcissism,"[104] but the questions arise, What kind of being is this narcissist? Who, precisely, are the fortunate creatures capable of objective knowledge? Who, or what, is the subject that has now been placed center stage?

PRAYING TO THE ALIENS

The traditional characterization of Kant's *Critique of Pure Reason*, then, prompted by the parallel he himself draws between his own radical intervention and the one effected by the esteemed astronomer, is as a "Copernican Revolution." Something of that great reversal is certainly apparent in an earlier work, at which we will look in a moment, in which Kant quotes "that witty author from The Hague":

> Those creatures which live in the forests on the head of a beggar, had long since considered their location as an immense ball, and themselves as the masterpiece of creation, when one of them, endowed by Heaven with a more refined spirit, a small Fontenelle of his species, unexpectedly became familiar with the head of a nobleman. Immediately he called together all the witty heads of his quarters and told them with excitement: "We are not the only living beings in nature; see, there, that new land, more **LICE** live there."[105]

100. Kant, *Prolegomena*, 80–82 (§36).
101. Kant, *Critique of Pure Reason*, 22 (Bxvi).
102. Prigogine and Stengers, *Order out of Chaos*, 87. On this "Copernican Revolution," see also Deleuze, *Kant's Critical Philosophy*, 13–14; Popper, "Kant's Critique and Cosmology," 180–81.
103. Prigogine and Stengers, *Order out of Chaos*, 86–89; Feyerabend, *Against Method*, 51.
104. Foucault, *Archaeology of Knowledge*, 203.
105. Quoted in Kant, *Universal Natural History*, 185 (177; parenthetical numbers refer to pages in the German edition). The identity of the writer of this satirical fable remains a mystery. The Fontenelle mentioned was one Bernard le Bovier de Fontenelle, whose popular astronomy text *Entretiens sur la pluralité des mondes* of 1686 had described imaginary journeys to other planets; Kant, *Universal Natural History*, 295n10; Crowe, *Extraterrestrial Life Debate*, 18–20.

53. LOUSE

One day the governess ordered our coachman to stop at several shops, where the beggars, watching their opportunity, crowded to the sides of the coach, and gave me the most horrible spectacle that ever a European eye beheld. There was a woman with a cancer in her breast, swelled to a monstrous size, full of holes, in two or three of which I could have easily crept, and covered my whole body. There was a fellow with a wen in his neck, larger than five wool-packs; and another, with a couple of wooden legs, each about twenty feet high. But the most hateful sight of all, was the lice crawling on their clothes. I could see distinctly the limbs of these vermin with my naked eye, much better than those of a European louse through a microscope, and their snouts with which they rooted like swine.

JONATHAN SWIFT, *Gulliver's Travels*, 128–29.

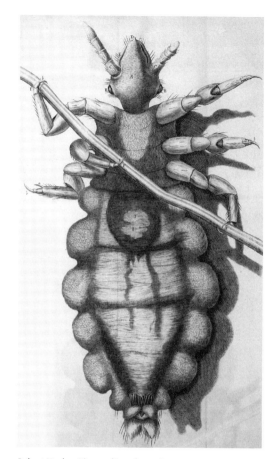

Robert Hooke, *Micrographia*, schematic 35.

Much like Nietzsche's self-absorbed gnat, these inattentive lice, up until the revelatory insight of one perceptive individual, similarly considered themselves the center of nature's aims.[106] Strictly speaking, however, the upheaval of Kant's Critique is quite the opposite to that wrought by Nicolaus Copernicus's heliocentric cosmology. Whereas Copernicus took humanity from its time-honored place at the center of the heavens and pushed it out toward the periphery, Kant assigns to human life a central position once more.[107] He reinstates, in fact, a familiar anthropocentrism. As Gilles Deleuze puts it, "The first thing that the Copernican Revolution teaches us is that it is we who are giving the orders."[108] Is this what Kant teaches? Is it indeed humans who take up this central, legislative role?

Kant seems to have had only humans in mind when discussing sensibility and understanding in the Critique and Prolegomena. Regarding the first pure form of intuition, Kant says, "It is, therefore, solely from the human standpoint that we can speak of space, of extended things, etc. If we depart from the subjective condition under which alone we can have outer intuition,

106. Kant, *Universal Natural History*, 185 (177).

107. Popper draws attention this restoration of human centrality; Popper, "Kant's Critique and Cosmology," 180–81.

108. Deleuze, *Kant's Critical Philosophy*, 14.

namely, liability to be affected by objects, the representation of space stands for nothing whatsoever."[109] The same is true of time[110] and thus of intuition in general: "But intuition takes place only in so far as the object is given to us. This again is only possible, to man at least (uns Menschen wenigstens), in so far as the mind is affected in a certain way."[111] And when discussing the understanding, Kant frequently calls it human understanding.[112] He congratulates himself for having isolated the "pure elements of human knowledge," and especially for having done so by discerning the system of which they are a part, rather than merely observing an aggregate of miscellaneous faculties. The beauty of such a scheme is, of course, that it is necessary and complete: "This same system, like every true system grounded on a universal principle, shows its inestimable use in that it also ejects all alien concepts [fremdartige Begriffe], which might otherwise slip in among the pure concepts of the understanding, and gives all knowledge its proper place."[113] The complete system that Kant describes, then, is the system of the human mind, the means by which humans are able to garner objective knowledge about the external world. The dog at whom Kant looked is never seen to be gazing back. But does Kant really wish to assert that objective knowledge is possible only for the human mind? Is he really that dogmatic?

Concerning the pure forms of intuition, Kant also suggested that "we cannot judge in regard to the intuitions of other thinking beings, whether they are bound by the same conditions as those which limit our intuition and which for us are universally valid."[114] In fact, "this mode of intuiting in space and time need not be limited to human sensibility. It may be that all finite, thinking beings necessarily agree with man in this respect, although we are not in a position to judge whether this is actually so."[115] Thus, Kant allows not only that there are other thinking beings but also that they might actually share the very same intuitions of space and time that make knowledge possible for human beings. On the other hand, in using the qualifying term human—"human sensibility" and "human understanding"—Kant thereby allows that there may well be sensibilities and understandings of other kinds. There may in fact be thinking beings with entirely different forms of sensibility and understanding, which would make possible for them entirely different apprehensions of those objects with which they come into contact. The phenomena of which they are aware would thus be of an entirely different kind from those with which humans are familiar.

---

109. Kant, *Critique of Pure Reason*, 71 (A26/B42).

110. Ibid., 77–78 (A34–35/B51).

111. Ibid., 65 (A19/B33); see also 84 (A45/B62).

112. Ibid., passim, but see for example 103 (A66/B91), 105 (A68/B93), as well as *Prolegomena*, 88 (§39), 97 (§46).

113. Kant, *Prolegomena*, 89 (§39).

114. Kant, *Critique of Pure Reason*, 72 (A27/B43); see also 82 (A42/B59), 270 (A252).

115. Ibid., 90 (B72).

So who are these other thinking beings, if such there be? Man, after all, is the single being upon Earth who possesses understanding, according to Kant. He left open, however, the question of thinking beings on other planets. Or rather, Kant chose not to address this matter in the Critique of Pure Reason, having already dealt with the question of extraterrestrials in that earlier, lousy work, his Universal Natural History and Theory of the Heavens. This short book concerns itself with "the constitution and mechanical origin of the whole universe, treated according to Newton's principles."[116] The first two parts deal with the composition of the Milky Way, the density of the planets, the origins of their moons and of Saturn's ring, and so on. The third part, however, deals with the question "of the inhabitants of the stars." Kant is unequivocal on the matter: "I am of the opinion that it is not even necessary to assert that all planets must be inhabited, although it would be sheer madness to deny this in respect to all, or even to most of them."[117] Taking as beyond doubt the fact that the purpose of nature is to ensure its own contemplation by intelligent beings, Kant finds it all but inconceivable that the vast majority of planets should fail to support rational creatures. Those planets that are not currently inhabited are most likely to be passing through a state of development, and they will surely support not just life but reflective beings at some time in the future. Jupiter, we are told, seems to be passing through just such a phase.[118]

Now, Kant says, it is a simple matter to discern the relative intellectual capacities of the various inhabitants of Mercury, Mars, Venus, and the other planets. First, Kant asserts that "spiritual faculties"—notions, representations, and the ability to think—depend on bodily matter. Just as the physical bodies of children develop, so too do their thinking natures, which will subsequently wane with the loss of bodily vigor in old age. Gross matter both makes possible and constrains the spiritual part of man that is the very "goal of his existence."[119] Matter, in turn, depends on the influence of the sun: as the heat diffuses out from the center of the "world-system," it excites to different degrees the matter from which the planets are made. Now it follows, Kant says, that the matter that makes up both Venus itself and the inhabitants who inevitably live there must be denser stuff than that of Earth; otherwise they would be destroyed by the great heat that reaches that planet owing to its close proximity to the sun. And conversely, the matter of planets further out from the sun, such as Saturn and Jupiter, must be lighter and more volatile, and their fibers more elastic, due to the relative paucity of solar influence.[120] Given, then, that the quality and

116. Kant, *Universal Natural History*, title page. On the relation between Kant's interest in extraterrestrials and his contribution to sidereal astronomy, see Crowe, *Extraterrestrial Life Debate*, 47–55.

117. Kant, *Universal Natural History*, 184 (174–75).

118. Ibid.

119. Ibid., 186–88 (180–84).

120. Ibid., 188–89 (184–86).

crudeness of matter affects a creature's intellectual capacities, it further follows

> that the excellence of thinking natures, the promptness in their reflections, the clarity and vivacity of the notions that come to them through external impression, together with the[ir] ability to put them together, finally also the skill in their actual use, in short, the whole range of their perfection, stand[s] under a certain rule, according to which these [natures] become more excellent and perfect in proportion to the distance of their habitants from the sun.[121]

In short, the extraterrestrial who lives on Mercury or Venus will be rather dim—dense even—compared to an Earthling, due to a "grosser build and the **slug**gishness of the elements of his structure," whilst the inhabitant of Saturn, and eventually Jupiter, blessed with a body "much lighter and more volatile," will be considerably brighter than his Earthly counterpart.[122] Kant further speculates that the inhabitants of the outer planets might well be "too noble and wise to degrade themselves to [the level of] that stupidity which is inherent in sin" and that the inhabitants of the inner planets, tied so closely to matter, might not be deemed responsible for their actions. Thus would sin be confined to Earth, "and perhaps Mars (so that we would not be deprived of the miserable comfort of having companions in misery)."[123] Moral implications aside, however, the question arises as to whether aliens employ the same basic capacities of the mind as do humans. Is it the case that Venusians employ a sensibility and understanding that are identical to those of humanity, but make less-effective use of them? Do Saturnites employ the same intuitions and concepts again, but with a proficiency that would astound an Earthling? Or do the Venusian and the Saturnite have entirely different sensibilities and understandings? Is there a single system that "ejects all alien concepts," or are there several such systems? Daniel Dennett suggests that mathematics and physics will be the same "throughout the entire universe," implying, at least on a Kantian model, that all intelligent beings must share the same sensibility and understanding (see "The Truth about Mice and Ducks" in chapter 2). Kant, however, is not so sure.

The objective knowledge that is the focus of his study in the *Critique of Pure Reason* is objective knowledge for humans. Kant explicitly leaves open the possibility that there may be other forms of sensibility and understanding and therefore other forms of knowledge. Ultimately, however, it is impossible to know whether the two fundamental capacities that he identifies in the human mind are unique or shared with other beings. Venusians and Saturnites may well be giving the orders too. Like the lice of the witty writer from The Hague, humans have a tendency to regard themselves as exist-

---

121. Ibid., 189 (186–87).
122. Ibid., 189 (185).
123. Ibid., 195 (197).

Photograph by author.

54. Slug
A familiar and unwelcome animal in the garden and field because of its voracious appetite. The slug rasps its way through carrion, fungi and plant tissues including cereals, clover, root and potato crops.

Book of the British Countryside, 423.

ing at the center of the world, as masterpieces of creation, but in allowing for the possibility of alien intelligence, nay, in asserting its necessity and in some cases its considerable superiority, Kant really does shift humankind to a cosmo-

logical periphery. Man may be titled the lord of nature on earth, but his intellectual and moral superiors elsewhere seem to hold a stronger claim to that station if we consider the universe in its entirety. In light of his *Universal Natural History and Theory of the Heavens*, the rotation that Kant set in motion with the *Critique of Pure Reason* turns out to be a genuinely Copernican revolution after all.

NOTHING TO PHONE HOME ABOUT

Kant embraces the existence of rational alien beings,[124] whilst Nietzsche, though he does not discuss them explicitly, is willing to adopt an extraterrestrial perspective in the disparaging opening paragraphs of his essay "On Truth and Lies" (see "The Philosopher and the Gnat" in chapter 2). The two were willing to put humans in their place, which is to say *alongside* other beings with perceptions and knowledges of their own. Kant, in fact, could be every bit as downbeat as Nietzsche concerning human folly:

> The question can be raised, whether our species should be considered a good race or an evil one (for we can also call it a *race*, if we conceive of it as a species of rational *beings* on *earth* in comparison with rational beings on other planets, as a multitude of creatures originating from one demiurge); and then I must admit that there is not much to boast about in it.[125]

Kant and Nietzsche share a good deal more than a low opinion of humankind, but before

124. It is true that Kant deleted the final section, dealing with extraterrestrials, from later editions of his treatise, but he continued to write about the inhabitants of other worlds up until his last work; see below, and D. L. Clark, "Kant's Aliens," 282n84.

125. Kant, *Anthropology*, 191–92 (331). See also his references to humanity's "folly and childish vanity" and to their "folly and caprice" in "Idea for a Universal History," 42, 51. As David L. Clark points out, however, for every "ambivalently anti-anthropocentric gesture" that Kant makes, there is an unashamedly anthropocentric corollary; D. L. Clark, "Kant's Aliens," 211–14. So it is with this quotation: Kant goes on to point out that "our very judgment of condemnation reveals a moral disposition in us, an innate demand of reason to counteract this tendency. So it presents the human species, not as evil, but as a species of rational beings that strives, in the face of obstacles, to rise out of evil in constant progress toward the good"; Kant, *Anthropology*, 192–93 (333).

examining these commonalities, we would do well to recall the extent to which they have been regarded as oppositional factions in philosophy.

In a lecture delivered in 1973, exactly one hundred years after "On Truth and Lies," Foucault argued that Nietzsche provided therein a "great break" from the Kantianism, or neo-Kantianism, that was rife at the time. In Nietzsche's later writings, to which Foucault turns perhaps too quickly, something like *la grande rupture* can be discerned. But here, in 1873, Nietzsche's relationship to Kant is by no means as clear-cut as Foucault would have us believe, as we can see both from "On Truth and Lies" itself and from Nietzsche's notebooks of the time. As Foucault rightly points out, Nietzsche certainly wishes to distance himself from any account of knowledge that would render it objective. To the extent that Nietzsche, in an "insolent and cavalier manner," seeks to demonstrate how knowledge is *invented*, he is indeed a long way from Kant's earnest attempt to provide a firm foundation for the truth of the natural sciences.[126] Nietzsche regards Kant's influence on philosophy in its entirety as particularly detrimental. Following the publication of the *Critique of Pure Reason*, we can no longer rely upon the controlling influence that philosophy had hitherto exercised over the small-minded, indiscriminate, grubby pursuit of knowledge for its own sake that characterizes contemporary science and history. Contrary, perhaps, to his explicit intentions, Kant is part of the process whereby philosophy has gradually lost its hold on the reins of science.[127]

Nietzsche's reception of Kant is equivocal, however. He describes, for instance, what he calls "Kant's tragic problem," that is, the "marvellous, heroic desire" of the human being, which is of course doomed by a "mendacious nature," to be completely truthful.[128] He finds especially appealing Kant's insight into what Nietzsche calls the "anthropomorphic" nature of all constructions, including all science.[129] Moreover, beyond this begrudging admiration, in the process of acknowledging Kant's baleful influence on philosophy, Nietzsche inherits key elements of his method. The controlling principle, upon which we can no longer rely, thanks to Kant, is the "thing in itself," which Nietzsche retains as part of his understanding of the relation between the world and its representation. It appears, as we saw, as a component within his discussion of the "stammering translation" from individual to idea.[130] Further, informing this sequence of metamorphoses are the "primal forms" (*Urformen*) of time and space, those innate conceptions through which humans are compelled to perceive the world (see "The Birds and the Bees"

126. Foucault, "Truth and Juridical Forms," 6.
127. Nietzsche, *Unpublished Writings*, 10–11 (19.28), 14–15 (19.37), 16 (19.39), 20–21 (19.51).
128. Ibid., 37 (19.104).
129. Ibid., 14–15 (19.37), 42 (19.125), 44–45 (19.134), 57 (19.180). See "The Philosopher and the Gnat" in chapter 2.
130. Nietzsche, "On Truth and Falsity," 178; *Unpublished Writings*, 10–11 (19.28), 24–25 (19.66), 46–47 (19.140). On Nietzsche's equivocal relationship to Kant's thing in itself, see Stack, "Nietzsche's Critique."

55. LIMPET

Limpets are snails with an unusual mode of growth. Snail shells are cones that expand slowly and wind around an axis during growth, producing the conventional corkscrew of increasing width. But the limpet cone expands so rapidly that the shell never winds around its axis for more than a fraction of a whorl. Thus, a large open end clamps tightly down upon a rock, or a food source, and this power of adhesion has made the limpet a symbol of tenacity and stubbornness in many languages and cultures. In England, for example, limpets are (according to the OED), "officials alleged to be superfluous but clinging to their offices."

STEPHEN JAY GOULD, "Losing a Limpet," 56–57.

Photograph by Machel Spence.

131. Foucault, "Truth and Juridical Forms," 6.

132. Ibid., 14 (translation modified).

133. Maudemarie Clark calls this Nietzsche's "naturalized Kantian theory of knowledge"; *Nietzsche on Truth*, 124. It is not quite a blend of Kantianism with empiricism due to Nietzsche's emphasis on the role of language, which adds an additional element to the mix.

134. Nietzsche's early understanding of Kant was significantly influenced by his reading of Schopenhauer; see M. Clark, *Nietzsche on Truth*, 79–83; Magee, *Philosophy of Schopenhauer*, 286–300; Janaway, *Willing and Nothingness*. In fact, as Christopher Janaway (5) has pointed out, the opening of Nietzsche's "On Truth and Lies" is a "virtual parody" of the opening of the second volume of Schopenhauer's *The World as Will and Representation* (3). But see also the discussion of Nietzsche's direct debt to Kant in Hill, *Nietzsche's Critiques*.

in chapter 2). Foucault argues that whereas for Kant time and space are forms of knowledge, for Nietzsche they are "primitive rocks" onto which knowledge attaches itself.[131] For all practical purposes, however, these two *Urformen* onto which knowledge clings, **LIMPET**like, function in Nietzsche's text as none other than Kant's two pure forms of intuition.

Foucault suggests of Nietzsche that "when he says that knowledge [*connaissance*] is always a perspective, he doesn't mean, in what would be a blend of Kantianism and empiricism, that, in man, knowledge is bounded by a certain number of conditions, of limits derived from human nature, the human body, or the structure of knowledge itself."[132] In fact, in 1873, the necessity with which man is compelled to cast forth these forms, a necessity that Nietzsche equates with that compelling a spider to spin a web, suggests an epistemology that comes very close to a blend of Kantianism and empiricism.[133] Whether the conditions of *Erkennen* derive for humans from their "nature" or their "body" is less important for Nietzsche than the fact that they *are* so determined for humanity, just as they are, in their heterogeneous ways, for all the other creatures he mentions in his essay. By clinging fast, on the one hand, to Kant's inaccessible x, the noumena of his account, and, on the other, to the forms of intuition that permit the knowing subject to receive representations, that is, to perceive phenomena, Nietzsche retains, albeit in a modified form, Kant's representationalism.[134]

Like Nietzsche, Kant had asked, "What is truth?" And he had replied, with equal confidence, "The nominal definition of truth, that it is the agreement of knowledge with its object, is assumed as granted: the question asked is as to what is the general and sure criterion of the truth of any and every knowledge."[135] Nietzsche does indeed grant this definition, disagreeing with Kant not on the matter of what would constitute truth but, rather, on whether such a thing is possible. Having retained the essence of Kant's noumenal world, which remains utterly inaccessible, for Nietzsche the "thing in itself" itself would be the only pure, unadulterated truth, an incoherent notion requiring knowledge to be identified with its object.[136] To Kant's phenomenal world he adds linguistic constructions, but in both cases what is known is of an entirely different order from that of the "unknown something" that lies beneath. In a well-known passage from *Twilight of the Idols*, a much later work, Nietzsche recounts "The History of an Error," that is, "How the 'True World' Ultimately Became a Fable." He traces the six-stage process through which philosophers' understanding of the world has passed. The third stage, following on the heels of Plato and Christianity, describes how the true world has become unattainable but remains as "a thought, . . . a comfort, . . . the idea has become sublime, pale, northern, Königs-

bergian."[137] Contrary to Foucault's claim, in this early essay Nietzsche himself still saw through Königsbergian eyes.[138] The characterization of knowledge as representation is shared by realist and relativist epistemologies. Whilst the realist holds to the belief or hope that the representation will correspond to the world it depicts, the relativist knows for sure that no representation will ever manage to model the world as it really is, that the representation itself is as close as we get. But on the nature of knowledge itself, on the question of what knowledge is, the realist and relativist are in broad agreement. Knowledge is a picture or copy, a reproduction or reflection, a representation.

So is Kant himself a realist or a relativist? On the one hand, his steadfast belief in the objective validity of scientific knowledge, in the possibility of knowing the truth about phenomena, warrants a realist label. His objective

135. Kant, *Critique of Pure Reason*, 97 (A58/B82).
136. Nietzsche, "On Truth and Falsity," 178. Compare Kant's suggestion that a divine understanding would intuit not representations of objects, thought according to the categories, but the objects themselves; *Critique of Pure Reason*, 161 (B145). For a concise summary of Kant's position and of the extent to which Nietzsche shares it, see M. Clark, *Nietzsche on Truth*, 55–61.
137. Nietzsche, *Twilight of the Idols*, 24–25. Kant was, famously, a native and life-long resident of Königsberg.
138. For a clear discussion of the Kantian elements of "Truth and Lies," see M. Clark, *Nietzsche on Truth*, chapter 3 (esp. 85–90). By the time of *Twilight of the Idols*, Nietzsche's ideas lay two full stages beyond Kant's comforting skepticism. On the stages of Nietzsche's understanding of truth and the degree to which they correspond to those described in this late passage, see M. Clark, *Nietzsche on Truth*, 109–17; and Leiter, "Perspectivism," 335. We will return to Nietzsche's mature thinking in chapter 4.

in the *Critique of Pure Reason*, after all, is nothing less than to establish, by means of his firmly grounded metaphysics, a solid foundation on which the advances of science can comfortably and confidently rest. On the other hand, however, Kant is equally certain that nothing is or can be known about the things in themselves of which the world is truly composed. He shares none of Christopher Norris's unabashed confidence in the capabilities of science to get a firm grasp on a "mind-independent and language-independent reality."[139] Rather, he is insistent that all we can ever know are the representations and appearances furnished by our minds. This is relativist talk, especially when we recall that Kant is open to the possibility that nonterrestrial rational beings may well have conceptual schemata entirely different from those possessed by humble Earthlings. So which is it? Is Kant a relatively sophisticated realist, or a really sophisticated relativist?

Rom Harré and Michael Krausz argue that Kant was a prime example of what they call a "capped" relativist, a species of thinker who has appeared throughout the history of philosophy, since at least the time of Aristotle.[140] Philosophers who capped their relativist insights can be

identified by the fact that seemingly irresistible relativist conclusions were "blocked by assumptions which were intrinsic to the positions of those who gave the most vigorous expression to these insights."[141] Kant's own presuppositions regarding the necessity of objective knowledge stop him short of the radically relativist conclusions to which his philosophy might otherwise lead. His insight into the constructed nature of representations, mediated as they are through the sensibility and understanding, particularly in light of the potential variety of competing extraterrestrial conceptual systems, ought perhaps to lead him to the kind of relativist salon philosophy that so irked Richard Dawkins. But they do not, and Kant settles instead on a transcendental idealism, or formal idealism, or critical idealism, or perhaps even an empirical realism, that stops short of such unpalatable conclusions and guarantees instead the objectivity of human representations.[142]

Nietzsche, on the other hand, has no intention of capping his philosophy. He goes the whole **HOG**, relishing the diverse and arbitrarily heterogeneous languages that make "snakes" sinuous and "trees" masculine and make enigmatically unobtainable all the many objects to which these languages refer. Truthfulness is only possible, he asserts, "in a very relative sense."[143] A tension arises between this relativism and Nietzsche's own idealism, however. On the one hand, he draws attention to the fact that different

139. C. Norris, *Against Relativism*, vii; see "The Truth about Mice and Ducks" in chapter 2.

140. Harré and Krausz, *Varieties of Relativism*, 15.

141. Ibid.

142. Cavell calls this Kant's "settlement" with skepticism; see Cavell, *In Quest of the Ordinary*, 29–31.

143. Nietzsche, *Unpublished Writings*, 37 (19.104).

Thomas Bewick, *The Common Hog*, 1790, in Blanche Cirker, ed.,
1800 Woodcuts by Thomas Bewick and His School, plate 18.

56. Hog

Thus says the prophet of the Turk,
Good Mussulman, abstain from pork;
There is a part in every swine
No friend or follower of mine
May taste, whate'er his inclination,
On pain of excommunication.
Such Mahomet's mysterious charge,
And thus he left the point at large.
Had he the sinful part express'd,
They might with safety eat the rest;
But for one piece they thought it hard
From the whole hog to be debarr'd;
And set their wit at work to find
What joint the prophet had in mind.
Much controversy straight arose,
These choose the back, the belly those;
By some 'tis confidently said
He meant not to forbid the head;
While others at that doctrine rail,
And piously prefer the tail.
Thus, conscience freed from every clog,
Mahometans eat up the hog.

WILLIAM COWPER, "The Love of the World Reproved;
or, Hypocrisy Detected," in *The Poems of William Cowper*,
412–13.

languages represent the world in different ways, but on the other, he argues that innate primal forms determine a distinctly human means of perceiving the world. The latter position he inherits from Kant, whilst the former position constitutes the flowering of the very conclusions that Kant could not, or would not, acknowledge. In his critique of truth, Nietzsche appeals both to the phenomena that are the result of human sensibility and to the metaphorical metamorphoses brought about by language that should, by rights, make such an idealist model epistemologically problematic. Having stopped short at phenomena, Kant was able to argue that objective knowledge is possible. Nietzsche, on the other hand, having taken the further step of acknowledging the relativity of diverse human languages, should not be able to rely on the notion of sensibly determined human phenomena. But, as we have seen, he invokes both the thing in itself and his own variety of Urformen. Nietzsche, like Kant, is a representationalist, but the realist and idealist elements that form part of his Kantian inheritance threaten to undermine his attempt to push the relativist implications of that inheritance to their logical conclusions.[144]

Neither of these two great thinkers can be described straightforwardly as relativists, then. If any he-goats have been milked, it seems that Kant is a likely suspect: the question he identifies as capable of a reasonable answer is the

144. On Nietzsche's retention of Kant's thing in itself, see M. Clark, *Nietzsche on Truth*, 85–90.

matter of educing the correct means of arriving at objective knowledge of subjective appearances. Nietzsche, meanwhile, following in his turn, attempts to provide a watertight response to Kant's enquiry by employing the sieve that constitutes the latter's fundamental premises.[145] But if Kant himself is not a full-blooded relativist, his representational idealism is the epistemological starting point for many a relativist to follow. Nietzsche was skeptical that the influence of Kant, that "quiet scholar," had really been as profound as is often claimed, but he warned that "should the moment ever arise in which Kant begins to have a popular effect, then we will become aware of it in the form of a corrosive and disintegrating skepticism and relativism."[146] Nietzsche, in fact, is only one of many succeeding philosophers and theorists who, consciously or otherwise, inherit from Kant a conception of knowledge that lends itself to some variety or other of relativism. We will examine two of these in the remaining sections of the chapter. First, however, we need to answer one last question concerning representation: does it, in either its realist or relativist guise, entail an anthropocentric outlook?

Despite his genuinely Copernican revolution, Kant *was* in fact anthropocentric. "Man" may have been demoted on some putative hier-

archy of intellects, but this evaluative conception of anthropocentrism was never the one that concerned us most. Kant's arguments in each of the two works we have considered exhibit precisely that first-and-foremost, epistemological anthropocentrism articulated by Protagoras (see the prelude and "Into Your Hand They Are Delivered" in chapter 1). Like Heidegger and Bataille, Kant feels compelled to start from the human, but having done so, he finds that the human is all he is then able to address with any confidence. Kant seemed to be aware of this danger, when he returned to the question of the shape and material composition of extraterrestrials in his last published work, *Anthropology from a Pragmatic Point of View*:

> It is noteworthy that the only form we can think of as suitable for a rational being is that of a man. Any other form represents, at most, a symbol of a certain quality in man—as the snake is an image of evil cunning—but not the rational being himself. So our imagination populates all the other planets only with human forms, although, in view of the different soil that supports and feeds them and the different elements they are composed of, these beings are probably formed very differently.[147]

Even beyond humanity's anthropomorphic inclinations, however, Kant himself displays a distinct lack of imagination when it comes to the intellectual capacities of his aliens. "Man" serves, in his *Universal Natural History and Theory*

145. On Nietzsche's full realization that he had been duped and his rejection of Kant and the problematic notion of the thing in itself, see "The Eyes Have It" in chapter 4.

146. Nietzsche, "Schopenhauer as Educator," 188.

147. Kant, *Anthropology*, 48 (172).

of the *Heavens*, "as the foundation and general reference point" for the enquiry, that is, as the starting point for Kant's sober extrapolations regarding the mental capabilities of the world-system's other inhabitants.[148] And in the *Critique of Pure Reason*, the assertion that "we are not in a position to judge" whether the identified mode of intuiting space and time is limited to human sensibility or not is an assumption based only on Kant's firm conviction that human capacities must be his point of departure. As a result, any attempt to speculate regarding the nature of other (nonhuman) minds, any attempt to step outside the human mechanisms that make his enquiry possible, inevitably seem to engage in those frivolous flights of fancy that manage only to dabble in "obscure and vain subtleties" and that, as Kant solemnly noted, have ruined many a good brain in the past. Kant is prevented from ever discerning the nature of alien minds not by their radical alterity, if indeed they are radically other, but by the premises of his own argument.[149]

The very fact that Kant permits the possibility that extraterrestrials may share "human" perceptual and conceptual faculties, and even that they might have entirely different ones, demonstrates, however, that a representationalist perspective need not be anthropocentric. The characterization of knowledge as representation is entirely compatible with the possibility that different beings, different creatures and species, might partake of such representations. Whether some portion of these representations might be true, or whether a multiplicity of representations demonstrates ipso facto that no such truth is ever possible, is a question over which the realist and relativist will inevitably disagree. But that such representations might be held by a diversity of nonhuman beings is a matter that neither need feel compelled to deny. In addition to Kant's aliens, who may well conduct themselves with the benefit of the very same sensibility and understanding as humans, there are a multitude of animals to whom Nietzsche has drawn our attention, animals who, he argues, comprehend the world in ways that are radically different both from one another and from those of the unfortunate, delicate, transient creatures, human beings (see "The Birds and the Bees" in chapter 2). Nietzsche urges us to imagine perceiving the world as if "each of us had for himself a different sensibility, if we ourselves were only able to per-

148. Kant, *Universal Natural History*, 186 (180).

149. Kant still did not know "how it is with the inhabitants of other planets and with their nature" when he returned to the question in "Idea for a Universal History" (47). He does indulge in what can only be described as a flight of fancy, though, in the final paragraph of *Anthropology*, where he permits himself to imagine a particular alien race: "It could well be that some other planet is inhabited by rational beings who have to think aloud—who, whether awake or dreaming, in company with others or alone, can have no thoughts they do not *utter*." Kant suggests that unless these aliens were all "as *pure as angels*," they could not possibly live peacefully together. It belongs, he asserts, to the basic composition of a *human* creature "to explore the thoughts of others but to withhold one's own." This dissimulation, he claims, soon becomes deception and then lying, an assessment not so far from Nietzsche's in "On Truth and Lies"; Kant, *Anthropology*, 192 (332). David L. Clark explores Kant's ambivalence regarding dissimulation throughout his essay "Kant's Aliens," esp. 211–25 and 248–53.

ceive sometimes as a bird, sometimes as a worm, sometimes as a plant," in short, as Kant puts it, as if "a man changed sometimes into this and sometimes into that animal form."[150] In doing so, these two representationalists help demonstrate that there is nothing in the notion of representation that necessitates anthropocentrism.[151]

Kant's own first-and-foremost anthropocentrism is not required, then, by his representationalist epistemology. After devoting his *Anthropology* to a lively examination of the nature of man, he admits in the closing pages that, strictly speaking, we cannot really know man at all, since we do not have nonterrestrial rational beings with which, or with whom, to compare humanity:

> In order to characterize a species of beings, two things are required: we have to apprehend it together with other species we are acquainted with under one concept, and to state its characteristic property (PROPRIETAS)—the quality by which it differs from the other species—and use this as our basis for distinguishing it from them. . . . Let the highest specific concept be that of a terrestrial rational being: we cannot name its character

because we have no knowledge of non-terrestrial rational beings that would enable us to indicate their characteristic property and so to characterize terrestrial rational beings among rational beings in general.[152]

Without concrete knowledge of extraterrestrial rational beings, we cannot understand the nature of terrestrial rational beings. Aliens, and an understanding of their ways, are, it turns out, a necessary condition for the very possibility of Kant's philosophy.[153] Heidegger suggested that the question concerning the nature of human beings had not been adequately asked (see "If a Lion Had Hands" in chapter 1); Kant is here forced, somewhat reluctantly, to the same conclusion. At the end of his *Universal Natural History and Theory of the Heavens*, Kant gazes wistfully up at a clear night sky, contemplating the starry firmament above. The spectacle furnishes a particular pleasure, he says, available only to "noble souls," a pleasure that is a corollary of the kind of contemplations with which his treatise has dealt. But despite his hope that the immortal human soul might one day "know at a closer range those faraway globes of the world-edifice and also the excellence of their establishments which excite so much her curiosity from a distance," Kant himself was never able to assess his off-world counterparts in the flesh.[154] His speculative flights of fancy, concerning the Saturnites, the Venusians, and their kin were, alas, as close as he ever got.[155]

150. Nietzsche, "On Truth and Falsity," 186; Kant, *Critique of Pure Reason*, 132 (A100).

151. Jakob von Uexküll explicitly adopted a Kantian epistemology in his own attempts to stroll through the *Umwelten* of other animals; see Uexküll, *Theoretical Biology*, xv–xvi; Buchanan, *Onto-Ethologies*, 12–16, 21–22.

152. Kant, *Anthropology*, 182–83 (321).

153. David L. Clark's essay "Kant's Aliens" closely examines the unavoidable role that aliens of all sorts play in Kant's philosophy, especially in his *Anthropology* and *Universal Natural History*.

154. Kant, *Universal Natural History*, 196 (199).

155. On the importance of alien others for the unstable distinction that Kant insisted on drawing between his metaphysical (rational) and anthropological

FROM NOUMENA TO NEBULA

Karl Popper once suggested that by emphasizing the pivotal role played by whoever is doing the knowing, "Kant made an indelible impression not only upon philosophy but also upon physics and cosmology."[156] Similarly, Umberto Eco notes that whilst a good number of contemporary writers, himself included, explicitly acknowledge the debt they owe to Kant, "many others again indulge in neo-Kantism all unawares."[157] In this section and the next, I would like to indicate how, once Kant has been uncapped, the way is opened for the full flood of the epistemological relativism he implies. Having examined the representationalism that relativism shares with realism, it is important to take note of the key respects in which the two epistemologies differ. Whilst realism looks always to the goal of an objective account of reality, whilst it pursues truths or even a single underlying truth, relativism insists, notoriously, that no such account is possible. A variety of competing and necessarily irreconcilable perspectives is all we have and all we can ever have. As Nietzsche has already said, there is no standard of right perception. This understanding of the validity of knowledge, of what knowledge posits, this *perspectivism*, constitutes the second key element of relativist epistemology. In the *Prolegomena*, Kant suggested that his search for the complete system of the pure concepts of the understanding was analogous to identifying the general rules of operation of language.[158] In order to explore perspectivism a little further, we will examine one such reflection on the structure of language, a reflection that has been of decisive importance to contemporary relativism. It is to the work of Ferdinand de Saussure and his industrious animals that we now turn.

In his *Course in General Linguistics*, Saussure famously examines the nature of language's basic unit, the linguistic sign.[159] The sign is composed, he asserts, of two distinct but mutually dependent elements: the concept or signified (*signifié*) and the sound-image or signifier (*signifiant*). Thus, the sign for a horse, Saussure's first cipherous animal, will comprise, on the one hand, the mental concept of a horse ("a solid-hoofed perissodactyl quadruped . . . having a flowing mane and tail, whose voice is a neigh"),[160] and on the other, the word *horse*. Both elements, Saussure stresses, are "psychological": the signified is not an actual horse but the mental concept of one, and the signifier is not a physical or material sound but a "sound-image," an "inner image" that we can recite to ourselves without actually vocalizing. Considered in its entirety,

---

(empirical) work, see D. L. Clark, "Kant's Aliens," 206–9. The possibility that there might be other rational but nonhuman beings on earth is not one that Kant chooses to contemplate. In "Idea for a Universal History," he self-consciously *assumes* that "one animal species was intended [by nature] to have reason" (44).

156. Popper, "Kant's Critique and Cosmology," 181.
157. Eco, *Kant and the Platypus*, 7.
158. Kant, *Prolegomena*, 85 (§39).
159. Saussure, *Course in General Linguistics*, 65–70. Page numbers refer to the Baskin translation, except where noted, and further references are in the text.
160. *Oxford English Dictionary*, 2nd ed., s.v. "horse."

57. Ox

Nearly all the house pets, farm, and field (game) animals have monosyllabic names: dog, cat, bull, cow, ox, and so on, whereas among the more remote wild beasts monosyllables are rare. The vocabulary is most elaborated in the farm category and most attenuated in the inedible house-pet and wild-beast categories. Thus farm animals have separate terms for (1) an intact male, (2) an intact female, (3) a suckling, (4) an immature female, (5) a castrated male (e.g., bull, cow, calf, heifer, bullock, with local variants). . . . Ox (Oxen)—properly the term for the species in general, but now archaic and where used at all refers to a castrated male. . . . The English language classification of animals is by no means a simple matter; it is not just a list of names, but a complex pattern of identifications subtly discriminated not only in kind but in psychological tone. Our linguistic treatment of these categories reflects taboo or ritual value, but these are simply portmanteau terms which cover a complex of feeling and attitude, a sense perhaps that aggression, as manifested either in sex or in killing, is somehow a disturbance of the natural order of things, a kind of necessary impiety.

EDMUND LEACH, "Anthropological Aspects of Language," 46, 49, 54.

Thomas Bewick, *Lancashire Ox*, 1791, in Blanche Cirker, ed., *1800 Woodcuts by Thomas Bewick and His School*, plate 12.

(65–67). Clever Hans himself could not hope for a clearer account.[161] The sign is also arbitrary in nature, which is to say that there is no necessary connection between the two elements. If we consider an **ox**, as Saussure urges us to do, we can see that the signified ("a large cloven-hoofed, often horned ruminant mammal")[162] is not linked "by any inner relationship" to the signifier (ox). This is apparent when we remember that, as Nietzsche pointed out, different languages will employ quite different signifiers: bœuf, Ochse, and so on (67–68). The apparent exception, onomatopoeic words, are in fact also "already to a certain extent arbitrary," and their imitation of sounds will be "already partly conventionalized." When French dogs vocalize, whether doing so faithfully or reluctantly, they will oua-oua, whereas German dogs, such as Anna Freud's Wolf or even Kant's four-footed friend, will wau-wau.[163] Given time, these words will mutate like all others, just as the Latin PIPIO, meaning

161. More than one introduction to semiology confuses this matter by suggesting either that the signifier is the sound made when a word is uttered or the marks made when it is written or that it is these sounds or marks as we perceive them. This is not the case, as is made clear both by Saussure's own unambiguous explanation (66) and by his editor's footnote on the same page. Quite apart from running contrary to Saussure's explicit description, this interpretation makes his account incoherent, as we will see in a moment.

162. *Oxford English Dictionary*, 2nd ed., s.v. "ox."

163. Saussure, *Course in General Linguistics*, trans. Harris, 69. Philocynics, Freudian or otherwise, may also be interested to learn that Russian dogs *gaff gaff* and Swedish dogs *skälla*, whilst Danish dogs *byaffe*; see Bellos, "Gaffing up a Russian Tree."

164. This transmutation of the pigeons' own vocalizing into Latin tweeting and thence into the French and English name for the three hundred or so species of *Columbiformes* might perhaps, after Nietzsche, be considered a "stammering translation" of sorts. With onomatopoeic terms there remains a clearer vestige of the percepts and nerve stimuli that lie behind the sign, though they take their place (their pigeonhole) within the columbarium of ideas, like all others. See "The Birds and the Bees" in chapter 2.

to chirp or pipe, began life as an onomatopoeic formation and eventually evolved into the modern day pigeon (69).[164]

These immaterial, arbitrary signs, Saussure goes on to explain, make coherent thought possible. Without words, thought is only "a shapeless and indistinct mass," jumbled ideas that are "chaotic by nature" (111–12). Sound, meanwhile, is a similarly "plastic substance," a vague plane with no clear divisions. It is only by means of signs that it is possible to make consistent, comprehensible distinctions amongst these two "shapeless masses." Like the surface of a lake, signs are the waves that simultaneously break into divisions both the air and the water. The lion, we remember from Bataille, is not the king of the beasts but one powerful wave amongst many, and it is the wave, the sign "lion," that, according to Saussure's model, makes it possible to distinguish lions at all.

> A linguistic system is a series of differences of sound combined with a series of differences of ideas; but the pairing of a certain number of acoustical signs with as many cuts made from the mass of thought engenders a system of values; and this system serves as the effective link between the phonic and psychological elements within each sign. (120)

Signs link thought and sound by means of a reciprocal delimitation, and language is "the domain of articulations" (112). We start then, as did Kant, with the whole, from which are derived distinct elements. Just as space, for Kant, is essentially one, with the notion of separate spaces depending on the introduction of limitations, so thought, for Saussure, is at base "a vague, uncharted nebula" that is subsequently marked out by signs.[165]

This marking out resembles the indicative marking off effected by Heidegger's hand (see "Into Your Hand They Are Delivered" in chapter 1), but Saussure's reciprocal delimitation is by no means the same as those disclosive demarcations. Whereas Heidegger addresses the universal human capacity for the word, Saussure is concerned with the significance of the *variety* of human languages. Different languages will chart the nebula of thought in diverse and potentially contradictory ways. Words do not stand for preexisting concepts or entities that are entrusted to humanity by Being. Were that the case, "they would all have exact equivalents in meaning from one language to the next; but this is not true" (116). French speakers can either herd or eat *mouton*, whereas an English speaker will conceive the objects of these two activities quite differently (115–16). Within any given language, words used to express similar or related ideas delimit one another reciprocally: in English one cannot have "mutton" without "sheep."[166] Each linguistic

---

165. Kant, *Critique of Pure Reason*, 69 (A25/B39); Saussure, *Course in General Linguistics*, 112. On the parallels between the transcendental deduction of Kant's *Critique of Pure Reason* and the a priori analysis of language in Saussure's *Course in General Linguistics*, see Rose, *Dialectic of Nihilism*, 112–24.
166. On the naming of animals as different kinds of meat, see Adams, *Sexual Politics of Meat*, 58–59, 78–81, and passim; Adams, *Neither Man nor Beast*, 29; Dunayer, *Animal Equality*, 139–40.

system, each language, is thus made up of a series of differences. Every language is, in effect, a system of values, and no single system need be preferred to any other. Just as for Nietzsche there was no standard of right perception, so for Saussure there is no standard of right articulation. The joints at which thought is divided are many and varied. Saussure makes this point about the very object of linguistics itself. The French word *nu* (naked, bare) could be considered as a sound, as an expression of an idea, or as an equivalent to the Latin NUDUM. Which of these it is does not antedate the viewpoint that one takes on the matter. Rather, "it is the viewpoint that creates the object," and "nothing tells us in advance that one way of considering the fact in question takes precedence over the others or is in any way superior to them" (8). Those who, naked or otherwise, are credited with an outlook will thus have a variety of viewpoints or perspectives, each more or less adequate and sufficient in its own terms.[167]

Saussure is, of course, a linguist, and language is his object of study. His concern is not with the concrete things of the world, and the blooming, buzzing confusion with which he deals is that of thought rather than reality. The *Course in General Linguistics* addresses neither the world beyond the linguistic system nor the interrelation between the two: as a linguist, Saussure has little to say regarding referents and is concerned, rather, with the elements of language, that is, with signs. It would be inappropriate, then, to suggest that Saussure himself is an epistemological relativist. But in concerning himself only with the "material" of linguistics, which is to say with entirely *immaterial* entities, Saussure implicitly marks out a chasm between the world and its representation more drastic even than that envisaged by Nietzsche. Eco has accused Nietzsche of failing to address the reckoning between world and language, of suggesting that metaphors are "free and inventive,"[168] and Foucault too emphasized the purely inventive side of Nietzsche's understanding of knowledge.[169] But Nietzsche in fact insisted on the sequence of metaphorical metamorphoses that pertain between object and idea. For Nietzsche there is a process of translation that we can follow, a process that, though "stammering" and "aesthetical," takes us from the thing to its representation (see "The Philosopher and the Gnat" in chapter 2). When it comes to the matter of language, it is in fact Saussure who makes possible a decisive break. The relationship between *signifié* and *signifiant* is, as we saw, entirely arbitrary, but further, in concerning himself with only these two, purely psychological entities, Saussure disregards the question of the relationship between

---

167. Just like Nietzsche before him, then, Saussure stresses both that signs are fundamentally arbitrary and that they refer principally not to things but to one another; see "The Philosopher and the Gnat" and "The Birds and the Bees" in chapter 2.

168. Eco, *Kant and the Platypus*, 44–46.

169. Foucault, "Truth and Juridical Forms," 5–9.

170. Eco has discussed the semiotic dimension to Kant's own theory of knowledge; see Eco, *Kant and the Platypus*, 66–75.

the immaterial sign and the material object to which it refers.

Kant assumed that something lies behind the phenomena that are experienced but was prevented from saying anything about that which must, by definition, remain unknown. Similarly, Saussure does not address that which lies behind or beyond his signs. He opens up a rift that proves to be unbridgeable, much as Kant did between noumena and phenomena. Just as, in identifying the pure forms of intuition, Kant sought out those elements that are not grounded on any particular experience, so Saussure identifies the operation of the sign irrespective of any particular language. Kant identified the grounds of the possibility of thought, whilst Saussure identifies the grounds of the possibility of language.[170] But whereas the unknown something was formerly apprehended and comprehended (though absolutely not as it is in itself) by means of the sensibility and understanding, now it is carved up (though certainly not at the joints) by an untold number of different languages, in diverse and unrelated ways. Saussure is an idealist of sorts, at least insofar as he concerns himself with the ontology of language, and this implicit idealism has been inherited by writers and thinkers who would emphasize the preeminence of language and build on it a relativist epistemology. Manuel DeLanda has argued that "postmodern linguistic relativism" thus retains an essentially

Kantian epistemology insofar as it rejects noumena in favor of "linguistically-defined phenomena."[171] In effect, Saussure and his followers manage, finally, to uncap Kant.

Once uncapped, two consequences can be drawn from a post-Kantian epistemology. First, the realist commitment to truth is rejected in favor of a perspectivism that permits a variety of competing and incommensurable viewpoints. Despite their mutual dependence on a representationalist framework, realism's rhetoric of truth is replaced for relativism by one of outlooks and perspectives. Does this perspectivism entail anthropocentrism? Do the diverse languages and discourses all inevitably partake of a Protagorean measuring? DeLanda suggests that despite declaring themselves antiessentialist, linguistic relativists "share with essentialism a view of matter as an inert material, only in their case form does not come from a Platonic heaven, or from the mind of God, but from the minds of humans (or from cultural conventions expressed linguistically). The world is amorphous, and we cut it out into forms using language."[172] When Louis Althusser suggests, for instance, that a child is but a "small animal," a "biological creature" like a mere "wolf-child," until the process of humanization is effected, his claim is that language is fundamental to this transformation. The transition, Althusser stresses, by which "mammiferous larvae" cross "the infinite divide that separates

171. DeLanda, "Deleuze and the Genesis of Form."
172. Ibid.

life from humanity" results in the formation of the unconscious, which, following Lacan, following Saussure, is structured like, indeed depends upon, language.[173] The supposition that language is confined to this single species, that language and cultural conventions manifest always and only in human animals, is akin to Kant's assumption that the sensibility and understanding are uniquely human. As Kant observed in his more cautious moments, however, these are matters that have yet to be ascertained. Perspectivism may perhaps rest on Protagorean prejudices, but since it is shared with relativism by a third epistemology, we will examine this alleged anthropocentrism in the next chapter (see "The Eyes Have It" in chapter 4). What, however, of the other consequence of Kant's uncapping? That consequence is a certain *interpretivism*, and it proves, in fact, to be the distinctive feature of relativism. It is this interpretivism with which linguistic relativism has been most closely associated, and which we now address.

THOSE WHO LIKE TO THINK SO

Benjamin Lee Whorf was an expert in Native American languages, including the hieroglyphic writing system of the Maya, and especially the language of the Hopis of Arizona. He argued that his comparative studies showed that the particular language we speak determines our very experience and understanding of the world and thus our behavior and actions. At the opening of his best-known and highly influential essay "The Relation of Habitual Thought and Behavior to Language," Whorf quotes his mentor Edward Sapir: "The fact of the matter is that the 'real world' is to a large extent unconsciously built up on the language habits of the group. . . . We see and hear and otherwise experience very largely as we do because the language habits of our community predispose certain choices of interpretation."[174] Observers are not led by the same physical evidence to the same picture of the universe; rather, their interpretations are shaped by the languages they speak. Whorf took this to be "a new principle of relativity."[175] He provides in his essays many examples of this "linguistic relativity," from the most trivial to the most profound:

> Sometimes the sway of pattern over reference produces amusing results, when a pattern engenders meanings utterly extraneous to the original lexation reference. The lower mind is thrown into bewilderment, cannot grasp that compelling formulas are at work upon it, and resorts wildly and with glad relief to its favorite obvious type of explanation, even "seeing things" and "hearing things" that help out such explanation. The word "asparagus," under the stress of purely phonetic English patterns . . . rearranges to "sparagus"; and then since "sparrer" is a dialectical form of "**SPARROW**," we find

173. Althusser, "Freud and Lacan," 189–90.
174. Sapir, "Status of Linguistics," 69; quoted in Whorf, "Relation of Habitual Thought and Behavior," 134.
175. Whorf, "Science and Linguistics," 214. The thesis is most often called the Sapir–Whorf hypothesis.

Thomas Bewick, *House Sparrow*, 1797, in Blanche Cirker, ed., *1800 Woodcuts by Thomas Bewick and His School*, plate 49.

58. Sparrow

Like spring itself, the asparagus crop takes us by surprise. Following a deep freeze, slow thaw, warmish rain and tentative sun, the spears appear suddenly, nudging their way upward in a matter of hours. The tips are thick with a lavender blush, and often hard to distinguish from grass, weeds and the wild lilies that join them in the field. Called "sparrowgrass" by the British for its timely return with the birds, asparagus is the first vegetable of the season. A green promise of golden days, it awakens passions and tickles desire.

BETH DOOLEY, "Taste: Asparagus."

"sparrow grass" and then religiously accepted accounts of the relations of sparrows to this "grass."[176]

Those who have learned to call this particular herbaceous perennial by the name "sparrow grass" are likely to see different things in it than those who know it as *Asparagus officinalis* or by some other name. We can see this more clearly still in a second example that Whorf provides:

> In parts of New England, Persian cats of a certain type are called **Coon cats**, and this name has bred the notion that they are a hybrid between the cat and the "coon" (**RACCOON**). This is often firmly believed by persons ignorant of biology, since the stress of the linguistic pattern (animal-name 1 modifying animal-name 2) causes them to "see" (or as the psychologists say "project") objective raccoon quality as located on the body of the cat—they point to its bushy tail, long hair, and so on. I knew of an actual case, a woman who owned a fine "Coon cat," and who would protest to her friend: "Why, just look at him—his tail, his funny eyes—can't you see it?" "Don't be silly!" quoth her more sophisticated friend. "Think of your natural history! Coons cannot breed with cats; they belong to a different family." But the lady was so sure that she called on an eminent zoologist to confirm her. He is said to have remarked, with unwavering diplomacy, "If you like to think so, just think so." . . . I am told that Coon cats received their name from one Captain Coon, who brought the first of these Persian cats to the State of Maine in his ship.[177]

Language, then, conditions how we see the world. This power of language does not depend wholly, or even principally, on individual words or signs, however. Sparrow grass and coon cats indicate how individual words can be leading

176. Whorf, "Language, Mind, and Reality," 261. The plant has also been called "sparrow's guts." "Asparagus" derives, in fact, from the Ancient Greek ἀσπάραγος; *Oxford English Dictionary*, 2nd ed., s.v. "asparagus."
177. Whorf, "Language, Mind, and Reality," 261–62.

59. Coon Cat

Around the origins of the Maine Coon cat swirls a fog of legend and conjecture as obscuring as the fogs of its homeland. . . . Of the many legendary tales of the Coon cat's beginnings, the one most completely discredited is the best known, the mating of the raccoon and the domestic housecat. . . . Now we come to the most romantic and embellished of the origin legends, the tale of Captain Samuel Clough of Wiscasset, Maine, Marie Antoinette, Queen of France, and the royal cats. . . . As the French Revolution drove to it bloody climax, . . . Clough . . . was to bring the queen to the United States in his ship, the *Sally*. . . . When the captain sailed, he had on board furniture, cloth, wallpaper, household china and silver, various ornamental knick-knacks, and . . . six of the queen's long-haired cats. . . . The cats went visiting, as cats do, to become the fur-cloaked, royal ancestors of the Maine Coon cat. . . . Delving far back into American history, one comes upon the Vikings, and with the Vikings may have come another potential ancestor for the Maine Coon, one known today in the European cat fancy as the Norweign Skogkatt. . . . It is not inconceivable that the practical Vikings might have taken some along to their settlements in Greenland and Vineland to keep down the rodent population in grain and food stores.

MARILIS HORNIDGE, *That Yankee Cat*, 1–8.

Photograph by Faye White, copyright 2010.

60. Raccoon

The original names for the raccoon and its closest relatives in Subfamily Procyoninae came from the tribal languages of Native Americans. All tribal names had descriptive meanings chosen to distinguish each kind of animal from others in some way.

Algonkin: *ah-rah-koon-em*, they rub, scrub, scratch [with their hands]

Aztec: *mapachitl*, they take everything in their hands

Delaware: *eespan*, one who picks up things; *wtakalinch*, one very clever with its fingers

Lenape: *eespan, hespan*, they handle things; *nachenum*, they use hands as a tool

Tschimshean: *que-o-koo*, washes with hands

Hopi: *shiuaa*, painted one

American-English: coon, rattoon

Canadian French: *chat, chat sauvage*, cat, European wildcat

Latin: Linnaeus, *Systema Naturae*, 1747: *Ursus cauda elongata*; 1748: *Ursus cauda annulata, fascia per oculos transversali*; 1758: *Ursus lotor*

VIRGINIA C. HOLMGREN, *Raccoons*, 23, 157–61.

Thomas Bewick, *Racoon*, 1790, in Blanche Cirker, ed., *1800 Woodcuts by Thomas Bewick and His School*, plate 20.

or even misleading, but "sentences, not words, are the essence of speech."[178] No word has an exact meaning; rather, the context in which it occurs determines meaning in each particular instance. Consider, Whorf suggests, the English word hand. If we take "his hand," the word refers to a part of the human body. But if we talk of an "hour hand," then we refer to a different object altogether. Similarly, "all hands on deck," "a good hand at gardening," and "he held a good hand (at cards)" all refer to entirely different entities, and if we suggest that someone "got the upper hand," the phrase refers to nothing concrete at all, "but is dissolved into a pattern of orientation."[179] It is in noticing the variety of meanings of a given word within different contexts that we begin to appreciate the extent to which our understanding of the world is conditioned by the patterns of language. Faithful Fido returns, this time with a companion, to emphasize this point: "The word 'Fido' said by a certain person at a certain time may refer to a specific thing, but the word 'dog' refers to a class with elastic limits. The limits of such classes are different in different languages."[180] In Hopi, the word pohko means "dog," but it also refers to any pet or domestic animal.[181] A pet eagle, for instance, will thus be an "eagle-dog." In many situations, a Hopi speaker might thus happily discuss a particular eagle by referring to him or her as someone's pohko. It is, Whorf argues, the linguistic context that will determine how we understand the words hand

or pohko, and thus how we understand hands (or clocks) and dogs (or eagles).

More important even than the context of individual words, however, in the determination of one's experience and understanding is the "patternment," the grammatical structure in the broadest sense, that underlies an entire language. Whorf demonstrates the extent to which this can be the case by means of a comparison between key aspects of what he calls SAE ("Standard Average European" languages, such as English, French, and German) and Hopi.[182] The contrast turns on the radically different ways in which SAE and Hopi deal with those two most fundamental of Kantian notions, space and time. SAE uses two basic kinds of noun to denote physical things: individual nouns that take an article (for example, "a tree, a stick, a man, a hill") and mass nouns that do not (for example, "water, milk, wood, granite, sand, flour, meat").[183] Relatively few materials described by means of mass nouns actually come as unbounded extents (for example, "air, water, snow") however, and ordinarily we are required to individualize the mass noun by means of body types (for example,

178. Ibid., 258.

179. Ibid., 260.

180. Ibid., 258.

181. Ibid., 259–60.

182. As Eco notes, in pointing out that different languages organize experience in different ways, Nietzsche's "On Truth and Lies" is a "prelude" to the Sapir–Whorf hypothesis; Eco, *Kant and the Platypus*, 44.

183. Whorf, "Relation of Habitual Thought and Behavior," 140. On the use of mass nouns and the politics of animal terms, including the grammatical treatment of "meat," see Adams, *Neither Man nor Beast*, 27–30 and passim.

"a stick of wood, a *cake of* soap") or containers (for example, "a glass of water, a *bottle of beer*"). On the model of these latter containers, the formula "individual noun plus a similar relator" (for example, "bottle of . . .") encourages us to think in terms of form and content, even in those cases where no container exists. When SAE speakers consider a "lump of dough," then, they will unconsciously be thinking of the dough as substance or matter, which is contained in the form of a lump. And this, says Whorf, is all the result of linguistic habit: "Our language patterns often require us to name a physical thing by a binomial that splits the reference into a formless item plus a form."[184] That the universe is composed of formless continua called "substances" or "matter" that are arranged into bodies or "forms" becomes, to the minds of SAE speakers, common sense (140–42, 147).

As a result of this binomial pattern, such speakers are accustomed to thinking in terms of spatial metaphors, even when such metaphors are, strictly speaking, inappropriate. If they need to describe degrees of intensity, perhaps of an emotion, they are required to use terms such as "large, great, much, heavy, light, high, low, sharp, faint," and so on, all of which derive in the first instance, Whorf says, from descriptions of physical bodies existing in space (145). Whorf calls this process "objectification," wherein all manner of nonspatial qualities, intensities, and potentials

are subsumed under an "imaginary space" (145–46). Within this imaginary space, these nonspatial objects are described as behaving precisely as if they were concrete objects. Thus,

> I "grasp" the "thread" of another's arguments, but if its "level" is "over my head" my attention may "wander" and "lose touch" with the "drift" of it, so that when he "comes" to his "point" we differ "widely," our "views" being indeed so "far apart" that the "things" he says "appear" "much" too arbitrary, or even "a lot" of nonsense! (146)

Such spatial metaphors permeate the language of SAE speakers, and, as a result, their understanding of the world.

Hopi, by contrast, neither distinguishes between individual and mass nouns nor relies on an "imaginary space" in order to describe nonspatial objects. In Hopi, Whorf explains, *all* nouns have an individual sense and both singular and plural forms. Since a noun is already individual, there is no need to employ body types or containers. A Hopi speaker who wants a glass of water will ask for ke.yi (literally "a water"), whilst one who wants to go paddling will seek out pa.he ("a pool of water"). Even the most vague or indefinite body of water will still be, to the Hopi mind, a particular existent that cannot be referred to as if it were mere "substance" that is subsequently decanted into an appropriate form. As a result, Whorf argues, Hopi does not employ spatial terms and metaphors for anything other than spatial objects. The Hopi language has in-

---

184. Whorf, "Relation of Habitual Thought and Behavior," 141. Further citations in the text.

stead a wide range of conjugational and lexical means for expressing intensities and tendencies directly. Verb "aspects" and "voices" achieve this, as do a distinct category of adverbials he calls "tensors," which express continuity or variation in strengths and intensities, as well as distinctions of degree, rate, constancy, repetition, increase and decrease, sequence, interruption, quality, and more. Whorf suggests that "while Hopi in its nouns seems highly concrete, here in the tensors it becomes abstract almost beyond our power to follow" (145–47).[185]

The SAE penchant for objectification by means of spatial metaphors is especially marked in its conception of time. SAE applies numbers to what Whorf calls "perceptible spatial aggregates" (for example, ten men) but also to "metaphorical aggregates" (for example, ten days). We cannot observe ten days, as we can ten men, but the patterns of SAE require its speakers, he says, to use the same formula for both, thereby encouraging them to think about cyclic sequence, "cyclicity," in the same way that they think about concrete aggregates (139). For SAE speakers, time, just like intensity, becomes objectified, and a "length of time" is pictured as a queue of similar units, "like a row of bottles" (140). They refer to particular times such as "summer, winter, September, morning, noon, sunset" by using nouns that serve to further enhance this objectification into segments or phases. But more than this, the individual nouns ("a summer," "a time") have

also become mass nouns ("summer," "time"), as if these were formless, undifferentiated substances. "A summer" thus consists of "a quantity of 'time'" (143). The three-tense system of SAE compounds the problem (143), and speakers end up thinking of time as "a ribbon or scroll marked off into equal blank spaces," a kind of "evenly scaled limitless tape measure" (154). Time has the character that it does for speakers of SAE largely because of the linguistic formulas used to discuss it.

In Hopi, Whorf tells us, there are no "imaginary plurals." Plurals and cardinal numbers are applied only to objects that can form a concrete group. One does not speak of "ten days" but, instead, uses ordinals to consider what happens on the "tenth day." There is no "length of time"; rather, there is "a relation between two events in lateness" (140). To refer to particular times of the day or year, such as "morning" or "summer," one uses not nouns but a distinct kind of temporal adverb. These temporals place a strong emphasis on the continuing duration of the time in question: one thinks not about something happening "in the morning" (a phrase relying on spatial metaphors of substance and containment) but, rather, of something happening "when it is morning," or "while morning-phase is occurring" (143). One cannot say, in Hopi, that "summer is hot," since summer is not a thing, region, or quantity that could get hot; summer is *when* conditions are hot. "Nothing is suggested

---

185. On Whorf's tensors, see Lee, "Whorf's Hopi Tensors."

about time except the perpetual 'getting later' of it" (143). Whorf suggests that Hopi verbs do not have tenses; instead, they use a range of means to denote time and duration. For instance, the "validity-form" of a verb indicates whether the speaker is reporting something (the rough equivalent of SAE past and present), expecting something (future), or making a general statement (gnomic present) (144–45). Thus, when the Hopi speaker considers the "tenth day," it is not as one more distinct day in a succession of similar, or even different, days. This would be an SAE characterization, as if days were objects and therefore potential or actual elements in a group. Rather, Hopi days are spoken of as the successive reappearance of the *same* day, which is now later and therefore changed as a result of what went before (148–52). Hopi, then, according to Whorf, does not have recourse to an objectification of time; rather, it considers events, persistence, and qualities of duration.

Whorf is clearly enamored with Hopi conceptions of space and time. "We say 'see that wave'—the same pattern as 'see that house.' But without the projection of language no one ever saw a single wave."[186] Rather, Whorf argues, what we actually see is "a surface in everchanging undulating motions," and those languages that cannot say "a wave" are thus "closer to reality."[187]

The Hopi *walalata* should be translated literally as "plural waving occurs," and though the Hopi speaker can draw attention to a particular wave, the term *wala* is best translated as "a slosh occurs."[188] Saussure's waves were clear-cut swells, vigorously chopping up the surface that is the meeting point of thought and sound. They were waves as SAE would characterize them, distinct entities with clear-cut borders, synchronically abstracted from the flow of time. But, as the Hopi language indicates, waves are not at all like this. Hopi here gets closer to reality itself, Whorf suggests, by recognizing the fundamental mutability of these beings through time. By avoiding the persistent SAE notion that entities of all kinds behave like quantities of matter enclosed within formative containers, Hopi better captures the fact that there are no waves, just ongoing waving.

In like manner, whilst SAE encourages a belief in objectified and neatly compartmentalized time, Hopi conveys a more immediate, subjective experience of duration and cyclicity. This is our basic sense of "becoming later and later."[189] "Instead of our linguistically promoted objectification of that datum of consciousness we call 'time,' the Hopi language has not laid down any pattern that would cloak the subjective 'becoming later' that is the essence of time."[190] If we inspect consciousness, says Whorf, "we find no past, present, future, but a unity embracing complexity. *Everything* is in consciousness,

186. Whorf, "Language, Mind, and Reality," 262.
187. Ibid.
188. Ibid.
189. Whorf, "Relation of Habitual Thought and Behavior," 139, 142.
190. Ibid., 140.

and everything in consciousness is, and is to-gether."[191] There is a "sensuous" component to this consciousness, made up of all that we are currently experiencing (the "present"), and there is a "nonsensuous" component, made up of both the image world of memory (the "past") and the realm of belief, intuition, and foresight (the "fu-ture"). All these elements are in consciousness together, and all are "getting later" in a variety of qualitatively different ways.[192] This ceaseless "lat-ering" or "durating" of events is, Whorf believes, the true subjective experience of time before SAE overlays it with misleading spatial and sub-stantive metaphors. Hopi, with its complex and varied means of adjusting verb forms, does not obscure the feeling of duration as it is actually experienced.

In suggesting that Hopi, or indeed any language, manages in part to provide a picture of the universe that is "closer to reality," Whorf simultaneously characterizes language as a rep-resentation and postulates a mind-independent reality that exists beyond that representation. He subscribes, in short, to the representationalism shared by realism and relativism. The suggestion that it is better to speak of waving rather than of individual waves carries with it the implication that, were we able to engage with it directly, we would find the underlying reality of the world to be composed of undulating swells, a kind of on-tological sloshing, perhaps, rather like the run-ning water that threatened Nietzsche's colum-

barium. This reality, which languages represent imperfectly, is not at all unlike Kant's realm of noumena, existing just beyond the human ca-pacity to access it without mediation.[193] Further, Whorf's assumption that everyone has a prelin-guistic "immediate and subjective" awareness of time as something that simply gets "later and later"[194] has a distinctly Kantian flavor. Whorf's "latering" recalls Kant's pure form of intuition, which was, we remember, the "inner sense" that allows us to intuit the relation of representations as either simultaneous or successive. Whorf, then, owes a good deal to Kant. Ultimately, how-ever, his linguistic relativism makes a decisive break from the Kantian model.

Whereas for Kant it is the sensibility and understanding that simultaneously make knowl-edge possible whilst ensuring that access to reality is impossible, for Whorf that function is performed by language, or, more precisely, lan-guages. Individuals' conceptions of the world will vary according to the particular languages they speak. "Concepts of 'time' and 'matter' are not given in substantially the same form by experi-

191. Ibid., 143–44.
192. Ibid., 144.
193. In the first part of "Language, Mind, and Reality," Whorf discusses his fer-vent hope that one day we might tap into the "unknown, vaster world—that world of which the physical is but a surface or skin, and yet which we *are in*, and *belong to*." His view is that "a noumenal world—a world of hyperspace, of higher dimensions—awaits discovery by all the sciences, which it will unite and unify, awaits discovery under its first aspect of a realm of *patterned relations*, inconceiv-ably manifold and yet bearing a recognizable affinity to the rich and systematic organization of *language*"; Whorf, "Language, Mind, and Reality," 247–48.
194. Whorf, "Relation of Habitual Thought and Behavior," 139.

61. Rabbit

RABBIT AND PORK, n. and v. A, or to, talk: rhyming s.: C. 20. . . . Often shortened to *rabbit*, as in "She can't arf rabbit."

BUNNY, v. To talk, to chat: low: since ca. 1945. (Norman.) Ex rabbit, v., 3. Red Daniells, 1980, quotes a Lambeth carpenter saying of his wife, "She's always bunnying to her mates on the dog and bone [telephone] but she won't bleedin' rabbit to me about nothin' serious."

ERIC PARTRIDGE, *A Dictionary of Slang and Unconventional English*, 953, 158–59.

Jacob Knight, *Liberatus* (detail), 1988. Painting in oils; privately owned.

ence to all men but depend upon the nature of the language or languages through the use of which they have been developed."[195] According to Whorf, space and especially time are not, *pace* Kant, powers or capacities of the mind by means of which we perceive the world outside us. They are, rather, linguistically constructed concepts, which operate as filters and differ radically from one group of languages to another. Whorf is quite explicit: "Newtonian space, time, and matter are no intuitions. They are recepts from culture and language. That is where Newton got them."[196] Science, and indeed any other form of human knowledge, is no simple matter of carving nature at the joints; as Whorf says, "languages dissect nature differently."[197] "Each language performs this artificial chopping up of the continuous spread and flow of existence in a different way."[198] Whorf inherits a Kantian representationalism in his belief in a set of mediating structures (language) and an underlying reality (noumena). But he goes the extra mile, if such a wantonly spatial metaphor can here be excused: in moving from innate and universal modes of perception to culturally diverse languages, Whorf uncaps Kant and articulates the fully fledged relativism from which the latter had recoiled.

Whorf's claims regarding the radical alterity of the Hopi language have been much criticized, but the accuracy of his individual analyses is

195. Ibid., 158.

196. Ibid., 152–53. In fact, Whorf is inclined to think that "the apprehension of space is given in substantially the same form by experience irrespective of language" but that "the *concept of space* will vary somewhat with language" since, as a concept, it is an "intellectual tool" closely tied to other, linguistically conditioned tools; Whorf, "Relation of Habitual Thought and Behavior," 158–59. On the "universal experiential parameters" that constrain linguistic processes in Whorf's account, see Lee, *Whorf Theory Complex*, 89–96.

197. Whorf, "Science and Linguistics," 208.

198. Whorf, "Language, Mind, and Reality," 253. On the different "isolates from experience" that contrasting processes of linguistic enculturation make meaningful, see Lee, *Whorf Theory Complex*, 89–109, 122–26.

less important here than the conception of language that his principle of linguistic relativity posits.[199] Whorf's point is that we fail to appreciate the power that a language has to forge our understanding of the world. The effortlessness with which we daily speak beguiles us; we are like the person whose ideas are based only on unreflective assumptions. Gazing out over a cloudless landscape, such a person—surely not one of Kant's contemplative noble souls—will tend to think that "the earth is flat; the sun and moon are shining objects of small size that pop up daily above an eastern rim. . . . The stars, tiny and rather near objects, seem as if they might be alive, for they 'come out' from the sky at evening like **RABBITS** or **RATTLESNAKES** from their burrows, and slip back again at dawn."[200] In fact, we all project a set of linguistic relations, peculiar to our language, onto the universe. Like the New Englander who *saw* the characteristic features of a raccoon in her cat, we cannot help but think things so. A powerful, masculine VERVEX will butt because he has VERMES in his head; a mule will be stubborn rather than wary or wise; those who are poor or inferior will be lousy; the "dense" Mercurian will be sluggish in his mind and movements; the redundant limpet will cling to office; the Muslim will be a cast as a whole-hog-eating hypocrite; the Cockney wife will be a garrulous prattler. Language, in short, shapes a "thought world," a kind of "habitual thought" on which we depend:

The forms of a person's thoughts are controlled by inexorable laws of pattern of which he is unconscious. These patterns are the unperceived intricate systematizations of his own language. . . . His thinking itself is in a language—in English, in Sanskrit, in Chinese. And every language is a vast pattern-system, different from others, in which are culturally ordained the forms and categories by which the personality not only communicates, but also analyzes nature, notices or neglects types of relationship and phenomena, channels his reasoning, and builds the house of his consciousness.[201]

There is a "give-and-take" between language and culture as a whole,[202] but it is the former that is primary: "In this partnership the nature of the language is the factor that limits free plasticity and rigidifies channels of development in the more autocratic way." As a system rather than a mere assemblage of norms, a language can change only very slowly, thereby restricting the evolution of the "mass mind."[203]

It is not entirely clear just how compelling Whorf believed these "fashions of speaking" to be.[204] He suggests that language has a profound effect on one's personal consciousness, or on what he calls one's "microcosm."[205] Linguistic

199. See especially Ekkehart Malotki's substantial and highly critical tome, *Hopi Time*, but, in response, Lee, *Whorf Theory Complex*, 139–41.
200. Whorf, "Language, Mind, and Reality," 250–51.
201. Ibid., 252.
202. Whorf, "Relation of Habitual Thought and Behavior," 147.
203. Ibid., 156.
204. Ibid., 158
205. Ibid., 147.

62. Rattlesnake

The segments of a rattlesnake's rattle consist of the dried epidermis of the enlarged terminal scale, retained when the rest of the skin is shed, and held loosely together by constrictions around their "waists." . . . Snakes' evolutionary history, which included a long spell as burrowing animals, has been the driving force behind some of the unique ways they have of sensing the world around them. Sight, for example, became largely superfluous when they lived underground, and their eyes therefore became redundant. . . . Advanced species, which made the move back to the surface, needed to reinvent the eye or a satisfactory substitute, leading to fundamental differences between their eyes and other animals' visual organs. For example, snakes' eyes focus not by changing the shape of the lens but by moving the lens backward and forward. This trait appears to be a limitation, and most snakes have poor eyesight; in particular, they are not very good at seeing stationary objects.

TIM HALLIDAY AND KRAIG ADLER, eds., *The New Encyclopedia of Reptiles and Amphibians*, 181.

Nature Reflections, photograph by Mike Woodhouse.

and mental phenomena, as well as significant behavior, are "ruled by a specific system or organization," that is, by the "geometry" and structure of a language, which is "imposed from outside."[206] This system is so influential that it makes of one's consciousness "a mere puppet whose linguistic maneuvrings are held in unsensed and unbreakable bonds of pattern."[207] One's "thought world," then, is "linguistically conditioned," or even "linguistically determined."[208] The linguistic patterns engage "even our unconscious personal reactions" and endow them with typical, habitual characters.[209] But, in addition to his talk of "behavioral compulsiveness" and the "far-reaching compulsion from large-scale patterning of grammatical categories,"[210] Whorf also argues that there are no direct "correlations" or "diagnostic correspondences" between linguistic patterns and cultural norms.[211] Languages as similar as Hopi and Ute have given rise, he says, to very different cultures.[212] At the close of "The Relation of Habitual Thought and Behavior to Language," which set out to determine just how tight a hold language has on individual and collective actions, Whorf refers instead to seemingly less prescriptive "connections" and urges that we study a culture and its language as a whole, in order to uncover the "concatenations" that link the two.[213]

Regardless of the precise extent to which language governs thought and behavior, Whorf's

206. Whorf, "Language, Mind, and Reality," 257.

207. Ibid.

208. Whorf, "Relation of Habitual Thought and Behavior," 159, 154.

209. Ibid., 154.

210. Ibid., 137.

211. Ibid., 159

212. Ibid., 139n1.

213. Ibid., 159. For a careful discussion of the extent of Whorf's determinism, see Lee, *Whorf Theory Complex*, chapter 3, esp. 84–89.

linguistic relativism points toward a significantly different conception of the utility of knowledge from that espoused by realism. As Christopher Norris illustrated, for realism, knowledge is a set of representations whose primary function is to tell us about the world, to explain how things are (see "The Truth About Mice and Ducks" in chapter 2). It is the accuracy of what is *known* that is of greatest import. The concerns of relativism are rather different. In focusing on the diversity of viewpoints, on the ways in which different languages produce entirely different sets of knowledge, the emphasis shifts from the known to the *knower*. Since knowledge is a matter of perspective, when we examine assertions about asparagus (or sparrow grass), coon cats (or *skogkatt*), and *pohko* (or eagle-dogs), we learn not about the creatures or objects to which these terms refer but about the beliefs and conceptions of those doing the asserting. The utility of the investigation is that we gain an understanding of a particular set of assumptions and ways of thinking (concerning cats and raccoons, for example), held at a particular time (the early twentieth century), in a particular part of the world (New England).

The philosopher of social science Brian Fay has called this approach *interpretivism*.[214] Comprehending human behavior, practices, and artifacts is a matter of "reconstructing the self-understandings" of those engaged in performing or creating those forms of behavior, practices, and artifacts.[215] In focusing on the "semantic dimension" of the processes and products of a culture we learn about the values and interpretations of its members. The objective is not to assess, as would a realist, whether those interpretations accurately explain the world, whether, when looking up at the night sky, we see distant stars and a waxing moon rather than a multitude of tiny creatures clustered around a shining calabash. What is now of import is what those interpretations tell us about the interpreters. For relativism, knowledge becomes partial both in the sense that it is incomplete and only ever furnishes part of any supposed total picture of the world and also in the sense that it is biased and dependent on the views of an interested group. Kant hoped that his careful dissection of the sensibility and understanding would provide a firm foundation for an objectively true modern science, but by insisting that we have access only to phenomenal representations, he prepared the way for perspectival relativism, the first stage of his uncapping. With a potentially unlimited range of representations now vying for the epistemologist's attention, knowledge becomes ungrounded. As the logic of Kant's epistemology is pushed further, and this is the second consequence of his uncapping, the relativist now attends solely to the systems of knowledge themselves, the interpretations of a particular cultural group, be they Hopi-speaking Native Americans, SAE-speaking Europeans, or simple New England folk.

214. Fay, *Contemporary Philosophy of Social Science*, 112–19.
215. Ibid., 113.

ONE RING TO RULE THEM ALL

The biblical King Solomon is probably best known today for the shrewd means by which he solved a dispute between two mothers, each of whom claimed that the baby brought before him was her own. Solomon ordered that a sword be fetched so that the child could be apportioned equally between them. The first of the two immediately begged that the child be spared and given over to the other, whilst the second was content that, if she could not have the child, then neither would her opponent. By this ruse Solomon discovered the first, compassionate woman to be the true mother and allowed her to keep the child.[216] A great many further stories are recounted concerning the king's vast wisdom, ranging from travel advice to the crafty and inventive ways in which he solved the unending legal disputes of his subjects, and even including an early application of forensic science.[217] So great was his encyclopedic learning that a tradition developed that his knowledge covered arcane and even supernatural matters. Further, Solomon was believed to be able to understand the speech of the birds and the beasts.[218] This latter feat, however, was only possible because the king possessed a magical ring, the Seal of Solomon. Legend has it that shortly after succeeding to the throne, the king was visited by eight angels, the rulers of the eight winds, who gave him four gems. Solomon had these placed into a ring, which he wore ever after and which gave him a range of magical powers, including that of interspecific communication.[219] Even the great magician Solomon, then, needed a divine artifact in order to understand the animals.

Magical rings notwithstanding, it has been long been believed that the birds and the beasts do not in fact employ language. Heidegger suggested, we will remember, that the abyssal difference between human and animal rests on the latter's lack of hand and thus of word (see "Into Your Hand They Are Delivered" in chapter 1). Animals may well communicate in a multitude of different ways, but they do not, it has been argued, speak. Any anthropomorphic claims to the contrary, we are urged, have an altogether hollow ring to them.[220] The radical disjunctions between

216. 1 Kings 3:16–28.

217. On Solomon's great wisdom, see Duling, *Testament of Solomon*, esp. 944–51. For a selection of the legends themselves, see Ginzberg, *Legends of the Jews*, 123–76 ("Solomon").

218. On Solomon's learning and magical abilities, see Josephus, *Jewish Antiquities*, 5: 592–97 (8.2.5). The suggestion that Solomon could talk to animals is believed to have resulted from a misreading of the biblical claim that he could talk authoritatively *of* animals: "He would speak of trees, from the cedar that is in the Lebanon to the hyssop that grows in the wall; he would speak of animals, and birds, and reptiles, and fish"; 1 Kings 4:33 (NRSV); see Lorenz, *King Solomon's Ring*, xix.

219. Blumberg, *Whose What?* 96–97. This account of the origin of Solomon's ring comes from Islamic tradition. In older Judaic versions the ring is given to Solomon by the archangel Michael so that he can imprison all demons and employ them to build Jerusalem; see Duling, *Testament of Solomon*, 962, and, on the introduction of the ring into the legends of Solomon, 947–51, 962 note k.

220. There is not room here to address the fiercely contested debate over animal language. See Savage-Rumbaugh and Lewin, *Kanzi*, esp. 223–50 (chapter 9), for a fascinating account of Savage-Rumbaugh's experience teaching sign language to chimpanzees; see Pinker, *Language Instinct*, 332–69 (chapter 11), for strongly

different "fashions of speaking" that Whorf discussed were, of course, disjunctions between different *human* languages: "The beasts may think, but they do not talk."[221] Whorf, the true relativist of our chapter, argues that one's "microcosm," one's interpretation and knowledge of the world, is determined (or perhaps shaped, engendered, conditioned, or governed) by one's language and that every culture's knowledge is thereby determined quite differently. But is Whorf's linguistic relativism *necessarily* anthropocentric? His understanding of the nature of language certainly goes hand in hand with his humanism. Whorf was especially keen on the notion of a universal brotherhood binding all humans together:

> For the scientific understanding of very diverse languages . . . is a lesson in brotherhood which is brotherhood in the universal human principle—the brotherhood of the "Sons of Manas." It causes us to transcend the boundaries of local cultures, nationalities, physical peculiarities dubbed "race," and to find that in their linguistic systems, though these systems differ widely, yet in the order, harmony, and beauty of the systems, and in their respective subtleties and penetrating analysis of reality, all men are equal.[222]

Far from pushing different cultures apart, the diversity of spoken languages helps indicate, to those prepared to look a little deeper, an enduring and fundamental community. The "great fact of human brotherhood" is that all humans are alike in their being determined by the patterns of language.[223] In the last few months of his life, in a short article entitled "A Brotherhood of Thought," Whorf wrote, "It is not sufficiently realized that the ideal of world-wide fraternity and co-operation fails if it does not include ability to adjust intellectually as well as emotionally to our brethren of other countries. . . . This requires linguistic research into the logics of native languages, and realization that they have equal scientific validity with our own thinking habits."[224] The "next great step," the "road out of illusion" lies in a greater understanding of language, which can be gained only by embracing a much broader humanistic perspective.[225]

Shortly after writing "A Brotherhood of Thought," Whorf reviewed Oliver L. Reiser's recently published *The Promise of Scientific Humanism.*[226] His critique is extremely positive, describing Reiser's text as "an important and highly significant book." Reiser argues that the grammar of "Western Aryan languages" was refined by Aristotle and his followers into the constraining logic of "Laws of Reason." These laws, which ap-

voiced arguments against the findings of several of those who have claimed to do such a thing, including Savage-Rumbaugh.

221. Whorf, "Linguistics as an Exact Science," 220.

222. Whorf, "Language, Mind, and Reality," 263. *Manas* can be translated roughly as "mind," though Whorf laments the fecundity of meaning that is thereby lost (252–53).

223. Ibid., 257.

224. Whorf, "Brotherhood of Thought," 13–14.

225. Whorf, "Language, Mind, and Reality," 263. On Whorf's ideas concerning the benefits of greater language awareness and on the "humanism which pervades his work" (225), see Lee, *Whorf Theory Complex*, chapter 6.

226. Whorf, "Dr. Reiser's Humanism."

pear to be common sense, compel us to consider the universe atomistically, in terms of separate and distinct objects. Whorf commends Reiser's attempt to move away from the "limited semantics" of this "straight thinking" and to pursue a new, holistic logic dubbed "organismic thinking." The political corollary is a kind of "global thinking" that rejects the separateness, egotism, nationalism, and arrogant "Pan-Westernism" of world affairs. This new way of thinking works instead toward a worldwide brotherhood and casts Man as "the evolving spirit of a planetary globe." Says Whorf, "for Reiser as for Nietzsche, Man is important not as a goal but as a bridge—a bridge to the superman." Reiser's superman will possess a range of powers and faculties that currently exist only in their infant stages, including extrasensory perception (ESP). Our "**OSTRICH**-like" resistance to these conclusions, Whorf and Reiser argue, is the result of the inadequate semantics of our current scientific culture, which cause us to reject such ideas out of hand. Man may, in fact, be in the process of evolving into "one great planetary Being," for whom ESP will be simply an embryonic "circulatory process." Humankind is destined, it is hoped, for a single, vast, egalitarian brotherhood.

Not unlike Kant, who capped off the relativistic consequences of his epistemology, Whorf seems to step back from the full, radically pluralistic implications of his linguistic relativism. The disparate worldviews that his linguistic studies unearth point not toward a fundamental incommensurability between communities, as might be expected, but, he argues, toward a common, encompassing Brotherhood of Man. In fact, Whorf cannot help hoping that those linguistic studies will themselves facilitate the convergence of the currently incongruent pockets of humankind. Similarly, Whorf is ultimately inclined to

---

63. OSTRICH

To escape detection, chicks as well as adults may lie on the ground with neck outstretched; a habit that may have given rise to the legend that the ostrich buries its head in the sand when danger threatens.

Encyclopaedia Britannica, 15th ed., s.v. "ostrich."

W. F. Keyl, *Ostrich and Nest*, engraved by G. Pearson, in J. G. Wood, *Bible Animals*, 454.

deny, or at least temper, the linguistic determinism that his analyses of the "inexorable laws of pattern" might have entailed (and to which his detractors have taken greatest exception). At the end of the day, to employ a temporal metaphor, Whorf is an honest-to-goodness humanist, committed to the dignity and autonomy of the human species and its members. In addition to the carefully compiled empirical data concerning diverse linguistic communities, Whorf's conclusions draw on the assumption that those communities, despite their differences, share a common humanity. Is it the case that linguistic relativism is thus anthropocentric? Will an epistemological anthropocentrism always, inevitably attend relativism in its representationalist, interpretivist, or perspectivist aspects?

As we saw at the start of the chapter, Kant was anthropocentrically inclined. Man, the lord of nature, was certainly always his starting point. But his musings on the intellectual capacities of Saturnites and Venusians demonstrated that this anthropocentrism *need* not be part of a representationalist epistemology. There is nothing in the representationalists' account that *requires* them to adopt an epistemological anthropocentrism, even if so many are inclined to do so. Indeed, as Dennett argued, it is entirely possible in principle that observers from another planet, if such there be, irrespective of any particular predilections or peccadilloes, might formulate an identical set of representations concern-

ing mathematics or physics. Epistemological anthropocentrism is neither entailed by nor an intrinsic part of representationalist accounts of the ontology of knowledge, in either their realist or relativist form.

Interpretivism concerns itself with the meanings, values, and interpretations articulated by the speakers of a language rather than with the workings of the world. As Whorf suggested, when we examine a particular language, a fashion of speaking, we examine the way in which a linguistic community understands the surrounding environment, evaluates the relationships between its members, and so on. Insofar as it is assumed that such values are articulated only by means of a human language, this aspect of relativist epistemology might indeed be called anthropocentric. Brian Massumi has argued that social constructivism's assertion that "everything . . . is constructed in discourse," coupled with the post-Lacanian claim that language is the "special preserve of the human," signals a return, in a new permutation, to a classical definition of the uniquely rational human being.[227] But the interpretivist is not obliged to adopt either supposition. As Derrida has argued:

> The idea according to which man is the only speaking being, in its traditional form or in its Heideggerian form, seems to me at once undisplaceable and highly problematic. Of course, if one defines language in such a way that it is reserved for what we call man, what is there to say?

227. Massumi, "Autonomy of Affect," 231.

But if one reinscribes language in a network of possibilities that do not merely encompass it but mark it irreducibly from the inside, everything changes. I am thinking in particular of the mark in general, of the trace, of iterability, of *différance*. These possibilities or necessities, without which there would be no language, *are themselves not only human*. It is not a question of covering up ruptures and heterogeneities. I would simply contest that they give rise to a single, linear, in-divisible, oppositional limit, to a binary opposi-tion between the human and the infra-human. And what I am proposing here should allow us to take into account scientific knowledge about the complexity of "animal languages," genetic coding, all forms of marking within which so-called human language, as original as it might be, does not allow us to "cut" once and for all where we would in general like to cut.[228]

Thus, on the one hand, we might take issue with the "highly problematic" claim that man is the only speaking being; there is nothing in the in-terpretivists' approach that prevents them from remaining open to the possibility that some nonhuman animals, or even aliens, might also have fashions of speaking and therefore values and interpretations of their own. On the other hand, even those who would balk at conceding the "undisplaceable" claim that language is the special preserve of the human, that it is reserved for what we call man, can still allow the possi-bility that animals and aliens might demonstrate desires, interpretations, and even values by non-linguistic means, a possibility we will explore in the next chapter. Epistemological anthropo-centrism is neither entailed by nor an intrinsic part of interpretivist accounts of the utility of knowledge.

Once Solomon had slipped the magical ring onto his finger—perhaps even his ANNU-LARIS—he was able to converse with all the creatures of the world. He became, one might say, a kind of biblical Doctor Doolittle. It is worth remembering, however, that John Doo-little M.D. of Puddleby-on-the-Marsh had no such supernatural help, even if, as a MEDICUS, he was entitled to wear a ring of his own. The altruistic doctor learned to speak with his animal patients only after intensive instruction from the PARROT Polynesia.[229] Hard work with pencil and notepad, not magic, was the key to his success.[230] Both the legends about Solomon and the many stories dealing with Doctor Doolittle's exploits depict animals as possessing languages of their

228. Derrida, "'Eating Well,'" 284–85. On this point, see Derrida's critique of the supposed distinction between mere animal reaction and true human response; Derrida, *Animal That Therefore I Am*, 119–40 (chapter 3); see also Wolfe, "In the Shadow of Wittgenstein's Lion," 73–75.

229. Lofting, *Story of Doctor Doolittle*, 29–41 (chapter 2).

230. Worryingly, it was the butcher's book in which Doctor Doolittle recorded his early lessons; ibid., 32. In fact, in some of the legends concerning King Solomon's extraordinary communicative feats, no ring is mentioned; see for instance Ginz-berg, *Legends of the Jews*, 138–41. Despite acknowledging the fact that the tales concerning Solomon's ability to talk with the animals almost certainly arose from a misunderstanding, the ethologist Konrad Lorenz felt inclined to accept them nonetheless: "I am quite ready to believe that Solomon really could do so, even without the help of the magic ring . . . and I have very good reason for crediting it; I can do it myself, and without the aid of magic, black or otherwise'; Lorenz, *King Solomon's Ring*, xxix.

Alex the Parrot, photographed by Arlene Levin-Rowe of The Alex Foundation.

64. PARROT

Alex, an African grey parrot, has been trained by psychologist Irene Pepperberg, who is researching the bird's cognitive abilities. . . . He knows the names of fifty objects, seven colours and five shapes. He can enumerate up to six objects and say which of two objects is smaller. . . . Pepperberg describes how, when Alex is scolded, "We say, 'No! Bad boy!' We walk out. And he knows what to say contextually, applicably. He brings us back in by saying, 'Come here! I'm sorry!'" Does he feel regret? "He bites, he says 'I'm sorry,' and he bites again," Pepperberg says somewhat irritably. "There's no contrition!" . . . [Once,] when Pepperberg turned to leave [Alex] in a veterinarian's office for lung surgery, Alex called out, "Come here. I love you. I'm sorry. I want to go back." He thought he had done something bad and was being abandoned as punishment.

JEFFREY MASSON AND SUSAN MCCARTHY, *When Elephants Weep*, 34–35, 217.

own, however, and it is only once Solomon and Doolittle can understand those languages that they begin to appreciate the huge variety of nonhuman perspectives. Solomon settles a heated dispute between a man and a serpent, each of whom feels wronged by the other, by interrogating the Scripture-quoting snake.[231] Doctor Doolittle, meanwhile, learns that a plow horse being treated for spavins simply needs spectacles and that wise old Polynesia is something of a misanthrope.[232] It seems that, given voice, serpents and parrots and plow horses view the world from their own particular perspectives. But we need not conceive these perspectives, and the values and interpretations they entail, in terms of relativism, linguistic or otherwise. Before we can agree with Doctor Doolittle and King Solomon that there are indeed nonhuman perspectives, that perspectivism need not be anthropocentric, we should examine a third epistemological paradigm: pragmatism. We begin by returning to Nietzsche, whose earlier focus on the perspectives of gnat, bird, and worm (see "The Birds and the Bees" in chapter 2) turns now to a terrifying, perplexing creature whom the adventurous Doctor Doolittle never encountered despite all his wide-ranging travels.

231. Ginzberg, *Legends of the Jews*, 134–35.
232. Lofting, *Story of Doctor Doolittle*, 29–41 (chapter 2).

The chapter title comes from "Et digitum minimum movere non potes ut non mundum universum excites" (You cannot move even your little finger, without awakening the whole world). These words have been erroneously attributed to Pierre-Simon Laplace, the determinist mathematician who wrote during the eighteenth and early nineteenth centuries. I have been unable to trace their true origin.

65. Sphinx

[The Sphinx] had the face of a woman, the breast and feet and tail of a lion, and the wings of a bird. And having learned a riddle from the Muses, she sat on Mount Phicium, and propounded it to the Thebans. And the riddle was this: What is that which has one voice and yet becomes four-footed and two-footed and three-footed?

APOLLODORUS, The Library, I: 346–49 (3.5.8).

Oedipus and the Sphinx, Gustave Moreau, 1864. Oil on canvas, Metropolitan Museum of Art.

DIGITO MINIMO MUNDUM
UNIVERSUM EXCITES
With Your Little Finger
You Would Awaken the Whole World

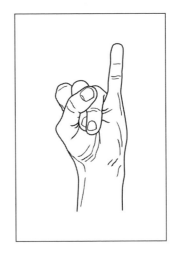

THE EYES HAVE IT

niquely terrifying, the **Sphinx** was the daughter of Echidna, one of the formidable Dracaenae who had the upper bodies of beautiful women but the long, coiling tails of serpents, or of the fire-breathing Chimera, who, in addition to a serpent tail, had the hindquarters of a goat, the foreparts of a lion, and three fearsome heads. The Sphinx had been sent by Hera, queen of the gods, as a scourge upon the recalcitrant city of Thebes. From Mount Phikios she assailed the populace, devouring all who failed to answer her infamous riddle:

> There is on earth a being two-footed, four-footed, and three-footed that has one name; and, of all creatures that move upon earth and in the heavens and in the sea, it alone changes its form. But when it goes propped on most feet, then is the swiftness in its limbs the weakest.[2]

One after another the citizens were dispatched as they failed to provide the correct answer. In desperation, when even his own son Haemon was killed, King Creon promised his sister Jocasta in marriage, plus all his kingdom, to whoever could solve the riddle and lift the curse. Oedipus, attempting to flee his fate, and having already unwittingly murdered his father, encountered the Sphinx on the road from Delphi. He answered her riddle correctly and in a rage she threw herself down a precipice. The Thebans were

The little finger or pinkie, known in Roman times as the DIGITUS MINOR or MINIMUS, was in later centuries called the AURICULARIS, a name deriving from the Latin word for ear. The reason, as John Napier explains, is that it is the digit employed for the purpose of extracting wax from the depths of that orifice. The surgeon Frederic Wood Jones argues that this is by no means the trivial matter that it might appear and notes that it is but one element in that important assemblage of processes, some few of which he deems unsuitable for polite discussion, subsumed under the heading "toilet operations." He points out that the choice of the little finger, its insertion into the external auditory meatus, and even, at the moment of insertion, the rotary motion imparted so that the nail makes an excursion of the passage, are all automatic. The business of keeping ears clean is vital to those creatures that have them, and some more or less specialized structure must evolve that can fulfill this function.[1]

1. Napier, *Hands*, 22–24; Isidore of Seville, *Etymologiarum sive originum*, 11.1.71; F. W. Jones, "Mammalian Toilet," 216–21; F. W. Jones, *Principles of Anatomy*, 134, 144.
2. Segal, *Oedipus Tyrannus*, 36; this is the earliest version to have survived. On the Sphinx's riddle, see Regier, *Book of the Sphinx*, 69–88 (chapter 4).

saved, and Oedipus not only took possession of what had been his father's kingdom but also married his own mother. As is well known, dire and tragic consequences inevitably followed.[3]

Oedipus is the thinker, the man of reason and intelligence, the truth seeker. Due to the reticence of his adoptive mother, Queen Periboea, Oedipus journeyed to Delphi to enquire of the Sibyl about his true parentage. Further, his victory over the Sphinx is achieved by means of intellect rather than force. Whereas Perseus beat the Gorgon Medusa in combat, by violent decapitation, Oedipus succeeds with a single word: "Man."[4] Only Man, he explains, is four-footed as a babe, goes on two feet as an adult, and then, in old age, has recourse to a third "foot," a walking stick. Oedipus is the ideal person to unravel a riddle about feet. His father, King Laius, forewarned by an oracle that his son would be his undoing, had pierced Oedipus's ankles when he was a newborn and left him exposed on Mount Cithaeron. He was rescued by shepherds, and his adoptive mother named him "Swollen-Feet" (Oidipous, from oideô, "to swell," and pous, "foot"). An alternative etymology suggests a more telling translation still: "He who knows the riddle of the feet" (oida, "I know," and pous, "foot").[5] Oedipus, then, is the one looking to know the truth. The answer he gives to the riddle of the Sphinx is the only answer that will do, the correct answer, the true answer. With her hybrid form and riddling cruelty, there is a sinister, mysterious ambiguity about the Sphinx. Nietzsche notoriously supposed truth to be a woman, and though she is part animal, the Sphinx is certainly all woman.[6] She points, for Nietzsche as for Oedipus, toward the truth, just as the riddle points toward Man. Truth may be elusive, even guarded, a wary creature on which it is hard to put one's finger, but it is there nonetheless for those with the wit or perception to uncover it.[7]

In Nietzsche' s essay of 1873, "On Truth and Lies in an Extra-Moral Sense," we saw the beginnings of his perspectivism. In that early essay he called upon the aid of a number of different animals in order to combat the naive assumptions of those who believe in transcendental truth. Nietzsche argued that each creature, whether bird, worm, or plant, perceives the

3. The story of Oedipus's meeting with the Sphinx is recounted by several ancient authors. See, for instance, Apollodorus, *Library*, 1: 343–51 (3.5.7–9); or, for alternatives, Graves, *Greek Myths*, 2: 9–15.

4. On the contrast between Oedipus's victory and that of other Greek mythic heroes, see Goux, *Oedipus, Philosopher*, 15–18; Segal, *Oedipus Tyrannus*, 49–50.

5. Segal, *Oedipus Tyrannus*, 36. On the interplay between knowledge and power in Sophocles's *Oedipus Rex*, see Foucault, "Truth and Juridical Forms," 17–32. On Oedipus's role as the one who knows, see ibid., 24, 28–30.

6. Segal points out that "in various versions of the myth, both literary and pictorial, the Sphinx preys on young men, carrying them off in a deadly, quasi-erotic embrace and devouring them"; Segal, *Oedipus Tyrannus*, 33. She is described as a "she-hawk" or as a "virgin or bitch"; Goux, *Oedipus, Philosopher*, 17. Goux argues that within the structure of what he calls the "Greek monomyth," it is most often against a monstrous *female* opponent that heroes succeed (Perseus overcomes the Gorgon, Bellerophon the Chimera); ibid., 7–8. On Nietzsche's supposition regarding truth, see Nietzsche, *Beyond Good and Evil*, 13 (preface). For varied responses to his characterizations of "woman," see Oliver and Pearsall, *Feminist Interpretations of Friedrich Nietzsche*; Burgard, *Nietzsche and the Feminine*.

7. On the concept of truth particular to Sophocles's *Oedipus Rex*, see Foucault, "Truth and Juridical Forms," 17–24.

world differently and that nature is "an extremely subjective structure."[8] A great many animals appeared in that short essay, as they do throughout Nietzsche's texts.[9] Why, then, when he returned to this theme in the 1880s, did he single out the Sphinx? Nietzsche cautioned, "There are many kinds of eyes. Even the Sphinx has eyes—and consequently there are many kinds of 'truths,' and consequently there is no truth."[10] Given that there are so many kinds of eyes, why pick out those of this particular, monstrous creature? Is she merely a cipher, plucked by chance from the mass of interchangeable and rhetorically equivalent beasts? But why "*even the Sphinx*"? What makes her a special case?

Nietzsche would have us remember that even the Sphinx, even the keeper of this most vital truth, has eyes. In virtue of that fact, she, like other living creatures, has her own distinctive ways of seeing, her own distinctive truths. Does this mean, then, that there can be more than one answer to the riddle of the Sphinx? The answer that Oedipus gives surely seems like the right answer. It has a certain finality to it, after all. Is not "Man," the measure of all things, always the final answer, the end to all questions?[11] Man, here represented by the inquisitive figure of Oedipus, recognizes himself, knows himself. As Charles Segal points out, "Of all creatures he alone uses his intelligence to change his mode of locomotion as he progresses through life. As the very existence of the riddle implies, he alone

is conscious of his uniqueness in nature."[12] Can Oedipus's answer really be just one amongst many? To an audience familiar with his tragic story, a second answer already suggests itself: Oedipus himself. When he answers the Sphinx, Oedipus does so as an adult in full health: Oe-di*pous* is still di*pous* ("two footed"). As an abandoned babe, however, Oedipus had crawled on all fours, weak and helpless with his pierced ankles. And it will not be long before, as a result of his clever answer, Oedipus will stand broken and infirm, "a stick tapping before him step by step."[13] There is, then, more than one true answer to this riddle.[14]

It might seem that Nietzsche's brief comment concerning the eyes of the Sphinx

8. Nietzsche, "On Truth and Falsity," 186; see "The Birds and the Bees" in chapter 2.
9. On Nietzsche's animals, see M. Norris, *Beasts of the Modern Imagination*, 73–100 (chapter 4); Ham, "Taming the Beast"; Langer, "The Role and Status of Animals"; Acampora and Acampora, *Nietzschean Bestiary*; Lemm, *Nietzsche's Animal Philosophy*.
10. Nietzsche, *Will to Power*, 291 (§540).
11. "Man, the amazing exception, the super-beast, the quasi-God, the mind of creation, the indispensable, the key-word to the cosmic riddle, the mighty lord of nature and despiser of nature, the creature that calls *its* history 'the history of the world'! Vanitas vanitatum homo"; Nietzsche, *Human, All-Too-Human*, 192–93 (2.12). See also Theodor Adorno and Max Horkheimer: "Oedipus' answer to the Sphinx's riddle: 'It is man!' is the Enlightenment stereotype repeatedly offered as information, irrespective of whether it is faced with a piece of objective intelligence, a bare schematization, fear of evil powers, or hope of redemption"; Adorno and Horkheimer, *Dialectic of Enlightenment*, 6–7.
12. Segal, *Oedipus Tyrannus*, 36.
13. The words are those of the oracle Teiresias in Sophocles's *Oedipus Rex*, quoted in Segal, *Oedipus Tyrannus*, 82.
14. On the two answers to the riddle, see Segal, *Oedipus Tyrannus*, 36–37. It was Thomas De Quincey who deduced this second, "full and final" answer, but Charles Sanders Peirce also proposed alternatives; see De Quincey, "The Theban Sphinx," 247–48; Regier, *Book of the Sphinx*, 74. We will uncover yet another answer to the

accords with his earlier arguments regarding the perceptions of different animals. There is a significant difference, however, between his youthful idealism and his mature perspectivism. The latter, in fact, constitutes a deliberate attempt to move away from Kant and to provide an alternative to those "sublime, pale, northern, Königsbergian" ways of seeing that constitute only a passing stage in Nietzsche's history of that erroneous notion, the "true world."[15] During the course of the final essay of *The Genealogy of Morals*, published in 1887, Nietzsche begins to wonder what the "ascetic priests," who disavow the basic impulses of the body and of earthly existence and who delight instead in denial and self-sacrifice, will accomplish when they turn their eyes to philosophy. They will look for

error, he says, in whatever was formerly considered most true and real: the body, pain, the ego, even reason itself. This is a kind of sadistic pleasure, "a lasciviousness which reaches its peak when ascetic self-contempt, the self-mockery of reason decrees: 'A realm of truth and freedom *does* exist, but reason is the very thing which is excluded from it!'"[16] Kant is, of course, one of those whom Nietzsche has in mind:

> Something of this lascivious contradictoriness of asceticism, with its love of turning reason against reason, persists even in the Kantian concept of the "intelligible character of things": for according to Kant, "intelligible character" means that things are constituted in such a way that they are understood only to the extent that the intellect acknowledges them as *completely beyond its grasp*.[17]

The "nominal definition of truth," Kant suggests, is "the agreement of knowledge with its object." This much he takes as having been granted.[18] Starting from his assumption that knowledge is a matter of representing the world and combined with what he discerns about the two "fundamental sources" from which all knowledge is derived, that is, the sensibility and the understanding, Kant is forced to conclude that noumena, "things in themselves," must exist but that we can say precisely nothing about them. The concept of noumena represents, he says, a problem that we can imagine but not solve.[19] And here's the rub. If it is impossible for

---

Sphinx's riddle in the final chapter: see "Four Hands Good, Two Hands Bad" in chapter 5.

　　There is a terrible irony to the fact that when Oedipus meets the Sphinx and correctly answers her riddle, he does *not* know himself, that is, does not know the truth about his parentage. He has eyes but does not know the truth, and soon he will gain the truth and lose his eyes. The tragedy of his story depends on the slow but inevitable process by which he comes to know himself. On the extent to which Oedipus is "the man knowing nothing," see Vellacoot, *Sophocles and Oedipus*, 170.

15. Nietzsche, *Twilight of the Idols*, 24–25. On the correspondence between the stages of Nietzsche's understanding of truth and those he describes in *Twilight of the Idols*, see M. Clark, *Nietzsche on Truth*, 109–17.

16. Nietzsche, *On the Genealogy of Morals*, 98 (3: 12). On the ascetic philosophers' impulse to deny the body, see also *Beyond Good and Evil*, 21–22 (§10).

17. Nietzsche, *On the Genealogy of Morals*, 98 (3: 12); see also Nietzsche, *Will to Power*, 253–54 (§461).

18. Kant, *Critique of Pure Reason*, 97 (A58/B82); see "Nothing to Phone Home About" in chapter 3.

19. Kant, *Prolegomena*, 77–78 (§34); see "An Unknown Something" in chapter 3.

us to know anything about noumena, argues Nietzsche, then we do not even know enough to be entitled to make the distinction between those noumena and mere appearances:[20]

> The sore point of Kant's critical philosophy has gradually become visible even to dull eyes: Kant no longer has a right to his distinction "appearance" and "thing-in-itself"—he had deprived himself of the right to go on distinguishing in this old familiar way, in so far as he rejected as impermissible making inferences from phenomena to a cause of phenomena.[21]

"Old Kant" gains possession of the thing in itself "surreptitiously," but this is a "ludicrous affair";[22] the very notion of the thing in itself is a "CONTRADICTIO IN ADJECTO."[23] In "On Truth and Lies," Nietzsche clung limpetlike to this redundant thing in itself, this unknown x, but from his notebooks of the time we can see that he had already begun to move away from the distinction, or opposition, between noumena and phenomena: "Against Kant we can still object, even if we accept all his propositions, that it is still possible that the world is as it appears to us. On a personal level, moreover, this entire position is useless. No one can live in this skepticism. We must get beyond this skepticism, we must forget it!"[24] We must forget this opposition because it is useless, because it does no work. Noumena are like the "wheels turning idly" in Wittgenstein's machine: they look like they are an important part of the mechanism, hard at work performing some vital function, but in fact they are connected to nothing, spinning happily but fulfilling no useful purpose.[25] If we cannot, by definition, know anything about noumena, positing their existence is altogether pointless.[26]

Nietzsche suggests that we should not be ungrateful for perverse, ascetic inversions such as Kant's, however. Adopting a new and unfamiliar perspective is a good preparation for the intellect, he says, as it journeys down the long road toward "eventual 'objectivity'" (einstmalige 'Objektivität').[27] This "'objectivity,'" always within quotation marks, is by no means the "inconceivable and nonsensical notion" of "disinterested contemplation," however. This myth of a "pure, will-less, painless, timeless knower" is entangled

20. Nietzsche, *Joyful Wisdom*, 296–300 (§354).

21. Nietzsche, *Will to Power*, 300 (§553).

22. Nietzsche, *Joyful Wisdom*, 261 (§335).

23. Nietzsche, *Beyond Good and Evil*, 27 (§16). For an elaboration of this point, see *Will to Power*, 301 (§555) and 302 (§558).

24. Nietzsche, *Unpublished Writings*, 42 (19.125).

25. Wittgenstein used this wonderful image several times; see *Philosophical Remarks*, 51; *Philosophical Investigations*, 95 (§271).

26. On the useless or even harmful notion of the "thing in itself," see also Nietzsche, *Human, All-Too-Human*, 20–21 (1.9–10) and *Will to Power*, 300–307 (§§553–69). On Nietzsche's increasing dissatisfaction with the thing in itself, see M. Clark, *Nietzsche on Truth*, 63–158 (chapters 3–5), esp. 95–103 (chapter 4.1). Nietzsche was by no means alone in rejecting the thing in itself as an incoherent or unnecessary fiction: see, for instance, the work of Kant's contemporary critics Friedrich Heinrich Jacobi and Salomon Maimon, recounted in Beiser, *Fate of Reason*, esp. 122–26, 306–9. On Lange's critique of the thing in itself, with which Nietzsche was familiar, see Stack, *Lange and Nietzsche*, 217–19. Hilary Putnam has suggested that "in the first Critique Kant himself repeatedly comes to the very point of seeing that the notion of the 'thing in itself' is empty, and always backs away from his own recognition of that fact"; Putnam, *Pragmatism*, 29.

27. Nietzsche, *On the Genealogy of Morals*, 98 (3: 12).

66. Octopus

The layman's octopus is an animal that consists of arms. In amongst the arms, somewhere in the middle, is a head with almost human eyes; children and cartoonists usually forget about the body. In a way the laymen, children and cartoonists are right; the arms make the octopus. They comprise the greater part of the weight of the body and they contain most of the nervous system. . . . *Octopus* uses its arms to move about, collect food, defend itself, and examine its surroundings. The animal is clearly able to discriminate between objects that it touches and . . . it can learn to distinguish between objects by touch as readily as it can learn to distinguish between figures by sight.

MARTIN J. WELLS, *Octopus*, 217.

Octopus, by Phoebe Cookson; privately owned.

within "the tentacles of such contradictory concepts as 'pure reason,' 'absolute spirituality,' 'knowledge in itself.'"[28] Nietzsche's position could not be further from that of the ascetic philosopher, studiously straining to become disinterested. Nietzsche's *einstmalige 'Objektivität'* is, rather, "the capacity to have all the arguments for and against *at one's disposal* and to suspend or implement them at will."[29] In this way we will be able, he says, to exploit the very *diversity* of perspectives and affective interpretations, in the interests of knowledge: "The more feelings about a matter which we allow to come to expression, the more eyes, different eyes through which we are able to view this same matter, the more complete our 'conception' of it, our 'objectivity', will be."[30] Attempting to eliminate the will, the feelings, all that permits us to adopt a perspective, amounts to the *castration of the intellect*.[31] "The **SNAKE** that cannot shed her skin perishes. So do the spirits who are prevented from changing their opinions; they cease to be spirit."[32] "'Objectivity,'" or knowledge, is a matter of gaining multiple opinions, perspectives, and eyes, and the more the better. His own form

28. Ibid. Christopher Janaway points out that this "pure, will-less, painless, timeless knower" is a direct but unattributed quotation from Schopenhauer, who conceives of this passive subject as a "mirror" of objective reality. Nietzsche's attack on this conception of objectivity here derives a good deal of its impetus from his reading of Schopenhauer, who remains, in Janaway's words, an "unnamed but scarcely disguised subtext"; see Janaway, "Schopenhauer as Nietzsche's Educator," 16, 27–36. On Schopenhauer's continuing influence on Nietzsche's conception of truth, knowledge, and objectivity, see M. Clark, "On Knowledge, Truth, and Value."

29. Nietzsche, *On the Genealogy of Morals*, 98 (3: 12).

30. Ibid.

31. Ibid., 99 (3: 12).

32. Nietzsche, *Daybreak*, 569 (§573) (translation modified).

of perspectivism, then, is Nietzsche's alternative to Kant.

Nietzsche's is no relativist perspectivism, however. Rejecting, finally, Kant's representationalism changes the tenor of his own antirealist epistemology. On the one hand, a perspective depends very much on the particular pair (or more) of eyes doing the seeing. The realist and the ascetic priest, who here amount to much the same thing, ask us to imagine

> an eye which is impossible to imagine, an eye which supposedly looks out in no particular direction, an eye which supposedly either restrains or altogether lacks the active powers of interpretation which first make seeing into seeing something—for here, then, a nonsense and non-concept is demanded of the eye. Perspectival seeing is the only kind of seeing there is, perspectival "knowing" the only kind of "knowing."[33]

The eyes that creatures have will affect what they see, in the most basic, bodily sense. There are many kinds of truth, in the first instance, because there are many kinds of eyes. Even resourceful Doctor Doolittle would have had trouble testing the eyesight of the Sphinx, but Nietzsche knew that, hybrid monster that she was, her eyes differed from those of Oedipus.[34] We have already encountered the trichromatic color vision of the dog-faced baboon, the lamplike eyes of the wolf, the exceptional eyesight of the falcon and the eagle, the compound eyes of the gnat, the ultraviolets and polarization per-

67. Snake

The skin of an animal is a complex organ which periodically undergoes renewal. The old dead layers of cells must come off to make room for the new layers of cells formed underneath. . . . Snakes normally shed their skin in one piece. This process is called ecdysis. This may occur from 4 to 12 times a year, with young, rapidly growing snakes shedding more frequently. Snakes lack eyelids, and instead have a clear scale called the spectacle to cover and protect the eye. During ecdysis the dead outer layer of the spectacle is shed.

   s. l. barten, "Shedding (Ecdysis)," 17.

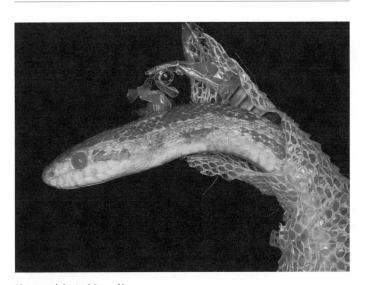

Photograph by José Bergadá.

33. Nietzsche, *On the Genealogy of Morals*, 98 (3: 12); see also *Will to Power*, 305–6 (§567).
34. On the different kinds of gaze, and therefore of knowledge, in *Oedipus Rex*—the gazes of the gods, of the slaves, and, situated between them, especially of Oedipus himself—see Foucault, "Truth and Juridical Forms," 23–24, 28–30. Foucault does not, alas, discuss the gaze of the Sphinx.

ceived by the bee, the eyespots of the worm, the dull vision of the snake and of the shortsighted spider. What one sees, the perspective that one has, depends on one's eyes.[35] But in speaking of eyes and perspectives, Nietzsche is not dealing with *representations*. His insistence on the corporeal nature of perception, on the fact that the observing subject *does* experience time, pain, feelings, and its own willful intentions, is a move away from disembodied, abstract representationalism in either its realist or relativist forms. And it is in the interests that arise as a result of this embodiment that we find a second important characteristic of Nietzsche's perspectivism.

Like the skin-shedding snake, Nietzsche himself suffered from poor eyesight, but perspectivism is not simply a matter of visual perception. Nietzsche stresses that all creatures' perspectives will be determined by their interests and values. Any and every understanding of the world will be *evaluative*. The notion of the thing in itself is redundant, but so too is the idea that we can understand a thing, even a phenomenon, without involving our own interests, prefer-

ences, and predilections. "That things possess a constitution in themselves quite apart from interpretation and subjectivity, is a quite idle hypothesis: it presupposes that interpretation and subjectivity are not essential, that a thing freed from all relationships would still be a thing."[36] It is our concerns that allow us to know a thing at all. "Coming to know means 'to place oneself in a conditional relation to something'; to feel oneself conditioned by something and oneself to condition it."[37] Attempting to know anything that is unconditioned by our desires and interests entails a contradiction between wanting to know something and the desire that it not concern us. "But why know at all, then?" asks Nietzsche.[38] "The question of values is more *fundamental* than the question of certainty: the latter becomes serious only by presupposing that the value question has already been answered."[39] Attempting to gain knowledge about the world is not a matter of trying to achieve certainties, truths, or absolute knowledge about a thing in itself, or even about a mere appearance. This, Nietzsche argued much earlier, is a white lie that people tell themselves (see "The Philosopher and the Gnat" in chapter 2). Rather, knowing something is a matter of interpreting the world in order to survive in life.[40] "There is no question of 'subject' and 'object,' but of a particular species of animal that can prosper only through a certain relative rightness; above all, regularity of its perceptions (so that it can accumulate experience)."[41] The "organs of

35. On the importance of the visual element for Nietzsche's perspectivism, see Leiter, "Perspectivism," esp. 343–47; Poellner, "Perspectival Truth," 88–98. On his use of the metaphor of the eye, see Kofman, *Nietzsche and Metaphor*, 101–8; but see also Cox, *Nietzsche*, 109–68 (chapter 3).
36. Nietzsche, *Will to Power*, 302–3 (§560).
37. Ibid., 301 (§555).
38. Ibid.
39. Ibid., 322–23 (§588).
40. Ibid., 322–23 (§588).
41. Ibid., 266–67 (§480).

knowledge" of any species are developed not so that it can avoid being deceived, but so that it can preserve itself and flourish.[42] Perspectives, then, involve not just a straightforward visual element, but also the values, in the broadest sense, that permit a creature to go about the important business of living.

Nietzsche's approach to interpretation differs here from that of Whorf. The linguist's concern with the values and viewpoints of different perspectives signaled a shift in emphasis from the known to the knower: Whorf was interested not in the nature of the *pohko* but in Hopi speakers' understanding of such a creature (see "Those Who Like To Think So" in chapter 3). Further, the relativist implication, where there is no standard of right perception, is that all perspectives will be of equal merit. Such a position is alien to Nietzsche's perspectivism.[43]

> That the value of the world lies in our interpretation . . . ; that previous interpretations have been perspective valuations by virtue of which we can survive in life, i.e. in the will to power, for the growth of power; that every elevation of man brings with it the overcoming of narrower interpretations; that every strengthening and increase of power opens up new perspectives and means believing in new horizons—this idea permeates my writings.[44]

Our objective, our *einstmalige 'Objektivität,'* should be the capacity to suspend or implement any of a number of perspectives at will. These perspectives, these interpretations, are certainly not of equal value. Part of the journey toward eventual "objectivity" is a matter of acknowledging that some interpretations are narrower than others, that it is better to overcome these interpretations, and that this overcoming will allow us to elevate ourselves. Some perspectives are better than others.[45]

The creatures that entertain these different perspectives are not, of course, only human. Even in "On Truth and Lies" the different perceptions of the world belonged not just to different language speakers but also to different species of animal. In yet another of his many attacks on the scientific belief in a "true world," the mature Nietzsche argues that such an approach omits "precisely this necessary perspectivism by virtue of which every center of force—and not only man—construes all the rest of the world from its own viewpoint, i.e., measures, feels, forms, according to its own force."[46] Human perspectives are not at all the only valid ones: "I think that we are today at least far from the lu-

---

42. Ibid.
43. In fact, Nietzsche has often been saddled with relativist beliefs in secondary literature. Brian Leiter calls this the "Received View"; see Leiter, "Perspectivism," 334–36.
44. Nietzsche, *Will to Power*, 330 (§616).
45. That Nietzsche was more than ready to pass judgment on diverging perspectives is one of Leiter's key contentions; see Leiter, "Perspectivism." On Nietzsche's navigation between relativism and dogmatism in his understanding of interpretations and perspectives, see Schrift, *Nietzsche and the Question of Interpretation*, esp. 144–68 (chapter 6); Cox, *Nietzsche*, esp. 109–68 (chapter 3).
46. Nietzsche, *Will to Power*, 339–40 (§636); see also 330 (§616) and 305–6 (§567).

Arthur Rackham, *King Log*, in Aesop, *Æsop's Fables*, trans. Jones, 63.

68. Frog

Brekekekex, ko-ax, ko-ax,
Brekekekex, ko-ax, ko-ax!
We children of the fountain and the lake
    Let us wake
Our full choir-shout, as the flutes are ringing out,
    Our symphony of clear-voiced song.
The song we used to love in the Marshland up above,
    In praise of Dionysus to produce,
    Of Nysaean Dionyus Dionysus, son of Zeus,
When the revel-tipsy throng, all crapulous and gay,
To our precinct reeled along on the holy Pitcher day,
    Brekekekex, ko-ax, ko-ax.

ARISTOPHANES, *The Frogs*, lines 209–220.

dicrous immodesty of decreeing from our nook that there *can* only be legitimate perspectives from that nook." Rather, the world has become "infinite": we cannot dismiss the possibility that it contains *infinite* interpretations.[47] Perspectivism is not simply a human affair. In an early section of *Beyond Good and Evil*, for instance, we find Nietzsche evaluating a certain philosophical perspective by drawing an analogy with the outlook of a particular lowly animal. Metaphysi-

cians of all ages, he tells us, have been inclined to ask themselves how the good and honored things, those of the highest value, such as truth or altruism, could possibly have originated except "in the womb of being . . . , in the intransitory, in the hidden god, in the 'thing in itself.'"[48] We would do better, Nietzsche asserts, to regard the very oppositions themselves, these routine antitheses of the good (the true, the genuine, the selfless) and the bad (appearance, deception, selfishness), as superficial estimates, as merely provisional viewpoints, perspectives from below: "**FROG**-perspectives."[49] In the next section we will examine the question of the appropriate grounds and means for evaluating perspectives, for choosing between viewpoints. For the moment we need only observe that the Sphinx's perspective is due not simply to the fact that she speaks, using the language of the man Oedipus,

47. Nietzsche, *Joyful Wisdom*, 340–41 (§374).
48. Nietzsche, *Beyond Good and Evil*, 16 (§2).
49. Ibid. A *Froschperspektive* is a view from below just as, in English, a "bird's-eye view" is a view from above. Nietzsche seems to have held frogs in particularly low regard. Zarathustra hears the croak of the frog in the swamp-smelling wisdom of dusty scholars, and he compares inflated windbags to the frog who has blown himself out for too long and eventually explodes; see Nietzsche, *Thus Spoke Zarathustra*, 147–49 ("Of Scholars") and 270 ("The Sorcerer"). Blown-out frogs also appeared in the preface to *Twilight of the Idols*, xviii.

but also to the fact that she has both eyes and values of her own, neither of which can truly be described as human. Her inhuman kenning depends on her peculiar visual and evaluative perspectives.

Now, then, the "true world" has become an "idea that no longer serves any purpose, that no longer constrains one to anything,—a useless idea that has become quite superfluous."[50] It stands condemned, like the notion of "disinterested contemplation," by those damning quotation marks. It is an *exploded* idea, says Nietzsche, so "let us abolish it!"[51] The perspectivism that stands in its place, which prompts all free spirits to "kick up a shindy,"[52] is a kind of pragmatism in which one's interpretations are variously enabling. No longer concerned with cold, dusty "representations," perspectival knowledge is a means by which one gets things done. It is our needs and drives that interpret the world.[53] "In order for a particular species to maintain itself and increase its power, its conception of reality must comprehend enough of the calculable and constant for it to base a scheme of behavior on it . . . a species grasps a certain amount of reality in order to become master of it, in order to press it into service."[54] Even before Heidegger argued that πράγμα (*pragma*) should be translated not simply as "thing" or "fact" but as "action" or "activity" (*Handlung*), Nietzsche emphasized the importance of our involvement, our "concernful dealings" (to use Heidegger's phrase), for a

proper understanding of our engagement with the world (see "Into Your Hand They Are Delivered" in chapter 1). It is when we set about a scheme of behavior, when we use objects and ideas, when we press reality into service, that we formulate understandings, interpretations, and perspectives.[55]

Pragmatism, understood in a broad sense, is the third and last of our schematic epistemological paradigms. It shares with relativism a perspectival conception of the validity of knowledge. Like the relativist, and quite unlike the realist, the pragmatist does not seek the truth but instead acknowledges a diverse, frequently incommensurable range of perspectives. As a pragmatically inclined thinker, Nietzsche was in fact perfectly at ease employing the word *truth*: it has a utility, a use, that cannot be denied. His objection was only to those attempts by ascetic metaphysicians to attain *the* truth, to arrive at a transcendental "truth" that was not provisional,

---

50. Nietzsche, *Twilight of the Idols*, 24–25.
51. Ibid.
52. Ibid.
53. Nietzsche, *Will to Power*, 267 (§481).
54. Ibid., 266–67 (§480); see also 305–6 (§567) and 339–40 (§636). This is not to say, of course, that Nietzsche, any more than contemporary pragmatists, is suggesting that we have carte blanche in our formulation of those understandings, interpretations, and perspectives. It is necessary that a creature or species comprehends what is "calculable and constant," thereby grasping "a certain amount of reality," before any action or activity is likely to be successful.
55. On characterizing Nietzsche's philosophy as a form of pragmatism, see Danto, *Nietzsche as Philosopher*, 54; Rorty, "Introduction"; Rorty, "Pragmatism as Romantic Polytheism." On the errors of doing so, see, for example, Boffetti, "Rorty's Nietzschean Pragmatism."

partial, perspectival: such an understanding of truth, of the "true world," has precisely no use at all. For Nietzsche, then, the Sphinx becomes the symbol not of truth but of "truth." The will to truth (*Wille zur Wahrheit*), whose mendacious origin in dissembling he had traced in his earlier essay, tempts us to many a hazardous enterprise.[56] It is, says Nietzsche, a Sphinx who asks us questionable questions. But in asking us these questions, these riddling puzzles, she teaches us too to ask questions. Just as Kant's perverse, ascetic inversions encourage us to add fresh perspectives to our armory, so the Sphinx prompts us to enquire after the origin and value of the will to truth itself. "The problem of the value of truth stepped before us—or was it we who stepped before this problem? Which of us is Oedipus? Which of us Sphinx?"[57] At this "rendezvous of questions and question-marks" we fix our eye on the problem, the hazard, of the value of the will to truth. The Sphinx asks us a riddle, a question that requires, on pain of death, a "true"

answer, but we are no longer concerned with the business of trying to achieve these "truths." Nietzsche deals now with truths as perspectives.

Richard Rorty, a self-confessed Nietzschean pragmatist, has suggested that the desire to know the truth is the desire to "recontextualize," that is, to accommodate new beliefs and conceptual frameworks by dropping or altering old ones. This desire is, he says, characteristically human in the sense that "we have little choice" but to keep doing it.[58] Just as Nietzsche suggested in his early essay that humans cannot help but conceive the world in terms of *Urformen*, casting them forth "with that necessity with which the spider spins,"[59] so for Rorty humans cannot help reweaving the webs of beliefs and desires that constitute a human mind. This desire, when taken to its logical and necessary conclusion, is the desire to keep coming up with new interpretations, "to recontextualize for the hell of it."[60] This will to perspectival truth is as characteristically human, he says, as the desire to use the opposable thumb.[61] We need not confine a Nietzschean *Willen zur Wahrheit* to human beings, however. Truths and interpretations are no longer to be conceived in terms of merely human perspectives: the centers of force are many and varied, as the tactile octopus and fusty frog help show. Nietzsche's pragmatism, his perspectivism, is not about grasping beings with a hallowed human hand. Perspectivism need not be anthropocentric: even the Sphinx has eyes.

56. Nietzsche, *Beyond Good and Evil*, 15 (§1); see "The Philosopher and the Gnat" in chapter 2.

57. Nietzsche, *Beyond Good and Evil*, 15 (§1).

58. Rorty, "Inquiry as Recontextualization," 110.

59. Nietzsche, "On Truth and Falsity," 186; see "The Birds and the Bees" in chapter 2.

60. Rorty, "Inquiry as Recontextualization," 110.

61. Strictly speaking, Rorty argues that this exuberant recontextualization is characteristic "not of the human species, but merely of its most advanced, sophisticated subspecies—the well-read, tolerant, conversable inhabitant of a free society"; ibid. In the next chapter we will look briefly at his charge that, in this regard, Foucault does not quite make the grade, before we deal more fully with the issue of opposable thumbs.

A TALE OF THREE FISH

The ancient Sanskrit *Panchatantra*, attributed to a wise royal adviser named Vishnu Sarma, is a political treatise that takes the form of a series of nested fables. Toward the end of the first book, it includes the following apologue:

> ONCE UPON A TIME three large fish dwelt in a certain big pond. Their names were Forethot, Ready-wit, and Come-what-will. Now once Forethot, as he was swimming around in the water, heard the words of some fishermen who were passing near by: "This pond has plenty of fish; so tomorrow we will catch the fish in it." And hearing this Forethot reflected: "They are sure to come back; so I will take Ready-wit and Come-what-will along and take refuge in another pond whose stream is not blockt." Thereupon he called his friends and askt them to go with him. Then Ready-wit said: "If the fishermen come here, then I will save myself by some means or other suited to the circumstances." But Come-what-will, whose end was at hand, paid no heed to his words, and took no steps to go. So seeing that both of them were determined to stay there, Forethot entered the stream of the river and went to another lake. And on the next day after he left the fishermen with their followers blockt the river from within and threw in a scoop-net and caught all the fish to the last one. When this had happened Ready-wit assumed the aspect of a dead fish, and made himself appear so as he lay in the net. And they thot: "This big fish is already dead;" and they took him out of the net and laid him down near the water. But

> thereupon he jumpt up and fled in great haste to another lake. But Come-what-will had no idea what to do, and he moved aimlessly about this way and that till he was caught in the net and killed with clubs.[62]

We will come back to these three instructive fish shortly, but we turn first to a pragmatic thinker who displayed ready wits, if not forethought, of his own.

Jacques Barzun once suggested that, by his "originality and force of mind," William James "met and subdued some of the old Sphinxes who challenge the earthly traveler, as always on pain of death."[63] Like Nietzsche, James was fond of walking in woods and mountains, but it was, thankfully, a squirrel rather than a Sphinx who presented to him the intriguing philosophical riddle with which we will here be concerned:

> Some years ago, being with a camping party in the mountains, I returned from a solitary ramble to find everyone engaged in a ferocious metaphysical dispute. The *corpus* of the dispute was a **SQUIRREL**—a live squirrel supposed to be clinging to one side of a tree-trunk; while over against the tree's opposite side a human being was imagined to stand. This human witness tries to get sight of the squirrel by moving rapidly round the tree, but no matter how fast he goes,

---

62. Edgerton, *Panchatantra Reconstructed*, 2: 314.

63. Barzun, *Stroll with William James*, 5. For James's own invocation of the Sphinx, whose "monotonous challenge" to humanity to produce "the Truth, conceived as one answer, determinate and complete" he rejected, see James, *Pragmatism*, 115.

the squirrel moves as fast in the opposite direction, and always keeps the tree between himself and the man, so that never a glimpse of him is caught. The resultant metaphysical problem now is this: *Does the man go round the squirrel or not?* He goes round the tree, sure enough, and the squirrel is on the tree; but does he go round the squirrel?[64]

James's fellow ramblers were divided equally on the matter and were thus most insistent that he take sides. Mindful of the adage that "whenever you meet a contradiction you must make a distinction," James suggests that "which party is right . . . depends on what you *practically mean* by 'going round' the squirrel" (27). Notwithstanding ensuing accusations of "shuffling evasion" and "quibbling or scholastic hair-splitting," James elaborates what he calls his "pragmatic method." This technique aims to settle philosophical questions by looking at the respective practical consequences of the possible answers. Does the man go round the squirrel? If by "going round" you mean that the man passes from north to east of the squirrel, and then to the south, west, and then north again, it is clear that he does indeed circumnavigate the squirrel. If, on the other hand, you mean that the man is first in front of the squirrel, then on his right, then behind him, then left, and finally in front again, then he patently fails, due to the compensating movements of the squirrel. The "principle of pragmatism"

Beatrix Potter, *The Tale of Squirrel Nutkin*, 18–19.

---

69. SQUIRREL

But Nutkin was excessively impertinent in his manners. He bobbed up and down like a little red *cherry*, singing—
"Riddle me, riddle me, rot-tot-tote!
   A little wee man in a red, red coat!
   A staff in his hand, and a stone in his throat;
   If you'll tell me this riddle, I'll give you a groat."
   Now this riddle is as old as the hills; Mr. Brown paid no attention whatever to Nutkin. He shut his eyes obstinately and went to sleep.

   BEATRIX POTTER, *The Tale of Squirrel Nutkin*, 18–19.

---

64. James, *Pragmatism*, 27. Further references are in the text.

Beatrix Potter, *The Tale of Squirrel Nutkin*, 56–57.

---

70. OWL

Old Brown carried Nutkin into his house, and held him up by the tail, intending to skin him; but Nutkin pulled so very hard that his tail broke in two, and he dashed up the staircase and escaped out of the attic window.

BEATRIX POTTER, *The Tale of Squirrel Nutkin*, 56–57.

---

ends the game of hide-and-seek by requiring that we look to the ways in which we actually use the phrase *going round*. Wittgenstein and Austin could have hoped for nothing more.

James attributes this principle of pragmatism to Peirce, though he traces the partial use of the pragmatic method back to John Locke, George Berkeley, and David Hume and further, to Socrates and Aristotle (28–30). Like Heidegger, he underlines the fact that the terms *practice* and *practical* derive from the Greek πράγμα (*pragma*), meaning "action." It is what we do here that counts. If there is no practical difference between alternatives, if the answers we give make no difference to our actions, then those alternatives, practically speaking, mean the same thing "and all dispute is idle" (28). When pressed by his metaphysically minded camping companions, James refuses to give a single, definitive answer to the riddle; what he actually does is to take a long, hard look at the question and to see it from a pair of different perspectives. So it is with Beatrix Potter's Old Brown, the taciturn inhabitant of Owl Island. When a disrespectful Squirrel Nutkin repeatedly, and with increasing impudence, quizzes the **OWL**, he remains silent. The answers to Nutkin's riddles, both obvious and irrelevant to a wise old owl, are never explicitly stated. The practical consequences of the act of riddling, however, have an ominous inevitability. Squirrel Nutkin, foolishly focused on his

Thomas Bewick, *Cows*, in Blanche Cirker, ed., *1800 Woodcuts by Thomas Bewick and His School*, plate 13.

71. Cow

A moral lesson this might teach
Were I ordained and called to preach;
For men are prone to go it blind
Along the calf-paths of the mind,
And work away from sun to sun
To do what other men have done.
They follow in the beaten track,
And out and in, and forth and back,
And still their devious course pursue,
To keep the path that others do.
They keep the path a sacred groove,
Along which all their lives they move;
But how the wise old wood-gods laugh,
Who saw the first primeval calf.
Ah, many things this tale might teach—
But I am not ordained to preach.

SAM WALTER FOSS, "The Calf-Path" in *Whiffs from Wild Meadows*, st. 7, lines 51–66.

provocative questions and oblivious to the owl's perspective, reaps his just deserts at the end of this tale about a tail. The practical consequences of a squirrel running round an owl become apparent.

James has a second, more urgent example than his squirrel chase, set within a similarly idyllic scene. His solitary rambling this time leads him to a more serious predicament: short on prior planning, he has become lost in the woods and is famished and unsure how to proceed. Casting around, he comes across what looks like a **cow** path, an ancient, winding trail through the wood. James realizes that "it is of the utmost importance that I should think of a human habitation at the end of it, for if I do so and follow it, I save myself" (98). How does James know that he has stumbled across a cow path and not one of the many wood paths (*Holzwege*) described by Heidegger that look so similar?[65] In German, to be on a wood path (*auf dem Holzweg sein*) is to wander up a blind alley or a cul-de-sac, to be on the wrong track, to be barking up the wrong tree. This would not do at all. In his discussion of this passage, Frank Lentricchia suggests that James's choosing to believe that it is a cow path is perhaps due to "irrefutable olfactory evidence."[66] Whether such evidence exists or not, what is important here is that James's interpretation of the path, his implicit theorizing about its origin and use, is undertaken as a means of getting himself out

65. "In the wood are paths that mostly wind along until they end quite suddenly in an impenetrable thicket. They are called woodpaths"; quoted by David Farrell Krell in Heidegger, *Basic Writings*, 34.
66. Lentricchia, *Ariel and the Police*, 106–7.

of a tight spot. Certain thoughts and ideas, he holds, are "invaluable instruments of action" (97), and their employment allows us "to do work in the world" (98). James's prior knowledge of the appearance and nature of cow paths here proves to be priceless. Knowledge is valuable because it is useful, because it explains things, and it is precisely because this particular path is well trodden, because the following of it has repeatedly proven useful to others, that James is able to save himself.

It matters not that this path meanders a little, nor that it is inhuman in origin. In this case, contra Nietzsche, following the route trampled by the herd is of great benefit.[67] And like Nietzsche, James employs the word *true* pragmatically rather than absolutely. "True ideas" are valuable because they prove to be useful. It is irrelevant, James says, whether we claim that "it is true because it is useful" or that "it is useful because it is true" (98). Like realism, pragmatism takes knowledge to be an *explanation of* things. Its interest lies less in the ideas, values, and interpretations of those doing the knowing than in the objects, processes, and relationships of the world. When James stumbles across a path through the forest, it matters little how or why he should arrive at the conclusion that he is on a cow path. That his supposition may or may not have derived from a priori modes of perception and judgment or from prior experiences that may or may not have been partially or wholly

determined by language (see chapter 3 above) is far less important than the fact that the path will lead him to safety. And quite *unlike* that of the realist, James's claim is not that he arrives at the "truth" because his account is conceptually adequate or because he has reasoned by means of inference to the best explanation (see "The Truth about Mice and Ducks" in chapter 2). Rather, his is an approach that explains, that is expedient, and that, on that account, is worth thinking of as true.[68]

From a pragmatic perspective, the whole question of inference to the best explanation is a red **HERRING**. The pragmatist looks not for *the* truth, for the single, essential explanation that must be considered definitive. He or she wants, rather, to deal with a particular matter at hand. Bas van Fraassen does not need an ultimate ontological explanation for the scratching in his wall or the patter of little feet at midnight; rather, he needs to know how best to deal with the theft of his cheese. Subject to further discoveries, acting as if his wall cavities are inhabited by mice, rather than by some variety of genetically modified, cancer-prone rodent, is likely to prove most useful. Similarly, the flapping, quacking creatures one encounters on a pond will, ordinarily, be best dealt with if they are assumed to

---

67. On the detested "herd mentality," see Nietzsche, *Beyond Good and Evil*, esp. 69–71 (§62), 104–6 (§201), and 186–87 (§268).

68. On James's consideration of the *variety* of types of expediency—usefulness for prediction, conservation of past doctrine, simplicity, coherence, and so on—see Putnam, *Pragmatism*, 8–12.

Blueback Herring (*Alosa aestivalis*). Image developed by Ellen Edmonson and Hugh Chrisp for the 1927–40 New York Biological Survey.

72. Herring

Literally, red herring are herring that have been salted and smoked, a traditional curing process that reddens the fish and imbues it with a strong pungent odor.... The official etymology of the idiom, as documented by the Oxford English Dictionary . . . is that at one time red herring were drawn across a track, presumably in an attempt to throw hunting dogs off the track for training purposes.... The olfactory senses of a hound dog, the sort most frequently used in fox hunting, are sensitive enough to differentiate between one fox and another; surely they can differentiate between a salted and dried fish and a living fox.... The red herring idiom was popularized by William Cobbett (1763–1865), an English political agitator who captured the attention of his nation by never letting truth get in the way of a good argument. In the February 14, 1807 edition of Cobbett's *Weekly Political Register*, Cobbett employs a literal red herring in a tall-tale concerning his youth.... Cobbett's story doesn't reflect an actual practice, it is an intentional fiction designed to cast the dogs' owner in a negative light.

ROBERT SCOTT ROSS, "Popularization of Red Herring by English Political Agitator William Cobbett," 62–69.

69. "We have no need of these certainties about the farthermost horizons in order to live a full and efficient human life, any more than the ant needs them in order to be a good ant"; Nietzsche, *Human, All-Too-Human*, 195 (2.16).

70. Neither van Fraassen nor Hacking are convinced that inference to the best explanation entails realism; see van Fraassen, *Scientific Image*, 19–23; Hacking, *Representing and Intervening*, 52–57.

be ducks rather than robotic imitations. This is not a matter of applying Occam's razor in order to reach the simplest explanation. The fact that, on some few occasions, it will be OncoMouse™ or RoboDuk whom we encounter or that sometimes the cow path will turn out to be a wood path after all does nothing to ruffle the pragmatist's feathers. She or he is not looking for a rule that will lead to a comprehensive, absolute, and conclusive truth. When a snake sheds her skin, she loses her current set of spectacles too. Her perspective changes, but there is no single, final moment when the scales fall from her eyes. The change in perspective, the shedding of one's skin, occurs over and over, indefinitely, like serpentine ecdysis.[69] The explanatory power of a theory or supposition is one of the means by which we evaluate and choose between these shifting perspectives, but we need not presume that we are attaining or even working toward the single, simplest, "best" explanation. Irrespective of whether inference to the best explanation entails realism,[70] the pragmatist is much more interested in inference to an explanation that is *good enough*. Wanderers through the woods are concerned not with strict rules of inference but with rough guides that will lead them to their objectives.

The physicist and philosopher Ludwig Boltzmann placed particular emphasis on this capacity of a theory or hypothesis to explain. Boltzmann was Nietzsche's exact contemporary

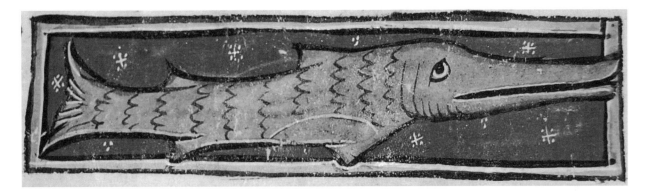

and shared his mistrust of metaphysics.[71] In a
paper entitled "On a Thesis of Schopenhauer's,"
he launched a blistering attack on that writer's
thinking and style, damning the former as a
philosophy from which nothing can arise and
the latter as a mode of expression "associated in
the past with fishwives."[72] Nietzsche had already
suggested, "We are possessors of our opinions
as of fish—that is, in so far as we are possessors
of a fish pond. We must go fishing and have
luck—then we have our fish, our opinions. I
speak here of live opinions, of live fish. Others
are content to possess a cabinet of fossils—and,
in their head, 'convictions.'"[73] Boltzmann hoped
to muddy Schopenhauer's ascetic waters, suggesting that it might be most useful to introduce
a **PIKE** into the complacent **CARP** pond of philosophy (193). It is our deeds, he argued, not
logic or metaphysics, that determine whether
something is true or false, and only those infer-
ences that lead to practical success should be
considered correct (192). In Boltzmann's own

Thirteenth-century medieval bestiary. Westminster Abbey Library, MS 22, fol. 43v.

73. PIKE
His wolfish greed has given the name of Lupus to the Pike, and it is difficult to catch
him. When he is encircled by the net, they say that he ploughs up the sand with his tail
and thus, lying hidden, manages to escape the meshes.

T. H. WHITE, *The Book of Beasts*, 202–3.

pond of opinions there is room for the dead
red herring of inference to the best explanation only if this fish is cunningly feigning death
in pursuit of some practical objective, such as
self-preservation. The task of philosophy should
be to formulate concepts of a sort that allow us
to engage and intercede in the world. The "laws
of thought must everywhere lead us to the inter-

71. Nietzsche and Boltzmann were both born in 1844, both became professors
in their mid-twenties, and both met untimely deaths (Nietzsche in 1900 and
Boltzmann in 1906) following poor mental health. William James, born in 1842,
outlived them both (1910).
72. Boltzmann, "On a Thesis of Schopenhauer's," 191, 185. Further references are
in the text.
73. Nietzsche, *Human, All-Too-Human*, 353 (2.317).

Common carp (*Cyprinus carpio*). Copyright Joseph R. Tomelleri; from *The Great Minnesota Fish Book*, by Tom Dickson, 55.

74. CARP

The common carp is very active when feeding and its movements often disturb sediments and increase turbidity, causing serious problems in some regions especially where the species is abundant. The species also retards the growth of submerged aquatic vegetation by feeding on and uprooting plants. . . . Silt resuspension and uprooting of aquatic plants caused by feeding activities can disturb spawning and nursery areas of native fishes . . . as well as disrupt feeding of sight-oriented predators, such as bass and sunfish.

LEO NICO, ERYNN MAYNARD, AND PAMELA J. SCHOFIELD, "Cyprinus carpio."

ventions in actual events in the way that experience shows to be desirable" (197).

Schopenhauer carped incessantly on the centrality of the Will, but for Boltzmann the Will is simply an inherited striving within us, a striving toward intervention into the material world (194–95). This notion of inheritance is central to Boltzmann's own outlook. A rationalistically inclined Kant had suggested that the sensibility and understanding are a priori faculties. This, according to Boltzmann, is an illusion: our

"laws of thought" (including our methods of inference) are the result of thousands of years of their being tried and tested in the arena of practical experience and experimentation. These laws are thus "innate" to the individual in the sense that they are physically inherited (192, 195). The true salvation for philosophy, according to Boltzmann, lies in the theories of Charles Darwin (193). Boltzmann argues that supposedly a priori faculties are in fact the result of generations of trial and error. Like Nietzsche's "live opinions," and quite unlike Kant's fossilized convictions, these mental mechanisms will change and evolve under the pressure of external stimuli.

The very impulse to ask questions is, Boltzmann claims, an evolved trait, and one that illustrates nicely how these "innate" impulses can sometimes "overshoot the mark." Due to the long established, hereditary custom of asking for the cause of things, we feel compelled to ask for the cause of the law of cause and effect (195–96). Rather like the predicament of Kant's misguided he-goat milkers, however, the "innate love of asking" here results in the "spiritual migraine that is called metaphysics" (192, 198). Similarly, Boltzmann suggests, the instinct for classification is another example of a wonderfully productive impulse that, if not kept in check, extends itself beyond all utility. Things are forced into a preconceived schema, are made to fit either by arbitrarily enlarging or shortening them, like the victims of Procrustes's fatal bed (196).[74] Boltzmann thus seeks simultaneously to explain the origin of "innate" ideas and, at the same time, the reason for metaphysicians' tendency to wander off down *Holzwege*.

Unlike the protagonists of Vishnu Sarma's cautionary tale, all of our three queer fish effect an escape. Boltzmann churned up the sand of philosophical opinion and worked hard to avoid becoming yet another ossified carp. James, on the other hand, found his way out of the woods by following the tried and tested tracks of his predecessors. Like Alice before him, who had the added advantage of finger-posts, he was pointed in the right direction through the trees by a well-established trail.[75] Finally, Nietzsche, our original odd fish, escaped the clutches of the Sphinx by adopting an appropriately self-questioning perspective. Like Oedipus, when he looked he saw a man ("ECCE HOMO"), but the Sphinx taught him to see with other eyes, to ask questions of questions. The real import of Oedipus's answer is not that it is true but that it produces a concrete effect: his answer leads to the death of the Sphinx and the freeing of the Thebans. These three practical souls (or soles) are less interested in the values and interpretations of others than in actions and activities that will gets things done. Our three fish escape, endure, and indeed flourish because they swim freely in a pragmatic pond of live, evolving opinions.

With regard to the utility of knowledge, it is a concern with the explanatory or instrumental property of knowledge that pragmatism shares with realism and that distinguishes these philosophies from relativism, with its interest in the values and interpretations of contrasting cultural groups. Does the pragmatist or the realist thereby commit to a Protagorean perspective, to an epistemological anthropocentrism? The *Panchatantra* tells us that, of the three allegorical fish, two at least escaped the king's frying pan through their quick wits. The first utilized his knowledge of the pond's topography to effect a fast exit, whilst the second appreciated how unappetizing a dead fish would be. Squirrel Nutkin knew the answers to his riddles; more important to him was the mischievous effect he hoped to achieve, rather unwisely, when he set about pestering Old Brown with them. Finally, that well-trodden cow path was not, of course, used only by errant ramblers. The beaten track owed its existence to the fact that countless cows, down through the ages, found it just as useful as did William James. The pragmatist need not conceive of the instrumental employment of knowledge as a uniquely human attribute. Is it appropriate to call these inhuman practices and behaviors *knowledge*, however? Is there any kind of *knowing* going on when the cows come home?

74. Such a schema perhaps resembles Nietzsche's sepulchral columbarium of ideas into which the whole of the empirical world was stuffed; see "The Birds and the Bees" in chapter 2.

75. Carroll, *Through the Looking Glass*, 205.

An answer to these questions lies in the final aspect of the pragmatist conception of knowledge,
which distinguishes this epistemology from
both realism and relativism. We come to pragmatism's understanding of what kind of thing
knowledge is. To explore this pragmatic ontology
of knowledge, we turn from three fish to a whole
flock of miscellaneous fowl.

HANDING ON AND GATHERING IN

In 1958, a few years after the death of Ludwig
Wittgenstein, Norman Malcolm published a
short memoir of his friend. In it he recounts an
anecdote, told to him by Wittgenstein himself,
concerning the spur that prompted the philosopher to reject the assumptions on which his
earlier, highly influential work had been based.
The account concerns a conversation he had had
with the Italian economist Piero Sraffa, who had
been lecturing at Cambridge at the time and was
a frequent disputant with Wittgenstein. Malcolm
relates the tale thus:

> One day (they were riding, I think, on a train)
> when Wittgenstein was insisting that a propo-
> sition and that which it describes must have
> the same "logical form," the same "logical
> multiplicity," Sraffa made a gesture, familiar to
> Neapolitans as meaning something like disgust

or contempt, of brushing the underneath of his
chin with an outward sweep of the finger-tips
of one hand. And he asked: "What is the logical
form of that?" Sraffa's example produced in Wittgenstein the feeling that there was an absurdity
in the insistence that a proposition and what it
describes must have the same "form." This broke
the hold on him of the conception that a proposition must literally be a "picture" of the reality
it describes.[76]

During the dogmatic slumbers from which
Wittgenstein was awoken by this harsh gesture,
he had persisted in considering language on a
representationalist model. The "picture theory"
of language that he held was in many ways akin
to Kant's epistemology, suggesting as it did a
necessary if somewhat mysterious correspondence between the world and its representation.
If Malcolm's anecdote is to be believed, Sraffa
changed the course of Wittgenstein's thinking
and of his whole conception of the function and
operation of language.[77]

Malcolm describes the hand gesture employed by Sraffa as being familiar to Neapolitans,
but this comment is a little misleading. The
principal meaning of the gesture, as Malcolm
explains, is as a strong indication of disinterest: it is an insult that says, in no uncertain
terms, "Stop bothering me" or "You bore me." In
France, where the chin flick is employed exten-
sively, it is called la barbe (the beard), a fact that
provides a clue to the gesture's origin, according
to research published in 1979 by Desmond Mor-

---

76. Malcolm, *Ludwig Wittgenstein*, 69.

77. In his *Philosophical Investigations*, Wittgenstein attributed to the stimulus of
Sraffa's unceasing criticism "the most consequential ideas of this book"; Wittgenstein, *Philosophical Investigations*, viii. Raymond Tallis briefly discusses the
Wittgenstein–Sraffa train conversation and the implications it had for Wittgenstein's philosophy; see Tallis, *Hand*, 86–88.

ris and his colleagues. By implicitly referring to the gesturer's beard, the flick effectively says, they argue, "I point my masculinity at you." (In the Middle East, a gesture with the same meaning of weary disinterest involves the gesturer indicating a long, imaginary beard that has grown during a boring conversation.) The chin flick also has another use, however: it can simply mean "no," just like the head shake from side to side employed in many countries across the world. This innocent indication of a straightforward negative carries none of the insulting connotations of the gesture's other meaning.[78]

Employed as a discourteous indication of disinterest, the chin flick is widespread in French-speaking countries, such as Belgium, France, and Tunisia, as well as in Yugoslavia and southern Sardinia. As a simple negative, it is common only in southern Italy, Sicily, northern Sardinia, Malta, and Corfu. One might expect that the gesture would be employed in northern Italy just as it is in the south, but this is not in fact the case: northern Italians employ the chin flick in the same manner as their French neighbors. Morris and his colleagues suggest that this allows us to formulate a speculative account of the chin flick's historical evolution and that the gesture has two quite distinct derivations. As a negative, the chin flick evolved from another gesture, the simple head toss, which has the same meaning. Here, the head is jerked sharply upwards and backwards and is often accompa-

nied by raised eyebrows and eye-rolling.[79] The addition of the chin flick to the head toss emphasizes the upward movement, they argue, and thus aids communication at longer distances. Both the head toss and the negative chin flick are common in southern Italy, and indeed this elaboration of the head toss is the only instance of the chin flick described in Andrea de Jorio's book of Neapolitan gestures, under the heading "Negativa, No."[80] So where did this head toss come from? Morris and his colleagues believe that it originated in Greece, where it is still common today, and that it was brought to southern Italy with the Greek settlement more than two millennia ago, a settlement that never reached the northern parts of the peninsula.[81] The chin flick, however, is more or less absent from mainland Greece, suggesting that

> the annoyance meaning for the chin flick is the ancient, basic one and that this became modified when it encountered the head toss in southern Italy. There it probably became infected by the simple, unannoyed negative meaning of the head toss, and gradually lost its irritability, becoming eventually no more than a long-distance amplification of the tossed "no."[82]

Sraffa, born and raised in Turin, in northern Italy, employed the chin flick in the older sense,

78. D. Morris et al., *Gestures*, 169–176 (§14).

79. Ibid., 161–68 (§13).

80. De Jorio, *Gesture in Naples*, 289–96 (222–29).

81. D. Morris et al., *Gestures*, 164–65. See also De Jorio, *Gesture in Naples*, 290n236.

82. D. Morris et al., *Gestures*, 175.

forcefully indicating a jaded disinterest in Wittgenstein's ideas. Though either of the two meanings would have illustrated his point equally effectively, we might perhaps do better to consider his gesticulation not a *Neapolitan* chin flick, which would be a mild, elaborated head toss, but rather a more forceful chin flick *Torinese*.[83]

Morris and his fellow researchers here attempt to reconstruct the evolving meaning and distribution of the chin flick. They suggest that its use as an indication of annoyance became "infected" by the temperate, negative head toss. An explicitly evolutionary, virological approach to cultural practices had been discussed and developed by Richard Dawkins just a few years earlier, in 1976.[84] Dawkins suggested that, in addition to genes, there might be other kinds of replicators that reproduce, mutate, and evolve according to the principles of natural selection. In *The Selfish Gene* he argues that just such a new kind of replicator emerged very recently, in the "primeval soup" that is human culture. These new replicators are units not of genetic but of cultural transmission, spreading by means of a process that, in a broad sense, can be called imitation. Searching for a suitable name for this new kind of replicator, Dawkins considers the Greek term μίμησις (mimesis), "imitation."

He discards *mimeme*, however, in favor of the abbreviated, monosyllabic *meme*, which conveniently rhymes with *gene* (192). Examples of memes would include "tunes, ideas, catchphrases, clothes fashions, ways of making pots or of building arches" (192) and a host of other cultural practices, including, he would later add, hand gestures.[85] Genes are passed from one body to another via sperms or eggs, but memes take a different route: "If a scientist hears, or reads about, a good idea, he passes it on to his colleagues and students. He mentions it in his articles and his lectures. If the idea catches on, it can be said to propagate itself, spreading from brain to brain" (192). Dawkins quotes N. K. Humphrey, who became infected by this new way of thinking after reading an early draft of Dawkins's work: "When you plant a fertile meme in my mind you literally parasitize my brain, turning it into a vehicle for the meme's propagation in just the way that a virus may parasitize the genetic mechanism of a host cell" (192). A meme, then, is a kind of cultural virus that is passed, often unwittingly, from one individual to another.

Dawkins suggests that, just as there are for genes, there are three key qualities that will ensure the survival, replication, and success of any given meme: longevity, fecundity, and copying fidelity (194–95). The duration of any given instance of a meme is relatively unimportant; a quick chin flick, for example, takes less than a second. But so long as people keep flicking and

---

83. A third use of the chin flick, to indicate disbelief, occurs much less frequently, in Greece and northern France; see D. Morris et al., *Gestures*, 174–76.
84. Dawkins, *Selfish Gene*, 189–201 (chapter 11). Further references are in the text.
85. Dawkins, *Extended Phenotype*, 109.

so long as others keep seeing and understanding the flick's implications, the meme is likely to endure; there is evidence that this particular gesture has lasted well over two millennia already. More important than its longevity, however, is a meme's fecundity. The replication of the chin flick has depended on its reception and duplication within the cultural environments in which it has been executed. Though doubtless those individuals to whom it has been addressed over the years have not welcomed it, this does not seem to have stopped them from reproducing the gesture themselves when occasion arose. The chin flick has proved remarkably popular. Finally, a meme must be a reasonably high-fidelity replicator. Although any individual performing a chin flick will necessarily give to it his or her own particular style or flourish, the essentials of the flick—the brushing of the underside of the chin with the backs of the fingers as they flick forward in an arc—must remain the same.[86] Any gesture that diverges too far from the norm is in danger of becoming no more than an ostentatious scratching.

The copying of memes, their successive imitation in the broadest sense, need not always be perfect, of course, and it is in fact the minor errors and mutations that creep in that account for the *evolution* of cultural traits. Dawkins recounts the examples of a pair of (not so) well-known songs. Few people remember all the words to "Auld Lang Syne," if they ever knew them at all,

but most know enough to end their efforts with the refrain "For the sake of auld lang syne." In fact, as Dawkins points out, this is not what Burns actually wrote: the correct words are simply "For auld lang syne." A mutant version has evolved and possesses the collective minds of New Year's Eve revelers year after year. Dawkins puts the endurance of the interpolated phrase down to its containing the "notoriously obtrusive" sibilant s sound, whose "survival value" has helped oust the less durable original wording. Something similar has happened with "Rule Britannia." The second line of the chorus of this stirring, nationalist song should be the imperative exhortation "Britannia, rule the waves." It is often rendered, however, as the merely indicative observation "Britannia rules the waves," with no comma and that persistent, susurrant s appearing once again (323–24).[87] The copying errors in each of these two cases have survived not because they sound better (Dawkins is persuaded that they do not) or because they benefit their host. So who profits from these mutations?

Dawkins is at pains to emphasize that when taking an evolutionary perspective on cultural practices we should not imagine that these prac-

86. On the key components of the chin flick and their variations, see D. Morris et al., *Gestures*, 170. On the question of what constitutes a single meme unit and therefore of how best to assess copying fidelity, see Dawkins, *Selfish Gene*, 194–96.
87. Dawkins believes the final test of any hypothesis to be experimental. Accordingly, he suggests that we might surreptitiously inject the hissing meme into another song and then monitor its survival, mischievously proposing "God *saves* our gracious Queen" as the experimental subject; *Selfish Gene*, 324.

tices evolve as they do because they bestow some kind of survival advantage on their carriers. The memes that survive and replicate successfully are not necessarily those that improve the lot of the infected organism (though this may help); rather, they are those that are simply good at replicating. A successful meme evolves as it does because it is advantageous to itself (199–200). From such a "meme's-eye view," any benefit to the meme's host is largely irrelevant. This is not to imply, of course, that memes are conscious or that they actively seek their own replication, any more than Dawkins is suggesting this of genes. But, just like genes, memes can be considered "selfish" replicators in the sense that they compete "'ruthlessly" with one another in the "meme pool" that is their environment. They vie for television time, billboard space, newspaper column inches, library shelf space, and so forth, but above all they must best their rivals when it comes to that relatively scarce and most accommodating of resources, the human brain (196–97). Dawkins takes as an illustrative example the threat of hellfire, one part of the coadapted stable set of mutually assisting memes that is organized religion. The fear of ghastly torments after death that infects believ-

ers, he argues, makes this particular technique of persuasion especially effective. The meme carrier gains no survival benefit,[88] but the meme itself replicates very effectively: "The idea of hell fire is, quite simply, self perpetuating, because of its own deep psychological impact. It has become linked with the god meme because the two reinforce each other, and assist each other's survival in the meme pool" (197–98).[89]

In *The Extended Phenotype*, Dawkins's sequel to *The Selfish Gene*, he set about refining the meme meme. Emphasizing the meme–gene analogy, he was concerned that he had been insufficiently clear in distinguishing between the meme itself, a "unit of information residing in a brain" (the memetic equivalent of a genotype), and its "meme products" (the memetic equivalent of a phenotype).[90] In his earlier work, the term *meme*, in referring to "units of imitation" such as hand gestures, might have been taken as applying equally to the individual instances of the gesture (Sraffa's particular flicking of the chin on that fateful train journey with Wittgenstein), to the idea or knowledge of the hand gesture (residing in the structures and synaptic connections of Sraffa's brain), or even to the hand gesture known as *la barbe* in general (irrespective of the individuals who are currently employing it or who are able to do so). In Dawkins's later formulation, the term *meme* refers only to the second of these cases, and the individual instances are regarded as a meme's

---

88. Indeed, Dawkins argues that in extreme circumstances of religious fundamentalism, this meme and its allies might even encourage martyrdom (198, 330–31).

89. For extended discussion of the cluster of religious memes that Dawkins believes to be tantamount to a form of mental illness, or even child abuse, see Dawkins, *Viruses of the Mind*; Dawkins, *God Delusion*.

90. Dawkins, *Extended Phenotype*, 109.

"phenotypic effects."[91] The information structures in a person's brain that enable him or her to understand the Neapolitan (or Torinese) chin flick and to know how to execute it constitute the meme, whilst any chin flickings in which that person chooses to indulge should be considered concrete practices that arise from it.

In fact, by describing memes and their effects in this way, Dawkins does not clarify his theory so much as revise it, as Derek Gatherer has pointed out.[92] In moving from the meme as "a unit of cultural transmission" to "a unit of information residing in the brain," Dawkins changes the focus from an understanding that includes physical items and patterns of behavior toward one that emphasizes unseen cerebral structures. Rather than considering the cultural trait or artifact in its own right, we must now suppose that an individual has been infected by a meme, which then manifests in a mode of behavior or the production of a concrete object: the meme is not the chin flick itself but the knowledge or competence to perform it. Daniel Dennett has argued that in fact people do not have memes; rather, memes take hold of people: "A human mind is itself an artifact created when memes restructure a human brain in order to make it a better habitat for memes. . . . Our existence as us, as what we as thinkers are . . . is not independent of these memes."[93] One's mind is perhaps best conceived in large part as an assemblage of memes, "a sort of dung heap in which

the larvae of other people's ideas renew themselves, before sending out copies of themselves in an informational Diaspora."[94]

Gatherer argues that this refinement, far from enhancing the utility of this new theoretical tool, introduces difficulties that have retarded the progress of memetics as an innovative and potentially productive new means of thinking about cultural developments. First, problems arise in attempting to assign memes to particular individuals. Given that, in the current state of neurobiology at least, it is impossible to see the meme itself, its existence can be inferred only from its products, be they behaviors or artifacts. If there are people who understand the chin flick but never actually flick their chins, ascertaining the frequency of this particular meme within a population proves difficult. And when, precisely, do people "have" a meme? Do they still have it even when they are not exercising it? Since we cannot get at the memes themselves, it becomes difficult, if not impossible, to establish a clear meme–host relationship or to attribute memes to individuals with any reliability or regularity. As a result, and this is Gatherer's main con-

91. For further clarification of this point, see Dawkins's discussion of origami Chinese junks; Dawkins, foreword to *Meme Machine*, ix–xii. Dawkins also here relates another Wittgenstein-related meme, the philosopher's habit when cogitating of screwing up his eyes and jerking his head down to his chest, which has since been inherited by his followers, their offspring, and even Dawkins himself (ibid., vii).

92. Gatherer, "Progress of Memetics."

93. Dennett, *Consciousness Explained*, 207–8.

94. Ibid., 202.

cern, it becomes impossible to quantify meme frequencies within a population. Memetics, as a dependable, scientific approach to culture, becomes considerably less useful, less practical, than one might wish.[95]

With Dawkins's refinement, we find ourselves contemplating abstract, internal, immeasurable entities of rather dubious ontological status.[96] Gatherer has an efficient solution, however: rather than adopt Dawkins's revision, he undertakes his own. Instead of pushing memes back into the mind and distinguishing them from "phenotypic effects," he argues that it is those very "effects" that should be regarded as the memes. Sraffa's gesture is the meme, not the informational structures in his brain. As Gatherer says:

> This is a behaviourist scheme, which treats memes as cultural events, behaviours or artefacts which may be transmitted or copied. Outside the occurrence of the event, the practice of the behaviour, or the lifetime of the artefact, the meme has no existence. The meme does not "go anywhere" when it is not manifested. It is not stored in some neural bank, some internal meme repository.[97]

The chin flick is a practice, a function, evolving within the meme pool that is daily life. Gatherer's behaviorist approach allows us to quantify and measure such memes. It is a supremely practical, pragmatically cogent understanding of the meme. One can, as Morris and his colleagues in fact did, undertake an extensive, empirical survey of the occurrence of a meme and on that basis posit statistically informed theories regarding its origin, evolution, and proliferation. The contest between the two competing, mutant varieties of meme theory continues, neither having established itself authoritatively within the niche of evolutionary epistemology that is contemporary memetics.[98] But Gatherer's interpretation draws attention to the pragmatic strain within all accounts of memes. Whether we call them memes or merely the "phenotypic effects" of memes, what is important in this evolutionary model is that social and cultural endeavors be considered as practices, concrete activities that are subject to a wide range of mechanisms of replication, mutation, sifting, and selection. They are evolving, immersive activities, developing and transforming within particular environments. In the next section we examine the survival and success of that matchless example of a practical meme, Charles Dar-

---

95. Gatherer addresses the problems of attribution and of quantification in the first two sections of his paper and of suggesting that memes "have" people in the penultimate section; Gatherer, "Progress of Memetics," §§1–2, 8.4.

96. On memes as information, mental representations, and the dangers of becoming embroiled in the mind–body problem, see Hull, "Taking Memetics Seriously," 58–61.

97. Gatherer, "Progress of Memetics," §4. As Gatherer says, this is basically Dawkins's original formulation "but with the mentalistic component of that meme definition stripped out." William Benzon, on whose work Gatherer draws, has suggested that not only should we consider items of physical culture as the memes, but that the corresponding psychological traits and brain states should be considered the cultural phenotypes; Benzon, "Culture as an Evolutionary Arena," 323–24.

Illustration by L. Wells, in Stonehenge [John Henry Walsh], *The Dog in Health and Disease*, 198–99.

75. BULLDOG

F. Cuvier has asserted that this dog has a brain smaller in proportion than any other of his congeners, and in this way accounts for his assumed want of sagacity. But though his authority is deservedly high, I must beg leave to doubt the fact as well as the inference; for if the brain is weighed with the body of the dog from which it was taken, it will be found to be relatively above the average, the mistake arising from the evident disproportion between the brain and the skull. . . . The mental qualities of the bulldog may be highly cultivated, and in brute courage and unyielding tenacity of purpose he stands unrivalled among quadrupeds, and with the single exception of the game-cock he has perhaps no parallel in these respects in the brute creation.

STONEHENGE [JOHN HENRY WALSH], *The Dog in Health and Disease*, 198–99.

win's own theory of evolution by natural selection, including the birds who made it possible.

BIRD BRAINS

On Saturday, June 30, 1860, the British Association for the Advancement of Science, known to the initiated as the British Ass, assembled at the impressive new Oxford University Museum. The meeting had been scheduled to take place in the lecture room, but when more than seven hundred people began to congregate, the proceedings had to be relocated to a larger room in the museum library. What occasioned this prodigious audience of science lovers? On the Origin of Species by Means of Natural Selection had been pub-

lished just a few months earlier, and the previous Thursday, Thomas Henry Huxley, who would later become known as Darwin's **BULLDOG**, had crossed swords with Richard Owen, England's foremost comparative anatomist and an outspoken critic of Darwin's theory of evolution. Huxley, having undertaken a careful investigation of the matter, had cited the similarity of ape and human brains as evidence for evolution. Owen, however, had argued that there were more differences between the brains of gorilla and human than between the gorilla and the lowliest of the primates. Huxley flatly contradicted him.[99] Word spread, and it was widely expected that the fireworks would resume at the Saturday meeting, when Samuel Wilberforce, bishop of Oxford, intended to demolish Darwinism. Wilberforce was an accomplished orator; his own nickname was "Soapy Sam," perhaps because he had a characteristic

98. For an overview of debates within memetics, see Aunger, *Darwinizing Culture*, esp. 1–23 (introduction).

99. Huxley published his criticisms a few years later; see Huxley, *Evidence*, 85, 94–103.

hand-washing gesture when speaking, or perhaps because, though often in hot water, he always came out with clean hands.[100] Either way, he was certainly considered a safe pair of hands by Darwin's opponents. The occasion of the meeting at the University Museum was thus, as Huxley's son Leonard later described it, "spiced with the personal element which appeals to one of the strongest instincts of every large audience."[101]

Wilberforce had reviewed Darwin's book, and it was on this text that his speech was based.[102] He spoke with eloquence and wit for about half an hour, concentrating on the fixity of forms: he spoke of the short-legged sheep and wild horses of America, and he asserted that rock pigeons were what rock pigeons had always been.

In his review, he initially affected an open mind toward the question of "our unsuspected cousinship with the mushrooms," which he called "our fungular descent," but as he spoke on that warm Saturday afternoon he was forced to conclude that Darwin's theory broke the principles of inductive science, that it was quite unphilosophical, and that it was founded on fancy rather than facts. There was cheering around the room as he drew to a close, but Wilberforce is best remembered for his parting shot, addressed directly to Huxley himself. Infamously, he begged to know whether it was through his grandfather or his grandmother that he claimed descent from a monkey? This, it is widely agreed, was an uncharacteristic mistake on the part of the bishop. In the first place, it was bad taste in a debate of this sort to descend to the level of the personal. In the second, one should certainly not bring ladies into the argument; Wilberforce, it was said, had "forgotten to behave like a gentleman."[103] Huxley later recounted that he turned to Sir Benjamin Brodie, sitting next to him on the platform, and said in an undertone, "The Lord hath delivered him into mine hands."[104]

Huxley, who up until this debate had tended to eschew public speaking, initially concentrated on scientific matters. But, unable to resist replying to the bishop's enquiry, he responded thus:

> If . . . the question is put to me, "would I rather have a miserable ape for a grandfather, or a man highly endowed by nature and possessed of

100. R. W. Clark, *Huxleys*, 55. Ambrose Bierce suggested, on the other hand, that the name derived from a (perhaps apocryphal) comment by Benjamin Disraeli that Wilberforce was "unctuous, oleaginous, saponaceous"; Bierce, *Devil's Dictionary*, s.v. "oleaginous."

101. Huxley, *Life and Letters*, 1: 181. There is no verbatim record of the Oxford meeting. For overviews of the existing accounts, see Huxley, *Life and Letters*, 1: 179–189; R. W. Clark, *Huxleys*, 54–61; Lucas, "Wilberforce and Huxley"; Thomson, "Huxley, Wilberforce, and the Oxford Museum."

102. The review was published anonymously in the July issue of *Quarterly Review*. Darwin thought it "uncommonly clever," and in a letter to his friend Joseph Hooker, who also spoke at the meeting, acknowledged that it "picks out with skill all the most conjectural parts, and brings forward well all the difficulties"; Darwin to Joseph Hooker, July 3, 1860, in Darwin, *Life and Letters*, 2: 324–25; quoted in Lucas, "Wilberforce and Huxley," 320.

103. Farrar to Leonard Huxley, July 12, 1899; quoted in Lucas, "Wilberforce and Huxley," 327.

104. Huxley to Francis Darwin, June 27, 1891, in Huxley, *Life and Letters*, 1: 187–88. Cunning memetic detective work by Keith Thomson provides evidence that Huxley's biblical reference (to Judges 7:15) was in fact a later embellishment, prompted by his reading of a misquotation (of Judges 15:8) in Hooker's account; Thomson, "Huxley, Wilberforce, and the Oxford Museum," 213.

Barmaid, a Dwarf Beagle, bred by Lord Gifford, by L. Wells, in Stonehenge [John Henry Walsh], The Dog in Health and Disease, *67–68.*

76. BEAGLE

The true beagle is a miniature specimen of the old Southern hound, except that, like almost all moderately reduced dogs as to size, he possesses more symmetry than his prototype. Where, however, this reduction is carried to extremes in order to produce a little hound capable of being carried in the pocket of a shooting-jacket, and slow enough to allow of his followers keeping up with him on foot, there is generally a loss of symmetry and of its ordinary accompaniment, a hardy constitution. In order to get a reduction of size in any breed, the smallest puppy in a litter is selected, and as this is also generally the most weakly, it is only to be expected that in the course of time a constant repetition of such selection will result in a loss of constitution.

STONEHENGE [JOHN HENRY WALSH], *The Dog in Health and Disease,* 67–68.

great means and influence, and yet who employs those faculties and that influence for the mere purpose of introducing ridicule into a grave scientific discussion"—I unhesitatingly affirm my preference for the ape.[105]

The impact of his riposte was undoubtedly dramatic: Huxley records that it was met with "indistinguishable laughter"; one writer reported that she jumped out of her seat; and a Lady Brewster was apparently so overcome that she fainted on the spot. The bishop, as one account would later have it, had been bearded,[106] and Soapy Sam's hands were no longer quite so clean. All parties later claimed victory, of course, but there can be no doubt that this was a defining moment for the reception of Darwin's theory. When he wrote

to Huxley a month later, Darwin believed that Oxford had done the subject much good, and he expressed the opinion that his book alone would have done "absolutely nothing."[107] As Leonard Huxley put it, the publicity that was generated "helped to save a great cause from being stifled under misrepresentation and ridicule," and "the new theories secured a hearing, all the wider, indeed, for the startling nature of their defence."[108]

It has been frequently noted that the environment into which Darwin's meme, his theory of evolution, was released at the end of November 1859 was not a welcoming one. Ideas about evolution were not new, but neither were they popular, and Darwinians were in a small minority. *On the Origin of Species* was the culmination of decades of meticulous research. Thirty years before the debate at Oxford, Darwin had set out on his five-year voyage aboard H. M. S. **BEAGLE**. In 1835, he had visited the Galápagos

105. Huxley to Henry Dyster, September 9, 1860, quoted in R. W. Clark, *Huxleys,* 59. The exact wording both of Wilberforce's question and of Huxley's reply has been much discussed.

Finches from Galápagos Archipelago: Large Ground Finch (*Geospiza magnirostris*), Medium Ground Finch (*Geospiza fortis*), Small Tree Finch (*Geospiza parvula*), and Warbler Finch (*Certhidea olivacea*), by T. Pritchett. In Charles Darwin, *Journal of Researches into the Natural History and Geology of the Countries Visited during the Voyage Round the World of H. M. S. Beagle*, 405.

77. FINCH

[Cactus finches] nest in cactus; they sleep in cactus; they often copulate in cactus; they drink cactus nectar; they eat cactus flowers, cactus pollen, and cactus seeds. . . . Two other species of Darwin's finches use tools. They pick up a twig, a cactus spine, or a leafstalk, and they trim it into shape with their beaks. Then they poke it into the bark of dead branches and pry out grubs. One finch eats green leaves, which birds are not supposed to do. Another, the vampire finch, . . . perches on the backs of boobies, pecks at their wings and tails, draws their blood, and drinks it. . . . They even drink the blood of their own dead. There is a vegetarian species that knows how to strip the bark off twigs into long curling ribbons like Geppetto's shavings, to get at the cambium and phloem. There are also species that perch on the backs of iguanas and rid them of ticks.

JONATHAN WEINER, *The Beak of the Finch*, 17.

106. Isabella Sidgwick, quoted in Lucas, "Wilberforce and Huxley," 313.
107. Darwin to T. H. Huxley, July 20, 1860, quoted in R. W. Clark, *Huxleys*, 61.
108. Huxley, *Life and Letters*, 1: 179, 189.
109. Darwin, *Journal of Researches*, 403–4 (chapter 17).
110. Quoted in Weiner, *Beak of the Finch*, 21.

Islands, equatorial home to the famous FINCHES that have since taken his name. In his *Journal of Researches*, often called *The Voyage of the Beagle*, Darwin had the following to say of these birds:

> The remaining land-birds form a most singular group of finches, related to each other in the structure of their beaks, short tails, form of body and plumage. . . . All these species are peculiar to this archipelago. . . . The males of all, or certainly of the greater number, are jet black; and the females (with perhaps one or two exceptions) are brown. The most curious fact is the perfect gradation in the size of the beaks in the different species of Geospiza, from one as large as that of a hawfinch to that of a chaffinch, and . . . even to that of a warbler. The largest beak in the genus Geospiza is shown above in Fig. 1, and the smallest in Fig. 3; but instead of there being only one intermediate species, with a beak of the size shown in Fig. 2, there are no less than six species with insensibly graduated beaks. . . . Seeing this gradation and diversity of structure in one small, intimately related group of birds, one might really fancy that from an original paucity of birds in this archipelago, one species had been taken and modified for different ends.[109]

In his diary, Darwin recorded that "the birds are Strangers to Man & think him as innocent as their countrymen the huge TORTOISES. Little birds, within 3 or four feet, quietly hopped about the Bushes & were not frightened by stones being thrown at them. Mr King killed one with his hat."[110] Darwin certainly had no trouble shooting thirty-one of them to be used as samples.

The finches illustrate perfectly the key idea of Darwin's theory of evolution by natural selection: from a common ancestor multiple species gradually evolve, as groups of individuals become reproductively isolated from their fellows and adapt, generation after generation, to a particular ecological niche. The Galápagos Islands represent a kind of natural laboratory in which this process can be seen especially clearly: not only is the archipelago of twenty or so islands far from the South American mainland (Ecuador is six hundred miles distant), but each island is in turn isolated from the others. There are thirteen distinct species recognized as "Darwin's finches" living on the Galápagos (a fourteenth exists on Cocos Island, four hundred miles to the northeast). As Darwin himself noted, the different finches are very similar in appearance, but it is the slight variation in their beaks, the "gradation and diversity of structure," that illustrates his theory. From a single ancestor evolved the blood-sucking Sharp-beaked Ground Finch (Geospiza difficilis), the well-endowed Large Ground Finch (Geospiza magnirostris), the tool-using Woodpecker Finch (Camarhynchus pallidus), and so on.[111]

It is this question of the instability of species, their "transmutation," as Darwin put it, from one into another that made his work so radical and, in certain quarters, unpalatable. Bishop Wilberforce was too astute a disputant to have missed the implications this instability had for a literal understanding of Genesis, but

78. Galápagos Tortoise

I have not as yet noticed by far the most remarkable feature in the natural history of this archipelago; it is, that the different islands to a considerable extent are inhabited by a different set of beings. My attention was first called to this fact by the Vice-Governor, Mr Lawson, declaring that the tortoises differed from the different islands, and that he could with certainty tell from which island any one was brought. I did not for some time pay sufficient attention to this statement, and I had already mingled together the collections from two of the islands. I never dreamed that islands, about fifty or sixty miles apart, and most of them in sight of each other, formed of precisely the same rocks, placed under a quite similar climate, rising to a nearly equal height, would have been differently tenanted. . . . Captain Porter has described those from Charles and from the nearest island to it, namely Hood Island, as having their shells in front thick and turned up like a Spanish saddle, whilst the tortoises from James Island are rounder, blacker, and have a better taste when cooked.

CHARLES DARWIN, Journal of Researches into the Natural History and Geology of the Countries Visited during the Voyage Round the World of H. M. S. Beagle, 419–20.

Galápagos tortoise (*Geochelone nigra*). Photo by Rob Kroenert.

111. On the complexity and importance of Darwin's Finches, see Weiner, *Beak of the Finch*; Grant, *Darwin's Finches*; Sulloway, "Darwin and His Finches," 1–3.

his insistence on the fixity of species was based, at least in his altercation with Huxley, on what he took to be sound scientific evidence. Wilberforce's ideas were by no means uncommon at the time, but Darwin was not sure that he himself was even able to define quite what a species was: not long before he published *On the Origin of Species*, when asked by a paleontologist, "How do you define a species?" he replied simply, "I cannot." In a letter to the botanist Asa Gray, he remembered:

> When I was at systematic work, I know I longed to have no other difficulty (great enough) than deciding whether the form was distinct enough to deserve a name; & not to be haunted with [the] undefined & unanswerable question whether it was a true species. What a jump it is from a well marked variety, produced by natural cause, to a species produced by the separate act of the Hand of God.[112]

The differences in their beaks aside, the plumage of the various species of finch is in many cases very similar: more than one ornithologist has complained that they are almost impossible to distinguish. Jonathan Weiner remarks that "some of them look so much alike that during the mating season they find it hard to tell themselves apart."[113]

It is commonly believed that infertility between two groups is a requirement of their being considered distinct species, but this is not in fact the case. The inability ordinarily to interbreed, rather than actual infertility, is sufficient, although it is often impossible to arrive at such a neat distinction. As Dennett points out, "Wolves and coyotes and dogs are considered different species, and yet interbreeding does occur. . . . Dachshunds and Irish wolfhounds are deemed to be of the same species, but unless their owners provide some distinctly unnatural arrangements, they are about as reproductively isolated as bats are from dolphins."[114] And as Weiner implied, individuals of the different species of finch do, in fact, occasionally interbreed. There is a still better avian example of this mutability of species, however, which, as Dennett muses, seems made to order for philosophers. In Britain, the **HERRING GULL** and the **LESSER BLACK-BACKED GULL** are two quite distinct species. They are relatively easy to tell apart and they do not interbreed. If one follows the population of herring gulls westward, however, to North America, then to Alaska, to Siberia, across Russia, and back into Europe, the gulls gradually begin to look more and more like lesser black-backed gulls, until, as one reaches Britain once more, they *are* lesser black-backed gulls. The gulls make up a *ring species* in which neighboring groups can

---

112. Darwin to Asa Gray, November 29, 1857, in Darwin, *Correspondence*, 493.
113. Weiner, *Beak of the Finch*, 17. David Lack suggests that "in no other birds are the differences between species so ill-defined"; Lack, *Darwin's Finches*. Michael Harris has said that, though the beaks are undoubtedly the key to correct identification, "it is only a very wise man or a fool who thinks that he is able to identify all the finches which he sees"; Michael Harris, *Field Guide*, 137.
114. Dennett, *Darwin's Dangerous Idea*, 45.

Mike Langman, *Herring Gull* and *Lesser Black-Backed Gull*.
rspb-images.com.

79. & 80. HERRING GULL AND LESSER BLACK-BACKED GULL

Under what circumstances speciation in sexually reproducing animals can occur
without geographical disjunction is still controversial. According to the ring-species
model, a reproductive barrier may arise through "isolation by distance" when
peripheral populations of a species meet after expanding around some uninhabitable
barrier. . . . The classical example that the ring-species model was based upon is the
herring gull (*Larus argentatus*) complex. This group comprises more than 20 taxa of
large gulls . . . , which together occupy a circumpolar breeding range in the Northern
Hemisphere. . . . What earlier authors . . . regarded as "the herring gull" turned out to
be an assemblage of several distinct taxa (*argentatus, vegae, smithsonianus*), which are
not each other's closest relatives. Our results show that the ring-species model does
not adequately describe the evolution of the herring gull group because . . . there is no
overlap between the endpoints of a ring of interbreeding taxa.

DORIT LIEBERS, PETER DE KNIJFF, AND ANDREAS J. HELBIG, "The Herring Gull
Complex Is Not a Ring Species," 893, 897.

81. ROCK PIGEON

We now come to the best-known rock-pigeon, the *Columba livia*, which is often designated in Europe preeminently as the Rock-pigeon, and which naturalists believe to be the parent of all the domesticated breeds. This bird agrees in every essential character with the breeds which have been only slightly modified. It differs from all other species in being of a slaty-blue colour, with two black bars on the wings, and with the croup (or loins) white.

CHARLES DARWIN, *The Variation of Animals and Plants under Domestication*, 1: 192.

The Rock Pigeon, or Columbia livia. The Parent-Form of All Domesticated Pigeons, by Luke Wells. In Charles Darwin, *The Variation of Animals and Plants under Domestication*, 1: 141.

and do interbreed, all the way around the world, but whose "ends" constitute two distinct species.[115] Whilst the Galápagos finches indicate the mutability of species diachronically, the gulls do so synchronically, and between them they help show just how unsystematic the hand of God can sometimes be.[116]

115. Ibid. These birds represent the classic example of a ring species and have been much discussed; see Ridley, *Problems of Evolution*, 6; Dawkins, "Gaps in the Mind," 82. The essential point concerning the mutability of species is in no way compromised by recent research that suggests that the gulls do not, in fact, comprise a ring species; see Liebers, de Knijff, and Helbig, "Herring Gull Complex." Given the didactic role they have played, it matters not that those things said to be true of the gulls may turn out to be mere tales of men, as Augustine well knew (see "An ABC of Animals" in chapter 1). What is more, Liebers, de Knijff, and Helbig suggest that the gulls may soon *become* a ring species, as lesser black-backed gulls expand ever westward (899). For an alternative ring species, see the Asian greenish warbler (*Phylloscopus trochiloides*), whose populations encircle the Tibetan Plateau; Irwin, Bensch, and Price, "Speciation in a Ring." On the history and unstable integrity of the ring-species concept, see Irwin, Irwin, and Price, "Ring Species as Bridges."

116. We will return to the question of species and biological systematics in chapter 5; see "Four Hands Good, Two Hands Bad."

117. Sulloway, "Darwin and His Finches," 46–47.

118. The collective name seems to have been coined by the ornithologist Percy R. Lowe when he presented a commemorative lecture to the British Association one hundred years after Darwin's visit to the Galápagos; see Weiner, *Beak of the*

The Galápagos finches have taken on an almost mythical status within the history of evolutionary theory. Darwin's encounter with them is often related as the decisive moment at which his daring new theory first began to take shape, a Damascene epiphany with monumental consequences.[117] The finches did not become known as "Darwin's finches" until 1935,[118] however, and in fact Darwin himself barely mentioned them in the diary he kept whilst voyaging on the *Beagle*. Indeed, insofar as he did consider them, he failed even to realize that they were all finches. Of the nine he collected, he identified only six as finches; the cactus finch looked to him like some kind of blackbird, and he thought others were wrens and warblers.[119] At the time of his visit, Darwin failed to pick up on any correlation between diet and beak size, and he did not notice the differences exhibited by finches living on different islands. Much to his later regret, he bundled all his specimens into a single bag, failing to record from which of the islands each came. Darwin, in short, did not appreciate what he was dealing with, and his understanding of the significance of the finches came much later. Mention of them was brief in the first edition, in 1839, of his *Journal of Researches*, and the famous passage concerning the gradation of beak sizes, cited above, appeared only in the second edition, in 1845, after his specimens had been examined and classified (and relabeled) by experts in London.[120] The Galápagos finches did not punctuate Darwin's equilibrium so much as chart the gradualist evolution of his ideas.[121]

Darwin never explicitly mentioned the exotic Galápagos finches in *On the Origin of Species*.[122] A different, rather mundane group of birds played a much more prominent role in the development and demonstration of his ideas. In his review of Darwin's book, Wilberforce had as-

serted that **ROCK PIGEONS** today remained what they had always been: honest-to-goodness rock pigeons. He mentioned these particular creatures because they play a key role early in Darwin's discussion of variation.[123] In the first chapter of *On the Origin of Species*, Darwin describes the huge variety of startlingly different fancy pigeons bred by enthusiasts: the fantails, pouters, runts, toys, carriers, tumblers, barbs, and turbits, as well as the Jacobin, the trumpeter, and the laugher.[124] Darwin argued, however, that "great as the differences are between the breeds of pigeons, I am fully convinced that . . . all have descended from the rock-pigeon (*Columba livia*)."[125] All the varieties can be intercrossed, and, the distinctive characteristics for which they are each bred aside, all the varieties are fundamentally similar to the rock pigeon in terms of constitution, habits, voice, coloring, and general structure.[126] The **TUMBLERS**

Finch, 54. The designation became established after David Lack used it for the title of his book in 1947; see Sulloway, "Darwin and His Finches," 45–46.

119. Sulloway, "Darwin and His Finches," 8–9; Weiner, *Beak of the Finch*, 22.

120. J. Browne, *Charles Darwin*, 358–61.

121. Sulloway, "Darwin and His Finches," 5–6. For a full account of what Sulloway calls "The Legend of Darwin's Finches," see 38–47.

122. Sulloway, "Darwin and His Finches," 39. The variety of finches in general is briefly mentioned in the first edition of *On the Origin of Species*, 28.

123. Darwin, *On the Origin of Species*, 20–29. Domestic pigeons occupy two full chapters of Darwin's subsequent *Variation of Animals and Plants under Domestication*, the first of a projected series of expansions of the ideas in *On the Origin of Species* (chapters 5 and 6).

124. Darwin, *On the Origin of Species*, 21–22.

125. Ibid., 23.

126. In fact, Darwin provided the first systematic account of the reasons for believing that fancy pigeons descended from a single wild stock; Secord, "Nature's Fancy," 180.

82. Short-Faced English Tumbler

These are marvellous birds, and are the glory and pride of many fanciers. In their extremely short, sharp, and conical beaks, with the skin over the nostrils but little developed, they almost depart from the type of the Columbidæ. Their heads are nearly globular and upright in front, so that some fanciers say "the head should resemble a cherry with a barley-corn stuck in it."

CHARLES DARWIN, *The Variation of Animals and Plants under Domestication*, 1: 159.

Short-faced English Tumbler, by Luke Wells. In Charles Darwin, *The Variation of Animals and Plants under Domestication*, 1: 160.

provide a particularly good example of the gradation between varieties to which Darwin wished to draw attention:

> In regard to the whole group of Tumblers, it is impossible to conceive a more perfect gradation than I have now lying before me, from the rock-pigeon, through Persian, Lotan, and Common Tumblers, up to the marvellous short-faced birds; which latter, no ornithologist, judging from mere external structure, would place in the same genus with the rock-pigeon.[127]

As James Secord has argued, this combination of wide divergence amongst varieties with a demonstrable common ancestor provided Darwin with the clearest possible illustration of the effectiveness of selection.[128] Starting from the pigeon varieties achieved by human selection over a few thousand years, Darwin argued by analogy

to the power of natural selection to transform, over many millions of years, entire species.[129]

Whilst writing On the Origin of Species, Darwin had initially hoped to avoid altogether the business of breeding pigeons. He considered the matter "no amusement, but a horrid bore,"[130] but he was soon won over, purchasing a huge range of different varieties, and eventually owning nearly ninety birds.[131] Darwin entered enthusiastically into the world of the pigeon fancier, attending shows, mixing with breeders, and even joining two of the London societies.[132] "I am hand & glove with all sorts of Fanciers, Spital-field weavers & . . . odd specimens of the Human species, who fancy Pigeons,"[133] he told a correspondent. When the naturalist or ornithologist considered the pigeon, it was most often with the eye of the taxonomist, concerned with the bird's correct classification. Scientists had long believed that the different breeds all

127. Darwin, *Variation of Animals and Plants*, 1: 161, quoted in Secord, "Nature's Fancy," 181.

128. Secord, "Nature's Fancy," 166.

129. See Gould, "What the Immaculate Pigeon Teaches," 358–60.

130. Darwin to W. D. Fox, March 19, 1855, quoted in Secord, "Nature's Fancy," 165.

131. Secord, "Nature's Fancy," 165–66.

132. Ibid., 174–78.

133. Darwin to James Dwight Dana, September 29, 1856, quoted in Secord, "Nature's Fancy," 178.

derived from a single wild species and so tended to ignore what they saw as degenerate variations brought about by artificial selection. The breeder, on the other hand, was interested in realizing and refining these distinct varieties. Insofar as taxonomic matters were considered at all, fanciers tended to believe that variations were the result of descent from several wild stocks.[134] Darwin was familiar, of course, with the approaches and arguments of the naturalists. By immersing himself so fully in the practices of the breeders, however, he was able to employ their methods to prove what the naturalists had simply assumed: a single common ancestor.

The experienced breeder, Darwin noted, had a keen eye for the tiniest of variations: "Those alone who have associated with fanciers can be thoroughly aware of their accurate powers of discrimination acquired by long practice, and of the care and labour which they bestow on their birds."[135] Darwin's own firsthand experience as a practicing pigeon breeder was invaluable. By employing for himself the "selecting hand,"[136] Darwin was able to understand and to demonstrate the extent to which the mechanism of selection can take the tiniest of variations and make of them entirely new forms. Much has been made of the intellectual environment in which Darwin found himself and of the degree to which this informed his thinking.[137] Many of the meetings of the London pigeon clubs were held in gin palaces south of the river, however,

and it has been suggested that "the clubs, and the working-class clubs in particular, offered a less restricted forum at which Darwin could openly discuss ideas about the transmutation of species—a matter that was still largely taboo in the conservative halls of mid-nineteenth-century establishment science."[138] The community of breeders, including those Spitalfields weavers and odd specimens of humanity, provided Darwin, Secord argues, with an irreplaceable "alternative vision."[139]

It would be inappropriate to imagine that this alternative vision was simply one more influence on Darwin's thinking. Together with the many other practices and behaviors in which he was immersed, the actions of the breeders constituted a set of pressures on Darwin's work: selection pressures. Nondiscursive as well as discursive practices constrained and channeled his activities; his interactions with naturalists, with breeders, and above all with the pigeons themselves focused and directed the course of his thought. To the ascetic outlook of the naturalist, Darwin added the pragmatic concerns of the fancier. The alternative vision of the breeders

134. Secord, "Nature's Fancy," 166–70.
135. Darwin, *Variation of Animals and Plants*, 1: 226.
136. The term is Secord's; see "Nature's Fancy," 165, 169.
137. See, for instance, Beer, *Darwin's Plots*, esp. 29–48 (chapter 1), on the influence of William Shakespeare, Thomas Malthus, John Milton, and Charles Lyell.
138. Hinchliffe, "Pigeons, Cities, and Unnatural Selection," 180. On the question of class, see also Secord, "Nature's Fancy," 174–78.
139. Secord, "Nature's Fancy," 174. Spitalfields is an area of London, known during the Victorian period both for its textile industry and for widespread deprivation and crime.

was an evaluative perspective, a way of seeing that involved a whole new set of interests, purposes, and objectives. Darwin, in short, involved himself in a concrete practice, in which the immediate practicalities of pigeon breeding could not be ignored. His thoughts on natural selection were of necessity a *working* theory, a nexus between abstract knowledge of the nature of species and the earthy mechanics of the processes of reproduction. The two needed to *fit*, like hand and glove.

Darwin demonstrated the transmutation of species, but in doing so he contributed to a transmutation of the very *concept* of species too. The pigeons with whom he dealt no longer lived in some great columbarium of ideas, a rigid cemetery of purified, petrified perceptions into which empiric content was subsequently stuffed (see "The Birds and the Bees" in chapter 2). Darwin's tumblers, turbits, and trumpeters were very far from being pigeonholed in this way. Nietzsche would argue, just a few years later, that not rock but running water provided the slight foundations for the peculiar pigeon cote that is linguistic and scientific representation. With his distinct but interbreeding varieties of pigeon, Darwin meanwhile demonstrated the plasticity of *Columba livia*. There were thus no dependable

rocks for Bishop Wilberforce either: just evolving rock pigeons. Concepts and ideas, like species, metamorphose and evolve.[140] Evolutionary theory itself is a set of discourses and endeavors, an immersive knowledge that is embedded in a range of actions and activities. It is, to adopt Gatherer's revision of Dawkins, a meme complex composed of cultural events, behaviors, and artifacts. Evolutionary theory, understood from the perspective of evolutionary theory itself, is thus a very practical form of knowledge. As such, it illustrates the final property of pragmatism, which distinguishes that epistemology from both realism and relativism: for pragmatism, knowledge is conceived as a practice, not a representation. It is something that one does rather than a collection of concepts or ideas that one has.

Darwin's was certainly not the first theory of evolution, and the discourse of "non-creation" has transmuted many times since his contribution.[141] As an ongoing practice, the success of Darwin's theory of evolution by natural selection has depended on its utility, ease of replication, and of course on the selection pressures of its environment. Owen and Wilberforce represented just two examples of the opposition it initially encountered, both in orthodox scientific circles and across Victorian society as a whole. As a meme, an evolving set of knowledge practices, however, Darwin's theory did not need to be true; it simply needed to replicate. The legend of Darwin's finches is, as we have seen, quite un-

140. The concept of species is a good one, then, not because it is "true" but because it is useful, even despite the problems Darwin and others had in arriving at a single, clear, and distinct definition; see Dupré, "In Defence of Classification."

141. In early manuscripts Darwin spoke of the "non-creation" of species; see J. Browne, *Charles Darwin*, 359.

true, but this has not stopped it from replicating extremely successfully, generating in the process a number of elaborations, embellishments, and, inevitably, variations.[142] We might observe too that it has worked as a selection pressure in favor of its parent theory: although the legend itself is untrue, it accurately communicates the gist of Darwin's ideas. As such, a bogus but captivating and widely reported story has helped disseminate the theory it illustrates.[143]

Part of the appeal of the myth of Darwin's finches is undoubtedly the fact that it invokes the image of the young adventurer, dashing from one exotic location to the next, alone but determinedly opposed to the scientific conformity of his day. As Frank Sulloway has suggested, "Through the legend, Darwin is continually celebrated as a scientific hero who single-handedly solved the biological riddle of the Sphinx when he recognized the different Galápagos finches for an extraordinary microcosmic example of evolution in action."[144] Rather this than a middle-aged recluse pottering about his pigeon sheds, and better, too, a blinding flash of insight than the slow accumulation of suspicions and intimations, the creeping realization of an abstract principle in amongst the laborious succession of mundane facts.[145] No matter that, once again, the categories of wild and tame prove insecure: the free-flying finches passively succumbed to the less-than-tender ministrations of Darwin and Mr. King, whilst the domestic pigeons inflexibly insisted on a radical new mode of thought. The finches, despite their drab appearance and relative superfluity, bring to the tale all the color and excitement of a tropical archipelago and win out over the pigeons who, despite their flamboyant plumage and vital contribution, connote only the humdrum commonplace of an urban landscape.[146] As a pragmatic St. Augustine argued earlier, the truth of these tales matters far less than the lessons they impart, the functions they perform, or the practices they effect (see "An ABC of Animals" in chapter 1).

We have employed the notion of the meme in order to examine the final, distinguishing property of pragmatic epistemology: the emphasis on knowledge as a practice. This practical aspect, already implicit within Dawkins's early formulation of memetics, was drawn out by a behavioristically inclined Gatherer. For the memeticist, knowledge becomes an open-ended subset of rituals and routines, what Foucault called "discursive" and "nondiscursive" practices,

142. See Sulloway, "Darwin and His Finches," 6–8, 38–47; Weiner, *Beak of the Finch*, 35–36.
143. Nietzsche, appreciative of the utility of deception and error, would surely have appreciated the irony, had he not harbored such a deep-seated and misplaced hostility toward Darwinism; see Ansell-Pearson, *Viroid Life*, 86–105 (chapter 4).
144. Sulloway, "Darwin and His Finches," 47.
145. Darwin commented that "my mind seems to have become a kind of machine for grinding general laws out of large collections of facts"; "An Autobiographical Fragment, Written in 1838," in *Charles Darwin and Thomas Henry Huxley Autobiographies*, by Gavin de Beer, quoted in Beer, *Darwin's Plots*, 30.
146. On the displacement of the pigeons by the finches, see Weiner, *Beak of the Finch*, 35.

within the broader framework of a society's culture. Darwin's theory of evolution by natural selection has itself been our key example of just such a knowledge meme complex. It would be unfitting, from the perspectives both of the pragmatist and of the memeticist, to ask whether this particular meme complex is *true*, but one cannot help but enquire how *successful* it has been. How widely has it replicated? The answer, in fact, is "not very." David Hull points out that "Darwin published his theory of evolution in 1859. A century and a half later, the vast majority of human beings have never heard of Darwinian evolution. Of those who have heard of it, the vast majority do not understand it. Of those few who do understand it, most do not accept it."[147] Why this poor distribution and reception? What enduring selection pressures have been aligned against Darwinian theory that have so impeded its expansion?

Alfred Russel Wallace, who had arrived at an identical theory of evolution, provided one explanation for this "utter inability of numbers of intelligent persons to see clearly, or at all, the self-acting and necessary effects of Natural Selection."[148] He argued that Darwin's term itself,

natural selection, was not the "best adapted" for the job at hand. Darwin's analogy with artificial selection had been a little too effective, and careless readers had come to believe that evolution required some "intelligent chooser." Wallace argued, in effect, that misunderstandings regarding natural selection were the result of Darwin's failure to articulate sufficiently the most important aspect of his theory: that there was no prime mover. He suggested that Darwin adopt instead the phrase *survival of the fittest*, first used by Herbert Spencer. Darwin was sympathetic to Wallace's suggestion and incorporated Spencer's phrase into subsequent editions of *On the Origin of Species*, but he had reservations, not the least of which was that "it cannot be used as a substantive governing a verb."[149] The importance for any meme of its relative elegance and convenience of use was not lost on Darwin. He was reluctant to leave off using *natural selection* altogether and resolved to let the two terms fight it out in a battle for the survival of the fittest.[150] Stephen Jay Gould suggested that Darwin's theory remains unpalatable principally because it confounds humanity's long-held assumptions concerning its own worth. No longer the culmination or centerpiece of creation, fashioned in God's image, humans are relegated to a miniscule, recent, and entirely contingent twig on the tree of life. Natural selection dashes any notions of progress, natural harmony, or higher purpose, and especially of human necessity and inherent su-

147. Hull, "Taking Memetics Seriously," 55.
148. Wallace to Charles Darwin, July 2, 1866, in Darwin, *More Letters*, 1: 267. Wallace will return in "The Rule of Thumb" in chapter 5.
149. Darwin to Alfred Russel Wallace, July 5, 1866, in Darwin, *More Letters*, 1: 270–71.
150. In his own discussion of this epistolary exchange, Dawkins argues that the phrase *survival of the fittest* caused more problems than its predecessor ever did. He is keenly aware of the dangers of a misleading nomenclature, following the objections to his own term, *selfish gene*; see Dawkins, *Extended Phenotype*, 179–81.

periority. With these former certainties, the conclusion has been drawn, die all spiritual hopes and aspirations.[151] If Darwin did indeed solve the riddle of the Sphinx, single-handedly or otherwise, the answer is no longer as reassuring as it was in the time of Oedipus.

From a memetic point of view, these two explanations amount to the same thing: the environment in which Darwin's meme has continued to struggle has not been a welcoming one. What, however, of the meme meme itself? How has this mutant variant of Darwin's theory fared? Dennett once suggested that its spread had been initially curtailed by a particularly aggressive array of filters set up by "'humanist' minds" and that there had been a kind of "immunological rejection" of a theory that appeared suspiciously sociobiological.[152] Having now infected a "card-carrying academic humanist," which is to say himself, he hoped that its chances of replication had improved.[153] Since it first emerged in Dawkins's book, the term *meme* has in fact recurred in a wide range of texts, many of which have nothing to do with technical discussions of cultural transmission. Dawkins compares *meme* with a rival term, *culturgen*, proposed by Edward O. Wilson and Charles Lumsden at about the same time and meaning much the same thing. His own term has been significantly more successful, and he speculates that in this Darwinian struggle the monosyllabic form and the "quasi-genetic subcoinings" that are thus pos-

sible—meme pool, memotype, memeticist, memoid, retromeme, and more—may have been decisive.[154] The term has even become sufficiently widespread to be canonized by inclusion in the Oxford English Dictionary.[155]

Are memes confined to human beings? Need these practices be conceived as a form of cultural transmission that manifests only amongst human populations? Dennett, the card-carrying academic humanist, suggests that "by and large" memes are visible only to humans. In keeping with evolutionary tradition, he considers the urban pigeon, arguing that for those who inhabit New York City, the constant assault of words, pictures, signs, and symbols has no effect: "It is nothing to the pigeon that it is under a page of the *National Enquirer*, not the *New York*

---

151. Gould, introduction to *Evolution*. Gould himself argues, with characteristic optimism, that, on the contrary, Darwinism is "intellectually exhilarating" and permits us to seek "ethical rectitude, or spiritual meaning . . . within other domains of human inquiry"; ibid., xiii.

152. Dennett, "Memes and the Exploitation of Imagination," 134.

153. Since it first appeared in 1990, Dennett's discussion of memes has itself replicated with minor variations: it reappears in his *Consciousness Explained* (199–208) and also in his *Darwin's Dangerous Idea* (361–68).

154. Dawkins, foreword to *Meme Machine*, xiii–iv. Like Darwin, Dawkins was keen to settle on a snappy name for his new theory; see Dawkins, *Selfish Gene*, 192. On culturgens, see Blackmore, *Meme Machine*, 32–36.

155. Dawkins, *Selfish Gene*, 322; Dawkins, foreword to *Meme Machine*, viii. David Hull sounds a note of caution, however. He points out that Dawkins's was not the first attempt to provide an evolutionary account of culture (Richard Semon proposed the study of *mnemes* in 1904) and that memetics did not become established as a research program for some time after the publication of Dawkins's book; see Hull, "Taking Memetics Seriously," 50–52. George Dyson suggests that Samuel Butler had anticipated Dawkins's notion of memes as far back as the 1880s; see Dyson, *Darwin among the Machines*, 28.

83. Tit

In 1921, in the south of England, tits (small garden birds) were seen prising open the wax-board tops of milk bottles left on the doorstep. Subsequently, the habit became widespread across England and some parts of Scotland and Wales, with other species of bird joining in, and foil tops being pecked as well. That the tits learned from each other was suggested by the way the trick spread gradually from village to village, and across different areas, although it was obviously independently reinvented many times.

SUSAN BLACKMORE, *The Meme Machine*, 48.

"Blue Tit," photograph by Daniel Powderhill, 2009.

156. Dennett, *Consciousness Explained*, 204.

157. Ibid., 208.

158. Blackmore, *Meme Machine*, 50.

159. Dawkins, *Selfish Gene*, 190.

160. Dawkins, *Extended Phenotype*, 109.

161. Blackmore, *Meme Machine*, 48–49. Blackmore's suggestion that memes are (almost) uniquely human depends on distinguishing them from mere "social learning," which, she argues, does not count as true imitation; see Blackmore, *Meme Machine*, 47–51; Blackmore, "Memes' Eye View," 26–29. This restricted definition of imitation deviates from Dawkins's emphasis on imitation "in the broad sense" and, it has been argued, unnecessarily constrains the scope of memetics and arbitrarily excludes animal memes; see Dawkins, *Selfish Gene*, 192; Hull, "Taking Memetics Seriously," 44–45; Reader and Laland, "Do Animals Have Memes?"

Times, that it finds a crumb."[156] Memetic evolution, he says, is "restricted to one species, *Homo sapiens*."[157] Susan Blackmore argues in her book *The Meme Machine* that "only humans are capable of extensive memetic transmission."[158] And even Dawkins has suggested that although examples of cultural evolution have been observed in birds and monkeys, these are just "interesting oddities" and that "it is our own species that really shows what cultural evolution can do."[159]

The bird brains who appear in the work of Blackmore and Dawkins insist that both writers concede the existence of nonhuman memetic practices, however. Dawkins includes in his list of exemplary cases of memetic transmission the liberation of cow's milk by enterprising British **TITS**.[160] Even Blackmore, who discounts the pecking tits and has a stricter definition of what counts as true memetic imitation, acknowledges that many instances of the "special case" of birdsong qualify as genuine memes.[161] Dawkins describes one of the best examples: on a small group of islands off the coast of New Zealand lives the **SADDLEBACK** (*Philesturnus carunculatus*), a species of passerine, so called due to a conspicuous chestnut-colored patch across the bird's back. The rigidly defined territories of saddleback couples are maintained by means of mutual avoidance behavior, which is mediated by especially loud songs sung by the male. Groups of neighboring males sing the same songs, and young males, having dispersed to a new territory, learn their songs not from their father but from their neighbors. The songs are in fact memes, passed on by imitation. Further, a new song will periodically arise as the result of a mutation in this copying process.[162] Just as Darwin's saddle-backed tortoises helped point out one kind of evolutionary process, so these voluble, avian saddlebacks indicate another. Dawkins is unequivocal: humans may be especially accomplished imitators, but "cultural transmission is not unique to man."[163]

GETTING STUCK IN

Even granting that enterprising tits and territorial saddlebacks swap memes amongst themselves, it is not immediately apparent that this process should qualify as the exchange of knowledge. The memeticist identifies parallels between the songs of humans and birds, but is it appropriate to imply that a saddleback knows something when he sings? A human singer will know (or not) the words to "Auld Lang Syne" or "God Saves the Queen," but what is the knowing involved in a saddleback song? These suspicions, these questionable questions, betray a representationalism that is at odds with a genuinely pragmatic epistemology. Gatherer argued that memes are best conceived as patterns of behavior, as more or less habitual actions and activities (see "Handing On and Gathering In," above). For the pragmatic memeticist, knowledge is a matter neither of units of information in the

Saddleback (*Creadion carunculatus*), hand-painted lithographic print by John Gerrard Keulemans, in Walter Lawry Buller, *A History of the Birds of New Zealand*, 18.

84. SADDLEBACK

The male rhythmical song is used exclusively by site-attached pair-bonded adult males. . . . New song forms have been shown to arise variously by change of pitch of a note, repetition of a note, the elision of notes and the combination of parts of other existing songs. . . . In all cases the nature of the preceding song being imperfectly copied was well known over a period of years so that the new variant was immediately recognisable. The appearance of the new form was an abrupt event and the product was quite stable over a period of years. Further, in a number of cases the variant was transmitted accurately in its new form to younger recruits so that a recognizably coherent group of like singers developed.

P. F. JENKINS, "Cultural Transmission of Song Patterns and Dialect Development in a Free-Living Bird Population," 53, 76–77.

162. Dawkins, *Selfish Gene*, 189–90; Jenkins, "Cultural Transmission of Song Patterns"; Attenborough, *Life of Birds*, 178–79. For further birdsong memes, see Mundinger, "Animal Cultures," 192–95, 207–14; Lynch et al., "Cultural Evolution of Chaffinch Song"; and M. C. Baker, "Singing Honeyeaters."
163. Dawkins, *Selfish Gene*, 189.

brain nor of structures and representations in the mind; knowledge is practice itself. The distinctive songs of the saddleback are practices by means of which each bird identifies where any given territory begins and ends, and thus where he should forage, seek a mate, or establish a territory of his own. The bottle-top pecking that tits learn from one another is a practice, a mutating meme, that enables them to feast on the cream beneath the wax-board, cardboard, or foil.

The impulse to enquire after the knowledge that lies behind a practice, that makes that practice possible, is a representationalist inclination. Realist and relativist epistemologies alike embrace this characterization of knowledge as a representation, a reflection of the world. Whereas the realist seeks ever-more-accurate representations, always "polishing the mirror" to use Richard Rorty's suggestive phrase,[164] the relativist finds instead the unavoidable assumptions and beliefs of an interested party. For the realist, knowledge tells us about the world, the object of knowledge, whilst for the relativist it tells us about the worldview of the knower, the subject. Both approaches depend, however, on an understanding of knowledge as an entity distinct from the world it represents. A defining characteristic of pragmatism, in all its diverse forms, is that in its conception of the ontology of knowledge, it shuns this reliance on representation and adopts instead what Rorty calls an "antirepresentationalist" perspective. Whatever else it may be or do, knowledge is not for the pragmatist a representation, transcending the objects or subjects to which it corresponds.[165]

Knowledge, for the pragmatist, is part of the world. Rorty suggests, following John Dewey, that beliefs are "adaptations to the environment."[166] Like Boltzmann's laws of thought, knowledge takes shape—evolves, in fact—under the pressure of external stimuli. But this is not just a matter of the same evolutionary processes, of mutation and selection, taking place at the memetic as well as at the material level. Rather, by focusing on knowledge as a practice, as a set of recurring, transforming behaviors, it is conceived as an immediate, immanent element of the environment itself. Perhaps, mutatis mutandis, Bataille was right after all: there is a sense in which every animal is in the world like water in water (see "Like Water in Water" in chapter 1). The behavior of creatures immersed in their environments, humans included, is just as much a part of the world as the physical, brute entities themselves. Like the DIGITUS MINIMUS, that specialized adaptation that evolved in such a way that it can be employed to undertake those vital toilet operations inside the AURICULA, knowl-

164. Rorty, *Philosophy and the Mirror of Nature*, 12.
165. On what distinguishes antirepresentationalism from representationalism and why the former is not simply a linguistic version of Kant's transcendental idealism, see Rorty, *Objectivity, Relativism, and Truth*, part 1. Cary Wolfe has discussed the failure of much contemporary theory to avoid the representationalism shared by realism and relativism, as well as the benefits and limitations of Rorty's own brand of pragmatism; see Wolfe, *Critical Environments*, xii–xvii, 12–22.
166. Rorty, *Objectivity, Relativism, and Truth*, 10.

edge is a matter of activity and intervention, of getting stuck in.

For pragmatism, as an antirepresentationalist epistemology, knowledge does not depict the world but instead makes possible modes of activity in the world. It permits creatures in the know to pursue particular practices, or rather, it is the very process of that pursuit. The ministrations of that mundane, practical little finger may seem insignificant, but they are, as Frederic Wood Jones noted, indispensable. Their consequences, like the infinite paths of evolution itself, are unpredictable; just as, with a mere hand gesture, an entire philosophical system might be overthrown, so with one's little finger one might awaken the whole world. Here, as Ian Hacking put it, "the final arbitrator in philosophy is not how we think but what we do."[167] This practice-based pragmatism embraces not just the contingent, uneven processes and principles of evolutionary theory and the explanatory emphases of James and Boltzmann but also, as we have seen, the anti-Kantian engagement of an evaluative perspectivism. It is an inclusive, "renovated pragmatism" that encompasses, as Cary Wolfe would have it, a Nietzschean commitment to "radical plurality, contingency, historicity, and difference."[168]

During their shared train journey, Sraffa managed to shunt Wittgenstein's thought away from a model of language as representation toward a pragmatic understanding of discursive practices, or "language-games," as the latter would go on to call them. The form of this gentle jolt, the Torinese chin flick, made apparent to Wittgenstein that no picture or representation need be involved: "What is the logical form of *that*?" Though Sraffa used a hand gesture to make his point, though he deployed the organ so often associated with human uniqueness, the practice that formed the basis of his intervention helps illustrate that memes are by no means confined to humankind. With no chin to call their own, saddleback males have never had the option to flick one, but the loud, distinctive songs with which they mark their territories have much the same function as *la barbe*: those on the receiving end are being told, quite unequivocally, to buzz off. Even the memeticist who argues that human minds are composed of memes, are artifacts forged by selfish memetic restructuring, need not subscribe to epistemological anthropocentrism.

Protagoras claimed that "man is the measure of all things" (see the prelude). Our objective in the preceding chapters has been to enquire whether the assertions that humanity cannot know the world except by means of human aptitudes and abilities, that human beings will inescapably, unavoidably be the measure of all things, are intrinsic, incidental, or entirely extraneous to a diverse range of epistemological outlooks. At Socrates' prompting, Theaetetus

167. Hacking, *Representing and Intervening*, 31.
168. Wolfe, *Critical Environments*, xiv, 1.

attempted to examine the nature of knowledge by considering it in turn as perception, as true belief, and as true belief with an explanatory account. I have employed an alternative Procrustean schema in order to take in hand Nietzsche's *Erkennen* and his evaluations, Saussure's *signifiés*, Whorf's patternment, Kant's *Vorstellungen*, Dawkins's memes, and an unruly variety of approaches to the question that beset Theaetetus. Three epistemological paradigms—realism, relativism, and pragmatism—have been explored, each conceived as addressing three qualities of knowledge. Concerning the ontology of knowledge, which is to say what it *is*, writers across the paradigms characterized knowledge either as mediating representation or as immersive practice. With regard to the utility of knowledge, which is to say what it *does*, knowledge was characterized either as explanation of the world or as the interpretations of a worldview.

Finally, concerning the validity of knowledge, which is to say what it *claims*, philosophers have characterized knowledge alternately as transcendental truth or as partial perspective. For none of these properties need the thinker or theorist commit to a first-and-foremost, epistemological anthropocentrism, though we found that many, nonetheless, exhibited an unwarranted Protagorean prejudice. Two questions remain. On the one hand, we have yet to enquire after the nature of that peculiar creature, *anthrōpos*, who has purportedly held the center, and to ask, with Heidegger, "Who is man?" (see "If a Lion Had Hands" in chapter 1). On the other hand, we need to address, in this five-fingered treatise, the last and most distinctive of the digits, the thumb. In chapter 5 we will find that these two questions are most profitably addressed at one and the same time.

The Thumb Is a Little Hand, Assistant to the Greater

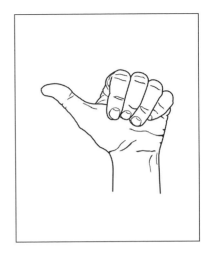

TO WE OR NOT TO WE

Something of our opening question remains unanswered. We began by asking whether a claim that has been asserted or assumed by a varied series of thinkers and theorists, that humanity can only ever know the world from an inescapable, distinctively human standpoint, was required by their epistemologies. We enquired, that is, into the necessity of the contention that humans are condemned to a first-and-foremost anthropocentrism. This Protagorean perspective, this particular form of humanist supposition, was found on reflection to be incidental or superfluous to the philosophies in which it so often occurred. Foucault argued that humanism is best understood as a set of themes and values that have reappeared, with significant variations and on several occasions, within European societies. These themes and values have been wide-ranging, divergent, and sometimes even contradictory. As such, "the humanistic thematic is in itself too supple, too diverse, too inconsistent to serve as an axis for reflec-

The chapter title comes from "Huic manui parva quaedam manus adiutrix data est, cui pollicis nomen" (To this hand a certain smaller hand is given as assistant, which is called the thumb); Albinus, *De ossibus corporis humani*, 290. Charles Bell invokes Albinus—"manus parva, maiori adiutrix"—in his own discussion of the thumb; see Bell, *Hand*, 114.

The importance of the thumb, often called the "fifth finger," has been recognized since ancient times. Galen tells us that Hippocrates called it the "great finger" (μέγας, megas), despite the fact that, as Aristotle later noted, it is actually the shortest of the fingers. It was known as the ἀντίχειρ (antikheir), meaning "another hand" or a "second hand," because, according to Macrobius, it "always has as much work to do as a whole hand." Isidore tells us that the thumb "opposes the other fingers with strength and power," for which reason it is called in Latin the POLLEX, from POLLERE (to be powerful, to exert influence). Montaigne devoted a short essay to this "master-finger," quoting from Martial, Horace, and Juvenal, amongst others. Albinus, the eighteenth-century anatomist, suggested that in the thumb the hand had been given an assistant, an additional "little hand." And, as the surgeon Charles Bell noted, "the loss of the thumb amounts almost to the loss of the hand."[1]

1. Galen, *Parts of the Body*, 107 (1: 22); Aristotle, *On the Parts of Animals*, 99–100 (687b); Macrobius, *Saturnalia*, 500 (7.13.7–14); Isidore of Seville, *Etymologiarum sive originum*, 11.1.70; Montaigne, "On Thumbs"; Albinus, *De ossibus corporis humani*, 290; Bell, *Hand*, 114; Bertelsen and Capener, "Fingers." The tale attributing to Isaac Newton the assertion, "In the absence of any other proof, the thumb alone would convince me of God's existence" is apocryphal.

tion."[2] Indeed, Heidegger's commentators failed to agree, in our first chapter, as to whether or not his thinking was anthropocentric, humanistic, or perhaps even hyperhumanistic (see "Into Your Hand They Are Delivered" in chapter 1). Heidegger himself rejected the term *humanism*, not because it was unstable or inconsistent but because in all its traditional forms, even in their "highest determinations," humanism failed to recognize the proper dignity of mankind, did not set the *humanitas* of humanity high enough.[3] In this final chapter we will find a convenient use for this supple term that was discarded, for different reasons, by both Foucault and Heidegger.

What, however, is the nature of the human being that provides the foundation, or axis of reflection, for humanism? Who or what is the *anthrōpos* that purports to be, or is accused of being, central? It was Heidegger who complained that the very question "Who is man?" has not been adequately asked. He argued that objections to humanization (*Vermenschung*) or to an-thropomorphism (*Vermenschlichung*), objections that trade in an implicit anthropocentrism, are mere idle talk if we have not yet asked this most basic of questions. We will have assumed, "ahead of time," that we know the answer to the question *Wer ist der Mensch?*[4] Have we approached our question backward, then? Should we have set out with Heidegger's more fundamental question at the start, rather than arriving at it here in our final chapter? Have we been engaged, all this time, in merely "superficial and specious discussion."[5] In his discussion of unfathomable animality, Georges Bataille privileged a human perspective, it was claimed, with his use of first-person pronouns (see "Like Water in Water" in chapter 1). But who was this first-and-foremost first person? Is it possible to interrogate anthropocentrism, or to ask after "our" knowledge and understanding, without first determining who that "we" is taken to be?

Richard Rorty has voiced similar suspicions concerning the validity of Foucault's political projects. In assessing Foucault's objectives, Rorty finds much to admire. He casts Foucault as a "knight of autonomy," a kind of "Romantic intellectual" valiantly pursuing a program of self-creation without recourse to illusory notions like a Kantian universal law.[6] At the same time, with his analyses of power, Foucault is "a useful citizen of a democratic country," attempting to achieve the same political consequences as any "good humanitarian bourgeois liberal" by seek-

---

2. Foucault, "What Is Enlightenment?" 44. Michael Hardt and Antonio Negri illustrate Foucault's point when they argue that since there are two distinct types of humanism—a humanism that conceives of humanity as fundamentally separate from nature and a revolutionary, antitranscendental Renaissance humanism—it is not paradoxical to suggest that in his later work Foucault himself, "the thinker who carried the banner of antihumanism throughout his career," was pursuing a "humanism after the death of Man"; Hardt and Negri, *Empire*, 91–92.

3. Heidegger, "Letter on Humanism," 233–34.

4. Heidegger, *Nietzsche*, 98–105 (chapter 13); see "If a Lion Had Hands" in chapter 1.

5. Heidegger, *Nietzsche*, 102.

6. Rorty, "Moral Identity and Private Autonomy," 194, 193.

ing to alleviate unnecessary suffering.[7] Foucault, Rorty suggests, is an up-to-date John Dewey.[8] Problems arise, however, when Foucault fails to separate these private (ethical) and public (moral) selves and begins to intimate that people have a moral duty to pursue inner autonomy. This is dangerous, Nietzschean, anarchistic posturing, wholly at odds with the liberal's tolerant pluralism. As a philosopher, Foucault is free to pursue as many projects of self-invention as he likes; they are nobody's business but his own. As a political writer, however, he should acknowledge the gains made by the modern liberal state, which, after all, makes possible, without prejudice, the eccentric pursuits of religious mystics, sexual fetishists, and even Romantic intellectuals.[9] As a philosopher, Rorty argues, Foucault can refuse to answer demands that he declare his allegiances and values, but as a good humanitarian bourgeois liberal he should really declare, proudly, "I stand with you as a fellow-citizen."[10]

Rorty takes Foucault to be mining one of those seams of Western humanism. The problem, as Rorty sees it, is that Foucault is not humanist enough. Unlike Dewey's, his vocabulary does not allow room for that "vital sense of human solidarity."[11] Even whilst pursuing his analyses of "normalizing power" in the arenas of madness, the clinic, sexuality, and so on, Foucault fails to acknowledge the fact that he himself belongs to a particular community of thinkers, a particular "we." Like those impetu-

ous thinkers making accusations or critiques of Vermenschung, Foucault, in essence, fails to pose a question that should be addressed first of all. Rorty suggests that it takes "no more than a squint of the inner eye to read Foucault as a stoic, a dispassionate observer of the present social order, rather than its concerned critic."[12] The self-denying philosopher "forbids himself the tone of the liberal sort of thinker who says to his fellow-citizens: 'We know that there must be a better way to do things than this; let us look for it together.' There is no 'we' to be found in Foucault's writings."[13]

Shortly before his death, Foucault addressed Rorty's criticisms in an interview with Paul Rabinow. Rabinow points out that Foucault has been read "as an idealist, as a nihilist, as a 'new

7. Ibid., 198, 195.
8. Ibid., 193; see also Rorty, "Method, Social Science, and Social Hope," 203–8.
9. Rorty, "Moral Identity and Private Autonomy," 194–95, 197.
10. Ibid. Cary Wolfe has criticized Rorty's failure here to appreciate "the very core of Foucault's work on the relationship between power and knowledge," his Romantic characterization of the liberal state, his homogenized "we," his debilitating humanism, and his ethnocentrism; see Wolfe, Critical Environments, 16–21, 88–101. See also Carol J. Adams's criticisms of the anthropocentrism implicit in this kind of autonomous, pluralist perspective; see Adams, Neither Man nor Beast, 121–23.
11. Rorty, "Method, Social Science, and Social Hope," 208. Rorty suggests that perhaps the most important thing the social sciences have done has been to make it possible to consider an exotic range of different specimens of humanity as "one of us" (203) without recourse to the notion of a common human nature or some other kind of "Brotherhood of Man" (207).
12. Rorty, "Habermas and Lyotard," 173.
13. Ibid., 174. Christopher Norris has argued that we might best interpret Rorty's "shrewdly angled misreading" as an "imminent critique of Foucault's entire project"; see C. Norris, "'What Is Enlightenment?'" 37–50, quotations at 50 and 47.

philosopher,' as an anti-Marxist, a new conservative, and so on." And so he is prompted to ask, "Where do you stand?"[14] Foucault is clearly delighted by the fact that he has, at one time or another, "been situated in most of the squares of the political checkerboard, one after another and sometimes simultaneously." He admits that he prefers not to identify himself with any political position. As he warms to his theme, he begins to develop this refusal into the outline of a methodology. He takes issue with the assumptions that underlie Rorty's criticism: "R. Rorty points out that in (my) analyses I do not appeal to any 'we'—to any of those 'we's' whose consensus, whose values, whose traditions constitute the framework for a thought and define the conditions in which it can be validated."[15] This accusation, however, misses Foucault's point:

> The problem is, precisely, to decide if it is actually suitable to place oneself within a "we" in

order to assert the principles one recognizes and the values one accepts; or if it is not, rather, necessary to make the future formation of a "we" possible, by elaborating the question. Because it seems to me that the "we" must not be previous to the question; it can only be the result—and the necessarily temporary result—of the question as it is posed in the new terms in which one formulates it.[16]

This was not a new theme for Foucault. In an interview conducted after the publication of *The Order of Things*, Paolo Caruso had also asked the question that Foucault always refused to answer: "Who are you, Professor Foucault?"[17] Caruso's first tactic for securing an answer is to ask Foucault about his "cultural education" and the route he has taken to reach his current thinking. Foucault is uncomfortable with the question: "It is rather difficult for me to describe the route that has led me to my current positions, for the very good reason that I hope, precisely, that I have not already got to the point of arrival. . . . The book I published last year . . . is a transitional book, a book which enables me, which I hope will enable me, to go further."[18] Foucault is equally unhappy with Caruso's next suggestion, that he indicate the direction in which he is heading. Foucault's objective, always, is not to reach a destination, to arrive at a position or stance, but rather to write in order to discover *new* ways of thinking, as he asserts in *The Archaeology of Knowledge*:

14. Foucault, "Polemics, Politics, and Problematizations," 383.

15. Ibid., 385.

16. Ibid. Rorty in response makes clear that it is precisely on the question of an explicitly acknowledged "we," and preferably "we liberals," that he disagrees most strongly with Foucault; see Rorty, *Contingency, Irony, and Solidarity*, 64.

17. Like Rorty and like Hardt and Negri, Caruso is insistent that Foucault still supports or harbors his own kind of humanism. Foucault will have none of it, describing humanism variously as "soft . . . sterile . . . noxious, harmful"; Foucault, "Who Are You, Professor Foucault?" 99–103.

18. Foucault, "Who Are You, Professor Foucault?" 87; see also Foucault, "Truth, Power, Self," 9. Foucault would often refuse to answer questions of an autobiographical nature. See especially the interview with Christian Delacampagne, first published anonymously in *Le Monde*, entitled "The Masked Philosopher," and also "Foucault," the short (auto)biography that he wrote under the pseudonym Maurice Florence.

85. MINOTAUR

[Pasiphae] gave birth to Asterius who was called the Minotaur. He had the face of a bull, but the rest of him was human; and Minos, in compliance with certain oracles, shut him up and guarded him in the Labyrinth. Now the Labyrinth which Daedalus constructed was a chamber "that with its tangled windings perplexed the outward way." . . . [Ariadne] besought Daedalus to disclose the way out of the labyrinth. And at his suggestion she gave Theseus a clue when he went in; Theseus fastened it to the door, and, drawing it after him, entered in. And having found the Minotaur in the last part of the labyrinth, he killed him by smiting him with his fists; and drawing the clue after him made his way out again.

APOLLODORUS, *The Library*, 1: 304–7 (3.1.4), 2: 134–37 (Epitome 1.8–9).

Illustration by Edmund Dulac, in Nathaniel Hawthorne, *Tanglewood Tales*, 46.

What, do you imagine that I would take so much pain and so much pleasure in writing, do you think that I would be so obstinate, head down, if I were not preparing—with a slightly feverish hand—a labyrinth into which I can venture, in which I can displace my proposal, undermine it with underground passages, bury it far from itself, find for it overhangs that condense and deform its course, in which I can lose myself and appear finally to eyes that I shall never have to meet again. More than one person, doubtless like myself, writes in order no longer to have a face. Do not ask me who I am, and do not tell me to stay the same: that is the question of a state bureaucracy; that morality keeps our papers in order. Spare us that morality when we write.[19]

Foucault's objective, then, is precisely not to declare his position, as a philosopher, a Romantic intellectual, a humanitarian bourgeois liberal, or a sexual fetishist, and certainly not as a good citizen of a democratic state. His continuing mission, rather, is to explore new worlds, to seek out new forms of life and civilization, to boldly go where no one has gone before. He

19. Foucault, *L'Archéologie du savoir*, 28, translated by Monica Tyler; compare this to the same passage in the standard English edition, translated by A. M. Sheridan Smith: Foucault, *Archaeology of Knowledge*, 17. Sheridan Smith's translation does not capture the full extent of the subterranean, labyrinthine imagery of Foucault's original. On the importance to Foucault, as an author, of an "ethics of thought" that works toward discovering "new forms of subjectivity," see Wolfe, *Critical Environments*, 98–101; Foucault, "Preface," 339.

writes in order to discover new directions, in order to excavate fresh, untraveled tunnels in a labyrinth of his own making.[20] His objective is to write toward a new, yet unknown "we." The "we" cannot, must not, precede the question. The "we" of our own analysis has, then, necessarily been left undefined. We have, perhaps with a slightly feverish hand, asked after the inevitability of anthropocentrism, without yet articulating, contra Heidegger and Rorty, the nature either of *anthrōpos* or of the "we" with which it is so often identified. It is time now to take the bull by the horns and to assess whether all the philosophical investigation, the labyrinthine tunneling, has brought us to the possibility of a new "we." We begin by returning to that distinctive, distinguishing human organ, the hand.

IF I HAD A HAMMER

In 1829, Francis Henry Egerton, eighth and last Earl of Bridgewater, died at the age of seventy-two. A zealous naturalist, he left instructions in his will, as well as the considerable sum of eight thousand pounds to see that they were carried out, directing the president of the Royal Society of London to nominate a person or persons to write, print, and publish a work

> on the Power, Wisdom, and Goodness of God, as manifested in the Creation; illustrating such work by all reasonable arguments,

as, for instance, the variety and formation of God's creatures in the animal, vegetable, and mineral kingdoms; the effect of digestion, and thereby of conversion; the construction of the hand of man, and an infinite variety of other arguments; as also by discoveries ancient and modern, in arts, sciences, and the whole extent of literature.[21]

Eight texts, called the Bridgewater Treatises, were produced during the 1830s by eight different authors, including *On Astronomy and General Physics* (by William Whewell), *On Geology and Mineralogy* (by William Buckland), and *On Chemistry, Meteorology, and the Function of Digestion* (by William Prout). The fourth Bridgewater Treatise, published in 1833, was written by the surgeon Charles Bell and entitled *The Hand: Its Mechanism and Vital Endowments as Evincing Design.*

Bell began his treatise in suitably reverent fashion: "If we select any object from the whole extent of animated nature, and contemplate it fully and in all its bearings, we shall certainly come to this conclusion: that there is Design in the mechanical construction, Benevolence in the endowments of the living properties, and that Good on the whole is the result."[22] The human body, like all else in nature, he argued, has been specially created to correspond with the external parts of the great system that is the world (7–8). The inhabitants of the planet have been shaped in relation to the whole, "planned together and fashioned by one Mind" (9). Whether one stud-

---

20. Foucault discusses how the labyrinth both hides and reveals the truth and nature of the Minotaur in *Death and the Labyrinth*, 87.

21. [Editor], "Notice," possibly quoting Egerton, in Bell, *Hand*, v.

22. Bell, *Hand*, 1. Further references are in the text.

ies the most minute or the most comprehensive subject, everywhere one will be made aware of "Prospective Design" (16–17). Given that this is the case, Bell argues, the objective, nay the duty of science, should rightly be the contemplation of God's work, and lack of such reflection amounts, in fact, to ingratitude. Linnaeus's acorn-eating brutes, who wander about the woods without ever looking up at the source of their food, might be forgiven, but as the sole species capable of comprehending and valuing the work of the "Beneficent Author," failure by man to reflect on God's work amounts to impiety and ungratefulness (10–11, 14). So complacent has man become, Bell continues, due to a continuing habit of inattention, that only the especially uncommon or monstrous rouses attention: we are more likely to marvel at the elephant's trunk than at that most beautiful, most accomplished, most outstanding of instruments, the human hand (14).

The hand, Bell argues, is the organ that corresponds most remarkably with man's capacities (2). In it, a large number of properties that are shared with the brutes are brought to perfection. The combination of strength with the ability to perform varied, extensive, and rapid motion; the power of the thumb and the form, relations, and sensibility of the fingers that permit unprecedented holding, pulling, spinning, weaving, and constructing: all these correspond to the superior mental capacities with which man has been endowed, allowing him to carry out what-

ever he conceives (252–53). "We ought to define the Hand as belonging exclusively to Man—corresponding in its sensibility and motion to the endowments of his Mind, and especially to that ingenuity which, through means of it, converts the being who is weakest in natural defence, to be the ruler over animate and inanimate nature" (18). Man is superior to the brutes with regard to his mind, allowing him to exist in every climate and to survive on every variety of nutriment, but it is the hand that makes all this possible and that, "by its correspondence with the intellect," allows him "universal dominion" (41). Bell refers time and again to the perfection of the human hand, a perfection that speaks simultaneously of the benevolence of a divine author and the preeminence of the recipient of that design (15, 252, and passim).

In pursuing his demonstration, Bell's wide-ranging treatise explores many different aspects of the hand. He dwells for several chapters on comparative anatomy; looks at the muscles of the hand and forearm; examines the sense of touch, which, he declares, is "seated in the hand" (190); discusses the dependence of the eye on the hand, and much more. All of these point, he argues, toward the existence of a comprehensive system that embraces not just man but all the creatures of the earth. Whenever we look at the organs of any animal, we find that they are "moulded with such a perfect accommodation to their uses," are adapted so exquisitely to the

Thomas Bewick, *The Sloth*, 1790, in Blanche Cirker, ed., *1800 Woodcuts by Thomas Bewick and His School*, plate 42.

86. SLOTH

Modern travellers express pity for these slow-paced animals. Whilst other quadrupeds, they say, range in boundless wilds, the sloth hangs suspended by his strong arms,—a poor ill-formed creature, deficient as well as deformed, his hind legs too short, and his hair like withered grass; his looks, motions, and cries, conspire to excite pity; and, as if this were not enough, they say that his moaning causes the tiger to relent and turn away. But that is not a true picture: the sloth cannot walk like many other quadrupeds, but he stretches out his arms, and if he can hook on his claws to the inequalities of the ground, he drags himself along. This condition it is which gives occasion to such an expression as "the bungled and faulty composition of the sloth." But if with his claws he can reach the branch or the rough bark of a tree, then will his progress be rapid; he will climb hand over head along the branches till they touch, thus getting from bough to bough, and tree to tree; in the storm he is most alive; it is when the wind blows, and the trees stoop, and the branches wave and meet, that he is upon the march.

CHARLES BELL, *The Hand*, 29–30.

creature's conditions and environment, that it is inconceivable that they could have been the result of some merely accidental external agency (166). If we compare the human hand to the extremities of the three-fingered **SLOTH** or with the horse's hoof or even with the wing of a bird, we find that "there is no regular gradation but, as I have often to repeat, a variety, which most curi-ously adapts the same system of parts to every necessary purpose" (29–39, 90). The same basic system of bones is preserved in each case, but it is "variously modified" so that it is appropriate for the uses to which it will be put (175). There are analogous body parts across all vertebrate spe-cies, and these have, in each case, been adapted perfectly by God to the function that they are required to play within each creature's particular environment. When Bell talks about adaptation, then, he does not mean the term in an evolu-tionary sense. Rather, just as the late earl had intended, his work elaborates an argument from design: "the Hand . . . presents the last and best proof in the order of creation, of that principle of adaptation which evinces design" (41). In the hand of man, we see the hand of God.

Kant had earlier suggested that it is by means of the hand that nature enables mankind to employ reason:

> The characterisation of man as a rational animal is already present in the form and organization of the human hand, partly by the structure and partly by the sensitive feeling of the fingers and fingertips. By this nature made him fit for ma-nipulating things not in one particular way but in any way whatsoever, and so for using reason, and indicating the technical predisposition—or the predisposition for skill—of his species as a rational animal.[23]

Nature, in other words, gives the hand to man, and only to man, because he alone amongst all the

23. Kant, *Anthropology*, 184–85 (323).

beasts and brutes is in a position to make use of it. The suggestion that this singular hand has been given only to man has a long and distinguished history. Galen opened his treatise *On the Usefulness of the Parts of the Body* with a book devoted entirely to the hand. He there points out that, thanks to the hands bestowed on him by nature, man surpasses the natural attributes of the beasts: his weapons are better than any claws, hooves, tusks, or horns, and his armor and defenses better than any skin. With his hands man can weave cloaks or fashion traps, write laws, raise altars and statues, build ships, make musical instruments, knives, and fire tongs, and even record commentaries on all these things.[24] "Thus man is the most intelligent of the animals and so, also, hands are the instruments most suitable for an intelligent animal. For it is not because he has hands that he is the most intelligent, as Anaxagoras says, but because he is the most intelligent that he has hands, as Aristotle says, judging most correctly."[25]

The passage Galen has in mind, and on which he draws heavily for his discussion of hands, is to be found in Aristotle's *On the Parts of Animals*, in which the great philosopher argues, like Bell, that all animals have been constructed with bodies that perfectly fit their nature and situation.[26]

> Now Anaxagoras said it was because they have hands that human beings are the most intelligent animals; it is reasonable, however, that it is because they are most intelligent that human

beings are given hands. For the hands are instruments and nature, like an intelligent human being, always apportions each instrument to the one able to use it. Surely it is more fitting to give flutes to the flautist than to provide the ability to play flutes to one who has them; for nature has provided the lesser to the greater and superior, not the more honourable and great to the lesser. So if it is better thus, and nature does, among the possibilities, what is best, it is not because they have hands that human beings are most intelligent, but because they are the most intelligent of animals that they have hands. For the most intelligent animal would use the greatest number of instruments well, and the hand would seem to be not one instrument, but many; indeed it is, as it were, an instrument for instruments. Accordingly, to the one able to acquire the most arts, nature has provided the most useful of instruments, the hand.[27]

Bell takes up this Aristotelian, teleological account of the hand:

> Seeing the perfection of the human Hand, both in structure and endowments, we can hardly be surprised at some philosophers entertaining the opinion of Anaxagoras, that the superiority of man is owing to his hand. . . . Nevertheless, the possession of the ready implement, is not the cause of man's superiority: nor is its aptness for execution, the measure of his attainments. So we

24. Galen, *Parts of the Body*, 67–69 (1: 2). Bell quotes approvingly from this passage; see Bell, *Hand*, 20.
25. Galen, *Parts of the Body*, 69 (1: 3).
26. Aristotle, *On the Parts of Animals*, 98–100 (4:687a–687b).
27. Ibid., 98–99 (4:687a). On this passage, see the editor's commentary (320–21) and Aulie, *Reader's Guide*, part 2.

Green Heron (*Ardea virescens*) by John James Audubon, engraved by Robert Havell, in John James Audubon, *The Birds of America*, plate 333.

87. HERON

In a city park in Japan, a hungry, green-backed heron picks up a twig, breaks it into small pieces, and carries one of these to the edge of a pond, where she drops it into the water. At first it drifts away, but she picks it up and brings it back. She watches the floating twig intently until small minnows swim up to it, and she then seizes one by a rapid thrusting grab with her long sharp bill. Another green-backed heron from the same colony carries bits of material to a branch extending out over the pond and tosses the bait into the water below. When minnows approach this bait, he flies down and seizes one on the wing.

DONALD R. GRIFFIN, Animal Minds, 2.

28. On the wide range of fishing techniques employed by different herons, including that described by Bell, see Griffin, *Animal Minds*, 2, 110–14.

rather say with Galen, that man has a hand, because he is the wisest of creatures, than ascribe to his possession of a hand, his superiority in knowledge. (252–53)

Passing over Aristotle's flautist, Bell seeks to demonstrate this point with rather different examples. Consider, he says, the **HERON**, still as a grey stone and hardly distinguishable from it, standing by the water and intently watching out for prey. We might be tempted to entertain the opinion that he acquired his particular mode of fishing from the use of his ideally suited stilt-like limbs, long bill, and flexible neck.[28] But consider, too, the **BLACK BEAR** carrying out the same task. He sits by the side of the stream on his hind extremities, patiently awaiting his opportunity. When the moment comes, he is every inch the perfect fisherman, despite the fact that he has no appropriate exterior organ like the heron (253). Does this not demonstrate, asks Bell, that it cannot be the organ that bestows the habit or instinct? Rather, "animals have propensities implanted in them, to perform certain motions to which their external organs are subservient" (256). As further illustration of this point, Bell recounts the story of a certain Russian bandit who, deprived of arms from birth, nonetheless set about highway robbery and murder. "His manner was to throw his head against the stomach of the person who was in the act of giving him charity, and having stunned him, to seize him with his teeth, and so drag him into the wood!" (256–57). The propensity can exist without the corresponding outward organs, but without the propensity these organs would be "useless appendages" (260).

What, however, of Anaxagoras himself, rebutted in turn by Aristotle, Galen, and Bell? Little of his work survives, and it does not include what he had to say about hands. Indeed, the only account of his thoughts on the matter is Aristotle's critique.[29] For an explicit argument that the hand came first, that, as Anaxagoras (allegedly) said, "it was because they have hands that human beings are the most intelligent animals," we turn to more recent authors. In his unfinished essay "The Part Played by Labour in the Transition from Ape to Man," Frederick Engels asserts, "[Labour] is the prime basic condition for all human existence, and this to such an extent that, in a sense, we have to say that labour created man himself."[30] But what, Engels feels compelled to investigate, made labor possible? Drawing on Darwin, Engels suggests that many hundreds of millennia ago a particularly highly developed race of anthropoid apes, who were "completely covered with hair, . . . had beards and pointed ears," came down from the trees (251).[31] Unlike their fellows, rather than "rest the knuckles of the fist on the ground and, with legs drawn up, swing the body through their long arms" (251), these enterprising apes began to adopt an increasingly erect posture. This, says Engels, was the decisive moment in the transition from ape

88. BLACK BEAR
A variety of techniques is used to catch fish and each bear has its own individual style. A commonly employed method is to plunge headfirst into the river from land and grab a fish with the front paws or the jaws; inexperienced bears may land with a "belly flop" (thereby scaring all the fish away!). Alternatively, a bear may use the centre of the river as a place of attack, sometimes even swimming under water, rushing at the fish with jaws open. At places where fish are able to jump clear of the rapids, bears may wait and snap the fish out of the air with paws or jaws.

PAUL WARD AND SUZANNE KYNASTON, *Bears of the World*, 97.

Photograph copyright 2010 by Darren Darbyshire.

to man. Freed from the business of locomotion, diverse new functions devolved upon the hands of these apelike ancestors. With increased use came increased dexterity and, in time, the evolution of the vastly superior, "perfected" human

29. For Anaxagoras's extant fragments, see Fairbanks, *First Philosophers of Greece*, 235–62.
30. Engels, "Transition from Ape to Man," 251. Further references are in the text.
31. See Darwin, *Descent of Man*, 50–53.

89. AUSTRALOPITHECUS

On the whole, the evidence indicates Lucy could climb trees to feed, but preferred to move on the ground. Evidence . . . indicates that *Australopithecus afarensis* had chimpanzee-like semicircular canals (an organ of balance found in the inner ear) and a gorilla-like shoulder blade, indicating it would have used its forelimbs for weight support, as do gorillas. *Australopithecus afarensis* ground movement would have included a two-legged gait, especially when feeding. Four-legged movements, however, were probably utilized when moving quickly or in heavy undergrowth. . . . *Australopithecus afarensis* remains predate tools by approximately half a million years.

ESTEBAN SARMIENTO, G. J. SAWYER, AND RICHARD MILNER, *The Last Human*, 69–72.

Australopithecus afarensis. "Lucy Eating." Copyright by Viktor Deak.

32. See, for instance, Eleanor Burke Leacock's 1972 introduction to Engels's essay; in Engels, "Transition from Ape to Man," 245–49.
33. Washburn, "Tools and Human Evolution," 62. On the key points of Washburn's article as they relate to the primacy of the hand, see F. R. Wilson, *Hand*, 15–18.
34. On the australopithecines, see also Washburn and Avis, "Evolution of Human Behavior," 429–35.
35. Washburn, "Tools and Human Evolution," 69.
36. Ibid., 69–71.

hand (252). Thereafter, a range of dependent developments followed, including increased sociability, language, larger brain size, superior senses, society, a meat diet, fire, and the domestication of animals. Labor itself, properly so called, began with the manufacture and use of tools (256). From our modern vantage point, Engels argues, all this is too readily and idealistically attributed to the mind, which so often plans labor but has it carried out by the hands of others (258). We forget the fundamental importance of the hand itself, the organ that made labor possible and was thus responsible for all the progressive refinements that distinguish humans from their bearded ancestors (252).

Engels's conjectures regarding the importance of tools seemed to be confirmed by research undertaken during the late 1950s and 1960s by the anthropologist Sherwood L. Washburn.[32] Washburn described humanity's direct ancestors, perhaps less evocatively than did Engels, as "not-fully bipedal, small-brained near-men, or man-apes."[33] He speculated that these creatures, the australopithecines, were able to run but not yet walk on two legs.[34] This limited bipedalism "left the hands sufficiently free from locomotor functions so that stones or sticks could be carried, played with and used."[35] The advantages that this restricted tool use gave to **AUSTRALOPITHECUS** led, Washburn argues, to increased bipedalism and thence to more-efficient tool use. The increased use of the hand,

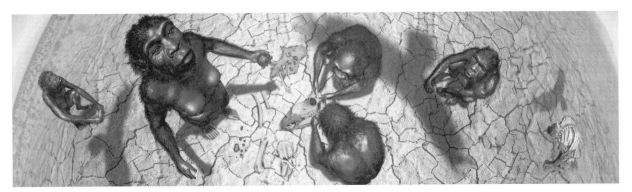

Homo habilis. "Lakebed Lunch." Copyright by Viktor Deak.

for a greater variety of tasks using tools, changed the selection pressures acting on the body, especially on the teeth, hands, and brain. As the functions of seizing and pulling were transferred from teeth to hands, canines became reduced and jaws shortened. The whole structure of the skull changed, and it eventually became much larger, as the brain grew in order to control an increasingly dextrous hand.[36] "The selection pressures that favored a large thumb also favored a large cortical area to receive sensations from the thumb and to control its motor activity. Evolution favored the development of a sensitive, powerful, skilful thumb."[37] In short, Washburn argues that the large human brain evolved as a result of increasing use of the hand amongst humanity's immediate ancestors.[38]

Washburn made his claims about the "man-apes" just as an especially significant set of fossils were being unearthed in the Olduvai Gorge of Tanzania, in East Africa. These were the remains

90. HANDY MAN

Throughout its lifespan at Olduvai, Homo habilis is associated with tools. In fact, its tool association provides an important part of its definition as a species. Tools found in Bed I upper member are of the Oldowan tradition, consisting of hammer-stones and simple flakes. Lower Bed II shows more advanced Oldowan tools, referred to as Developed Oldowan, in which stones are worked on two sides producing bifaces. Animal bones found in the H. habilis deposits show cut marks indicating meat was stripped from the bone. . . . Most of the fossil skulls upon which this species is based are those of females and/or immature individuals. . . . In a 1964 April issue of Nature, Louis Leakey, Phillip Tobias, and [John] Napier described the new species H. habilis. . . . They also revised the definition of Homo to better differentiate it, and the new fossils they included in it, from Australopithecus. At the suggestion of Raymond Dart, "habilis" (which in Latin means "able, handy, mentally skilful, vigorous") was chosen as the species name to emphasize this hominid's mental capacity and toolmaking skills.

ESTEBAN SARMIENTO, G. J. SAWYER, AND RICHARD MILNER, *The Last Human*, 125–30.

---

37. Ibid., 73.

38. Washburn and Avis, "Evolution of Human Behavior," 434–35. For a fascinating survey and critique of Washburn's work, see Haraway, *Primate Visions*, 203–217.

of a previously unknown hominid species, which the archaeologist Louis Leakey believed to be the earliest yet identified member of the genus *Homo*. Australopithecines were part of human ancestry, but this, he argued, was the earliest human. Accordingly, the new species was named *Homo habilis*, the **HANDY MAN**.[39] *Homo habilis* had a much thinner cranium, smaller cheek teeth, and a significantly larger brain than any of the various species of *Australopithecus*. In naming this new creature a species of *Homo*, however, Leakey broke with established anthropological

convention. The brain capacity calculated from the fragment of cranium was only 650 cubic centimeters, a full 100 cubic centimeters short of the "cerebral Rubicon" long accepted as the minimum necessary for a species to qualify as a member of the genus *Homo*. Leakey felt justified in this appellation on account of the more humanlike, less robust cranium and on the supposition, based on primitive stone artifacts found at the site, that members of the new species were toolmakers.[40] Washburn had claimed that "most of the obvious differences that distinguish man from ape came after the use of tools," that is, as the result of the increased use of the hand.[41] His suggestion has fallen out of favor,[42] and there is doubt too as to whether Leakey's *Homo habilis* should in fact be considered a direct human ancestor.[43] Nonetheless, for Leakey as for Washburn and Engels, it was the hand that made humanity possible.

Bell, following Aristotle, Galen, and Kant, argues that intelligence is primary. Washburn, following Anaxagoras, Darwin, and Engels, argues that the hand is more fundamental. But in *what sense* does each party suggest that one or the other is foremost? Although the hand was clearly of paramount importance for Washburn, he is also careful to point out that the brain became enlarged as a result of a system of feedback between tool use and bipedalism, in which each was both cause and effect of the other's advances.[44] Hand and brain moved forward by

39. The first of these fossils was discovered in 1959, although the new species would not be named until 1964; see Sarmiento, Sawyer, and Milner, *Last Human*, 130; F. R. Wilson, *Hand*, 319–20n7.

40. Leakey, *Origin of Humankind*, 26–29; Kingdon, *Lowly Origin*, 221–22; Sarmiento, Sawyer, and Milner, *Last Human*, 127–28, 130; Corbey, *Metaphysics of Apes*, 96–107 (4.1).

41. Washburn, "Tools and Human Evolution," 63; see also Washburn and Avis, "Evolution of Human Behavior," 427–28.

42. Louis Leakey's son, Richard, argues that bipedalism evolved about 7 million years ago as a more efficient means of locomotion and had nothing at all to do with tool use or an increased brain size, which did not appear until about 2.5 million years ago; see Leakey, *Origin of Humankind*, 12–19. The beginnings of a bipedal gait, along with so much else in the ongoing attempt to recount human origins, is a contentious and unresolved issue; speculations take place, as Jonathan Kingdon puts it, within "a theater for intellectual daring"; Kingdon, *Lowly Origin*, 16. That an erect gait provides the "great conceptual divide" between "Apes" and "Hominids" is the principal theme of Kingdon's own book (2). For a concise list of thirteen or so different hypotheses concerning the origin of bipedalism, see Kingdon, *Lowly Origin*, 16–17; for a survey of evolving explanations of increased brain size, see Leakey, *Origin of Humankind*, 10–12; for a fuller account of changing anthropological fashions, see Haraway, *Primate Visions*, 186–229 (chapter 8).

43. Kingdon, *Lowly Origin*, 341; Sarmiento, Sawyer, and Milner, *Last Human*, 129–30. This is also true of Lucy; see Kingdon, *Lowly Origin*, 23, 170–78; Sarmiento, Sawyer, and Milner, *Last Human*, 74. On successive reconstructions of human ancestry, see especially the diagrams in Kingdon, *Lowly Origin*, 9, 232.

increments, and in reality they evolved together. Similarly, although Aristotle asserts that it is because they are most intelligent that human beings are given hands, the order of precedence here is not chronological. Precisely because he does not believe in the transmutation of animal forms, there can be no sense, for Aristotle, of one faculty or organ preceding another. For both parties, then, the hand and the capacity to make use of it come into being together. The key disagreement here concerns not temporal precedence but, rather, that venerable opposition between evolution and design. On the one hand, for those writers concerned with a created universe, such as Aristotle and Bell, the questions one needs to ask of the structure or of any part of an organism are what purpose it serves and why it was created as it was. Answers will tend to be teleological, since they will attempt to explain the ends that the creator (nature, the gods, God) had in mind when any given structure or part was designed. The hand was created to serve particular functions and purposes, as Aristotle, Galen, and Bell explain: it evinces design.[45]

On the other hand, for writers concerned with an evolving universe, such as Engels or Washburn, the questions that need to be asked are, What are the *antecedents* that produced this structure? How did it develop? We need not posit any objective or end for which the organ has been composed. It has evolved historically, and the function it (currently) fulfills must be

explained as a temporal, temporary adaptation. Lucy used her hands, if Washburn is to be believed, for carrying stones and sticks, which eventually led, according to Leakey, to the use of stone flakes by *Homo habilis*. Neither of these developments were planned or inevitable.

Despite these differences, however, and they are significant, there is a key respect in which the two parties are in agreement. Both consider the hand to be distinctively and tellingly human. For both Aristotle and Engels, for both Kant and Leakey, it is the hand that marks out what is special about this particular animal, so adept at manipulation, that they call "man." For both parties, the hand and humanity go together, hand in hand. The Scottish anatomist John Goodsir, writing just a little after Bell, perhaps put it most succinctly: "The human hand is the only perfect or complete hand."[46] This emphasis on the humanity of the hand, this insistence on tying the hand to what is most human, pervades the work of physician and philosopher alike, but there is something just a little underhanded about these time-honored arguments. On the one hand, we are told that the hand is a distinctively human organ; as Bell argues, "We ought to define the Hand as belonging exclusively to Man," cor-

44. Washburn, "Tools and Human Evolution," 69, 75. Compare Engels's claim that "the hand is not only the organ of labour, *it is also the product of labour*"; Engels, "Transition from Ape to Man," 252.
45. On the teleology or "finalism" of Aristotle's biology, see Aulie, *Reader's Guide*, part 2.
46. Goodsir, *Anatomical Memoirs*, 1: 238, quoted in F. W. Jones, *Principles of Anatomy*, 299, and in F. W. Jones, *Arboreal Man*, 44.

responding as it does to the endowments of his Mind (18). On the other hand, we are also told that only humans have true hands; as Aristotle made clear, the hand was given to man precisely because he alone is in a position to make use of it. How do we know that we should define the hand as exclusively human, or the human as the sole owner of the hand? Which takes priority here, the definition of the hand or the definition of the human? In fact, both parties rely on a particular understanding of the human in order to define the hand, since only humans have a true, "perfect or complete" hand, and, simultaneously, both parties rely on a particular understanding of the hand in order to define what is human, since only those with true hands, like the handy man *Homo habilis*, can properly be considered human. Rather like those truth seekers so castigated by Nietzsche, who "discovered" that camels are mammals, our humanistic writers conveniently manage to uncover the very thing they themselves surreptitiously secreted away (see "The Birds and the Bees" in chapter 2). This is indeed an expedient discovery, what we might call a *handy humanism*.

In short, the arguments here are circular. Which came first, the hand or the human? As for the perpetually regressing chicken and egg riddle, there is no clear answer: hand and human arise together in a mutually dependent nexus that seems to need no origin. Heidegger suggested earlier that it is in the use of things that one arrives at them. It is in the process of employing things as ready-to-hand equipment that they can be appreciated "in a way which could not possibly be more suitable."[47] It is in hammering that the tool user enters into the most primordial relationship with the hammer and comes closest to encountering it as that which it is. "The hammering itself uncovers the specific 'manipulability' [*Handlichkeit*] of the hammer."[48] The hand is crucial here: it is only those beings who have hands, those beings for whom equipment manifests itself as ready to hand, who can enter into this concernful relationship to things. *Homo habilis* is to be considered the first true human precisely because he was a "handy man," who did not merely grasp those Paleolithic stone flakes but also fashioned them, manipulated them, scraped and hammered with them, and thereby discovered their readiness to hand as equipment. The other beings, the other *animals*, those creatures who had no hands, remained mere entities that were accessible, ready to hand, for man.[49]

What use is being made of the hand itself, then, in the work of Heidegger, of Aristotle, and of Washburn? At what do we arrive, when we employ this tool of tools, this instrument for instruments, this supremely manipulable hand? The hand, according to Heidegger, serves by means of its concernful dealings to disclose what

47. Heidegger, *Being and Time*, 98 (69); see "Into Your Hand They Are Delivered" in chapter 1.
48. Heidegger, *Being and Time*, 98 (69).
49. See Heidegger, *Being and Time*, 100 (70).

is concealed, to uncover by means of demarcation (see "Into Your Hand They Are Delivered" in chapter 1). The delimitation that is here brought about, the marking off that is effected, is the differentiation of a particular kind of being: human being. But this is a hasty discrimination that conflates too readily the hand with the human and all those mere claws, talons, and "grasping organs" with the animal. The function that the hand performs, the use to which it is put, is to distinguish Man from Animal. Foucault suggested that despite appearances, mankind itself has no purpose, no great end. Rather, it merely functions, whilst continually creating justifications for that functioning. Humanism, he says, is the last great justification.[50] The hand that pointed out for Bell the existence of a benevolent designer, in whose image man is made, becomes for Leakey an index for the existence of humanity itself. For both, the hand evinces, then, just as it does for Heidegger, the distinctiveness of matchless, inimitable Man. If we are to avoid this evaluative anthropocentrism, we must circumvent the circular arguments of the handy humanists. Or rather, we must take our own hammer to these eternal idols, strike them as with a tuning fork, and hear the hollow sounds of their inflated ringing.[51] We turn, then, to the question of inhuman hands.

THE RULE OF THUMB

Three common myths are recounted regarding the thumb. The first concerns that durable phrase *rule of thumb*, which dates back at least to the seventeenth century and means, roughly speaking, an approximate but serviceable method based on experience rather than precise calculation. It has been alleged that the expression derives from the tradition in British common law that permitted a husband to "chastise" his wife so long as the switch or rod used was no thicker than his thumb. Calls have been made to boycott the use of the phrase on account of this distasteful derivation. In fact, there is no evidence to suggest that the phrase originated in domestic abuse: it does not appear in legal history, in which use of the thumb as any kind of standard is rare. On the other hand, however, irrespective of whether the phrase itself was officially deployed, it is clear from eighteenth- and nineteenth-century documents that there certainly existed a belief, both in England and America, that, within these "reasonable" limits, wife beating was tolerable. Thus, although the origin of the perfectly innocent phrase *rule of thumb* does not lie with violent abuse, it seems that the thumb has been employed as a de facto standard in this regard.[52]

50. Foucault, "Who Are You, Professor Foucault?" 102.
51. See Nietzsche, *Twilight of the Idols*, xviii.
52. The key text here is Kelly, "*Rule of Thumb*," though compare his interpretation of the evidence with that of Freyd and Johnson, "Domestic Violence, Folk Etymologies." The suggestion that woodworking provided the true origin of the phrase also has no supporting evidence; Kelly, "*Rule of Thumb*," 342n6.

The truth of the second myth is similarly gruesome. It is generally believed that the "thumbs up" gesture, widely employed across Europe and elsewhere, originated in the Roman Colosseum. When a bested gladiator lay prone, the crowd would advise the emperor on his fate either by crying "MITTE!" (Release him!) whilst showing upturned thumbs or by calling out "IUGULA!" (Slay him!), with their thumbs turned down, POLLICE VERSO. The emperor would confirm their verdict or not, according to his whim. From this grisly origin, it is supposed, come modern thumb signals meaning "okay" and "not okay." In fact, POLLICE VERSO means not specifically a down-turned thumb but simply a turned or moving thumb: those who wanted the gladiator slain presented their thumb in full sight, perhaps jabbing it in the motion of a stabbing.[53] Those who wanted to spare him, meanwhile, kept their thumbs out of sight, POLLICE COMPRESSO. Thus, simply showing one's thumb in any way meant just one thing: "IUGULA!"[54] In the Colosseum, then, we find a different but no less oppressive rule of thumb.

Finally, the third myth is in fact one that we have encountered already. In the previous chapter, we saw Rorty suggest that the desire to recontextualize is as characteristically human as "the desire to use an opposable thumb" (see "The Eyes Have It" in chapter 4). Although Rorty does not quite say so himself, we often hear that it is opposable thumbs that make humans the unique kind of being that they are. Aristotle was in no doubt as to its value:

> One finger extends out of the side of the hand, and is short and thick, not long; for just as, if there were not a hand at all, one could not grasp, so too one could not grasp if this finger were not growing out of the side. For it squeezes from below upwards, while the others squeeze from above downwards. And this must happen if it is to bind things together strongly, like a strong clamp, in order that, though one, it may be equal to many.[55]

For the ancient Greeks, the thumb was the ἀντίχειρ (antikheir), a digit that was equivalent to the hand itself. The prefix anti- means both equal and opposed to: the thumb may have been, as Albinus suggested, an ADIUTRIX MANUI (an assistant to the hand), but it was an able assistant precisely because it was equal in strength to the other fingers and because it opposed them. The anthropologist Marvin Harris has argued that "the length and strength of the human thumb give us a uniquely precise grip, powerful yet delicate. This grip, almost as much a hallmark of humanity as bipedalism and braininess, has helped to make us the supreme artisans of the animal kingdom."[56] And in September 2008, scientists

53. See Juvenal, *Saturae*, 34–35 (3, line 36).

54. It seems that outside the amphitheater a down-turned thumb was actually a sign of approbation, and an upturned thumb its opposite; see the thorough account of the myths and misunderstandings surrounding ancient thumb gestures in D. Morris et al., *Gestures*, 185–96 (chapter 16).

55. Aristotle, *On the Parts of Animals*, 99 (687b).

56. Marvin Harris, *Culture, People, Nature*, 28.

Charles Bell, *The Hand*, 19.

91. SPIDER MONKEY
This is a sketch of the Coaita, or Spider Monkey, so called from the extraordinary length of its extremities, and from its motions. The tail answers all the purposes of the hand, and the animal throws itself about from branch to branch, sometimes swinging by the foot, sometimes by the fore extremity, but oftener, and with a greater reach, by the tail. The prehensile part of the tail is covered with skin only, forming an organ of touch as discriminating as the proper extremities.

CHARLES BELL, *The Hand*, 19.

hunting for the genetic enhancers most likely to have contributed to human evolution, seeking, that is, to "understand, at a molecular level, what it means to be human," announced in a press release accompanying research published in *Science* that the fastest-evolving noncoding sequence of the human genome yet identified turned out "to play a unique human-specific gene activating role in a region of the developing limb that eventually forms the junction of the wrist and thumb, and also extends partially into the developing thumb." The press release suggested that this genomic region "may have contributed to the evolution of the uniquely opposable human thumb."[57] If the hand is the mark of the human, then the thumb is the quintessence of the hand, a hand in miniature: a "little hand." It is these marvelous, uniquely opposable thumbs, we are told, that

permit humans to engage in all those dextrous, significant activities that make them veritable masters of animate and inanimate nature. Accounts of the importance of opposable thumbs entail, then, a rule of thumb all their own.

What should we make of this "romance of the hand and its apposable thumb," as Stanley Cavell has characterized it.[58] Are opposable thumbs the key to the hand? Is the thumb, with the grip it provides, really a "hallmark of humanity"? Is it the thumb, that "little hand," that makes the human hand a *true* hand, the only perfect and complete hand? Could there be such a thing as a nonhuman hand? An animal thumb? What would such an inhuman member look like?

There are certainly creatures, even Bell admitted, who possess appendages that look or function, more or less, like hands, some of which come equipped with what seem, to a greater or lesser extent, like thumbs. The remarkable tail of the **SPIDER MONKEY**, he notes, "answers all the

57. The team called this element "human-accelerated conserved noncoding sequence 1" or "HACNS1"; see "HACNS1 Gene Enhancer"; Prabhakar et al., "Human-Specific Gain of Function."
58. Cavell, *This New Yet Unapproachable America*, 41–42.

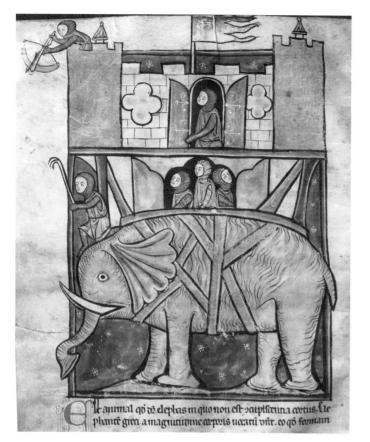

Thirteenth-century medieval bestiary. Westminster Abbey Library, MS 22, fol. 20v.

92. ELEPHANT

Next the Lucanian oxen with turreted backs, hideous creatures, snake-handed, were taught by the Carthaginians to endure the wounds of war, and to confound the great hosts of Mars.

> LUCRETIUS [TITUS LUCRETIUS CARUS], On the Nature of Things, 478–79 (bk. 5, lines 1302–4).

59. The Romans, in fact, also called bear paws "MANUS."

60. See "The Eyes Have It" in chapter 4. Several species of frog have six digits on their hind feet; see Gould, "Eight Little Piggies," 74, 76.

61. See "Prickly Porcupines and Docile Dogs" in chapter 1; F. W. Jones, *Arboreal Man*, 67.

purposes of the hand," and a "vulgar admiration is excited by seeing the spider-monkey pick up a straw, or a piece of wood, with its tail" (19, 15). This, of course, is not a hand, and further, when we look at the end of the monkey's arm we find the "thumb" to be so small that it has almost disappeared (90). The **ELEPHANT** possesses "an instrument, like a hand, in the proboscis,—to minister to the mouth, to grasp the herbage, and lift it to its lips" (332). This trunk, although called MANUS in Latin, is surely not a hand, however. Bell defended the supposedly "faulty composition" of the sloth and even noted that he climbed "hand over head," but he most often refers to those three-fingered appendages as claws (30). Of the light-boned bats (Chiroptera), the hand-wings, Bell notes that "the phalanges or the rows of bones of the fingers, are elongated so as hardly to be recognised" (74–75). But what of those other creatures, many of whom we have met already, whose limbs' ends are more clearly comparable to human hands than are the claws and wings of sloth and bat? What of the panda's dextrous paw, complete with extended, gripping thumb?[59] What of those frogs, perhaps members of Nietzsche's Dionysian chorus, who possess not five but six fingers to a limb?[60] What of Austin's chameleons, who have two opposable digits on each hand?[61] Is the tale told of uniquely human opposable thumbs another myth, another suspect attempt to rule by thumb?

The anatomist and anthropologist Frederic

Wood Jones distrusted paeans to the hand, both old and new:

> It would be a difficult matter to find the author who, writing of the human forearm and the human hand, has not seen in them the very highest and most perfect development of the fore-limb found anywhere in the animal kingdom. It has long been customary to lavish praise upon this culmination of human perfections, or climax of evolutionary advances, as writers of different periods have judged it.[62]

Jones observes that changes in these "almost inexhaustible eulogies" after 1859, the date of publication of Darwin's On the Origin of Species, were largely superficial. The hand and forearm came to be regarded "not as a wonderful and specially designed structure, but as the perfected products of accumulated ages of evolution—the last thing in animal development and specialization" (45). Here, in miniature, was the classic misunderstanding of Darwinian theory: evolution as progress. Humanity is no longer specially created but is instead specially evolved, the culmination and acme of evolutionary processes (45–46). Humans, now sitting at the very top of the great chain of being, gaze down first at the horses, dogs, and their fellow mammals, and then on to the lizards, fish, and assorted series of "lower" creatures. "A foolish argument," says Jones, "may be permitted in dealing with a folly" (45). We should imagine, he suggests, an equine anatomist producing a Bridgewater Treatise on

The Construction of the Hoof of the Horse, followed shortly after by a Descent of the Horse. The human forelimb would undoubtedly suffer badly, and these hypothetical works would thus, he suggests, be a most healthy tonic for human anatomists and philosophers alike.

The hand, far from being a specialized highpoint of the evolutionary process, is in fact a rather archaic appendage. Aristotle drew special attention to the fact that the five fingers are separate and distinct,[63] but as Jones demonstrates, pentadactylism is the "hallmark of primitiveness."[64] These five fingers collectively point, he shows, toward "something extraordinarily primitive about the hand that has been preserved and passed on to man" (20).[65] The pentadactyl limb is an ancient attachment, predating even mammalian life. Separate and distinct digits belong to numerous members of the massive superclass Tetrapoda, the four-limbed vertebrates, which includes amphibians, reptiles, birds, and mammals. It was from the very earliest tetrapods, the so-called four-footed fish who would go on to drag themselves into the inviting new shallows and wetlands of the late Devonian, 365 million years ago, that modern, human tetrapods inherited their flexible fingers. The Yokuts were only half right, then, when they suggested that humans were denied the hand of the coyote: in fact,

62. F. W. Jones, Arboreal Man, 43. Further references are in the text.
63. Aristotle, On the Parts of Animals, 99 (687b).
64. F. W. Jones, Principles of Anatomy, 22.
65. On this primitiveness, see also F. W. Jones, Arboreal Man, 46; Tuttle, "Hands from Newt to Napier," 3.

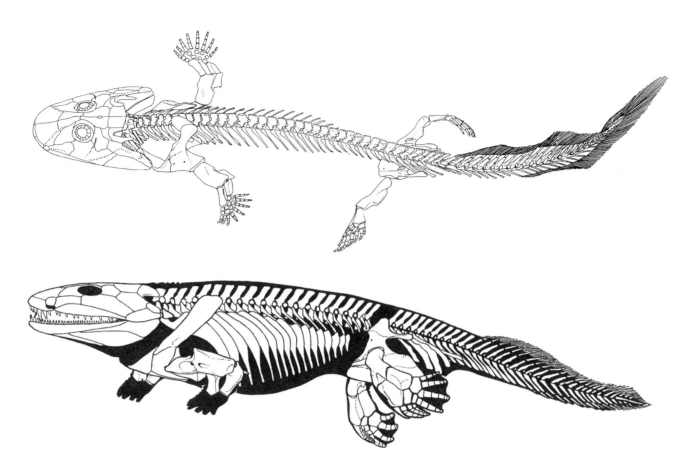

Images courtesy of Mike Coates.

93. & 94. ACANTHOSTEGA AND ICHTHYOSTEGA

New specimens of the earliest known tetrapod limbs show them to be polydactylous. The forelimb of *Acanthostega* has eight digits and the hindlimb of *Ichthyostega* has seven. Both of these come from the Upper Devonian of East Greenland, complementing the only other known Devonian tetrapod limb, that of *Tulerpeton* from Russia, which has six digits. The morphology of the specimens suggests that limbs with digits may have been adaptations to an aquatic rather than a terrestrial environment.

M. I. COATES AND J. A. CLACK, "Polydactyly in the Earliest Known Tetrapod Limbs," 66.

it was not the lizard who generously shared his fingers but his ancestor, a prehistoric fish. The origins of the five-fingered human hand reach back a long way indeed.

The division of the hand is certainly what makes it so flexible, so versatile, but that does not make it either unique to humanity or an evolutionary highpoint. In fact, the creatures whom we might more deservingly describe as "advanced" are those that have evolved beyond the ancient pentadactyl condition. This move away from the "primitive"[66] toward increasing specialization, manifests as a diminution in the number of digits. The most ancient of the Devonian tetrapods were **ACANTHOSTEGA** and **ICHTHYOSTEGA**. As Stephen Jay Gould explains in his essay "Eight Little Piggies," research published in the 1990s demonstrated that members of these two genera, though still confined entirely to water, had not five, but six, seven, or even eight digits on each limb.[67] Fingers have actually been lost in the intervening millennia, as species specialize. It is amongst the ungulates, the hoofed beasts, that this "digital reduction" has been most fully accomplished.[68] Bell himself discusses that "most perfect piece of mechanism," the horse's hoof, so well suited to the extensive plains and steppes where these great creatures originally roamed (94–98). Bell considers the remarkable combination of strength and elasticity in this fine apparatus and observes that there is just a single digit enclosed in the horse's bony hoof. It is this specialization that allows the horse to run such great distances at such high speed. But, as Jones points out, the unspecialized human forelimb "is far more like that of a tortoise than it is like that of a horse" (46). If the authors of those hypothetical texts *The Construction of the Hoof of the Horse* and *Descent of the Horse* had sought to derive their highly specialized limbs from those of a more primitive form, they would, "with far more justice" than humans, have regarded their race as the last effort in evolutionary chronology (45).[69]

Horses' hooves are clearly not hands. So just how many fingers does a hand have to lose before it becomes some other appendage? Is it just the thumb, the digit that, as in the case of Bell's spider monkey, is usually the first to go?[70] What of those, like the six-fingered frogs and the polydactylous *Acanthostega* and *Ichthyostega*, who have more than five digits? Can a hand have too many fingers? We return to the question: what makes a hand? Wittgenstein provided a playful image with which to illustrate the state of affairs, so often encountered by philosophers, wherein they seem to know what it is they wish

---

66. The human hand is not primitive in the sense that it is *crude*, of course: successive modifications and refinements have made it an extremely delicate and accomplished manipulative organ; see F. R. Wilson, *Hand*, 127–46 (chapter 7).
67. See Clack, *Gaining Ground* for the research to which Gould refers.
68. F. W. Jones, *Principles of Anatomy*, 21.
69. Jones concedes that such arguments are likely to appeal only to comparative anatomists from the kingdom of the Houyhnhnms; Jones, *Arboreal Man*, 46.
70. See Gould's discussion of the loss of digit number one; Gould, "Eight Little Piggies," 69–74.

to discuss but manage to perplex themselves from the outset:

> I have been talking about the game of "thumb-catching." What's wrong with that? "Thumb-catching": holding the right thumb, say, in the left hand, then trying to grasp it with the right hand. The thumb "mysteriously" disappears before it can be grasped.[71]

How are we to avoid the Scylla of simply defining the hand as exclusively human, as did Bell, and the Charybdis of getting caught in Wittgenstein's thumb-catching game, whereby a seemingly simple working definition remains permanently elusive?[72] The concepts of analogy and homology, as deployed by evolutionary biology, will prove helpful.

When he tussled with a tenacious Thomas Huxley in 1860, the comparative anatomist Richard Owen had long since parted ways with Darwin (see "Bird Brains" in chapter 4). Earlier in their careers the two had been on good terms, though: Owen had, in fact, worked on the fossil specimens brought back by Darwin on the *Beagle*.[73] Owen was the first English writer to distinguish clearly, and thereby to standardize, the terms *analogy* and *homology*. An analogue (from the Greek ἀνά, *ana*, meaning "up to," and λόγος, *logos*, meaning "ratio") is the appropriate description for "a part or organ in one animal which has the same function as another part or organ in a different animal."[74] A homologue, on the other hand (deriving from ὁμός, *homos*, meaning "the same"), is "the same organ in different animals under every variety of form and function."[75] Owen was not entirely clear in explaining just what counts as "the same" organ in different animals, but Darwin himself adopted Owen's terms and elaborated definitions of his own that went some way to addressing the issue. Analogous structures are those that depend on similarity of function, as do the wings of insects and of birds for instance, whereas homologous organs result from "their development from corresponding embryonic parts . . . as in the case of the arm of man, the fore-leg of a quadruped, and the wing of a bird."[76] Analogues, we might say, are those parts that have the same function, though they need not be the same organs; homologues, on the other hand, are the same organs, though they need not have the same function. The elephant's trunk, grasping at appetizing herbage, may in some ways be analogous to the human hand, but it is by no means a homologue of that appendage. Similarly, the panda's "thumb," though it appears in roughly the right position and is very effectively employed to grip bamboo, is not a true thumb, since, as Gould explained, it derives from the radial sesamoid bone rather than from the cor-

71. Wittgenstein, *Lectures and Conversations*, 27n5.

72. On the problems associated with defining the hand anatomically, see F. R. Wilson, *Hand*, 8–9.

73. See J. Browne, *Charles Darwin*, 348–51.

74. Owen, *Lectures on the Invertebrate Animals*, 668.

75. Ibid., 674.

76. Darwin, *On the Origin of Species*, 430, 434–35.

responding bones in a human hand (see "If a Lion Had Hands" in chapter 1).

Owen developed the concept of an *archetype* to explain the homological organs evident across vertebrate species. He viewed this archetype as a kind of Platonic model from which the frames of actual species are constructed. He used a picture of the archetype for his personal emblem and chose an appropriate maxim: "The motto is 'the one in the manifold,' expressive of the unity of plan which may be traced through all the modifications of the pattern, by which it is adapted to the very habits and modes of life of fishes, reptiles, birds, beasts, and human kind."[77] As Gould explains, Darwin considered this archetype "as more than idea," understanding it to represent, in fact, an ancestral vertebrate form.[78] In amending the concept of homology to designate "development from corresponding embryonic parts," Darwin gave to it a more immediately material meaning than Owen had intended. Owen, an evolutionist but one who rejected Darwin's theory of natural selection, had in mind a purely abstract "primal pattern," not some ancestral species. Bell, however, writing a little before Owen and Darwin, was deeply critical of all those "modern works on Natural History" that suppose "that the same elementary parts belong to all animals" (43). He recognized, as we saw, that different creatures have similar organs in similar positions, but he argued that all of those creatures were individually designed,

specially "adapted," to their environments. Similarities between the organs of different species are the result of similarities in the functions they need to fulfill (42–43, 166–70). In every case, organs are molded by a benevolent creator with "perfect accommodation" to their uses (166), and attempts to find some underlying structure are no more than "very trifling pursuits" that have the effect of "diverting the mind from the truth" (43). Bell denied altogether the "very curious opinion" (168) that elementary parts are "transposed" (43) in order to modify an archetypical creature to a particular environment. In short, Bell denied homology, in either its idealist or materialist forms.

For Bell, then, species are individually created and therefore essentially unrelated, a view that the philosopher of science Ron Amundson has dubbed "taxonomic nominalism."[79] The taxonomic nominalist does not deny the reality of species per se; they exist as distinct and unique entities in the world, to be sure. But for such a nominalist, the taxonomic categories into which these entities are placed—genus, family, class, and so on—do not represent objectively real relationships: such categories are purely human creations. Those similarities between species or organs that might be identified are just that, mere similarities of form, coincidences that

---

77. Owen to his sister Maria, 1852, quoted in Gould, "Eight Little Piggies," 63. On Owen's archetype and Darwin's transformation of it into an ancestor, see Amundson, *Changing Role of the Embryo in Evolutionary Thought*, 76–106.

78. Gould, "Eight Little Piggies," 63.

79. Amundson, *Changing Role of the Embryo in Evolutionary Thought*, 32–34.

are due entirely to similarities of function. For the taxonomic nominalist, then, similar organs in different species are never, strictly speaking (homologically), "the same." Traces of this determinedly antihomological perspective persist in the writings of those who would separate, absolutely, the human hand from the terminal organs of all inhuman limbs. Heidegger, as we saw, would countenance no relation between the human hand and other varieties of vertebrate appendage. The human body is, for Heidegger, "something essentially other than an animal organism"[80] precisely because it possesses the hand, which is "infinitely different" from the mere "grasping organs"—paws, claws, or fangs—of other creatures.[81] His insistence on this distinction displays an implicit special adaptationism in which the hand evinces man's unique place within Being.

To the extent that humanistic thinkers insist on an absolute difference between species or between appendages, they exhibit a taxonomic nominalism as pronounced as Bell's. When the human body is characterized as "essentially other" than an animal organism, or the opposable thumb as "uniquely" human, taxonomic nominalism has already been assumed. The writer who denies that there might be inhuman hands, who asserts that the difference between

human hand and animal paw is "infinite," does no more than *define* the hand as human. Homology is by no means adequate to establish identity: hooves are not hands. But an implicit and uncritical anthropocentrism here manifests as a vestigial taxonomic nominalism, a denial of structural homology, which precludes the very possibility of recognizing identity between similarly located appendages in different species. Degrees and kinds of functional similarity, which might be measured or assessed, become irrelevant when the opportunity to identify appendages as "the same" has already been ruled out. Such taxonomic nominalism sustains thereby a prejudicial rule of thumb, a long accepted, rough-and-ready measure of all things, which upholds humanity as "the ruler over animate and inanimate nature."

Schopenhauer was outraged at the deceitful double-dealing so often encountered in considerations of the animal kingdom. More than once he felt compelled to draw attention to the "vile and mean trick" whereby the terms employed to describe the activities and bodies of animals differ from those used for their human equivalents.[82] This miserable artifice is, he says, undoubtedly the work of "European priests and parsons," and it is thus that they "conceal under a diversity of words the perfect and complete identity of the thing."[83] This duplicitous practice is evident when we consider the question of the inhuman hand. Even should we grant Bell that

---

80. Heidegger, "Letter on Humanism," 228.

81. Heidegger, *What Is Called Thinking?*, 16; see "Into Your Hand They Are Delivered" in chapter 1.

82. Schopenhauer, *Parerga and Paralipomena*, 2: 370.

83. Schopenhauer, *On the Basis of Morality*, 176–77.

the elephant's proboscis is only analogically a MANUS and concede to Gould his observations regarding the nonhomological nature of the panda's thumb, there yet remain many pairs of hands that, though they do not belong to human beings, should nonetheless be called by no other name. In his discussion of the thumb, Bell turns to the chimpanzee. He provides an illustration of the extremity of an "adult Chimpanzee, from Borneo," to demonstrate that the thumb extends no further than the root of the fingers, which peculiarity distinguishes this member from the human hand. This five-fingered appendage he calls instead a *paw* (113–14).

Earlier in his treatise, Bell has already argued that *monkeys* do not have hands. He tells us that although we might be tempted to describe the hand as "an extremity in which the thumb and fingers are opposed to each other, so as to form an instrument of prehension," we would thereby include the organs of monkeys. But those monkey members are, he suggests, more properly to be considered *feet*, employed as they are for the purpose of progression by climbing and leaping through the branches of trees (18–19). The pragmatist and social psychologist George Herbert Mead reiterated precisely this point when he drew attention to the fact that the dominant function of a monkey's "so-called hands" is locomotion.[84] And the physician and primatologist John Napier, who had worked with Leakey on *Homo habilis*, could not quite bring

himself, in his engaging book *Hands*, to classify the monkey's appendages as "true hands." Employed in both a locomotor and manipulatory role, these organs constitute a compromise, he argues: the combination of "expert handling of objects with efficient locomotion" justifies our referring to a "foot-hand."[85]

Denying to monkeys the possession of "true hands," or suggesting that they bear only feet on the grounds that their grasping organs are employed for brachiation, is unwarranted. Napier opens the chapter of his book devoted to the function of the hand with a discussion of opposition. This is, he says, perhaps the hand's most important movement, the one that underlies all the skilled procedures of which it is capable. "The hand without a thumb is at worst, nothing but an animated fish-slice, and at best a pair of forceps whose points don't meet properly" (55). But although opposition of the thumb is one of the hallmarks of humanity, it is not, Napier emphasizes, unique to that species (56). Napier defines opposition more

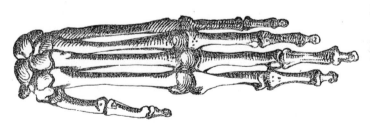

BONES OF CHIMPANZEE'S PAW.

84. Mead, "Concerning Animal Perception," 65.
85. Napier, *Hands*, 76; further references are in the text.

precisely than is usual, as the movement "by which the pulp surface of the thumb is placed squarely in contact with—or diametrically opposite to—the terminal pads of one or all of the remaining digits" (55). In addition to the requisite rotation of the thumb, a key factor in achieving this pulp-to-pulp contact is the proportionate lengths of thumb and index finger: the shorter a creature's thumb, the more difficult opposition becomes. The ratio of these two digits is expressed as the "opposability index," a figure calculated by multiplying the length of an individual's thumb by 100 and then dividing by the length of the index finger (57). The opposability index provides a useful indication of the manipulatory capacity of different hands. The mean calculation for those dextrous human hands, for instance, is 65. Most Old World monkeys are fully capable of opposing their thumbs, and the baboons and mandrills in particular, whose opposability index lies closest to that of humans (with a mean of 57–58), are expert manipulators.[86] Napier himself recounts the delicate thumb and finger movements employed both in feeding on seeds, grains, and young grass shoots and in the important activity of grooming. Though these appendages are also tasked with the business of locomotion, they remain without question supreme

manipulatory organs. They are, as Schopenhauer would surely insist, hands by virtue of both their structure and their function.[87]

Even were we to permit Bell his monkey feet, what of that chimpanzee "paw"? What should we make of the five-fingered appendages of the apes? Bell argues that "it is upon the length, strength, free lateral motion and perfect mobility of the thumb, that the superiority of the human hand depends" (113–14), and in this he was essentially correct. Opposition is by no means unique to the human hand, but what is distinctive about the "perfect" opposition of which the human thumb and fingers are capable, as Napier demonstrates, is the "broad area of intimate contact between the finger-tip pulps of the opposing digits" (56). This greater area of sensitive contact, along with the complex underlying movements of opposing human fingers, makes possible the considerably more accomplished manipulation of small or fragile items than is possible for other apes. Napier distinguished two basic patterns of prehensile action, the power grip and the precision grip (62–66), and it is in the latter, which depends on a sophisticated form of opposition, that the human hand excels.[88] The chimpanzee thumb, by contrast, although it is certainly opposed, is smaller and less dextrous than the human (the mean opposability index of chimpanzees is 43). A chimpanzee will struggle to bring the thumb across the hand to touch the tips of the ring and

86. Lacking rotation and thus pulp-to-pulp contact, New World monkeys and prosimians exhibit only what has been called "pseudo-opposability"; see Napier, *Hands*, 58.

87. Napier refers to them as such, in fact, throughout the rest of his text.

88. On the chimpanzee's powerful "double-locking grip," see Napier, *Hands*, 27–28.

little fingers, and these same fingers have difficulty crossing the hand in "ulnar opposition" to the base of the thumb.[89] As a result, the grip of the chimpanzee hand is neither so precise nor so versatile as that of the human.[90]

Galen long ago drew attention to the imperfections of the ape hand. He was quite emphatic on the matter when he came to discuss the thumb:

> Tell me, O noble sophists and clever accusers of Nature, have you ever seen in the ape this finger that is commonly called the antihand and that Hippocrates calls the great finger? And if you have not seen the ape's thumb, will you have the effrontery to say that it is just like the human thumb? If you have indeed seen one, I suppose you saw that it is short, slender, distorted, and altogether ridiculous, just as the ape's whole body is. . . . Then what advantage is there in having four fingers well formed if the thumb is so poorly arranged that it cannot even be called the great finger? Surely this is its condition in the ape, where it is separated only slightly from the forefinger, and is utterly ridiculous besides. And so, in this instance also, Nature is just, as Hippocrates often used to call her, because she has bestowed a ridiculous body on an animal with a ridiculous soul.[91]

Galen has a good deal more to say about how ludicrous the ape is, pretty to children, as "one of the Ancients" tells us, but no more than a plaything, a "laughable toy."[92] The hand and body of the ape are no more than caricatures

of the human hand and body, he suggests. But we should note that though this thumb may be small—perhaps even ridiculously small—and the hand may seem to Galen a ludicrous, laughable distortion, he does not doubt for a moment either that it is a thumb or that we are dealing here with a hand.

Napier insists that apes possess true hands. Even when employed to assist in terrestrial locomotion, these members are not placed flat on the ground like the "foot-hand" of the monkey but, rather, are made to bear weight on the semi-clenched dorsal side, just as Engels described, in the characteristic knuckle walk of the GORILLA and the chimpanzee. These apes, Napier argues, walk not on feet but on their hands. Further, like monkeys, apes are expert in the handling of objects. Chimpanzees in particular, despite their small thumbs and low opposability index, are enthusiastic tool users, employing a wide-ranging tool kit for a huge variety of tasks, from termite "fishing rods" to hammer stones and

---

89. See F. R. Wilson, *Hand*, 24.

90. On chimpanzee precision grips, see Butterworth and Itakura, "Precision Grips in Chimpanzees"; Marzke, "Precision Grips," 96–97, 103–4. On the importance of the overall "grasping repertoire" of the whole hand, and not just the flexibility of the thumb, see F. R. Wilson, *Hand*, 128–29, and especially Marzke, whose work complicates the degrees and modes of precision gripping and moves beyond its equation with relative thumb length. On the evolution of the human thumb, its muscles, and the complex range of movements of which it is capable, see F. R. Wilson, *Hand*, 136–39.

91. Galen, *Parts of the Body*, 107–8 (1: 22). The "apes" dissected by Galen were actually baboons and Barbary macaques, a species of tailless monkey; see R. Morris and D. Morris, *Men and Apes*, 123.

92. Galen, *Parts of the Body*, 107 (1: 22).

95. GORILLA

Whinny was followed by a bright-eyed, inquisitive ball of fluff who came to be known as Digit because of a twisted middle finger that appeared once to have been broken. . . . If I was alone, he often invited play by flopping over on to his back, waving stumpy legs in the air, and looking at me smilingly as if to say, "How can you resist me?" At such times, I fear, my scientific detachment dissolved. . . . It was Ian who found Digit's mutilated corpse lying in the corner of a blood-soaked area of flattened vegetation. Digit's head and hands had been hacked off; his body bore multiple spear wounds. Ian and Nemeye left the corpse to search for me and Kanyaragana, patrolling in another section. They wanted to tell us of the catastrophe so that I would not discover Digit's body myself.

DIAN FOSSEY, *Gorillas in the Mist*, 167, 182, 206.

Digit, aged eleven in 1972; from *Gorillas in the Mist*, by Dian Fossey.

weapons.[93] Napier's talk of "true hands" (76, 151) implies at times a prescriptive characterization that recalls Heidegger's absolute separation of hand from mere "grasping organ," and Napier's references to "'perfect' opposition" (56, 59), despite the scare quotes, cannot help but evoke Bell's contention that the matchless human hand demonstrates divine design. Despite these echoes of an antievolutionary anthropocentrism, however, Napier is fully committed to the essential relatedness of primate hands. Though ape and human hands may be superficially unalike, laughably so if we share Galen's sense of humor, Napier is emphatic that they "are cast from the same mould" and that "dissimilarities between ape and human hands are largely quantitative" (76). These hands *are* homologous. It is by rejecting a prejudicial taxonomic nominalism, a humanistic belief in hands that are "infinitely different" from all other organs, that we are able to recognize particular modes and *degrees* of similarity. This is not to replace absolute difference with "perfect and complete identity": the disparities between the hands of humans and those of other apes are many and varied.[94] Similarly, though opposable thumbs are by no means unique to human beings, even by Napier's more demanding reckoning, they are employed by different species in different ways. But in recall-

93. See McGrew, *Chimpanzee Material Culture*, 177–97, especially the tables listing tools organized by regional differences amongst cultural groups. On orangutan material culture, see van Schaik et al., "Orangutan Cultures."

94. See F. R. Wilson, *Hand*, 130–32; Marzke, "Precision Grips," 99.

Wolfgang Reitherman, director, *The Jungle Book* (movie).

96. ORANGUTAN

Now I'm the king of the swingers
Oh, the jungle VIP
I've reached the top and had to stop
And that's what botherin' me
I wanna be a man, mancub
And stroll right into town
And be just like the other men
I'm tired of monkeyin' around!

Oh, oobee doo
I wanna be like you
I wanna walk like you
Talk like you, too
You'll see it's true
An ape like me
Can learn to be human too.

RICHARD M. SHERMAN AND ROBERT B. SHERMAN, composers, "I Wan'na Be Like You," performed by Louis Prima (as King Louie), in *The Jungle Book* (movie, Disney, 1967).

ing the commonality of origin, the development from corresponding "embryonic parts," we are prompted to appreciate that sufficient similarity exists here to designate ape and human appendage alike as hands. Bell presents us not with a "chimpanzee's paw," as he would have it, but a chimpanzee's hand. Or does he?

Bell was wrong about the limb, but he was also mistaken regarding the identity of its owner: it was not a paw, and it did not belong to a chimpanzee. That short, thin thumb is characteristic of the **ORANGUTAN**, as Napier points out (76), native to the islands of Borneo and Sumatra

in Southeast Asia; the chimpanzee, who has a slightly larger thumb, is an African ape.[95] The naturalist and explorer Alfred Russel Wallace, who would censure Darwin for his use of the phrase *natural selection* (see "Bird Brains" in chapter 4), took a particular interest in orangutans during his expedition to the Malay Archipelago (1854–62). Having shot and examined a good number, he engaged in the ongoing debate, to

95. The size, shape, and arrangement of the metacarpals, phalanges, and scaphoid bones further indicate that this can only have belonged to an orangutan; Colin Groves, personal communication. Illustrations comparing the hands of a number of apes and monkeys can be found in Schultz, *Life of Primates*, 58 and 59 (partially reprinted in L. A. Jones and S. J. Lederman, *Human Hand Function*, 13, and in F. R. Wilson, *Hand*, 22), and in de Waal and Lanting, *Bonobo*, 27.

which Owen himself had contributed, regarding the ape's correct classification.[96] In a paper published in 1856, he recounts how, after killing a mother orangutan, he acquired a baby and resolved to raise him.[97] The naturalist describes the infant's endearing antics as he was suckled with rice water and bathed, as he dangled nonchalantly from his specially constructed climbing frame, and as he clung "cruelly tight" to Wallace's beard.[98] "When restless it would struggle about with its hands up to catch hold of something, and might often be seen quite contented when it had some bit of rag or stick grasped in two or three of its hands."[99] Wallace became quite enamored and was most upset when the inevitable came to pass. Maintained on an inadequate diet of biscuits and sweet potatoes, the orphaned orangutan died after just three months of captivity: "I much regretted the loss of my little pet ... which had afforded me daily amusement and pleasure by its curious ways and the inimitably ludicrous expressions of its little countenance."[100] Wallace's laughable toy was a plaything no more.

It was just two years later, whilst suffering from some tropical fever, that, according to his own account, the principle of evolution by natural selection occurred to Wallace in an Archimedean flash.[101] He dashed off a paper describing his theory, prompting a reluctant Darwin finally to make public the findings on which he had been sitting for so many years. Wallace's paper was presented, alongside Darwin's, to the Linnaean Society in July 1858. Famously, however, Wallace would later break with Darwin not just on the matter of the phrase *natural selection* but also on the extent to which the theory itself should be employed as an explanatory principle. Although he believed the theory could probably account for "all the varieties of structure, all the wonderful adaptations, all the beauty of form and of colour, that we see in the animal and vegetable kingdoms,"[102] Wallace developed reservations when it came to the question of humanity. In a paper titled "The Limits of Natural Selection as Applied to Man," Wallace argued that humans possess a number of traits that go far beyond immediate biological need—brain size, abstract thought, nakedness, voice, moral sense, consciousness—and that must therefore have developed by some means other than by natural selection.[103] Additionally, he was unable to see how an organ as remarkable and "perfect" as the human hand, so full of latent capacities that had remained unrealized by "palæolithic man and his still ruder predecessors," could have

---

96. By his own count, Wallace shot sixteen orangutans during the expedition; see Wallace, "On the Orang-Utan"; Wallace, *Malay Archipelago*, 51–74.

97. Wallace, "Infant 'Orang-Utan'"; the account is repeated, with minor changes, in *Malay Archipelago*, 53–57.

98. Wallace, "Some Account of an Infant 'Orang-Utan,'" 387.

99. Ibid.

100. Ibid., 390.

101. Wallace, *Wonderful Century*, 380–81; Wallace, *My Life*, 1: 360–63.

102. Wallace, "Limits of Natural Selection," 332.

103. This essay developed ideas that Wallace had briefly voiced, anonymously, the year before; see Wallace, "Sir Charles Lyell," in which he refers to that "admirable volume" on the hand by Charles Bell (392).

evolved unless in anticipation of the needs of civilized man.[104] Apes, he asserted, "make little use of their separate fingers and opposable thumbs. They grasp objects rudely and clumsily, and look as if a much less specialized extremity would have served their purpose as well." An "intelligent power" seemed to Wallace a much more likely explanation than mere natural selection for this remarkable appendage that, he argued, is fully utilized as a hand only by humanity.[105]

These were the old prejudices of human exceptionalism, of an expedient, handy humanism. Darwin, soon to publish *The Descent of Man*, was concerned for the welfare of their theory: "I hope you have not murdered too completely your own and my child."[106] On reading Wallace's arguments, he wrote to him, "As you expected, I differ grievously from you, and I am very sorry for it. I can see no necessity for calling in an additional and proximate cause in regard to man."[107] Just as Wallace's inadequate care had killed the infant orangutan, by seeking hands and "higher developments" outside the processes of his own theory, Wallace deprived human evolution of its natural environment. A rule of thumb, as we saw, is an approximate but serviceable method based on past experience rather than on precise calculation. Such pragmatism has its place, but dangers arise when we fail to reflect on that experience, when an uncritical reliance on a tried and tested rule of thumb sanctions the repressive exercise of privilege and prejudice, when the

thumb itself rules our thinking. The hand makes humans, we are told, not just "the supreme artisans of the animal kingdom," as Marvin Harris would have it, but also, according to Bell, "the ruler[s] over animate and inanimate nature." That oppressive, opposable thumb, the master finger, secures universal dominion. But just as we should free ourselves from the conviction that the down-turned thumb began as a fate-sealing signal in the Colosseum and from the belief that the phrase *rule of thumb* derived from domestic abuse, so we should eschew the myth that opposable thumbs, and thus perfect hands, originate with humanity. There is no one, true Hand, evincing design or anything else, but a multitude of particular *hands*, each gripping and grasping after its own fashion. Philosophers and scientists must guard against the long-established practice of assigning to humanity and its members some exceptional, mythic origin, lest they endanger both the integrity of their thought and the welfare of those to whom they would deny a common ancestry and homological affinity.

In his observations of his ill-fated orangutan, there were in fact truths that Wallace himself failed to notice. He took amusement in the ludicrous expressions of his adopted charge, hanging onto the crude climbing frame or from the naturalist's beard. But Wallace casually observed, too, that the orangutan would "struggle

104. Wallace, "Limits of Natural Selection," 349.
105. Ibid., 349–50.
106. Darwin to Wallace, March 27, 1869, in Darwin, *More Letters*, 2: 39.
107. Darwin to Wallace, April 14, 1869, in Darwin, *Life and Letters*, 2: 116.

about with its hands up to catch hold of something." Like Galen's similarly laughable caricature, this ape had hands. Further, Wallace also records seeing "some bit of rag or stick grasped in two or three of its hands." Not only did this orangutan have hands, but he had more than two of them. In fact, Wallace mentions more than once that the baby orangutan would grasp and grab with all four of his hands. Here we find a mischievous ape who does not simply want to be like man. Not content with just two hands, this king of the swingers has the temerity to possess twice as many as does the average human. The importance of having the right number of hands, and its significance for assigning to humanity its proper place within animate and inanimate nature, will occupy us next.

FOUR HANDS GOOD, TWO HANDS BAD

Wallace was left in no doubt that it was with powerful hands that the young orangutan clung tenaciously to his beard. But at the same time, the naturalist was equally sure that hands, like the higher developments of the brain, were properly employed only by humans. Like so many handy humanists before and since, his inclination was to place humans, alone subject to "the action of some unknown higher law,"[108] in a class of their own. Wallace was no taxonomic

nominalist, but he sought nonetheless to separate humans from their kin, to orphan them as he had the infant orangutan. Determining clearly demarcated categories has always been a problem for the taxonomist, of course, nominalist or otherwise. Darwin himself had complained of the difficulties he experienced whilst at systematic work (see "Bird Brains" in chapter 4). No one has highlighted the undefined and unanswerable questions that haunted Darwin and his fellow systematists with quite such flare, however, as Jorge Luis Borges.

In the short essay "John Wilkins' Analytical Language," first published in 1942, Borges describes several attempts to construct a universal language, that is, a language in which each word defines itself. Such a language would, as Borges puts it, speculate on "the words, definitions, etymologies, and synonymies of God's secret dictionary."[109] He mentions the system proposed in 1850 by one C. L. A. Letellier, in which "*a* means animal; *ab*, mammalian; *abo*, carnivorous; *aboj*, feline; *aboje*, cat; *abi*, herbivorous; *abiv*, equine," and so on.[110] He recounts a similar example from Wilkins's own "undoubtedly ingenious" system: although the English word *salmon* tells us nothing, "*zana*, the corresponding word, defines (for the person versed in the forty categories and the classes of those categories) a scaly river fish with reddish flesh."[111] Borges is alarmed by some of Wilkins's categories and divisions, however; the whale becomes, for instance, "a viviparous,

108. Wallace, "Limits of Natural Selection," 332.

109. Borges, "John Wilkins' Analytical Language," 231.

110. Ibid., 230.

111. Ibid., 232; Wilkins, *Philosophical Language*, 142, 415.

oblong fish."[112] The "ambiguities, redundancies, and deficiencies" of Wilkins's system recall, he suggests, a certain Chinese Encyclopaedia:

> In its distant pages it is written that animals are divided into (a) those that belong to the emperor; (b) embalmed ones; (c) those that are trained; (d) suckling pigs; (e) **MERMAIDS**; (f) fabulous ones; (g); stray dogs; (h) those that are included in this classification; (i) those that tremble as if they were mad; (j) innumerable ones; (k) those drawn with a very fine camel's-hair brush; (l) etcetera; (m) those that have just broken the flower vase; (n) those that at a distance resemble flies.[113]

A distinctive kind of disorder manifests here within the heart of the encyclopedic system. In his discussion of Borges's text, Foucault distinguishes the confusion of the merely incongruous from the true turmoil of the heteroclite.[114] The former is apparent, he suggests, in the unusual juxtaposition of creatures listed by Eusthenes when he declares, "I am no longer hungry. . . . Until the morrow, safe from my saliva all the following shall be: Aspics, Acalephs, Acanthocephalates, Amoebocytes, Ammonites, Axolotls, Amblystomas, Aphislions, Anacondas, Ascarids, Amphisbaenas, Angleworms, Amphipods, Anaerobes, Annelids, Anthozoans . . . ."[115] Ordinarily these creatures would certainly not be found together, but that they might meet on the site of Eusthenes's saliva, as they do in his list, is at least a theoretical possibility. The disorder

Louis A. Sargent, *Manatees*, in Frank Finn, *The Wild Beasts of the World*, 2: 144.

97. MERMAID

The Manatee is probably the origin of the mermaid legend, and this may have come about because they have a habit of standing up in the water with their head and shoulders above the surface. When doing this, the females often hold a baby manatee in one flipper to enable it to suckle at the breast. The Manatee and the Dugong are a puzzle for the zoologists, as among the mammals, for anatomical reasons, it has been necessary to place them in a group by themselves. They are almost hairless and live entirely in the water, but unlike the whales they are completely herbivorous. The hind limbs have evolved into a fleshy horizontal paddle. The general opinion is that they are very distantly related to the elephants. They are the last survivors of about twenty fossil genera.

A. F. GOTCH, *Mammals*, 193.

112. Borges, "John Wilkins' Analytical Language," 231; Wilkins, *Philosophical Language*, 132.

113. Borges, "John Wilkins' Analytical Language," 231.

114. Foucault, *Order of Things*, xi–xxi (preface).

115. Ibid., xvi. Eusthenes is a character in Rabelais's satirical novels *Gargantua and Pantagruel*.

of Borges's "Heavenly Emporium of Benevolent Knowledge" is another matter. Here, Foucault notes, the "fragments of a large number of possible orders glitter separately in the dimension, without law or geometry, of the *heteroclite*."[116] Each of the categories belongs to a different system. There is not even the possibility of a common locus where the creatures could convene, and yet the continuity of the alphabetical sequence obliterates the distances between the categories. The disorder here, Foucault explains, is the internal incoherence of the paradox.

Heteroclite systems are, Borges suspects, inevitable. Universal languages, and indeed all attempts at classification, do not and cannot hold because "there is no universe in the organic, unifying sense of that ambitious word."[117] In short, "there is no classification of the universe that is not arbitrary and speculative."[118] But, Borges asserts, the impossibility of constructing a perfect taxonomy, of reproducing God's secret dictionary, should by no means discourage us from the attempt. Systems and orders will always be provisional, but that in itself is no reason to abandon them. Taxonomy, that branch of biological science concerned with the task of classifying species and other taxa, learned long ago to hypothesize rather than to hypostatize. We will return to this noble endeavor in a moment, but first we must exchange Borges's heteroclite disordering for a little incongruity.

In a rich, inspiring essay entitled "Gaps in the Mind," Richard Dawkins endeavors to close the distance that Wallace would place between ape and human. Dawkins describes what he calls "the discontinuous mind," an outlook characterized by the desire to impose inappropriately rigid distinctions on real-world continua. Dawkins presents the example of a sophistic lawyer who, noticing that speciation allegedly occurs by means of infinitesimal, gradual variation, will attempt to argue that since a member of one species could never give birth to a member of another, Darwin's theory of evolution must surely be at fault.[119] The lawyer creates a gap where none exists. These gaps that are found or imposed by the discontinuous mind tend to be momentous: they are huge, yawning chasms, infinite divides of the sort we encountered with Bataille and Heidegger. Dawkins points out that it is convenient for our naming rituals that intermediate species have usually died out, but he invokes that globe-spanning ring species of gulls to demonstrate that this need not be the case (see "Bird Brains" in chapter 4). "Footling debates" that seek to establish sharp divisions where none exist entirely miss the point, and the import, of Darwin's discovery.

116. Ibid., xvii.

117. Borges, "John Wilkins' Analytical Language," 231.

118. Ibid. In her own discussion of Borges and Foucault, Carol J. Adams reproduces a heteroclite disorder all the more startling for its familiarity. The rationale behind the everyday categories by which animals are organized is, she demonstrates, "the arbitrary logic of the oppressor"; see Adams, *Neither Man nor Beast*, 188–90.

119. Dawkins, "Gaps in the Mind," 81–82. Further references are in the text.

Dawkins would not just peer into the un-fathomable depth of animality; rather, he would cross the abyss that it allegedly constitutes. "The word 'apes,'" Dawkins suggests, "usually means chimpanzees, gorillas, orangutans, gibbons and siamangs. We admit that we are like apes, but we seldom realise that we *are* apes" (82). In fact, he notes, humans are African apes and are more closely related to chimpanzees and gorillas than either of those two species are to orangutans (82–84). Dawkins proposes a thought experiment to demonstrate that there is no great divide, no yawning abyss, separating human from ape. He suggests that the reader imagine him- or herself standing on the shore of the Indian Ocean in southern Somalia, facing north. "In your left hand you hold the right hand of your mother. In turn she holds the hand of her mother, your grandmother. Your grandmother holds her mother's hand, and so on" (84). Following this "human chain," we will have hardly started across the width of our home continent before we reach our common ancestor with the chimpanzee. If this "arch-ancestress" then turns east and takes in her left hand her other daughter, from whom chimpanzees are descended, a parallel chain can be followed all the way back to the coast. The reader will now stand face-to-face with his or her modern chimpanzee cousin, the two of them joined by an unbroken sequence of linked hands. Like a kind of diachronic ring species, there are no gaps in this chain of beings.

Anyone who walked up and down this chain might pass members of *Homo erectus*, perhaps *Homo habilis*, the "handy man," or even *Australopithecus afarensis*, and other species besides. They would also pass individuals who could not comfortably be classified as belonging to any particular species. These individuals can be considered members of "intermediate species" only to those gazing down the line with the benefit of taxonomic hindsight. This hindsight is necessarily based on such historical contingencies as which species flourished, which became extinct, and which left the fossil remains on which modern classification depends.[120] The true importance of Darwin's work was not that he demonstrated the origin of any species but that he showed just how specious the notion of species can be.[121] To whatever species these individuals did or did not belong, however, and irrespective of the number of hands they each employed to form that chain, all were African

120. Dawkins notes that it is sheer bad luck that the intermediates have died out and that it would take "only a handful of [surviving] intermediate types to be able to sing: 'I've bred with a man, who's bred with a girl, who's bred with a chimpanzee'" (85). Genetic research has suggested that interspecies mating did in fact take place for over a million years after human and chimpanzee lineages first diverged; see Patterson et al., "Genetic Evidence." On the ethical consequences of discovering living intermediates, or a human–chimpanzee hybrid, see Dawkins, "Gaps in the Mind," 85–87; Dawkins, "Word Made Flesh."
121. On the subtleties of the concept of species and the problems of accurately representing descent graphically, see Dennett, *Darwin's Dangerous Idea*, 85–103 (chapter 4). See also John Dupré's discussion of the distinction between species considered as units of evolution and species considered as units of classification, which argues for the pragmatic utility of the latter over the former; Dupré, "In Defence of Classification."

98. Chimpanzee

But the Part, in the Formation and its Function too, being liker a Hand, than a Foot; for the distinguishing this sort of Animals from others, I have thought, whether it might not be reckoned and call'd rather Quadru-manus than Quadrupes, i.e. a four-handed, than a four-footed Animal. And as it uses its hinder Feet upon any occasion, as Hands; so likewise I observed in our Pygmie, that it would make use of its Hands, to supply the place of Feet. But when it went as a Quadruped on all four, 'twas awkwardly; not placing the Palm of the Hand flat to the Ground, but it walked upon its Knuckles, as I observed it to do, when weak, and had not strength enough to support its Body. So that this Species of Animals hath the advantage of making use of their Feet as Hands, and their Hands as Feet as there is occasion.

EDWARD TYSON, Orang-outang, sive Homo sylvestris, 12–13.

Edward Tyson, Orang-outang, sive Homo sylvestris, fold-out plate.

apes. There were transitions, to be sure, but not, pace Engels, from ape to man.

Dawkins's lineup ends with a single individual, one contemporary cousin standing opposite the reader, but there is in fact more than one species of chimpanzee. Chimpanzees (Pan troglodytes) have been known to the Western world since at least the seventeenth century. In 1699, the comparative anatomist Edward Tyson, a distant relative of Darwin's, dissected a juvenile **CHIMPANZEE**. He published an account, with superb anatomical drawings by William Cowper, as The Anatomy of a Pygmie.[122] Tyson's stated objective was to demonstrate that "the pygmies, the cynocephali, the satyrs, and sphinges of the ancients" were actually apes or monkeys, not men, and that his own subject was the connecting link in the great chain of being between animal and man. He depicted his pygmie standing upright, supported by a walking stick on account of his failing health.[123] It was not until the early

122. The full title of Tyson's book is Orang-outang, sive Homo sylvestris; or, The Anatomy of a Pygmie Compared with That of a Monkey, an Ape, and a Man. The individual Tyson dissected was unquestionably a chimpanzee; early classification of apes was far from standardized (see below).
123. On Tyson's account, see Montagu, Edward Tyson, 225–345 (chapters 8–9); Gould, "To Show an Ape"; Nash, Wild Enlightenment, 15–41 (chapter 1). The skeleton of Tyson's chimpanzee can be seen in the British Museum today. Nicolaas Tulp's earlier account of an "Indian Satyr," in 1641, has been taken as a descrip-

twentieth century that a second species of chimpanzee was identified. In 1928, a skull previously thought to be that of a young chimpanzee was recognized as belonging to an adult, albeit one with an unusually small head. The following year the subspecies *paniscus* was announced; a few years later, it was reclassified as a new species.[124] The name was simply a diminutive of the genus name, *Pan*, and the "new" species has often been called the "pygmy chimpanzee." In fact, though the skull is smaller and the build slimmer, the bonobo's body is of comparable size to that of *Pan troglodytes*.[125] The origin of the preferred name for this ape, **BONOBO**, is unknown, and may well have derived from a misspelling on a shipping crate.[126] The common chimpanzee and the pygmy chimpanzee are closely related, and the one has in the past often been confused with the other, but that they constitute separate species is now officially recognized.[127]

Kanzi, used by permission of the Great Ape Trust.

99. BONOBO

Bonobos manifest a more intricate socio-communicative repertoire, including the use of more gestures and more vocalization, than common chimps do. . . . Not only was Kanzi using the keyboard as a means of communicating, but he also knew what the symbols meant—in spite of the fact that his mother had never learned them. For example, one of the first things he did that morning was to activate "apple," then "chase." He then picked up an apple, looked at me, and ran away with a play grin on his face. . . . Kanzi was using specific lexigrams to request and name items, and to announce his intention—all important symbol skills that we had not recognized Kanzi possessed. . . . Kanzi appeared to know all the things we had attempted to teach Matata, yet we had not even been attending to him—other than to keep him entertained. Could he simply have picked up his understanding through social exposure, as children do? It seemed impossible.

SUE SAVAGE-RUMBAUGH AND ROGER LEWIN, *Kanzi*, 125, 135–36.

It does not matter, for the purposes of Dawkins's demonstration, whether the *Pan* whom his reader faces is a *troglodytes* or a *paniscus*: humans are as closely related to the one as to the other. There is an alternative conclusion we might draw from his observations, however, regarding the nomenclature of this African ape family. As has often been noted, humans

tion of a chimpanzee (Huxley) or a Bonobo (Reynolds), but it seems most likely to have been an orangutan (Rijksen and Meijaard). See Tulp, *Observationes Medicae*, 271 (3: 56); Huxley, *Evidence*, 8; Reynolds, "Ape Described by Tulp"; Rijksen and Meijaard, *Our Vanishing Relative*, 421–27.

124. On the ignominious events surrounding the discovery of *paniscus*—both Harold Coolidge and Ernst Schwarz claimed credit—see Gribbin and Gribbin, *Being Human*, 4–5; de Waal and Lanting, *Bonobo*, 5–6. Behavioral scientists had an inkling that there might be more than one species of chimpanzee earlier in the century; see de Waal and Lanting, *Bonobo*, 5–6.

125. Gribbin and Gribbin, *Being Human*, 18.

126. There is a town called Bolobo in the Democratic Republic of the Congo (formerly Zaire), the only nation in which this endangered species has survived; see de Waal and Lanting, *Bonobo*, 7.

127. Though see Watson, Easteal, and Penny, "Homo Genus," 315–16.

are genetically extremely close to chimpanzees, sharing 98.4 percent of their DNA.[128] Jared Diamond has pointed out that willow warblers and chiffchaffs share less than this, at 97.4 percent, and yet are placed together in the same genus, *Phylloscopus*. Similarly, the red-eyed and white-eyed vireos, two North American birds, both belong to the genus *Vireo* whilst sharing only 97.1 percent of their DNA.[129] In short, were the same criteria to be applied to the great apes as to these other species, humans and chimpanzees would be acknowledged as members of the same genus. Diamond's argument is based on cladistics, the school of taxonomy that depends on the objec-tive criteria of genetic distance between species, rather than on traditional or phenetic classifica-tion systems that rely on subjective evaluations of the relative importance of anatomical or be-havioral traits.[130] Since the genus name *Homo* was proposed first, then, according to the rules of taxonomic nomenclature, it must take prior-ity. Diamond thus argues that "there are not one but three species of genus *Homo* on Earth today: the common chimpanzee, *Homo troglodytes*; the pygmy chimpanzee, *Homo paniscus*; and the third chimpanzee or human chimpanzee, *Homo sapi-ens*."[131] The African ape who stands gazing back at Dawkins's reader on the coast of the Indian Ocean is a chimpanzee, though she is not a *Pan* at all but a fellow *Homo*.

It was the Swedish naturalist Carl Lin-naeus who devised both the taxonomic ranking method and the binomial system of nomencla-ture still used today.[132] Characterized by contem-poraries as a second Adam, Linnaeus set himself the task of giving true names to the earth's creatures and thereby accurately representing the order of nature.[133] His work constituted an attempt to peek at God's secret dictionary. In the Linnaean system, which quickly replaced a bewildering, heteroclitic assortment of compet-ing classificatory methods, each species is des-ignated by two Latinate names, the first generic, the second specific.[134] In his *Systema Naturae*, a scientific bestiary for the modern age, Linnaeus displaced the lion from his traditional, prime

128. The figure of 1.6 percent divergence in human and chimpanzee DNA refers to corresponding synonymous (functionally relatively unimportant) DNA sites. The figure actually rises to 99.4 percent for nonsynonymous (functionally much more important) DNA sites; see Wildman et al., "Implications of Natural Selec-tion." On the caution that must be exercised in drawing conclusions from DNA comparisons, see Pinker, *Language Instinct*, 351, and especially Taylor, *Not a Chimp*. On the persistent focus on homologues of human intelligence amongst chimpan-zees, at the expense of other species, see Beck, "Chimpocentrism."

129. Diamond, *Third Chimpanzee*, 19–21.

130. Ibid., 14–21; Tudge, *Variety of Life*, 33–62 (chapter 3), esp. 49–51; Groves, *Primate Taxonomy*, 3–14, 303; Corbey, *Metaphysics of Apes*, 103–5, 147–47. On a radical "post-Linnaean" classification that extols species pluralism, see Ereshef-sky, *Poverty of the Linnaean Hierarchy*; but see also Tudge's "neolinnaean impression-ist" argument for retaining traditional great ape nomenclature; Tudge, *Variety of Life*, 485–92.

131. Diamond, *Third Chimpanzee*, 20–21. Diamond was not the first to propose this revision; see Watson, Easteal, and Penny, "Homo Genus," 313–16, and Taylor, *Not a Chimp*, 12–15, who describe the work of Morris Goodman, amongst others.

132. Groves, *Primate Taxonomy*, 40.

133. Harrison, "Linnaeus as a Second Adam?"; Corbey, *Metaphysics of Apes*, 45.

134. Ritvo, *Platypus and the Mermaid*, esp. 1–50 (chapter 1). Linnaeus's method of nomenclature was often accepted even when his classifications were not; see ibid., 51–84 (chapter 2).

position. He began instead with the primates, and indeed with humans (genus *Homo*), whom he divided from the apes (genus *Simia*).[135] More than a century before Darwin, however, Linnaeus found himself wrestling with the unanswerable questions of taxonomy:

> I demand of you, and of the whole world, that you show me a generic character—one that is according to generally accepted principles of classification—by which to distinguish between Man and Ape. I myself most assuredly know of none. I wish somebody would indicate one to me. But, if I had called man an ape, or vice versa, I would have fallen under the ban of all ecclesiastics. It may be that as a naturalist I ought to have done so.[136]

In fact, Linnaeus had himself already complicated this distinction between Man and Ape. He divided the genus *Homo* into two species, *Homo sapiens* and *Homo troglodytes*. The former, also called *Homo diurnus*, comprised various subspecies or races, including *Homo americanus*, *Homo europaeus*, and even *Homo monstrosus*, a miscellany of oddities including the Patagonian giant, the dwarf of the Alps, the monorchid Hottentot, and others. *Homo troglodytes*, identified as *Homo nocturnus*, was a creature reported by travelers to exist in Africa and Asia, about whom Linnaeus recorded:

> It lives within the boundaries of Ethiopia (Pliny), in the caves of Java, Ambiona, Ternate. Body white, walks erect, less than half our size. Hair white frizzled. Eyes orbicular: iris and pupils golden. Vision lateral, nocturnal. Life-span twenty-five years. By day hides; by night it sees, goes out, forages. Speaks in a hiss. Thinks, believes that the earth was made for it, and that sometime it will be master again, if we may believe the travellers.[137]

According to Colin Groves, this golden-eyed anthropoid included "some undoubted orangutans and possibly chimpanzees."[138] Some of the great apes, at least, counted as *Homo*. King Louie wanted, more than anything else, to be a man, and for Linnaeus and his early followers, he was.[139]

Jared Diamond does not mention Linnaeus's early primate classification. In suggesting, however, that even today's cladistically inclined taxonomists are anthropocentric and that "the lumping of humans and chimps into the same genus will undoubtedly be a bitter pill for them to swallow," he is surely correct. The impetus to isolate humans within their own genus betrays

135. Linnaeus, *Systema Naturae*, 1: 20–29. *Systema Naturae* was first published in 1735; on the development of Linnaeus's classification of human and ape through successive editions, see Douthwaite, *Wild Girl*, 15–17.

136. Linnaeus to J. G. Gmelin, February 14, 1747, quoted in E. L. Greene, "Linnæus as Evolutionist," 25. Giorgio Agamben has argued that Linnaeus *does* identify a means to distinguish man: the ability to recognize himself as human; see Agamben, *Open*, 23–27 (chapter 7).

137. Linnaeus, *Systema Naturae*, 1: 24; translation from R. Morris and D. Morris, *Men and Apes*, 134–35.

138. Groves, *Primate Taxonomy*, 40; see also R. Morris and D. Morris, *Men and Apes*, 134.

139. Huxley had proposed that humans and the African apes should be placed in the same taxonomic order as far back as the 1860s, just a few years after Darwin published *On the Origin of Species*; see Huxley, *Evidence*, 104.

a heteroclitic humanism that goes beyond mere incongruity. Nevertheless, Diamond continues, "There is no doubt . . . that whenever chimpanzees learn cladistics . . . they will unhesitatingly adopt the new classification."[140] That is, we might add, whenever *we* learn to accept the new system of classification. Despite the speciousness of species, despite the lack of clear gaps in the continuum, despite the fact that we cannot read God's dictionary, we should not cease the attempt to keep compiling and revising systems of classification. The impossibility of penetrating the divine scheme of the universe should not, Borges asserts, dissuade us from devising our own schemes, even if it is clear that they are provisional.[141] The very nature of classifications, like dictionaries, is that they must be supplemented and amended.

Changing the names of species is nothing new. As we saw, *Pan paniscus* has changed name once already, but Groves lists forty-seven different names by which the several subspecies of ape now subsumed under *Pan troglodytes* have been known since the time of Linnaeus.[142] The International Code of Zoological Nomenclature requires that an existing genus name must take priority over any subsequently proposed names.[143] Diamond abides by these rules when he proposes that although humans are "the third chimpanzee," the genus name *Homo* should be adopted for the three species: *Homo* dates back to the official starting point for zoological nomenclature, 1758, when the tenth edition of Linnaeus's *Systema Naturae* was published, whereas *Pan* was not employed as a genus name until 1816.[144] There is a danger here, however, of reduplicating the same anthropocentrism that Linnaeus decried in himself when he imprudently separated Man and Ape. His very description of the genus *Homo* was in fact the phrase NOSCE TE IPSUM (know yourself).[145] Reclassifying chimpanzees as humans suggests once more that humans are in some sense prior to, or preeminent among, the great apes. Our objective should not be to welcome a few new, privileged members into the charmed circle of human affairs.[146] If we wish to avoid this evaluative anthropocentrism and if, following Foucault, we are writing in order to discover a new "we," it is vital that we find a different way to amend our primate nomenclature.

The genus name of the chimpanzee comes from the Greek god of shepherds and their flocks, Pan (Παν).[147] Depicted with a human torso but the hindquarters, beard, and horns of

140. Diamond, *Third Chimpanzee*, 21.

141. Borges, "John Wilkins' Analytical Language," 231.

142. Groves, *Primate Taxonomy*, 303–7. For a lively survey of the history of primate taxonomy and of the colorful characters who fill it, see ibid., 39–49.

143. Jeffrey, *Biological Nomenclature*, 23–28.

144. Ibid., 24; Groves, *Primate Taxonomy*, 303.

145. Linnaeus, *Systema Naturae*, 1: 18, 20.

146. Dawkins says as much in his qualified endorsement of the Great Ape Project, which campaigns to have the rights of nonhuman great apes recognized by international law; see Dawkins, "Gaps in the Mind," 87.

147. de Waal and Lanting, *Bonobo*, 6. The common name, *chimpanzee*, is the name for this ape in Angola in south-central Africa.

a goat, Pan was a lustful deity, pursuing nymphs and maenads around Arcadia, accompanied by his lascivious satyrs. Legends have long persisted of the prurient ape, and Linnaeus used the name *satyrus* for one of the species of his genus *Simia*.[148] The name *Pan* is usually taken to derive from *paein* (Πάειν), meaning "to pasture,"[149] but an ancient Homeric Hymn to Pan, chanted at religious festivals, suggests an alternative etymology. It recounts that the gods gave him the name they did because, as a rowdy child, full of merry laughter, "he delighted them all" (φρένα πᾶσιν ἔτερψεν).[150] Pan, here, is the stem of the Greek adjective meaning "all." It is most appropriate, then, that this name should apply to *every* one of the species within our chimpanzee genus, including the so-called shepherd of Being. For the human chimpanzee, anthropocentrism becomes, perhaps, panthropocentrism. But if humans should take the genus name *Pan*, what of their specific name?

In his *Anatomy of a Pygmie*, Tyson wondered whether it might be more appropriate to describe his chimpanzee as "Quadru-manus" rather than "Quadrupes."[151] Buffon, who was well acquainted with Tyson's text and was critical of Linnaeus's inclusion of *troglodytes* within the genus *Homo*, would go on to use the terms "quadrumanous" and "bimanous" of ape and man in his *Nomenclature of the Apes*.[152] It was not until 1795, however, that Johann Friedrich Blumenbach came to employ these two terms

in a specifically classificatory sense. In the third edition of his *On the Natural Varieties of Mankind*, Blumenbach suggested that despite the pioneering nature of the work of "the immortal Linnaeus," his *Systema Naturae* was now more than sixty years old and in need of revision.[153] Accordingly, and despite protesting, "I am very far indeed from that itch for innovation which afflicts so many of the moderns," he proposed a new taxonomy of his own (152n1).

Blumenbach rejected naturalists' long-established commitment to the continuity or gradation of nature, the chain of being that had still held Tyson captive, and argued instead that there are "large gaps" between classes and genera and kingdoms of creatures (150–51). He proposed ten distinct orders of mammalia; the first of them, the Bimanus, included only the genus *Homo* (152). He argued that man's unique, erect stature gives him "that highest prerogative of his external conformation, namely, *the freest use of two most perfect hands*" (171). The anthropomorphous animals, the apes, monkeys, and lemurs, however, have on their hind feet a second thumb, not

---

148. On the history of the virile ape, see R. Morris and D. Morris, *Men and Apes*, 53–82 (chapter 3); Janson, *Apes and Ape Lore*, 261–86 (chapter 9). On the pivotal roles that sexual relations play within bonobo societies, see de Waal and Lanting, *Bonobo*, 99–132 (chapter 4).

149. Graves, *Greek Myths*, 1: 102; *Oxford Classical Dictionary*, 3rd ed., s.v. "Pan."

150. *Homeric Hymns*, 198–203 (19).

151. Tyson, *Anatomy of a Pygmie*, 13.

152. J. C. Greene notes that this appeared in the fourteenth volume of Buffon's colossal, thirty-six-volume *Histoire naturelle, générale et particulière* (1749–1788); J. C. Greene, *Death of Adam*, 179–82.

153. Blumenbach, *Varieties of Mankind*, 150. Further references are in the text.

100. Pan bimanus

Man may be excused for feeling some pride at having risen, though not through his own exertions, to the very summit of the organic scale; and the fact of his having thus risen, instead of having been aboriginally placed there, may give him hope for a still higher destiny in the distant future. But we are not here concerned with hopes or fears, only with the truth as far as our reason permits us to discover it; and I have given the evidence to the best of my ability. We must, however, acknowledge, as it seems to me, that man with all his noble qualities, with sympathy which feels for the most debased, with benevolence which extends not only to other men but to the humblest living creature, with his god-like intellect which has penetrated into the movements and constitution of the solar system—with all these exalted powers—Man still bears in his bodily frame the indelible stamp of his lowly origin.

CHARLES DARWIN, *The Descent of Man, and Selection in Relation to Sex*, 619.

"A Venerable Orang-outang: A Contribution to Unnatural History," *Hornet*, March 22, 1871.

the great toe that is given to man alone. As such they ought not to be considered either bipeds or quadrupeds; rather, they belong in a distinct order of their own, the Quadrumana (171–73).[154] Only humans are fully bipedal,[155] a posture made possible precisely by the lack of Aristotle's instrument of instruments on their hind extremities. It is not the hand that distinguishes human beings but, rather, the fact that they have only two of them. With his two new orders, the Bimanus and the Quadrumana, Blumenbach thus definitively separated humans from all the other great apes, a taxonomic distinction that has persisted to the present day.[156] The distinguishing feature of the human chimpanzee is the fact that members of the species do not have four hands, like the majority of the other primates, nor "the hand," as Heidegger insisted, but a pair, as G. E. Moore ably demonstrated. Appropriating Blumenbach's term but tempering the rigidity of the divisions he described by recalling Dawkins's chain of beings joined by their hands, humans might then best be considered **Pan bimanus**.

Bishop Wilberforce gently mocked the "fungular descent" indicated by Darwin's theory (see "Bird Brains" in chapter 4). Huxley, however, was proud to affirm his ape ancestry through

154. Blumenbach's dissertation was first published in 1775, when he argued that apes should be considered quadrupeds; ibid., 86–87. He did not propose the order Quadrumana until the third edition of 1795.

155. Blumenbach discounts "the manati, birds (especially the penguins)," and "the lizard *Siren*"; ibid., 87.

156. Corbey, *Metaphysics of Apes*, 50–51.

either of his grandparents, whilst Engels described the "transition stages from walking on all fours to walking on two legs," by which his hairy, bearded ancestors distinguished themselves from the other knuckle-walking, anthropoid apes (see "If I Had a Hammer," above). Cousinship with the mushrooms may well have been unsuspected, and the relationship remains distant, but human beings are not simply close to the apes: as Dawkins illustrates, they *are* apes. Darwin well knew that the hand of God did not create discrete species but instead traced a proliferation of related lineages. The hand itself, shared by all the great apes and many other creatures besides, is no index of human being. Anthrōpos, or *Pan bimanus*, retains only half the number of this primitive instrument as do its two sister species.[157] In challenging Oedipus to know himself, the Sphinx was perhaps closer to the mark when she focused on feet rather than on hands (see "The Eyes Have It" in chapter 4). But even that fearsome guardian of truth failed to anticipate a third answer to her riddle: the being that is four-footed as a babe, two-footed in adulthood, and, just like Tyson's pygmie, three-footed when infirm, is a chimpanzee.

A REPORT TO AN ACADEMY

In Kafka's short story "A Report to an Academy," a chimpanzee named Rotpeter, who has been educated to the "cultural level of an average European," finds himself in something of a dilemma:[158] "Honored members of the Academy! You have done me the honor of inviting me to give your Academy an account of the life I formerly led as an ape [*äffisches Vorleben*]. I regret that I cannot comply with your request to the extent you desire" (250). Rotpeter explains that although only five years have passed "since I was an ape [*Affentum*]" and that although he can recount something of his capture, his incarceration, and the training and personal exertion that led to his becoming human, of his time in the forests of the Gold Coast he can say nothing.[159] The door through which he passed has now closed, and the strong wind that blew after him from his past is today no more than a gentle puff that plays about his heels (250). Bataille suggested in our first chapter that "nothing, as a matter of fact, is more closed to us than this animal life from which we are descended,"[160] a sentiment Rotpeter reaffirms when he tells the members of the Academy that "your life as apes, gentlemen, insofar as something of that kind lies behind you, cannot be farther removed from you than mine is from me" (250). The first-and-foremost anthropocentrism that beset Bataille

157. The hand turns out to be a poor symbol for "man" on several counts. Despite its masculine appearance, MANUS is in fact a fourth-declension *feminine* noun.
158. Kafka, "Report to an Academy," 258. Further references are in the text. Rotpeter refers to himself as an ape in his report, but he is identified by a third party specifically as a chimpanzee in an earlier fragment of Kafka's story; ibid., 260.
159. Note that Kafka's adjective and adjectival noun—*äffisches* (apish) and *Affentum* (ape existence)—become substantives in translation. We will return to this in a moment.
160. Bataille, *Theory of Religion*, 20; see "Like Water in Water" in chapter 1.

is the same as that which prompts Kafka's ape to claim, "What I felt then as an ape I can represent now only in human terms" (253). Rotpeter is now a human before he is an ape.

There is another, more appropriate tale with which to end this report to an academy, however. Pierre Boulle opens his most famous novel with Jinn and Phyllis, "a wealthy leisured couple," who are holidaying in space "as far as possible from the inhabited stars."[161] They spend their time sailing their solar-powered spacecraft and taking pleasure in one another's company. By chance, they intercept an old-fashioned message in a bottle that, as they read it, becomes the main body of Boulle's novel. Jinn and Phyllis shake their heads in disbelief as they complete the manuscript, which reports the trials and tribulations of an astronaut, one Ulysse Mérou, who has been stranded on a world populated by rational chimpanzees, gorillas, and orangutans, a veritable planet of the apes. "A likely story,"

says Jinn, which shows only that "there are poets everywhere, in every corner of the cosmos, and practical jokers too."[162] And so, in the closing words of the novel,

> [Jinn] let out the sail, exposing it to the combined rays of the three suns. Then he began to manipulate the driving levers, using his four nimble hands, while Phyllis, after dismissing a last shred of doubt with an energetic shake of her velvety ears, took out her compact and, in view of their return to port, touched up her dear little chimpanzee muzzle.[163]

Rotpeter appears at first to be an ape, but it soon becomes clear, if his repeated protestations are to be believed, that he is now human. Jinn and Phyllis, on the other hand, we assume to be human, right up until the point at which their quadrumanous nature and chimpanzee muzzles reveal them to be apes. Rotpeter is still an ape, however, despite his cultured ways. He tells us that "the first thing I learned was to give a handshake; a handshake betokens frankness" (251),[164] but it is clear from his report that he has not been entirely forthright with his captors, trainers, and audience. From the moment he realized that there was only one way out of his confinement, his assumption of human ways has been an elaborate and effective performance, an object lesson in Nietzsche's distinctively human dissimulation.[165] Is Rotpeter lying about his anthropocentric amnesia? Who can say? But his well-groomed fur and tail betray the fact that he

161. Boulle, *Monkey Planet*, 7.

162. Ibid., 174.

163. Ibid. The novel was, of course, made into a spectacularly successful and critically acclaimed film, *Planet of the Apes*, starring Charlton Heston, in 1968. The narrative fulfills the dream of Linnaeus's *Homo troglodytes*, who believed, we will remember, "that the earth was made for it, and that sometime it will be master again"; see "Four Hands Good, Two Hands Bad," above.

164. On wild chimpanzee hand-clasps, see Nakamura, "Grooming-Hand-Clasp"; McGrew, *Cultured Chimpanzee*, 137–43.

165. Rotpeter is, in fact, at pains to point out that his achievement was a matter of necessity rather than choice: "I repeat: there was no attraction for me in imitating human beings; I imitated them because I needed a way out, and for no other reason"; Kafka, "Report to an Academy," 257. On Rotpeter's wily, Nietzschean imitation, see M. Norris, *Beasts of the Modern Imagination*, 65–72.

remains an ape (252).[166] Rotpeter presents his report as a human, but he is in fact a chimpanzee,
just as Jinn and Phyllis seem to be human whilst
reading the astonishing account upon which they
have stumbled, only to turn out to be chimpanzees. And so it is with this report, honored members of the academy. Our lives as apes are not so
far removed and do not lie behind us.

In considering the question of ape and
human from the perspective of cladistics, our
proposed revision broke the taxonomic imperative of temporal preeminence. Homo came first
not only according to the author of Genesis but
also according to that second Adam, Linnaeus.
What justification, then, can be offered for this
willful itch for innovation? In retaining and indeed extending the use of Homo, I suggested, the
rules of nomenclature manifest, in this instance,
a form of evaluative anthropocentrism. Linnaeus
himself acknowledged that as a good naturalist,
he should have done otherwise. This anthropocentrism is a kind of self-centeredness, a species
of narcissism, a species narcissism.[167] The fact
that humans did not evolve from but, rather,
continue to be apes need not of itself prevent
their being self-centered, of course. Homo might
well be erased as a distinct genus, like a taxon
drawn in the sands of genealogical time, but this
does not bring to a close all possible forms of
narcissism. Indeed, Derrida has suggested that
one will always narcissistically appropriate the
other in one's own image:

I believe that without a movement of narcissistic
reappropriation, the relation to the other would
be absolutely destroyed, it would be destroyed
in advance. The relation to the other—even if it
remains asymmetrical, open, without possible
reappropriation—must trace a movement of reappropriation in the image of oneself for love to
be possible, for example. Love is narcissistic.[168]

What we think of as "non-narcissism" is in general "but the economy of a much more welcoming, hospitable narcissism." "Narcissism! There
is not narcissism and non-narcissism; there are
narcissisms that are more or less comprehensive, generous, open, extended."[169] There is, we
might say, more than one self-image in which
the other might be cast and with which one
might fall in love.

The seemingly incongruous claim that humans are chimpanzees is made possible not by
a listing of names, like Eusthenes's inventory of
edible snakes, but by the branching of an inclusive taxonomic hierarchy. Charles Jeffrey advises
that we imagine this hierarchy

as a series of containers, with adjacent walls and
bases, placed one inside another, and differ-
ing only in height. The containers themselves
then represent the taxonomic categories. The
levels of the roofs of the containers represent
the taxonomic ranks. The contents of the con-

166. Apes, unlike most monkeys, are in fact tailless.
167. On species narcissism, see "If a Lion Had Hands" in chapter 1.
168. Derrida, "There Is No One Narcissism," 199.
169. Ibid.

tainers—the groups of organisms we place in them—represent the taxa.[170]

The individual organisms that make up any given taxon belong, necessarily, to multiple categories. The *bimanus* belong to the genus *Pan*, the family Hominidae, the order Primates, the class Mammalia, the phylum Chordata, and the kingdom Animalia. Derrida suggests that there are "little narcissisms" and "big narcissisms,"[171] and here, in the component classes of our nested taxonomic schema, we can identify multiple differences, heterogeneities, and ruptures and therefore assorted scales of self-image.

In addition to these incongruously inclusive narcissisms, however, there are many more asymmetrically heteroclite clusters we might move to appropriate. The individual *Pan bimanus* that was Charles Darwin, for instance, was (1) male, (2) middle-class, (3) a parent, (4) included in the current classification, (5) etcetera. Mapping genealogical and evolutionary categories will not exhaust what an individual was, is, or might become. In our first chapter we traced the transformation not just of ciphers into indices, of CIFERAE into CI FERAE, but also of these substantives into adjectives: the animals turned out to be both *cipherous* and *indexical* (see "An ABC of Animals" in chapter 1). The politics of adjectives and articles requires that the being inclined to see itself as human pay due care and attention to the parts of speech employed in claims to self-identity. Whereas the substantive is liable to define and delimit, the adjective permits a more inclusive multiplicity of relations. One might choose, then, to acknowledge one's *animal* being rather than to be *an animal*, to see oneself as *mammalian* rather than as *a mammal*, to prefer *ein äffisches Leben* (an apish life) or *Affentum* (ape existence) to "a life as ape," and perhaps, even, to be *human* rather than *a human being*. Whereas the substantive tends to domesticate and foreclose, the adjective leaves open the possibilities both of an itinerant meander down the unbroken lineage of an evolutionary past and of an unruly roam, a wandering hither and thither, across a heteroclite expanse of untamed identities.

This report to an academy has examined the alleged inevitability of a Protagorean perspective. Anthropocentric thinkers will assume, first and foremost, an abyssal limit differentiating Human from Animal. For Heidegger it was "the hand" that marked out the edges of this unfathomable chasm. But as Derrida has pointed out,

> Every time it is a question of hand and animal—but these themes cannot be circumscribed—Heidegger's discourse seems to me to fall into a rhetoric which is all the more peremptory and authoritarian for having to hide a discomfiture. In these cases it leaves intact, sheltered in obscurity, the axioms of the profoundest metaphysical humanism: and I do mean the profoundest.[172]

170. Jeffrey, *Biological Nomenclature*, 3.
171. Derrida, "There Is No *One* Narcissism," 199.
172. Derrida, *Of Spirit*, 11–12.

Heidegger's profound metaphysical humanism, his handy humanism, manifests, Derrida says, in his treatment of one kind of animal in particular. When Heidegger suggests that apes "have organs that can grasp, but they have no hand," his claim is "most significant, symptomatic, and seriously dogmatic. Dogmatic also means metaphysical, coming under one of those 'common representations' that risk compromising the whole force and necessity of the discourse right here."[173] Heidegger's peremptory and authoritarian discourse, his attempted rule of thumb, is compromised at precisely the point at which he puts pen to paper not as a member of Homo humanus,[174] or even of Homo sapiens, but as a member of Pan bimanus.

Heidegger assumes a single narcissism. His first-and-foremost anthropocentrism depends on a single "we." It is true, as Derrida points out, that "'we' is always said by a sole person. . . . It is always me who says 'we'; it is always an 'I' who utters 'we.'"[175] And it is true that Derrida himself will not, "for a single moment," take it upon himself to contest the thesis of a rupture or abyss "between those who say 'we men,' 'I, a human,' and what this man among men who say 'we,' what he calls the animal or animals."[176] There will always be gaps in the mind, and such a disregard for difference would simply be "too asinine." The point, however, is that this is not the only difference, the only abyss or gap or rupture. Derrida has given his attention, he says,

not just to difference, but to differences, to heterogeneities and abyssal ruptures.[177] Rotpeter chooses to narrate his history, to recount his particular kind of being, by stressing a single difference, but there are other tales he might have told, and the "we" to whom Heidegger devotes his attention is not the only "we" on whose behalf a sole person, an individual "I," can speak. Heidegger precludes a more expansive interrogation of differences and the possibility of saying not just "we humans" but also "we tetrapods," "we vertebrates," "we animals." The rule of thumb was ever a provisional, makeshift judgment, a useful injunction to be sure, but ultimately one that was botched, approximate, and open to revision. And so, to follow Derrida, the autobiographical animal, one final time, we might choose to ask:

> Where then are we? Where do we find ourselves? With whom can we still identify in order to affirm our own identity and to tell ourselves our own history? First of all, to whom do we recount it? One would have to construct oneself, one would have to be able to invent oneself without a model and without an assured addressee. This addressee can, of course, only ever be presumed, in all situations of the world. But the schemas of this presumption were in this case so rare, so

173. Derrida, "Geschlecht II: Heidegger's Hand," 173; Heidegger, *What Is Called Thinking?*, 16.
174. Heidegger, "Letter on Humanism," 245; see "Into Your Hand They Are Delivered" in chapter 1.
175. Derrida, *Resistances of Psychoanalysis*, 43; on Heidegger's "we," in relation to his hand, see Derrida, "Geschlecht II: Heidegger's Hand."
176. Derrida, *Animal That Therefore I Am*, 30.
177. Ibid.

obscure, and so random that the word "invention" seems hardly exaggerated.[178]

Heidegger argued that the question "Who is man?" had not been adequately asked, whilst Rorty complained that "there is no 'we' to be found in Foucault's writings" (see "If a Lion Had Hands" in chapter 1 and "To We or Not to We" above). For Foucault, however, the objective is "not to discover what we are but to refuse what we are."[179] It is to write so that we can "make the future formation of a 'we' possible, by elaborating the question."[180] In asking "Where then *are* we?," in seeking to discover with whom we can identify in order to affirm our identity, the sole person who says "we" will construct or invent or affirm a "we" that comprises both addresser and addressee, both the writer and the reader of the report. "The 'we' must not be previous to the question," says Foucault; rather, "it can only

be the result—and the necessarily temporary result—of the question as it is posed in the new terms in which one formulates it."[181] By posing, and reformulating, the question of anthropocentrism, I, who presume to say "we," have proposed a new genus of welcoming, hospitable narcissism that would include both author (Rotpeter no less than Mérou), and audience (Jinn and Phyllis no less than the honored members of the academy). The new "we," that I would say, is "we chimpanzees."

This is not quite a *new* "we," of course: "we" have always been chimpanzees. Nietzsche opened his *Genealogy of Morals* with the words "We are unknown, we knowers, ourselves to ourselves: this has its own good reason. We have never searched for ourselves—how should it then come to pass, that we should ever *find* ourselves?"[182] Since the time of Linnaeus, few knowers have searched for a "we" amongst the chimpanzees. Of central importance to Nietzsche's own philosophy was the entreaty that we "become what we are,"[183] an aphorism he took from Pindar's second Pythian ode.[184] Pindar's exhortation was that, having learned what one is, one should strive to manifest it in one's actions, disregarding the judgments and opinions of less discerning souls.[185] With this phrase Nietzsche urged his readers to construct or create a self, to "'give style' to one's character."[186] One of the chief means by which one should take up this pursuit, according to

---

178. Derrida, *Monolingualism of the Other*, 55–56.

179. Foucault, "Subject and Power," 336.

180. Foucault, "Polemics, Politics, and Problematizations," 385.

181. Ibid.; see above, "To We or Not to We."

182. Nietzsche, *Genealogy of Morals*, 1 (preface, §1).

183. Nietzsche, *Joyful Wisdom*, 209 (§270), 263 (§335). Nietzsche also used this aphorism as the subtitle for his philosophical (and physiological) autobiography, *Ecce Homo*, and elsewhere. Alexander Nehamas traces Nietzsche's use of the phrase through his work in "How One Becomes What One Is," 255–56.

184. Γένοι' οἷος ἔσσί μαθών (*genoi'hoios essi mathōn*), Pythian Ode 2, line 72, in Pindar, *Olympian Odes, Pythian Odes*, 238–39.

185. Pindar, *Works of Pindar*, 3: 128–30. Scholars disagree as to quite how forcefully we should interpret Pindar's pithy words to Hieron, the king whose chariot-racing victory this ode commemorates; see Burton, *Pindar's Pythian Odes*, 125–26; Pindar, *Olympian and Pythian Odes*, 253–56, 264.

186. Nietzsche, *Joyful Wisdom*, 223–25 (§290); Nehamas, "How One Becomes What One Is," 270.

Nietzsche, is to identify oneself with *all* that one is.[187] If, with Foucault, we are to refuse what we are, refuse to be good bourgeois liberal humanists, it is in order that we might, with Nietzsche, become what we are, which is to say, far more than such a narrow pluralism would permit. Nietzsche's becoming is not the realization of a state or condition, not a matter of achieving a static goal, a well-established "we," a single, final narcissism. It is, rather, a process, a provisional alignment, a necessarily temporary result. We chimpanzees must become what we are, and we must continue to do so.

187. Nehamas, "How One Becomes What One Is," 269–80.

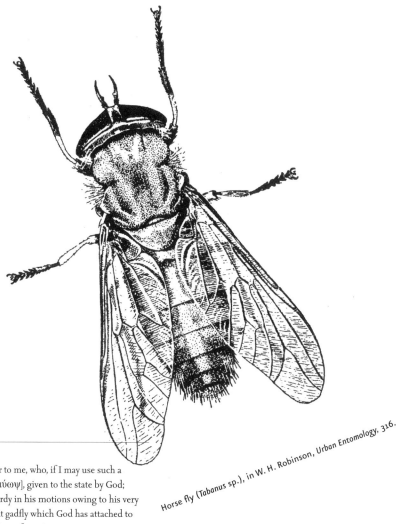

Horse fly (*Tabanus* sp.), in W. H. Robinson, *Urban Entomology*, 316.

101. Gadfly

If you kill me you will not easily find a successor to me, who, if I may use such a ludicrous figure of speech, am a sort of gadfly [μύωψ], given to the state by God; and the state is a great and noble steed who is tardy in his motions owing to his very size, and requires to be stirred into life. I am that gadfly which God has attached to the state, and all day long and in all places am always fastening upon you, arousing and persuading and reproaching you. You will not easily find another like me, and therefore I would advise you to spare me.

PLATO, "Apology," 124 (30e–31a).

Coda

Listen, and become what you are. Children prattle that
the ape is "pretty"—pretty indeed!

PINDAR, Pythian Ode 2

When he discussed the thumb, Galen claimed,
following "one of the Ancients," that the ape,
a ridiculous caricature of the human, was a
"laughable toy for children at play."[1] The ancient
source on which he drew was in fact the very
same line of the same Pythian ode that had so
appealed to Nietzsche. The translation is difficult and the verse dense with allusion, but the
little ape (πίθων) here represents the flatterer
who is fair to behold only to those whose child-
like naivety prevents them from seeing through
his tricks and deceptions.[2] Pindar's πίθων, at
least as Galen understands him, is a ludicrous
parody, a fawning mimic who apes human abilities. We have encountered more than once this
tradition of the imitative ape, aspiring to human
status. Disney's King Louie, tired of "monkeyin'
around," wanted nothing more than to "stroll

right into town," to "learn to be human," to "be
a man," whilst Kafka's reporter to the academy,
believing that he had left his ape existence entirely behind, thought that he had entered and
established himself "in the world of men."[3] This
is, of course, just another means of catching,
confining, and taming wild animals, of curtail-
ing the freedom to which they are accustomed
by nature, of denying their own wishes, by which
they would be governed. These are animals who
have been taken in hand, who are MANSUETA,
brought under the hand (see "Taking Animals in
Hand" in chapter 1).

As Pindar suggests, however, those who
would become what they are must not be fooled
by appearances, and we must not be taken in
by this misrepresentation of apes as petty or

---

1. Galen, *Parts of the Body*, 107 (1: 22); see "The Rule of Thumb" in chapter 5.
2. Burton, *Pindar's Pythian Odes*, 126; L. R. Farnell, in Pindar, *Works of Pindar*, 2: 129; Basil L. Gildersleeve, in Pindar, *Olympian and Pythian Odes*, 255; Frank J. Nisetich in Pindar, *Pindar's Victory Songs*, 162.
3. Sherman and Sherman, "I Wan'na Be Like You"; Kafka, "Report to an Academy," 250, 251; see "The Rule of Thumb" and "A Report to an Academy" in chapter 5.

presumptuous or jealous.[4] The bestiarist believed that the SIMIAE are so called because a great similarity (SIMILITUDO) to human reason can be observed in them, but also on account of their distinctively squashed noses (σιμός, simos).[5] Apes are no mere mimics, no pretty pets foolishly attempting to simulate human ways or take the place of human beings, like Linnaeus's envious Ethiopian anthropoid or the primates who rule Boulle's planet. Apes should be indices, like the rest of our 101 wild animals, proceeding always in their characteristic, inimitable ways, wandering hither and thither, wherever the spirit (ANIMUS) leads them. In ancient Rome, one who was enslaved, who had been claimed as a possession, was called MANCIPIUM, literally "taken by hand."[6] The slave was required to answer, of course, to the wants and wishes of those who had taken them in hand, but the prospect remained, for a lucky few, of release from this life of servitude. One who was discharged from service, who was finally emancipated, became MANUMISSUS, "released from the hand." Those animals who have been taken in hand, who have been tamed and enslaved, as ciphers or stereotypes, as anthropomorphic apologues or instances of the Animal, require their own, individual MANUMISSIO.

Protagoras was criticized by Socrates, in his discussion with Theaetetus, for claiming that "man is the measure of all things" (see the prelude). He may just as well have said, Socrates suggests, that a pig or a dog-faced baboon or some still stranger creature is the measure of all things. In fact, this is precisely what Protagoras supposed. In the dialogue that takes his name, Protagoras argues that just as some things are expedient or not for man, such as certain meats, drinks, medicines, and "ten thousand other things," so it is for horses, oxen, dogs, and even trees. That which is good for one may well be injurious to the other. In fact, Protagoras does not even wish to pronounce generally for all humanity or all horses or all oxen or all dogs; rather, he suggests that the good is relative to each individual, or even to parts of individuals: the manure that feeds a tree's roots would be damaging if applied to its shoots, just as olive oil will, he says, nourish a person's outer parts, the hair and body, but should be consumed internally only sparingly.[7] Rejecting the absolute assurances of realism, Protagoras subscribed to a contextual relativism or, perhaps more accurately, to an evaluative, pragmatic perspectivism.[8] For Protagoras, then, apes and other creatures do not aspire to be like Man, and each is its own measure of all things.

Nietzsche once suggested that "even great spirits have only their five-fingers' breadth of experience—just beyond it their thinking ceases and

4. See also Reginald Burton's critique of the interpretation of Pindar's ape as a mimic; Burton, *Pindar's Pythian Odes*, 126–27.

5. T. H. White, *Book of Beasts*, 34–35; W. B. Clark, *Medieval Book of Beasts*, 132–33.

6. Long, "Mancipium"; Fitzgerald, *Slavery*, 90.

7. Plato, "Protagoras," 157 (334).

8. On Protagoras's "practical program," see Versenyi, "Protagoras' Man-Measure Fragment," 182–84.

their endless empty space and stupidity begins."[9] Animals who have not been domesticated and disciplined, who are not MANSUETA or MAN-CIPIA, are FERAE, wild animals who can point beyond the five fingers' breadth of experience to which humans would confine themselves. They indicate modes of thinking that become possible when "we" cease to consider ourselves, preeminently or exclusively, as human: the 101 gesture with hand or paw toward the limits of our thinking *as human beings*. The endless empty space across which they point and through which they disclose a passage is the stupidity of the fathomless abyss that would separate, by a single, infinite divide, human from other animals. Thought may always be tamed and constrained, but this need not be by hands, and hands, of course, are not human: humanity need not be the measure of all things, even for humans. Manumission releases from the hand both those animals who would be wild and those humans, bound by a belief in human exceptionalism, who find themselves laboring under the burden of a handy humanism.

Wittgenstein took issue with Socrates' approach to the question of knowledge. He objected to the contemptuous attitude toward the particular that characterized Socrates' attempts

to define the fundamental nature of knowledge. Wittgenstein sought instead, by diagnosing and dissolving the suppositions on which this craving for generality depends, to eliminate the mental cramp that is their product. He sought to free the fly from the fly-bottle. The particular fly we have attempted to release is the assumption that the anthropocentric measuring of all things is inevitable. That fly has seen fit to alight on a diverse range of epistemologies and has been joined throughout by a succession of other animals who have intervened and interfered, persuading and reproaching us. Like that infamous Athenian GADFLY, they have fastened upon us, aroused us from dogmatic slumbers, and stirred us into life. Wittgenstein was in the business of freeing flies, but Socrates, responding to his accusers in the courthouse, claimed to be a fly, buzzing remorselessly around the imprudent assertions of his interlocutors. He called on those thinkers not to crush him, no matter that he vexed them. William Blake had swatted at flies, one summer's day, but following those offhand swipes he too, with something like contrition, had mused, "Am not I / A fly like thee?" Like the poet, we flies must be careful what we do with our thoughtless hands.

9. Nietzsche, *Daybreak*, 226 (§564).

Bibliography

Acampora, Christa Davis, and Ralph R. Acampora, eds. A Nietzschean Bestiary: Becoming Animal beyond Docile and Brutal. Lanham, Md.: Rowman and Littlefield, 2004.

Adams, Carol J. Neither Man nor Beast: Feminism and the Defense of Animals. New York: Continuum, 1994.

———. The Sexual Politics of Meat: A Feminist-Vegetarian Critical Theory. 10th anniversary ed. New York: Continuum, 2000.

Adorno, Theodor, and Max Horkheimer. Dialectic of Enlightenment. Translated by John Cumming. London: Verso, 1979. Originally published in German in 1944.

Adrados, Francisco Rodríguez. History of the Graeco-Latin Fable. Translated by Leslie A. Ray and Rojas del Canto. Revised by F. R. Adrados and Gert-Jan van Dijk. 3 vols. Leiden: Brill, 1999–2003.

Aesop. Aesop's Fables. Translated by Laura Gibbs. Oxford: Oxford University Press, 2008.

———. Æsop's Fables. Translated by V. S. Vernon Jones. Introduction by G. K. Chesterton. Illustrated by Arthur Rackham. 1912. New York: Franklin Watts, 1967.

———. The Fables of Æsop, Selected, Told Anew, and Their History Traced. Edited by Joseph Jacobs. Illustrated by Richard Heighway. London: Macmillan, 1894.

———. Three Hundred Æsop's Fables, Literally Translated from the Greek. Translated by George Fyler Townsend. London: George Routledge and Sons, 1867.

Agamben, Giorgio. The Open: Man and Animal. Translated by Kevin Attell. Stanford: Stanford University Press, 2004.

Albinus, Bernhard Siegfried. De ossibus corporis humani, ad auditores suos. Leidae Batavorum: Apud Henricum Mulhovium, 1726.

Alexander, Michael, trans. The Earliest English Poems. 3rd rev. ed. Penguin Classics. London: Penguin, 1992.

Althusser, Louis. "Freud and Lacan." In Lenin and Philosophy and Other Essays, translated by Ben Brewster, 177–202. London: NLB, 1971. Essay originally published in French in 1964.

Amundson, Ron. The Changing Role of the Embryo in Evolutionary Thought: Roots of Evo-Devo. Cambridge: Cambridge University Press, 2005.

Ansell-Pearson, Keith. Viroid Life: Perspectives on Nietzsche and the Transhuman Condition. London: Routledge, 1997.

Apollodorus. The Library. Translated by James

George Frazer. 2 vols. Loeb Classical Library 121 and 122. Cambridge, Mass.: Harvard University Press, 1921.

Aquila, Richard E. *Representational Mind: A Study of Kant's Theory of Knowledge*. Bloomington: Indiana University Press, 1983.

Aristophanes. "The Knights," "Peace," "The Birds," "The Assemblywomen," "Wealth." Translated by David Barrett and Alan H. Sommerstein. Harmondsworth, U.K.: Penguin, 1978.

———. "The Peace," "The Birds," "The Frogs." Translated by Benjamin Bickley Rogers. Loeb Classical Library. London: Heinemann, 1924.

Aristotle. *The History of Animals*. Translated by d'A. W. Thompson. In *The Complete Works of Aristotle: The Revised Oxford Translation*, edited by Jonathan Barnes, 2 vols., Bollingen Series, 1: 774–993. Princeton: Princeton University Press, 1984.

———. *Metaphysics*. Translated by W. D. Ross. In *The Complete Works of Aristotle: The Revised Oxford Translation*, edited by Jonathan Barnes, 2 vols., Bollingen Series, 2: 1552–728. Princeton: Princeton University Press, 1984.

———. *On the Heavens*. Translated by W. K. C. Guthrie. Aristotle in Twenty-Three Volumes, vol. 6. Loeb Classical Library 338. London: Heinemann, 1939.

———. *On the Parts of Animals*. Translated by James G. Lennox. Oxford: Clarendon Press, 2001.

Attenborough, David. *The Life of Birds*. London: BBC Books, 1998.

Audubon, John James. *The Birds of America*. London, 1827–38.

Augustine. *St. Augustine: Exposition on the Book of Psalms (Enarrationes in Psalmos)*. Edited by A. Cleveland Coxe. 1888. The Early Church Fathers, Nicene and Post-Nicene Fathers, series 1, St. Augustine Volumes, Christian Classics Ethereal Library, 8. http://www.ccel.org/ccel/schaff/npnf108.toc.html (accessed June 30, 2009).

Aulie, Richard P. *A Reader's Guide to "Of Pandas and People."* National Association of Biology Teachers, 1998. http://www.stephenjaygould.org/ctrl/archive/design/aulie_of-pandas.html (accessed October 1, 2011).

Aunger, Robert, ed. *Darwinizing Culture: The Status of Memetics as a Science*. Oxford: Oxford University Press, 2000.

Austin, J. L. *Sense and Sensibilia*. Reconstructed by G. J. Warnock. Oxford: Clarendon Press, 1962. Lectures delivered between 1947 and 1959.

Babrius and Phaedrus. Translated by Ben Edwin Perry. London: Heinemann, 1965.

Baker, Myron C. "Depauperate Meme Pool of Vocal Signals in an Island Population of Singing Honeyeaters." *Animal Behaviour* 51, no. 4 (1996): 853–58.

Baker, Steve. *Picturing the Beast: Animals, Identity, and Representation*. Champaign: University of Illinois Press, 2001.

———. "Sloughing the Human." In *Zoontologies: The Question of the Animal*, edited by Cary Wolfe, 147–64. Minneapolis: University of Minnesota Press, 2003.

Barten, S. L. "Shedding (Ecdysis)." In *Care in Captivity: Husbandry Techniques for Amphibians and Reptiles*, edited by E. Beltz, 17–18. Chicago: Chicago Herpetological Society, 1989.

Barthes, Roland. "Inaugural Lecture, Collège de France." In *A Barthes Reader*, edited by Susan Sontag, 457–78. London: Vintage, 1982. Lecture delivered in 1977.

———. "Myth Today." In *Mythologies*, translated by Annette Lavers, 109–59. London: Vintage, 1993. Essay originally published in French in 1957.

Barzun, Jacques. *A Stroll with William James*. Chicago: University of Chicago Press, 2002. Originally published in 1983.

Bataille, Georges. *Theory of Religion*. Translated by Robert Hurley. New York: Zone, 1989. Written in 1948 and first published in French in 1974.

Beck, Benjamin B. "Chimpocentrism: Bias in Cognitive Ethology." *Journal of Human Evolution* 11 (1982): 3–17.

Beer, Gillian. *Darwin's Plots: Evolutionary Narrative in Darwin, George Eliot, and Nineteenth-Century Fiction*. London: Ark, 1983.

Beiser, Frederick C. *The Fate of Reason: German Philosophy from Kant to Fichte*. Cambridge, Mass.: Harvard University Press, 1987.

Bell, Charles. *The Hand: Its Mechanism and Vital Endowments as Evincing Design*. 5th ed. Fourth Bridgewater Treatise. London: John Murray, 1852. First edition published in 1833.

Bellos, Alex. "Gaffing up a Russian Tree." *Guardian*, n.d., Weekend Guardian, 9.

Benzon, William. "Culture as an Evolutionary Arena." *Journal of Social and Evolutionary Systems* 19 (1996): 321–62.

Bertelsen, Arne, and Norman Capener. "Fingers, Compensation, and King Canute." *Journal of Bone and Joint Surgery* 42b, no. 2 (May 1960): 390–92.

Bestall, Alfred E. "Rupert and the Sky-Boat." In *Rupert: The Daily Express Annual*. London: Beaverbrook Newspapers, 1970.

Bhabha, Homi K. "The Other Question . . ." *Screen* 24, no. 6 (November–December 1983): 18–36.

Bierce, Ambrose. *The Unabridged Devil's Dictionary*. Edited by David E. Schultz and S. T. Joshi. Athens: University of Georgia Press, 2001.

Blackmore, Susan. *The Meme Machine*. Oxford: Oxford University Press, 1999.

———. "The Memes' Eye View." In *Darwinizing Culture: The Status of Memetics as a Science*, edited by Robert Aunger, 25–42. Oxford: Oxford University Press, 2000.

Blake, William. "The Fly." In *Songs of Innocence and of Experience: Shewing the Two Contrary States of the Human Soul*, no pagination. [London, 1794]. An online edition is available at http://www.rarebook-room.org/Control/blkin1/index.html.

Blumberg, Dorothy Rose. *Whose What? Aaron's Beard to Zorn's Lemma*. New York: Holt, Rinehart and Winston, 1969.

Blumenbach, Johann Friedrich. *On the Natural Varieties of Mankind (De generis humani varietate nativa)*. Translated by Thomas Bendyshe, 1865. New York: Bergman, 1969. Originally published in Latin in 1775.

Boffetti, Jason M. "Rorty's Nietzschean Pragmatism: A Jamesian Response." *Review of Politics* 66, no. 4 (Autumn 2004): 605–31.

Boltzmann, Ludwig. "On a Thesis of Schopenhauer's." Translated by Paul Foulkes. Originally published in German in 1905. In *Theoretical Physics and Philosophical Problems, Selected Writings*, edited by Brian McGuinness, 185–98. Dordrecht: D. Reidel, 1974.

Book of the British Countryside. 2nd ed. London: Drive Publications, 1974.

Borges, Jorge Luis. "John Wilkins' Analytical Language." In *Selected Non-Fictions*, edited by Eliot Weinberger, translated by Esther Allen, Suzanne Jill Levine, and Eliot Weinberger, 229–32. New York: Penguin, 1999. Essay originally published in Spanish in 1942.

Boulle, Pierre. *Monkey Planet*. 1963. Translated by Xan Fielding. Harmondsworth, U.K.: Penguin, 1975. Originally published in French in 1963.

Bradley, Melvin. *The Missouri Mule: His Origin and Times*. 2 vols. Missouri: University of Missouri, 1993.

Browne, Janet. *Charles Darwin: A Biography*. Vol. 1, *Voyaging*. London: Jonathan Cape, 1995.

Browne, Thomas. *Pseudodoxia Epidemica; or, Enquiries into Very Many Received Tenents and Commonly Presumed Truths*. 6th ed. London: Nath. Ekins, 1672. First edition published in 1646. http://penelope.uchicago.edu/pseudodoxia/ (accessed September 29, 2009).

Buchanan, Brett. *Onto-Ethologies: The Animal Environments of Uexküll, Heidegger, Merleau-Ponty, and Deleuze*. Albany: State University of New York Press, 2008.

Budiansky, Stephen. *If a Lion Could Talk: How Animals Think*. London: Phoenix, 1998.

Buller, Walter Lawry. *A History of the Birds of New Zealand*. 2nd ed. London, 1887–88.

Burgard, Peter J., ed. *Nietzsche and the Feminine*. Charlottesville: University Press of Virginia, 1994.

Burghardt, Gordon M. "Animal Awareness: Current Perceptions and Historical Perspective." *American Psychologist* 40, no. 8 (August 1985): 905–19.

Burton, Reginald William Boteler. *Pindar's Pythian Odes: Essays in Interpretation*. London: Oxford University Press, 1962.

Butterworth, George, and Shoji Itakura. "Development of Precision Grips in Chimpanzees." *Developmental Science* 1, no. 1 (1998): 39–43.

Calarco, Matthew. "Heidegger's Zoontology." In *Animal Philosophy: Essential Readings in Continental Thought*, edited by Peter Atterton and Matthew Calarco, 18–30. London: Continuum, 2004.

———. *Zoographies: The Question of the Animal from Heidegger to Derrida*. New York: Columbia University Press, 2008.

Candland, Douglas Keith. *Feral Children and Clever Animals: Reflections on Human Nature*. New York: Oxford University Press, 1993.

Carroll, Lewis. *Alice's Adventures in Wonderland and Through the Looking Glass*. Illustrated by Harry Rountree. London: Collins' Clear-Type Press, 1928. Originally published in 1866 (*Alice's Adventures in Wonderland*) and 1871 (*Through the Looking Glass*).

Cavell, Stanley. *In Quest of the Ordinary: Lines of Skepticism and Romanticism*. Chicago: University of Chicago Press, 1988.

———. *This New Yet Unapproachable America*. Albuquerque, N.M.: Living Batch Press, 1989.

Chappell, Timothy. "Plato on Knowledge in the *Theaetetus*." In *Stanford Encyclopedia of Philosophy* (Winter 2008 Edition), edited by Edward N. Zalta. http://plato.stanford.edu/archives/win2008/entries/plato-theaetetus/ (accessed July 6, 2009).

Churchill, Sue. *Australian Bats*. Sydney: Reed New Holland, 1998.

[Cicero, Marcus Tullius]. *Ad C. Herennium de ratione dicendi (Rhetorica ad Herennium)*. Translated by Harry Caplan. Loeb Classical Library 403. London: Heinemann, 1954.

———. *De re publica, de legibus*. Translated by Clinton Walker Keyes. Loeb Classical Library 213. Cambridge, Mass.: Harvard University Press, 1928.

———. "Pro Murena." In *The Speeches*. Translated by Louis E. Lord. Loeb Classical Library 324. London: Heinemann, 1953.

Cirker, Blanche, ed. *1800 Woodcuts by Thomas Bewick and His School*. New York: Dover, 1962.

Clack, Jennifer A. *Gaining Ground: The Origin and Evolution of Tetrapods*. Bloomington: Indiana University Press, 2002.

Clark, David L. "Kant's Aliens: The Anthropology

and Its Others." *Centennial Review* 1, no. 2 (Autumn 2000): 201–89.

Clark, Maudemarie. *Nietzsche on Truth and Philosophy*. Cambridge: Cambridge University Press, 1990.

———. "On Knowledge, Truth, and Value: Nietzsche's Debt to Schopenhauer and the Development of His Empiricism." In *Willing and Nothingness: Schopenhauer as Nietzsche's Educator*, edited by Christopher Janaway, 37–78. Oxford: Clarendon Press, 1998.

Clark, Ronald W. *The Huxleys*. London: Heinemann, 1968.

Clark, Willene B. *A Medieval Book of Beasts: The Second-Family Bestiary; Commentary, Art, Text, and Translation*. Woodbridge, U.K.: Boydell, 2006.

Coates, M. I., and J. A. Clack. "Polydactyly in the Earliest Known Tetrapod Limbs." *Nature* 347, no. 6288 (September 6, 1990): 66–69.

Corbey, Raymond. *The Metaphysics of Apes: Negotiating the Animal–Human Boundary*. Cambridge: Cambridge University Press, 2005.

Cowper, William. *The Poems of William Cowper*. Edited by John D. Baird and Charles Ryskamp. Vol. 1, 1748–1782. Oxford: Oxford University Press, 1980.

Cox, Christoph. *Nietzsche: Naturalism and Interpretation*. Berkeley: University of California Press, 1999.

Crowe, Michael J. *The Extraterrestrial Life Debate, 1750–1900*. Mineola, N.Y.: Dover, 1999.

Culler, Jonathan. "Commentary." In "On Metaphor," special issue, *New Literary History* 6, no. 1 (Autumn 1974): 219–29.

Danto, Arthur C. *Nietzsche as Philosopher*. Exp. ed. New York: Columbia University Press, 2005.

Darwin, Charles. *The Correspondence of Charles Darwin*. Edited by Frederick Burkhardt and Sydney Smith. Vol. 6, 1856–1857. Cambridge: Cambridge University Press, 1990.

———. *The Descent of Man, and Selection in Relation to Sex*. 2nd ed. London: John Murray, 1882. First edition published in 1871.

———. *Journal of Researches into the Natural History and Geology of the Countries Visited during the Voyage Round the World of H.M.S. Beagle*. 11th ed. London: John Murray, 1890. First edition published in 1839.

———. *The Life and Letters of Charles Darwin, Including an Autobiographical Chapter*. Edited by Francis Darwin. 3 vols. London: John Murray, 1887.

———. *More Letters of Charles Darwin*. Edited by Frances Darwin and A. C. Seward. 2 vols. London: John Murray, 1903.

———. *On the Origin of Species by Means of Natural Selection; or, The Preservation of Favoured Races in the Struggle for Life*. London: John Murray, 1859.

———. *The Variation of Animals and Plants under Domestication*. 2nd ed. 2 vols. London: John Murray, 1875. First edition published in 1868.

Daston, Lorraine, and Gregg Mitman, eds. *Thinking with Animals: New Perspectives on Anthropomorphism*. New York: Columbia University Press, 2005.

Dawkins, Richard. *The Blind Watchmaker*. New York: Norton, 1986.

———. "Don't Turn Your Back on Science." *Observer*, May 21, 2000. http://www.guardian.co.uk/Archive/Article/0,4273,4020558,00.html (accessed August 17, 2009).

———. *The Extended Phenotype: The Gene as the Unit of Selection*. Oxford: W. H. Freeman, 1982.

———. Foreword to *The Meme Machine*, by Susan Blackmore, vii–xvii. Oxford: Oxford University Press, 1999.

———. "Gaps in the Mind." In *The Great Ape Project: Equality beyond Humanity*, edited by Paola Cavalieri and Peter Singer, 80–87. London: Fourth Estate, 1993.

———. *The God Delusion*. London: Bantam, 2006.

———. *River out of Eden*. London: Weidenfeld and Nicolson, 1995.

———. "Science, Delusion, and the Appetite for Wonder." Richard Dimbleby Lecture, BBC 1, November 12, 1996. http://richarddawkins.net/articles/3-science-delusion-and-the-appetite-for-wonder (accessed October 1, 2011).

———. *The Selfish Gene*. 30th anniv. ed. Oxford: Oxford University Press, 2006. First edition published in 1976.

———. "Viruses of the Mind." In *Dennett and His Critics: Demystifying Mind*, edited by Bo Dahlbom, 13–27. Cambridge, Mass.: Blackwell, 1993.

———. "What's Wrong with the Paranormal?" http://www.simonyi.ox.ac.uk/dawkins/WorldOfDawkins-archive/Dawkins/Work/Articles/1998-02-08paranormal.shtml (accessed September 18, 2009).

———. "The Word Made Flesh." *Guardian*, December 27, 2001, Science section, 13.

de Jorio, Andrea. *Gesture in Naples and Gesture in Classical Antiquity*. 1832. Translated by Adam Kendon. Bloomington: Indiana University Press, 2000.

DeLanda, Manuel. "Deleuze and the Genesis of Form." *Art Orbit* 1 (March 1998). http://www.artnode.se/artorbit/issue1/f_deleuze/f_deleuze_delanda.html (accessed November 17, 2009).

———. *Intensive Science and Virtual Philosophy*. London: Continuum, 2002.

Deleuze, Gilles. *Kant's Critical Philosophy*. Translated by Hugh Tomlinson and Barbara Habberjam. Minneapolis: University of Minnesota Press, 1984. Originally published in French in 1963.

———. "Nomad Thought." Translated by Jacqueline Wallace. *Semiotext(e)* 3, no. 1 (1978): 12–21. Originally published in French in 1973.

Deleuze, Gilles, and Félix Guattari. *A Thousand Plateaus: Capitalism and Schizophrenia*. Translated by Brian Massumi. London: Athlone Press, 1988. Originally published in French in 1980.

Dennett, Daniel C. *Consciousness Explained*. London: Allen Lane, 1991.

———. *Darwin's Dangerous Idea: Evolution and the Meanings of Life*. London: Allen Lane, 1995.

———. *The Intentional Stance*. Cambridge, Mass.: Bradford Books, 1987.

———. *Kinds of Minds*. New York: Basic Books, 1996.

———. "Memes and the Exploitation of Imagination." *Journal of Aesthetics and Art Criticism* 48, no. 2 (Spring 1990): 127–35.

De Quincey, Thomas. "The Theban Sphinx." In *The Caesars and Other Papers*. De Quincey's Works, 9: 237–52. Edinburgh: Adam and Charles Black, 1862.

Derrida, Jacques. *The Animal That Therefore I Am*. Edited by Marie-Louise Mallet. Translated by David Wills. New York: Fordham University Press, 2008. Originally published in French in 2006.

———. "'Eating Well'; or, The Calculation of the Subject: An Interview with Jacques Derrida." Translated by Peter Connor and Avital Ronell. In *Points . . . : Interviews, 1974–1994*, edited by Elisabeth Weber, translated by Peggy Kamuf et al., 255–87. Stanford: Stanford University Press, 1995. Interview originally given in French in 1988.

———. "Geschlecht II: Heidegger's Hand." In *Deconstruction and Philosophy: The Texts of Jacques Derrida*, edited by John Sallis, 161–96. Chicago: University of Chicago Press, 1987.

———. *Margins of Philosophy*. Translated by Alan Bass. Chicago: University of Chicago Press, 1982. Originally published in French in 1972.

———. *Monolingualism of the Other; or, The Prosthesis of Origin*. Translated by Patrick Mensah. Stanford: Stanford University Press, 1996. Originally published in French in 1996.

———. *Of Spirit: Heidegger and the Question*. Translated by Geoffrey Bennington and Rachel Bowlby. Chicago: University of Chicago Press, 1989. Originally published in French in 1987.

———. *The Post Card: From Socrates to Freud and Beyond*. Translated by Alan Bass. Chicago: University of Chicago Press, 1987. Originally published in French in 1980.

———. *Resistances of Psychoanalysis*. Translated by Peggy Kamuf, Pascale-Anne Brault, and Michael Naas. Stanford: Stanford University Press, 1998. Originally published in French in 1996.

———. "There Is No One Narcissism (Autobiophotographies)." In *Points . . . : Interviews, 1974–1994*, edited by Elisabeth Weber, translated by Peggy Kamuf et al., 196–215. Stanford: Stanford University Press, 1995. Essay originally published in French in 1986.

de Waal, Frans. *The Ape and the Sushi Master: Cultural Reflections by a Primatologist*. London: Allen Lane, 2001.

de Waal, Frans, and Frans Lanting. *Bonobo: The Forgotten Ape*. Berkeley: University of California Press, 1997.

Diamond, Jared. *The Rise and Fall of the Third Chimpanzee*. London: Vintage, 1992.

Dickson, Tom. *The Great Minnesota Fish Book*. Minneapolis: University of Minnesota Press, 2008.

Diodorus of Sicily. *The Library of History*. Translated by C. H. Oldfather. Vol. 3. Loeb Classical Library 340. Cambridge, Mass.: Harvard University Press, 1993. Translation originally published in 1939.

Dooley, Beth. "Taste: Asparagus—Splendor in the Grass." *Minneapolis Star Tribune*, April 24, 2002. http://www.startribune.com/lifestyle/taste/11408616.html (accessed May 16, 2009).

Douthwaite, Julia V. *The Wild Girl, Natural Man, and the Monster: Dangerous Experiments in the Age of Enlightenment*. Chicago: University of Chicago Press, 2002.

Doyle, Arthur Conan. "The Adventure of Silver Blaze." In *Sherlock Holmes: The Complete Illustrated Short Stories*, 229–50. London: Chancellor Press, 1985. Originally published in 1892.

Duling, Dennis C. New translation of and introduction to the Testament of Solomon. In *The Old Testament Pseudepigrapha*, edited by James H. Charlesworth. Vol. 1, *Apocalyptic Literature and Testaments*, 935–87. London: Darton, Longman and Todd, 1983.

Dunayer, Joan. *Animal Equality: Language and Liberation*. Derwood, Md.: Ryce, 2001.

Dupré, John. "In Defence of Classification." In *Humans and Other Animals*, 81–99. Oxford: Clarendon Press, 2002.

Dyer, Richard. "The Role of Stereotypes." In *The Matter of Images: Essays on Representations*, 2nd ed., 11–18. London: Routledge, 2002.

Dyson, George. *Darwin among the Machines*. London: Allen Lane, 1997.

Eco, Umberto. "Horns, Hooves, Insteps: Some Hypotheses on Three Types of Abduction." In *The Sign of Three: Peirce, Holmes, Dupin*, edited by Umberto Eco and Thomas A. Sebeok, 198–220. Bloomington: Indiana University Press, 1983.

———. *Kant and the Platypus*. Translated by Alastair McEwen. London: Secker and Warburg, 1999.

Edgerton, Franklin, trans. and ed. *The Panchatantra Reconstructed.* 2 vols. New Haven: American Oriental Society, 1924.

Eldred, Michael. "As: A Critical Note on David Farrel Krell's Daimon Life." Version 1.2 (April 2002). Artefact: A Site of Philosophy. http://192.220.96.165/as_krell.html (accessed March 20, 2009).

Engels, Frederick. "The Part Played by Labour in the Transition from Ape to Man." In *The Origin of the Family, Private Property, and the State,* edited by Eleanor Burke Leacock. London: Lawrence and Wishart, 1972. Essay originally published in 1876.

Ereshefsky, Marc. *The Poverty of the Linnaean Hierarchy: A Philosophical Study of Biological Taxonomy.* Cambridge: Cambridge University Press, 2001.

Fairbanks, Arthur, ed. and trans. *The First Philosophers of Greece.* London: Kegan Paul, Trench, Trubner, 1898.

Fay, Brian. *Contemporary Philosophy of Social Science: A Multicultural Approach.* Oxford: Blackwell, 1996.

Fenton, M. Brock. *The Bat: Wings in the Night Sky.* Shrewsbury, U.K.: Swan Hill Press, 1998.

Feuerbach, Ludwig. *Principles of the Philosophy of the Future.* In *The Fiery Brook: Selected Writings of Ludwig Feuerbach.* Translated by Zawar Hanfi. Garden City, N.Y.: Anchor Books, 1972. Manifesto originally published in German in 1843.

Feyerabend, Paul. *Against Method.* 3rd ed. London: Verso, 1993. First edition published in 1975.

Finn, Frank. *The Wild Beasts of the World.* 2 vols. London: T. C. and E. C. Jack, 1909.

Fischer, Steven Roger. *A History of Writing.* London: Reaktion, 2001.

Fitzgerald, William. *Slavery and the Roman Literary Imagination.* Cambridge: Cambridge University Press, 2000.

Foss, Sam Walter. *Whiffs from Wild Meadows.* Boston: Lee and Shepard, 1905. Originally published in 1895.

Fossey, Dian. *Gorillas in the Mist.* London: Penguin, 1985. Originally published in 1983.

Foucault, Michel. *The Archaeology of Knowledge.* Translated by A. M. Sheridan Smith. London: Tavistock Publications, 1972. Originally published in French in 1969.

———. *L'Archeologie du savoir.* Paris: Gallimard, 1971. Originally published in 1969.

———. *Death and the Labyrinth: The World of Raymond Roussel.* Translated by Charles Ruas. London: Athlone Press, 1987. Originally published in French in 1963.

——— [Maurice Florence, pseud.]. "Foucault." Translated by R. Hurley. In *Aesthetics, Method, and Epistemology,* edited by James D. Faubion, vol. 2 of *Essential Works of Foucault,* 459–63. London: Allen Lane, 1998. Essay originally published in French in 1984.

———. "The Masked Philosopher." Interviewed by Christian Delacampagne. Translated by John Johnston. In *Foucault Live: Collected Interviews, 1961–1984,* edited by Sylvère Lotringer, 302–8. New York: Semiotext(e), 1996. Interview, originally in French, from 1980.

———. *The Order of Things: An Archaeology of the Human Sciences.* [Translated by A. M. Sheridan Smith, 1970.] London: Routledge, 1994. Originally published in French in 1966.

———. "Polemics, Politics, and Problematizations." Interviewed by Paul Rabinow. Translated by Lydia Davis. In *The Foucault Reader: An Introduction to Foucault's Thought,* edited by Paul Rabinow, 381–90. London: Penguin, 1984. Interview, originally in French, from 1984.

———. "Preface to *The History of Sexuality,* Volume

II." Translated by William Smock. In *The Foucault Reader: An Introduction to Foucault's Thought*, edited by Paul Rabinow, 333–39. London: Penguin, 1984.

———. "The Subject and Power." Part 2 translated by L. Sawyer. In *Power*, edited by James D. Faubion, vol. 3 of *Essential Works of Foucault*, 326–48. London: Allen Lane, 2001. Essay originally published in 1982; part 2 originally published in French.

———. "Truth and Juridical Forms." Translated by R. Hurley. In *Power*, edited by James D. Faubion, vol. 3 of *Essential Works of Foucault*, 1–89. London: Allen Lane, 2001. Lecture originally delivered in 1973.

———. "Truth, Power, Self: An Interview with Michel Foucault, October 25, 1982." Interviewed by Rux Martin. In *Technologies of the Self: A Seminar with Michel Foucault*, edited by Luther H. Martin, Huck Gutman, and Patrick H. Hutton, 9–15. Amherst: University of Massachusetts Press, 1988.

———. "What Is Enlightenment?" Translated by Catherine Porter. In *The Foucault Reader: An Introduction to Foucault's Thought*, edited by Paul Rabinow, 32–50. London: Penguin, 1984. Essay originally published in French in 1978.

———. "Who Are You, Professor Foucault?" Interviewed by Paolo Caruso. Translated by Lucille Cairns. In *Religion and Culture by Michel Foucault*, edited by Jeremy R. Carrette, 87–103. Manchester, U.K.: Manchester University Press, 1999. Interview, originally in French, from 1967.

Fox, Robert, Stephen W. Lehmkuhle, and David H. Westendorf. "Falcon Visual Acuity." *Science* 192, no. 4236 (April 16, 1976): 263–65.

Freud, Sigmund. "From the History of an Infantile Neurosis." Translated by Alix and James Strachey. In *An Infantile Neurosis and Other Works*, vol. 17 of *The Standard Edition of the Complete Psychological Works of Sigmund Freud*, edited by James Strachey, 1–122. London: Hogarth Press, 1955. Essay originally published in German in 1918.

———. *Group Psychology and the Analysis of the Ego*. Translated by James Strachey. Vol. 18 of *The Standard Edition of the Complete Psychological Works of Sigmund Freud*, edited by James Strachey. London: Hogarth Press, 1955. Originally published in German in 1921.

———. "The Return of Totemism in Childhood." Translated by James Strachey. In *Totem and Taboo*, vol. 13 of *The Standard Edition of the Complete Psychological Works of Sigmund Freud*, edited by James Strachey, vi–161. London: Hogarth Press, 1960. Essay originally published in German in 1913.

Freyd, Jennifer J., and J. Q. Johnson. "Commentary: Domestic Violence, Folk Etymologies, and 'Rule of Thumb.'" University of Oregon, 1998. http://dynamic.uoregon.edu/~jjf/essays/ruleofthumb.html (accessed February 3, 2010).

Gaita, Raimond. *The Philosopher's Dog*. London: Routledge, 2002.

Galen [Claudius Galenus]. *On the Usefulness of the Parts of the Body*. Translated by Margaret Tallmadge May. Ithaca, N.Y.: Cornell University Press, 1968.

Gardiner, Muriel, ed. *The Wolf-Man and Sigmund Freud*. Harmondsworth, U.K.: Penguin, 1973.

Gatherer, Derek. "Why the 'Thought Contagion' Metaphor Is Retarding the Progress of Memetics." *Journal of Memetics—Evolutionary Models of Information Transmission* 2, no. 2 (December 1998). http://cfpm.org/jom-emit/1998/vol2/gatherer_d.html (accessed January 9, 2010).

Gaylin, Willard. *Adam and Eve and Pinocchio: On Being and Becoming Human*. New York: Viking, 1990.

Gellius, Aulus. *Attic Nights*. Translated by J. C. Rolfe.

3 vols. Loeb Classical Library 195, 200, and 212. Cambridge, Mass.: Harvard University Press, 1927.

Genosko, Gary. *Undisciplined Theory*. London: Sage, 1998.

Geronimi, Clyde, Hamilton S. Luske, and Wolfgang Reitherman, directors. *One Hundred and One Dalmatians* (movie). Burbank, Calif.: Walt Disney Productions, 1961.

Ginzberg, Louis. *The Legends of the Jews*. Translated by Henrietta Szold. Vol. 4, *Bible Times and Characters from Joshua to Esther*. Philadelphia: Jewish Publication Society of America, 1936. Originally published in German.

Glendinning, Simon. "From Animal Life to City Life." *Angelaki* 5, no. 3 (December 2000): 19–30.

———. "Heidegger and the Question of Animality." *International Journal of Philosophical Studies* 4, no. 1 (1996): 67–86.

———. *In the Name of Phenomenology*. London: Routledge, 2007.

Goodsir, John. *The Anatomical Memoirs of John Goodsir*. Edited by William Turner. 2 vols. Edinburgh: Adam and Charles Black, 1868.

Gotch, A. F. *Mammals: Their Latin Names Explained*. Poole, U.K.: Blandford, 1979.

Gould, Stephen Jay. "Double Trouble." In *The Panda's Thumb: More Reflections in Natural History*, 35–44. New York: Norton, 1980.

———. "Eight Little Piggies." In *Eight Little Piggies: Reflections in Natural History*, 63–78. London: Jonathan Cape, 1993.

———. Introduction to *Evolution: The Triumph of an Idea*, by Carl Zimmer, ix–xiv. London: Heinemann, 2002.

———. "Losing a Limpet." In *Eight Little Piggies: Reflections in Natural History*, 52–60. London: Jonathan Cape, 1993.

———. "The Panda's Thumb." In *The Panda's Thumb: More Reflections in Natural History*, 19–26. New York: Norton, 1980.

———. "SETI and the Wisdom of Casey Stengel." In *The Flamingo's Smile: Reflections in Natural History*, 403–13. New York: Norton, 1985.

———. "To Show an Ape." In *The Flamingo's Smile: Reflections in Natural History*, 263–80. New York: Norton, 1985.

———. "What the Immaculate Pigeon Teaches the Burdened Mind." In *Eight Little Piggies: Reflections in Natural History*, 355–70. London: Jonathan Cape, 1993.

Goux, Jean-Joseph. *Oedipus, Philosopher*. Translated by Catherine Porter. Stanford: Stanford University Press, 1993. Originally published in French in 1992.

Grant, Peter R. *Ecology and Evolution of Darwin's Finches*. Princeton: Princeton University Press, 1986.

Graves, Robert. *The Greek Myths*. Rev. ed. 2 vols. Harmondsworth, U.K.: Penguin, 1960.

Greene, Edward L. "Linnæus as Evolutionist." *Proceedings of the Washington Academy of Sciences* 11 (March 31, 1909): 17–26.

Greene, John C. *The Death of Adam: Evolution and Its Impact on Western Thought*. Ames: Iowa State University Press, 1959.

Gribbin, Mary, and John Gribbin. *Being Human: Putting People in an Evolutionary Perspective*. London: Dent, 1993.

Griffin, Donald R. *Animal Minds*. Chicago: University of Chicago Press, 1992.

———. *The Question of Animal Awareness: Evolutionary Continuity of Mental Experience*. 2nd ed. New York: Rockefeller University Press, 1981.

Groves, Colin. *Primate Taxonomy*. Washington, D.C.: Smithsonian Institution Press, 2001.

Grzimek, Bernhard. *Grzimek's Animal Life Encyclo-pedia*. Vol. 6, *Reptiles*. New York: Van Nostrand Reinhold, 1971.

Guynup, Sharon. "Conservationists Fight to Save Harpy Eagles." *National Geographic News*, June 3, 2002. http://news.nationalgeographic.com/news/2002/06/0603_020603_TVharpyeagle.html (accessed February 5, 2010).

Hacking, Ian. *Representing and Intervening: Introductory Topics in the Philosophy of Natural Science*. Cambridge: Cambridge University Press, 1983.

———. *The Social Construction of What?* Cambridge, Mass.: Harvard University Press, 1999.

"HACNS1 Gene Enhancer May Have Contributed to Evolution of the Human Opposable Thumb." Agency for Science, Technology and Research, Singapore, September 5, 2008. http://www.a-star.edu.sg/biomedical_sciences/394Technical-Release?iid=552 (accessed August 3, 2009).

Halliday, Tim, and Kraig Adler, eds. *The New Encyclo-pedia of Reptiles and Amphibians*. Oxford: Oxford University Press, 2002.

Ham, Jennifer. "Taming the Beast: Animality in Wedekind and Nietzsche." In *Animal Acts: Configuring the Human in Western History*, edited by Jennifer Ham and Matthew Senior, 145–63. London: Routledge, 1997.

Hammond, Claudia. *Finger Prints*. BBC Radio 4, March 18 to April 15, 2003. http://www.bbc.co.uk/radio4/science/fingerprints.shtml.

Hansell, Jean. *The Pigeon in History; or, The Dove's Tale*. Bath, U.K.: Millstream Books, 1998.

Haraway, Donna. *Modest_Witness@Second_Millenium. FemaleMan©_Meets_OncoMouse™: Feminism and Technoscience*. New York: Routledge, 1997.

———. *Primate Visions: Gender, Race, and Nature in the World of Modern Science*. New York: Routledge, 1989.

Hardt, Michael, and Antonio Negri. *Empire*. Cambridge, Mass.: Harvard University Press, 2000.

Harré, Rom, and Michael Krausz. *Varieties of Relativism*. Oxford: Blackwell, 1996.

Harris, Marvin. *Culture, People, Nature: An Introduction to General Anthropology*. 7th ed. New York: Longman, 1997.

Harris, Michael. *A Field Guide to the Birds of Galapagos*. Illustrated by Barry Kent McKay. Rev. ed. London: Collins, 1982. First edition published in 1974.

Harrison, Peter. "Linnaeus as a Second Adam? Taxonomy and the Religious Vocation." *Zygon* 44, no. 4 (Dec 2009): 879–93.

Harter, Jim. *Animals: 1419 Copyright-Free Illustrations of Mammals, Birds, Fish, Insects, etc.; A Pictorial Archive from Nineteenth-Century Sources*. New York: Dover, 1979.

Hawthorne, Nathaniel. *Tanglewood Tales*. Illustrated by Edmund Dulac. London: Folio Society, 2002. First published in 1853; illustrations first published in the 1918 edition.

———. *A Wonder Book for Girls and Boys*. Illustrated by Walter Crane. Boston: Houghton, Mifflin, 1892. First published in 1852; illustrations first published in the 1892 edition.

Heidegger, Martin. "The Anaximander Fragment." In *Early Greek Thinking*, translated by David Farrell Krell and Frank A. Capuzzi, 13–58. New York: Harper and Row, 1975. Essay written in German in 1946.

———. *Aristotle's Metaphysics Θ 1–3: On the Essence and Actuality of Force*. Translation by Walter Brogan and Peter Warnek. Bloomington: Indiana University Press, 1995. Lecture course originally delivered in German in 1931.

———. *Basic Writings.* Edited by David Farrell Krell. 2nd ed. London: Routledge, 1993.

———. *Being and Time.* Translated by John Macquarrie and Edward Robinson. Oxford: Blackwell, 1962. Originally published in German in 1927.

———. *The Fundamental Concepts of Metaphysics: World, Finitude, Solitude.* Translated by William McNeill and Nicholas Walker. Bloomington: Indiana University Press, 1995. Lecture course originally delivered in German in 1929–30.

———. *Introduction to Metaphysics.* Translated by Gregory Fried and Richard Polt. New Haven: Yale University Press, 2000. Written in German in 1935.

———. "Letter on Humanism." Translated by Frank A. Capuzzi and J. Glenn Gray. In *Basic Writings,* edited by David Farrell Krell, 2nd ed., 217–65. London: Routledge, 1993. Essay written in German in 1947.

———. *Nietzsche.* Vol. 2, *The Eternal Recurrence of the Same.* Translated by David Farrell Krell. New York: HarperSanFrancisco, 1984. Lecture course originally delivered in German in 1937.

———. *Parmenides.* Translated by André Schuwer and Richard Rojcewicz. Bloomington: Indiana University Press, 1992. Lecture course originally delivered in German in 1942–43.

———. *What Is Called Thinking?* Translated by Fred D. Wieck and J. Glenn Gray. New York: Harper and Row, 1968. Lecture course originally delivered in German in 1951–52.

Herbermann, C. G., Edward A. Pace, Condé B. Pallen, Thomas J. Shahon, and John J. Wynne, eds. *Catholic Encyclopedia.* New York: Robert Appleton, 1907–14.

Hill, R. Kevin. *Nietzsche's Critiques: The Kantian Foundations of His Thought.* Oxford: Oxford University Press, 2003.

Hinchliffe, Steve. "Pigeons, Cities, and Unnatural Selection." In *City A–Z,* edited by Steve Pile and Nigel Thrift, 179–82. London: Routledge, 2000.

Hollier, Denis. "The Dualist Materialism of Georges Bataille." In *Bataille: A Critical Reader,* edited by Fred Botting and Scott Wilson, 59–73. Oxford: Blackwell, 1998.

Holmgren, Virginia C. *Raccoons: In History, Folklore, and Today's Backyards.* Santa Barbara, Calif.: Capra Press, 1990.

Holtsmark, Erling B. "Critiques of 'Proto-Guru' Xenophanes, a Precursor to Plato: Xenophanes Fragments 11–12." *Daily Iowan,* February 22, 1994, 6b.

Homeric Hymns, Homeric Apocrypha, Lives of Homer. Edited and translated by Martin L. West. Loeb Classical Library 496. Cambridge, Mass.: Harvard University Press, 2003.

Hooke, Robert. *Micrographia; or, Some Physiological Descriptions of Minute Bodies Made by Magnifying Glasses.* London: J. Martyn and J. Allestry, 1665.

Hornidge, Marilis. *That Yankee Cat: The Maine Coon.* 3rd edition. Gardiner, Maine: Tilbury House, 2002.

Howe, Nathan R., and Younus M. Sheikh. "Anthopleurine: A Sea Anemone Alarm Pheromone." *Science* 189, no. 4200 (August 1, 1975): 386–88.

Hoyningen-Huene, Paul. "Context of Discovery and Context of Justification." *Studies in History and Philosophy of Science* 18, no. 4 (1987): 501–15.

Hull, David L. "Taking Memetics Seriously: Memetics Will Be What We Make It." In *Darwinizing Culture: The Status of Memetics as a Science,* edited by Robert Aunger, 43–67. Oxford: Oxford University Press, 2000.

Hume, David. *Dialogues Concerning Natural Religion.* New York: Hafner / Macmillan, 1977. Originally published in 1779.

Huxley, Thomas Henry. *Evidence as to Man's Place in Nature.* London: Williams and Norgate, 1863.

———. *Life and Letters of Thomas Henry Huxley.* Edited by Leonard Huxley. 2 vols. London: Macmillan, 1900.

Irwin, Darren E., Staffan Bensch, and Trevor D. Price. "Speciation in a Ring." *Nature* 409, no. 6818 (Jan 18, 2001): 333–37.

Irwin, Darren E., Jessica H. Irwin, and Trevor D. Price. "Ring Species as Bridges between Microevolution and Speciation." *Genetica* 112–13 (2001): 223–43.

Isidore of Seville. *Isidori Hispalensis Episcopi etymologiarum sive originum libri XX.* Edited by W. M. Lindsay. Oxford: Clarendon Press, 1911.

Jacobs, Gerald H. "Color Vision Polymorphisms in New World Monkeys: Implications for the Evolution of Primate Trichromacy." In *New World Primates: Ecology, Evolution, and Behavior,* edited by Warren G. Kinzey, 45–74. New York: Aldine de Gruyter, 1997.

James, William. *Pragmatism.* Cambridge, Mass.: Harvard University Press, 1975. Originally published in 1907.

———. *Principles of Psychology.* 2 vols. London: Macmillan, 1890.

Janaway, Christopher. "Schopenhauer as Nietzsche's Educator." In *Willing and Nothingness: Schopenhauer as Nietzsche's Educator,* edited by Christopher Janaway, 13–36. Oxford: Clarendon Press, 1998.

———, ed. *Willing and Nothingness: Schopenhauer as Nietzsche's Educator.* Oxford: Clarendon Press, 1998.

Janson, H. W. *Apes and Ape Lore in the Middle Ages and the Renaissance.* London: Warburg Institute, 1952.

Jeffrey, Charles. *Biological Nomenclature.* 3rd ed. London: Edward Arnold, 1989. First edition published in 1973.

Jenkins, P. F. "Cultural Transmission of Song Patterns and Dialect Development in a Free-Living Bird Population." *Animal Behaviour* 26, no. 1 (1978): 50–78.

Jones, Frederic Wood. *Arboreal Man.* London: Edward Arnold, 1916.

———. "The Mammalian Toilet and Its Biological Implications." In *Life and Living,* 215–63. London: Kegan Paul, Trench, Trubner, 1939.

———. *The Principles of Anatomy as Seen in the Hand.* 2nd ed. London: Baillière, Tinddall and Cox, 1942. First edition published in 1919.

Jones, Lynette A., and Susan J. Lederman. *Human Hand Function.* Oxford: Oxford University Press, 2006.

Josephus. *Jewish Antiquities.* Books 5–8. Translated by H. St. J. Thackeray and Ralph Marcus. Loeb Classical Library. Cambridge, Mass.: Harvard University Press, 1958. Written in Greek circa A.D. 93–94.

Juvenal [Decimus Iunius Iuvenalis]. *Saturae.* Translated by G. G. Ramsay. London: Heinemann, 1940.

Kafka, Franz. "Report to an Academy." Translated by Willa and Edwin Muir. In *The Complete Stories,* edited by Nahum N. Glatzer, 250–59. New York: Schocken, 1971. Short story originally published in 1917.

Kant, Immanuel. *Anthropology from a Pragmatic Point of View.* Translated by Mary J. Gregor. The Hague: Martinus Nijhoff, 1974. Originally published in German in 1798.

———. *Critique of Judgment.* Translated by Werner S. Pluhar. Indianapolis, Ind.: Hackett, 1987. Originally published in German in 1790.

———. *Critique of Pure Reason*. Translated by Norman Kemp Smith. London: Macmillan, 1964. Originally published in German in 1781 (1st edition) and 1787 (second edition).

———. "Idea for a Universal History with a Cosmopolitan Purpose." In *Kant's Political Writings*, edited by Hans Reiss, translated by H. B. Nisbet, 2nd enlarged ed., 41–53. Cambridge: Cambridge University Press, 1970. Originally published in German in 1784.

———. *Prolegomena to Any Future Metaphysics That Will Be Able to Present Itself as a Science*. Translated by Peter G. Lucas. Manchester, U.K.: Manchester University Press, 1953. Originally published in German in 1783.

———. *Universal Natural History and Theory of the Heavens*. Translated by Stanley L. Jaki. Edinburgh: Scottish Academic Press, 1981. Originally published in German in 1755.

Kate, Maggie. *Big Book of Bird Illustrations*. Mineola, N.Y.: Dover, 2001.

Kelly, Henry Ansgar. "Rule of Thumb and the Folklaw of the Husband's Stick." *Journal of Legal Education* 44, no. 3 (September 1994): 341–65.

Kennedy, John S. *The New Anthropomorphism*. Cambridge: Cambridge University Press, 1992.

Kingdon, Jonathan. *Lowly Origin: Where, When, and Why Our Ancestors First Stood Up*. Princeton: Princeton University Press, 2003.

Kirkman, F. B., ed., *The British Bird Book: An Account of All the Birds, Nests, and Eggs Found in the British Isles*. London: T. C. and E. C. Jack, 1911.

Knowlson, T. Sharper. *The Origins of Popular Superstitions and Customs*. London: T. Werner Laurie, 1910.

Kofman, Sarah. *Nietzsche and Metaphor*. Translated by Duncan Large. London: Athlone Press, 1993. Originally published in French in 1972.

Krell, David Farrell. *Daimon Life: Heidegger and Life-Philosophy*. Bloomington: Indiana University Press, 1992.

Kroeber, A. L. *Indian Myths of South Central California*. University of California Publications in American Archaeology and Ethnology, vol. 4, no. 4. Berkeley: University Press, 1907.

Lack, David. *Darwin's Finches: An Essay on the General Biological Theory of Evolution*. Gloucester, Mass.: Peter Smith, 1968. Originally published in 1947.

Lamont, Corliss. *The Philosophy of Humanism*. 8th ed. Washington, D.C.: Humanist Press, 1997. First edition published in 1949.

Land, Michael F., and Dan-Eric Nilsson. *Animal Eyes*. Oxford: Oxford University Press, 2005.

Langer, Monika. "The Role and Status of Animals in Nietzsche's Philosophy." In *Animal Others: On Ethics, Ontology, and Animal Life*, edited by H. Peter Steeves, 75–92. New York: State University of New York Press, 1999.

Leach, Edmund. "Anthropological Aspects of Language: Animal Categories and Verbal Abuse." In *New Directions in the Study of Language*, edited by Eric H. Lenneberg, 23–63. Cambridge: MIT Press, 1966.

Leakey, Richard. *The Origin of Humankind*. London: Weidenfeld and Nicolson, 1994.

Lee, Penny. "Whorf's Hopi Tensors: Subtle Articulators in the Language/Thought Nexus?" *Cognitive Linguistics* 2, no. 2 (January 1991): 123–47.

———. *The Whorf Theory Complex: A Critical Reconstruction*. Amsterdam: John Benjamins, 1996.

Leiter, Brian. "Perspectivism in Nietzsche's Genealogy of Morals." In *Nietzsche, Genealogy, Morality: Essays on Nietzsche's "On the Genealogy of Morals,"* edited by Richard Schacht, 334–57. Berkeley: University of California Press, 1994.

Lemm, Vanessa. Nietzsche's Animal Philosophy: Culture, Politics, and the Animality of the Human Being. New York: Fordham University Press, 2009.

Lentricchia, Frank. Ariel and the Police: Michel Foucault, William James, Wallace Stevens. Madison: University of Wisconsin Press, 1988.

Lewes, George Henry. Sea-Side Studies at Ilfracombe, Tenby, the Scilly Isles, and Jersey. Edinburgh: Blackwood, 1860.

Lewis, Charlton T., and Charles Short. A Latin Dictionary. Oxford: Clarendon Press, 1879.

Liebers, Dorit, Peter de Knijff, and Andreas J. Helbig. "The Herring Gull Complex Is Not a Ring Species." Proceedings of the Royal Society, B: Biological Sciences 271, no. 1542 (May 7, 2004): 893–901.

Linnaeus, Carl. Systema Naturae. 10th ed. 2 vols. Holmiae [Stockholm]: Laurentii Salvii, 1758. First edition published in 1735.

Lippmann, Walter. Public Opinion. New York: Free Press, 1949. Originally published in 1922.

Lockwood, Randall. "Anthropomorphism Is Not a Four-Letter Word." In Perceptions of Animals in American Culture, edited by R. J. Hoage, 41–56. Washington, D.C.: Smithsonian Institution Press, 1989.

Lofting, Hugh. The Story of Doctor Doolittle. London: Jonathan Cape, 1922.

Long, George. "Mancipium." In A Dictionary of Greek and Roman Antiquities, edited by William Smith, 2nd ed., 727–28. Boston: Little, Brown, 1859.

Lorenz, Konrad. King Solomon's Ring: New Light on Animal Ways. London: Methuen, 1952.

Low, David. The Breeds of the Domestic Animals of the British Islands. 2 vols. London: Longman, Orme, Brown, Green, and Longmans, 1842.

Lucas, J. R. "Wilberforce and Huxley: A Legendary Encounter." Historical Journal 22, no. 2 (1979): 313–30.

Luckhardt, C. Grant. "Lion Talk," Philosophical Investigations 18, no. 1. (January 1995): 1–12.

Lucretius [Titus Lucretius Carus]. On the Nature of Things. Translated by W. H. D. Rouse. Revised by Martin Ferguson Smith. 2nd ed. Loeb Classical Library 181. Cambridge, Mass.: Harvard University Press, 1982.

Lynch, Alejandro, Geoffrey M. Plunkett, Allan J. Baker, and Peter F. Jenkins. "A Model of Cultural Evolution of Chaffinch Song Derived with the Meme Concept." American Naturalist 133, no. 5 (1989): 634–53.

Macrobius Ambrosius Theodosius. The Saturnalia. Translated by Percival Vaughan Davies. New York: Columbia University Press, 1969.

Magee, Bryan. The Philosophy of Schopenhauer. Oxford: Clarendon Press, 1997.

Magyar, László András. "Digitus medicinalis—The Etymology of the Name." In Actes du XXXIIe Congrés international d'histoire de la médecine, Anvers, 3–7 Septembre 1990, edited by Eric Fierens, Jean-Pierre Tricot, Thierry Appelboom, and Michel Thierry, 175–80. Antwerp: Societas Belgica Historiae Medicinae, 1991.

Malcolm, Norman. Ludwig Wittgenstein: A Memoir. London: Oxford University Press, 1958.

Malotki, Ekkehart. Hopi Time: A Linguistic Analysis of the Temporal Concepts in the Hopi Language. Berlin: Mouton, 1983.

Marler, Peter. "Bird Calls: A Cornucopia for Communication." In Nature's Music: The Science of Birdsong, edited by Peter Marler and Hans Willem Slabbekoorn, 132–77. San Diego, Calif.: Elsevier, 2004.

Marsden, Jill. "Bataille and the Poetic Fallacy of Animality." In *Animal Philosophy: Essential Readings in Continental Thought*, edited by Peter Atterton and Matthew Calarco, 37–44. London: Continuum, 2004.

Martial, Marcus Valerius. *Epigrams*. Translated by D. R. Shackleton Bailey. 3 vols. Loeb Classical Library 94, 95, and 480. Cambridge, Mass.: Harvard University Press, 1993.

Marzke, Mary W. "Precision Grips, Hand Morphology, and Tools." *American Journal of Physical Anthropology* 102 (1997): 91–110.

Masson, Jeffrey, and Susan McCarthy. *When Elephants Weep: The Emotional Lives of Animals*. London: Jonathan Cape, 1994.

Massumi, Brian. "The Autonomy of Affect." In *Deleuze: A Critical Reader*, edited by Paul Patton, 217–39. Oxford: Blackwell, 1996.

McGrew, William C. *Chimpanzee Material Culture: Implications for Human Evolution*. Cambridge: Cambridge University Press, 1992.

———. *The Cultured Chimpanzee: Reflections on Cultural Primatology*. Cambridge: Cambridge University Press, 2004.

McLuhan, Marshall. *Understanding Media: The Extensions of Man*. 3rd printing, with a new preface. New York: McGraw-Hill, 1964.

McNeill, Will. *Heidegger: Visions, of Animals, Others, and the Divine*. Warwick, U.K.: University of Warwick, 1993.

———. "Spirit's Living Hand." In *Of Derrida, Heidegger, and Spirit*, edited by David Wood, 103–17. Evanston, Ill.: Northwestern University Press, 1993.

Mead, George Herbert. "Concerning Animal Perception." In *Essays in Social Psychology*, edited by Mary Jo Deegan, 59–65. New Brunswick, N.J.: Transaction, 2001.

———. *Mind, Self, and Society from the Standpoint of a Social Behaviorist*. Edited by Charles W. Morris. Chicago: University of Chicago Press, 1934.

Menninger, Karl. *Number Words and Number Symbols: A Cultural History of Numbers*. Translated by Paul Broneer. New York: Dover, 1992. Originally published in German in 1957–58; translation originally published in 1969.

Midgley, Mary. "The End of Anthropocentrism?" In *Utopias, Dolphins, and Computers: Problems in Philosophical Plumbing*, 97–106. London: Routledge, 1996.

———. "What Is Anthropomorphism?" In *Animals and Why They Matter*, 125–33. Athens: University of Georgia Press, 1983.

Mitchell, R. W., N. S. Thompson, and H. L. Miles, eds. *Anthropomorphism, Anecdotes, and Animals*. Albany: State University of New York Press, 1997.

Montagu, M. F. Ashley. *Edward Tyson, M.D., F.R.S., 1650–1708, and the Rise of Human and Comparative Anatomy in England*. Philadelphia: American Philosophical Society, 1943.

Montaigne, Michel de. "On Thumbs." In *The Complete Essays*, translated by M. A. Screech, 784–85. London: Penguin, 1993.

Moore, G. E. "A Defence of Common Sense." In *Philosophical Papers*, 32–59. London: George Allen and Unwin, 1959. Essay originally published in 1925.

———. "Proof of an External World." In *Philosophical Papers*, 127–50. London: George Allen and Unwin, 1959. Essay originally published in 1939.

———. "The Refutation of Idealism." In *G. E. Moore: Selected Writings*, edited by Thomas Baldwin, 23–44. London: Routledge, 1993. Essay originally published in 1903.

Morgan, T. H., C. B. Bridges, and A. H. Sturtevant.

Contributions to the Genetics of Drosophila Melanogaster. Washington, D.C.: Carnegie Institution,
1919.

Morris, Desmond, Peter Collett, Peter Marsh, and
Marie O'Shaughnessy. Gestures: Their Origins and
Distribution. London: Jonathan Cape, 1979.

Morris, Ramona, and Desmond Morris. Men and
Apes. London: Hutchinson, 1966.

Mundinger, Paul C. "Animal Cultures and a General
Theory of Cultural Evolution." Ethology and Socio-
biology 1, no. 3 (1980): 183–223.

Nagel, Thomas. "What Is It Like to Be a Bat?" Philosophical Review 83 (1974): 435–50.

Nakamura, Michio. "Grooming-Hand-Clasp in
Mahale M Group Chimpanzees: Implications
for Culture in Social Behaviours." In Behavioural
Diversity in Chimpanzees and Bonobos, edited by
Christophe Boesch, Gottfried Hohmann, and
Linda F. Marchant, 71–83. Cambridge: Cambridge
University Press, 2002.

Napier, John. Hands. Revised by Russell H. Tuttle.
Princeton: Princeton University Press, 1993. First
edition published in 1980.

Nash, Richard. Wild Enlightenment: The Borders of
Human Identity in the Eighteenth Century. Charlottesville: University of Virginia Press, 2003.

Nehamas, Alexander. "How One Becomes What One
Is." In Nietzsche, edited by John Richardson and
Brian Leiter, 255–80. Oxford: Oxford University
Press, 2001.

Nico, Leo, Erynn Maynard, and Pamela J. Schofield.
"Cyprinus carpio." USGS Nonindigenous Aquatic
Species Database, Gainesville, Fla. (revised August
18, 2009). http://nas.er.usgs.gov/queries/factsheet.
asp?speciesID=4 (accessed January 11, 2010).

Nietzsche, Friedrich. Beyond Good and Evil: Prelude to
a Philosophy of the Future. Translated by R. J. Hollingdale. Harmondsworth, U.K.: Penguin, 1973.
Originally published in German in 1885.

———. The Birth of Tragedy; or, Hellenism and Pessi-
mism. Translated by William A. Haussmann. The
Complete Works of Friedrich Nietzsche, edited
by Oscar Levy, vol. 1. Edinburgh: T. N. Foulis,
1909. Originally published in German in 1872;
reissued in 1886.

———. Daybreak: Thoughts on the Prejudices of Morality. Translated by R. J. Hollingdale. Cambridge:
Cambridge University Press, 1997. Originally
published in German in 1881.

———. Ecce Homo: How One Becomes What One Is.
Translated by Anthony M. Ludovici. The Com-
plete Works of Friederich Nietzsche, edited by
Oscar Levy, vol. 17. Edinburgh: T. N. Foulis, 1911.
Originally published in German in 1888.

———. The Genealogy of Morals: A Polemic. Translated
by Horace B. Samuel. The Complete Works of
Friederich Nietzsche, edited by Oscar Levy, vol.
13. Edinburgh: T. N. Foulis, 1913. Originally published in German in 1887.

———. Human, All-Too-Human: A Book for Free Spirits.
Part 1. Translated by Helen Zimmern. The Works
of Friederich Nietzsche, edited by Oscar Levy,
vol. 6. Edinburgh: T. N. Foulis, 1910. Originally
published in German in 1878.

———. Human, All-Too-Human: A Book for Free Spirits.
Part 2. Translated by Paul V. Cohn. The Works
of Friederich Nietzsche, edited by Oscar Levy,
vol. 7. Edinburgh: T. N. Foulis, 1911. Originally
published in German in 1879–80.

———. The Joyful Wisdom (La Gaya Scienza).
Translated by Thomas Common. The Works
of Friederich Nietzsche, edited by Oscar Levy,
vol. 10. Edinburgh: T. N. Foulis, 1910. Originally
published in German in 1882.

———. On the Genealogy of Morals: A Polemic. Translated by Douglas Smith. Oxford: Oxford University Press, 1996. Originally published in German in 1887.

———. "On Truth and Falsity in Their Ultramoral Sense." Translated by M. A. Mügge. In Early Greek Philosophy and Other Essays, 171–92. The Works of Friederich Nietzsche, edited by Oscar Levy, vol. 2. Edinburgh: T. N. Foulis, 1911. Essay written in German in 1873.

———. "On Truth and Lie in an Extra-Moral Sense" (selection). In The Portable Nietzsche, translated and edited by Walter Kaufmann, 42–47. London: Penguin, 1954. Essay written in German in 1873.

———. "On Truth and Lies in a Nonmoral Sense." In Philosophy and Truth: Selections from Nietzsche's Notebooks of the Early 1870s, translated and edited by Daniel Breazeale, 79–91. Atlantic Highlands, N.J.: Humanities Press, 1979. Essay written in German in 1873.

———. "On Truth and Lying in a Non-Moral Sense." Translated by Ronald Speirs. In The Birth of Tragedy and Other Writings, edited by Raymond Geuss and Ronald Speirs, 141–53. Cambridge: Cambridge University Press, 1999. Essay written in German in 1873.

———. Philosophy and Truth: Selections from Nietzsche's Notebooks of the early 1870s. Translated and edited by Daniel Breazeale. Atlantic Highlands, N.J.: Humanities Press, 1979.

———. "Schopenhauer as Educator." In Unfashionable Observations, translated by Richard T. Gray. The Complete Works of Friedrich Nietzsche, edited by Ernst Behler, 2: 169–255. Stanford: Stanford University Press, 1995. Essay originally published in German in 1874.

———. Thus Spoke Zarathustra. Translated by R. J. Hollingdale. Harmondsworth, U.K.: Penguin, 1961. Originally published in German in 1883–85.

———. The Twilight of the Idols. Translated by Anthony M. Ludovici. The Complete Works of Friederich Nietzsche, edited by Oscar Levy, vol. 16. New York: Russell and Russell, 1964. Originally published in German in 1888.

———. "Über Wahrheit und Lüge im aussermoralischen Sinne." In Nachgelassene Werke: Aus den Jahren 1872/73–1875/76, 189–207. 2nd, completely rev. ed. Leipzig: C. G. Naumann, 1903. Essay originally published in 1873.

———. Unpublished Writings from the Period of Unfashionable Observations. Translated by Richard T. Gray. The Complete Works of Friedrich Nietzsche, edited by Bernd Magnus, vol. 11. Stanford: Stanford University Press, 1995. Originally written in German in 1872–74.

———. The Will to Power. Edited by Walter Kaufmann. Translated by Walter Kaufmann and R. J. Hollingdale. New York: Vintage, 1968. Originally written in German.

Norris, Christopher. Against Relativism: Philosophy of Science, Deconstruction, and Critical Theory. Oxford: Blackwell, 1997.

———. "'What Is Enlightenment?': Foucault on Kant." In The Truth about Postmodernism, 29–99. Oxford: Blackwell, 1993.

Norris, Margot. Beasts of the Modern Imagination: Darwin, Nietzsche, Kafka, Ernst, and Lawrence. Baltimore, Md.: The Johns Hopkins University Press, 1985.

Oliver, Kelly, and Marilyn Pearsall, eds. Feminist Interpretations of Friedrich Nietzsche. University Park: Pennsylvania State Press, 1998.

Ovid [Publius Ovidius Naso]. Metamorphoses. Edited by Samuel Garth. Translated by John Dryden,

Alexander Pope, Joseph Addison, William Congreve, et al. London: Jacob Tonson, 1717.

Owen, Richard. *Lectures on the Comparative Anatomy and Physiology of the Invertebrate Animals.* 2nd ed. London: Longman, Brown, Green and Longmans, 1855. First edition published in 1843.

Palmquist, Stephen. *Kant's System of Perspectives: An Architectonic Interpretation of the Critical Philosophy.* Lanham, Md.: University Press of America, 1993.

Parker, Andrew. *Seven Deadly Colours: The Genius of Nature's Palette and How It Eluded Darwin.* London: Free Press, 2005.

Parker, Holt N. "The Teratogenic Grid." In *Roman Sexualities,* edited by Judith P. Hallett and Marilyn B. Skinner, 47–65. Princeton: Princeton University Press, 1997.

Parkes, Malcolm Beckwith. *Pause and Effect: An Introduction to the History of Punctuation in the West.* Aldershot, U.K.: Scolar Press, 1992.

Partington, Angela, ed. *The Oxford Dictionary of Quotations.* 4th ed. Oxford: Oxford University Press, 1996.

Partridge, Eric. *A Dictionary of Slang and Unconventional English.* Edited by Paul Beale. 8th ed. London: Routledge and Kegan Paul, 1984.

Patterson, Nick, Daniel J. Richter, Sante Gnerre, Eric S. Lander, and David Reich. "Genetic Evidence for Complex Speciation of Humans and Chimpanzees." *Nature* 441, no. 7097 (June 29, 2006): 1103–8.

Peirce, Charles S. *Collected Papers of Charles Sanders Peirce.* Edited by Charles Hartshorne and Paul Weiss. Cambridge, Mass.: Belknap Press / Harvard University Press, 1931–35.

Pfungst, Oskar. *Clever Hans (The Horse of Mr. von Osten): A Contribution to Experimental Animal and Human Psychology.* Edited by Robert Rosenthal.

New York: Holt, Rinehart and Winston, 1965. Originally published in 1911.

Phaedrus. *Phaedri Avgvsti liberti fabvlae Aesopiae.* Translated by Lucianus Mueller. Leipzig: B. G. Teubner, 1903.

Pindar. *The Olympian and Pythian Odes.* Edited by Basil L. Gildersleeve. London: Macmillan, 1907.

———. *Olympian Odes, Pythian Odes.* Translated by William H. Race. Cambridge, Mass.: Harvard University Press, 1997.

———. *Pindar's Victory Songs.* Translated by Frank J. Nisetich. Baltimore, Md.: The Johns Hopkins University Press, 1980.

———. *The Works of Pindar.* Translated by L. R. Farnell. 3 vols. London: Macmillan, 1932.

Pinker, Steven. *The Language Instinct: The New Science of Language and Mind.* London: Allen Lane, 1994.

Plato. "Apology." In *The Dialogues of Plato,* translated by Benjamin Jowett, 3rd ed., 2: 95–135. London: Oxford University Press, 1892.

———. *Gorgias and Phaedrus.* Translated by James H. Nichols Jr. Ithaca, N.Y.: Cornell University Press, 1998.

———. "Protagoras." In *The Dialogues of Plato,* translated by Benjamin Jowett, 3rd ed., 1: 113–87. London: Oxford University Press, 1892.

———. "The Republic." In *The Dialogues of Plato,* translated by Benjamin Jowett, 3rd ed., 3: 1–338. London: Oxford University Press, 1892.

———. *Theaetetus. Sophist.* Translated by Harold North Fowler. Loeb Classical Library 123. Cambridge, Mass.: Harvard University Press, 1921.

Plumwood, Val. *Feminism and the Mastery of Nature.* London: Routledge, 1993.

Poellner, Peter. "Perspectival Truth." In *Nietzsche,* edited by John Richardson and Brian Leiter, 85–117. Oxford: Oxford University Press, 2001.

Polo, Marco. The Travels of Marco Polo. Translated by Aldo Ricci from the text of L. F. Benedetto. London: Routledge and Kegan Paul, 1931.

Popper, Karl R. "Kant's Critique and Cosmology." In Conjectures and Refutations: The Growth of Scientific Knowledge, 4th ed., 175–83. London: Routledge and Kegan Paul, 1972. Essay originally published in 1954.

———. The Logic of Scientific Discovery. 2nd ed. New York: Harper and Row, 1959.

———. Objective Knowledge: An Evolutionary Approach. Oxford: Clarendon Press, 1972.

———. The Philosophy of Karl Popper. Edited by P. A. Schilpp. 2 vols. La Salle, Ill.: Open Court, 1974.

———. Realism and the Aim of Science. Vol. 1 of Postscript to "The Logic of Scientific Discovery." London: Routledge, 1983.

———. "What Is Dialectic?" In Conjectures and Refutations: The Growth of Scientific Knowledge, 4th ed., 312–35. London: Routledge and Kegan Paul, 1972. Essay originally published in 1937.

Popper, Karl, and John C. Eccles. The Self and Its Brain: An Argument for Interactionism. London: Routledge, 1984.

Potter, Beatrix. The Tale of Squirrel Nutkin. London: Frederick Warne, 1903.

Prabhakar, Shyam, et al. "Human-Specific Gain of Function in a Developmental Enhancer." Science 321, no. 5894 (September 5, 2008): 1346–50.

Prigogine, Ilya, and Isabelle Stengers. Order out of Chaos. Rev. English ed. London: Heinemann, 1984. First edition published in French in 1979.

Purves, William K. "Why Is Spider Silk So Strong?" Scientific American, July 15, 2002. http://www.scientificamerican.com/article.cfm?id=why-is-spider-silk-so-str (accessed September 8, 2009).

Putnam, Hilary. Pragmatism: An Open Question. Oxford: Blackwell, 1995.

Reader, Simon M., and Kevin N. Laland. "Do Animals Have Memes?" Journal of Memetics—Evolutionary Models of Information Transmission 3, no. 2 (December 1999). http://cfpm.org/jom-emit/1999/vol3/reader_sm&laland_kn.html (accessed January 20, 2010).

Regier, Willis Goth. Book of the Sphinx. Lincoln: University of Nebraska Press, 2004.

Reid, Constance. From Zero to Infinity: What Makes Numbers Interesting. 4th ed. Washington, D.C.: Mathematical Association of America, 1992.

Reitherman, Wolfgang, director. The Jungle Book (movie). Burbank, Calif.: Walt Disney Productions, 1967.

Rescher, Nicholas. "Choice without Preference: The Problem of 'Buridan's Ass.'" In Essays in the History of Philosophy, 77–114. Aldershot, U.K.: Avebury, 1995.

Reynolds, V. "On the Identity of the Ape Described by Tulp 1641." Folia Primatologica 5 (1967): 80–87.

Ridley, Mark. The Problems of Evolution. Oxford: Oxford University Press, 1985.

Rijksen, H. D., and E. Meijaard. Our Vanishing Relative: The Status of Wild Orangutans at the Close of the Twentieth Century. Dordrecht: Kluwer Academic, 1999.

Ritvo, Harriet. The Platypus and the Mermaid and other Figments of the Classifying Imagination. Cambridge, Mass.: Harvard University Press, 1997.

Robinson, W. H. Urban Entomology: Insect and Mite Pests in the Human Environment. London: Chapman and Hall, 1996.

RoboDuk Decoys. http://www.roboduk.com/decoys.html (accessed October 15, 2009).

Rorty, Richard. *Contingency, Irony, and Solidarity.* Cambridge: Cambridge University Press, 1989.

———. "Habermas and Lyotard on Postmodernity." In *Essays on Heidegger and Others, Philosophical Papers,* vol. 2: 164–76. Cambridge: Cambridge University Press, 1991. Essay originally published in 1984.

———. "Inquiry as Recontextualization: An Anti-Dualist Account of Interpretation." In *Objectivity, Relativism, and Truth, Philosophical Papers,* vol. 1: 93–110. Cambridge: Cambridge University Press, 1991.

———. "Introduction: Pragmatism and Post-Nietzschean Philosophy." In *Essays on Heidegger and Others, Philosophical Papers,* vol. 2: 1–6. Cambridge: Cambridge University Press.

———. "Method, Social Science, and Social Hope." In *Consequences of Pragmatism (Essays: 1972–1980),* 191–208. Brighton, U.K.: Harvester Press, 1982.

———. "Moral Identity and Private Autonomy: The Case of Foucault." In *Essays on Heidegger and Others, Philosophical Papers,* vol. 2: 193–98. Cambridge: Cambridge University Press, 1991. Essay originally published in 1988.

———. *Objectivity, Relativism, and Truth.* Philosophical Papers, vol. 1. Cambridge: Cambridge University Press, 1991.

———. *Philosophy and the Mirror of Nature.* Princeton: Princeton University Press, 1979.

———. "Pragmatism as Romantic Polytheism." In *The Revival of Pragmatism: New Essays on Social Thought, Law, and Culture,* edited by Morris Dickstein, 21–36. Durham, N.C.: Duke University Press, 1998.

Rose, Gillian. *Dialectic of Nihilism: Post-Structuralism and Law.* Oxford: Blackwell, 1984.

Ross, Robert Scott. "Popularization of Red Herring by English Political Agitator William Cobbett." *Comments on Etymology* 38, nos. 1–2 (October–November 2008): 62–69.

Roze, Uldis. *The North American Porcupine.* Washington, D.C.: Smithsonian Institution Press, 1989.

Russell, Bertrand. *An Outline of Philosophy.* London: George Allen and Unwin, 1927.

Ryder, M. L. *Sheep and Man.* London: Duckworth, 1983.

Ryle, Gilbert. "Discussion: Meaning and Necessity." *Philosophy* 24, no. 88 (January 1949): 69–76.

———. "The Theory of Meaning." In *British Philosophy in the Mid-Century: A Cambridge Symposium,* edited by C. A. Mace, 239–64. London: George Allen and Unwin, 1957.

Sandis, Constantine. "The Lion for Real: On §327 of the Typescript Previously Known as Part II of the *Philosophical Investigations.*" Unpublished manuscript.

Sapir, Edward. "The Status of Linguistics as a Science." In *Culture, Language, and Personality,* edited by David G. Mandelbaum, 65–77. Berkeley: University of California Press, 1956. Essay originally published in 1929.

Sarmiento, Esteban, G. J. Sawyer, and Richard Milner. *The Last Human: A Guide to Twenty-Two Species of Extinct Humans.* Reconstructions and photographs by G. J. Sawyer and Viktor Deak. New Haven: Yale University Press, 2007.

Saussure, Ferdinand de. *Course in General Linguistics.* Translated by Wade Baskin. Edited by Charles Bally and Albert Sechehaye with Albert Reidlinger. 3rd ed. London: Fontana, 1974. Originally published in French in 1916.

———. *Course in General Linguistics.* Translated by Roy Harris. London: Duckworth, 1983. Originally published in French in 1916.

Savage-Rumbaugh, Sue, and Roger Lewin. *Kanzi: The Ape at the Brink of the Human Mind.* London: Doubleday, 1994.

Scarpitti, Michael A., and Susann Möller. "Verschlimmbesserung: Correcting the Corrections in Translations of Kant." *Semiotica* 111, nos. 1–2 (1996): 55–73.

Scarry, Richard. *Richard Scarry's What Do People Do All Day?* Glasgow: Collins, 1977.

Schiappa, Edward. *Protagoras and Logos: A Study in Greek Philosophy and Rhetoric.* Columbia: University of South Carolina Press, 2003.

Schilpp, Paul Arthur, ed. *The Philosophy of G. E. Moore.* 2nd ed. New York: Tudor, 1952. First edition published in 1942.

Schopenhauer, Arthur. *On the Basis of Morality.* Translated by E. F. J. Payne, rev. ed. Providence, R.I.: Berghahn Books, 1995. Originally published in German in 1839.

———. *Parerga and Paralipomena.* Translated by E. F. J. Payne. 2 vols. Oxford: Clarendon Press, 1974. Originally published in German in 1851.

———. *The World as Will and Representation.* Translated by E. F. J. Payne. 2 vols. New York: Dover, 1966. First edition published in German in 1818; revised edition in 1844.

Schrift, Alan D. "Arachnophobe or Arachnophile? Nietzsche and His Spiders." In *A Nietzschean Bestiary: Becoming Animal beyond Docile and Brutal*, edited by Christa Davis Acampora and Ralph R. Acampora, 61–70. Lanham, Md.: Rowman and Littlefield, 2004.

———. *Nietzsche and the Question of Interpretation: Between Hermeneutics and Deconstruction.* New York: Routledge, 1990.

Schultz, Adolph Hans. *The Life of Primates.* New York: Universe Books, 1969.

Scruton, Roger. *Kant.* Oxford: Oxford University Press, 1982.

Secord, James A. "Nature's Fancy: Charles Darwin and the Breeding of Pigeons." *Isis* 72, no. 262 (June 1981): 162–86.

Segal, Charles. *"Oedipus Tyrannus": Tragic Heroism and the Limits of Knowledge.* 2nd ed. New York: Oxford University Press, 2001.

Sextus Empiricus. *Outlines of Pyrrhonism.* Translated by R. G. Bury. Loeb Classical Library 273. Cambridge, Mass.: Harvard University Press, 1933.

Shakespeare, William. *The Third Part of King Henry VI.* Edited by Andrew S. Cairncross. Arden Shakespeare, 2nd ed. London: Methuen, 1965.

Sherman, Richard M., and Robert B. Sherman, composers. "I Wan'na Be Like You." Performed by Louis Prima (as King Louie). In *The Jungle Book* (movie). Burbank, Calif.: Walt Disney Productions, 1967.

Sinclair, Sandra. *How Animals See: Other Visions of Our World.* Beckenham, U.K.: Croom Helm, 1985.

Skinner, B. F. "A Case History in Scientific Method." *American Psychologist* 11, no. 5 (May 1956): 221–33.

Smith, David Eugene, and Louis Charles Karpinski. *The Hindu-Arabic Numerals.* Boston: Ginn, 1911.

Smith, Elmer Boyd. *Chicken World.* New York: Knickerbocker Press, 1910.

Smythe, R. H. *Vision in the Animal World.* London: Macmillan, 1975.

Spandl, Klara. "Exploring the Round Houses of Doves." *British Archaeology* 35 (June 1998): 6–7.

Stack, George J. *Lange and Nietzsche.* Berlin: Walter de Gruyter, 1983.

———. "Nietzsche's Critique of Things-in-Themselves." *Diálogos* (Rio Piedras) 15, no. 36 (1980): 33–57.

Stonehenge [John Henry Walsh]. *The Dog in Health*

and Disease. 3rd ed. London: Longmans, Green, 1879. First edition published in 1859.

Stricherz, Vince. "First Complete Fossil of Fierce Prehistoric Predator Found in South Africa." *University of Washington News,* December 8, 1998. http://www.washington.edu/news/archive/id/3499 (accessed February 10, 2010).

Sulloway, Frank J. "Darwin and His Finches: The Evolution of a Legend." *Journal of the History of Biology* 15, no. 1 (1982): 1–53.

Swift, Jonathan. *Gulliver's Travels.* London: Oxford University Press, 1963. Originally published in 1726.

Syed, Zainulabeuddin, and Walter S. Leal. "Acute Olfactory Response of Culex Mosquitoes to a Human- and Bird-Derived Attractant." *Proceedings of the National Academy of Sciences* 106, no. 44 (November 3, 2009): 18803–8.

Tallis, Raymond. *The Hand: A Philosophical Enquiry into Human Being.* Edinburgh: Edinburgh University Press, 2003.

Taylor, Jeremy, *Not a Chimp: The Hunt to Find the Genes That Make Us Human.* Oxford: Oxford University Press, 2009.

Thomson, Keith. "Huxley, Wilberforce, and the Oxford Museum." *American Scientist* 88, no. 3 (May–June 2000): 210–13.

Tudge, Colin. *The Variety of Life.* Oxford: Oxford University Press, 2000.

Tulp, Nicolaas. *Observationes Medicae.* Amstelredami [Amsterdam]: Apud Henricum Wetstenium, 1685. Originally published in 1641.

Tuttle, Russell H. "Hands from Newt to Napier." In *Evolutionary Biology, Reproductive Endocrinology, and Virology,* edited by S. Matano, R. H. Tulle, H. Ishida, and M. Goodman, Topics in Primatology 3, 3–20. Tokyo: University of Tokyo, 1992.

Tyson, Edward. *Orang-outang, sive Homo sylvestris; or, The Anatomy of a Pygmie Compared with That of a Monkey, an Ape, and a Man.* London: Thomas Bennet and Daniel Brown, 1699.

Uexküll, Jakob von. "A Stroll through the Worlds of Animals and Men: A Picture Book of Invisible Worlds." Translated by Claire H. Schiller. *Semiotica* 89, no. 4 (1992): 319–91. Originally published in German in 1934.

———. *Theoretical Biology.* Translated by D. L. Mackinnon. London: Kegan Paul, Trench, Trubner, 1926. Originally published in German in 1920.

Valéry, Paul. *Tel Quel.* Vol. 2. Paris: Gallimard, 1943.

van Fraassen, Bas C. *The Scientific Image.* Oxford: Clarendon Press, 1980.

van Schaik, Carel P., Marc Ancrenaz, Gwendolyn Borgen, Birute Galdikas, Cheryl D. Knott, Ian Singleton, Akira Suzuki, Sri Suci Utami, and Michelle Merrill. "Orangutan Cultures and the Evolution of Material Culture." In *The Animals Reader: The Essential Classic and Contemporary Writings,* edited by Linda Kalof and Amy Fitzgerald, 104–10. Oxford: Berg, 2007.

Varro. *On Agriculture.* Translated by W. D. Hooper and Harrison Boyd Ash. Loeb Classical Library 283. Cambridge, Mass.: Harvard University Press, 1934.

Vellacoot, Philip. *Sophocles and Oedipus: A Study of "Oedipus Tyrannus" with a New Translation.* London: Macmillan, 1971.

"A Venerable Orang-outang: A Contribution to Unnatural History." *Hornet,* March 22, 1871.

Versenyi, Laszlo. "Protagoras' Man-Measure Fragment." *American Journal of Philology* 83, no. 2 (April 1962): 178–84.

Wallace, Alfred Russel. "The Limits of Natural Selection as Applied to Man." In *Contributions to the*

Theory of Natural Selection: A Series of Essays, 332–71. London: Macmillan, 1870.

———. The Malay Archipelago: The Land of the Orangutan, and the Bird of Paradise. Oxford: Oxford University Press, 1986. Originally published in 1869.

———. My Life: A Record of Events and Opinions. 2 vols. London: Chapman and Hall, 1905.

———. "On the Orang-utan or Mias of Borneo." Annals and Magazine of Natural History, June 1856, 471–76.

———. "Sir Charles Lyell on Geological Climates and the Origin of Species." Quarterly Review 126, no. 252 (April 1869): 359–94.

———. "Some Account of an Infant 'Orang-utan.'" Annals and Magazine of Natural History, May 1856, 386–90.

———. The Wonderful Century: The Age of New Ideas in Science and Invention. 5th ed. London: Swan Sonnenschein, 1903. First edition published in 1898.

Wang, Xiaoming, and Richard H. Tedford. Dogs: Their Fossil Relatives and Evolutionary History. Illustrated by Mauricio Antón. New York: Columbia University Press, 2008.

Ward, Paul, and Suzanne Kynaston. Bears of the World. London: Blandford, 1995.

Washburn, Sherwood L. "Tools and Human Evolution." Scientific American 203, no. 3 (September 1960): 62–75.

Washburn, Sherwood L., and Virginia Avis. "Evolution of Human Behavior." In Behavior and Evolution, edited by Anne Roe and George Gaylord Simpson, 421–36. New Haven: Yale University Press, 1958.

Watkins, Peter, and Erica Hughes. A Book of Animals. London: Julia MacRae Books, 1985.

Watson, Elizabeth E., Simon Easteal, and David Penny. "Homo Genus: A Review of the Classification of Humans and the Great Apes." In Humanity from African Naissance to Coming Millennia: Colloquia in Human Biology and Paleoanthropology, edited by Phillip V. Tobias, Michael A. Raath, Jacopo Moggi-Cecchi, and Gerald A. Doyle, 307–18. Firenze, Italy: Firenze University Press, 2001.

Weiner, Jonathan. The Beak of the Finch: A Story of Evolution in Our Time. London: Jonathan Cape, 1994.

———. Time, Love, Memory: A Great Biologist and His Quest for the Origins of Behavior. New York: Alfred A. Knopf, 1999.

Wells, Martin J. Octopus: Physiology and Behaviour of an Advanced Invertebrate. London: Chapman and Hall, 1978.

White, E. B. Charlotte's Web. Illustrated by Garth Williams. New York: Harper, 1952.

White, T. H. The Goshawk. London: Readers Union / Jonathan Cape, 1953.

———. The Book of Beasts: Being a Translation from a Latin Bestiary of the Twelfth Century. London: Readers Union, 1956.

Whittell, Hubert Massey. The Literature of Australian Birds: A History and a Bibliography of Australian Ornithology. Perth: Paterson Brokensha, 1954.

Whorf, Benjamin Lee. "A Brotherhood of Thought." Main Currents in Modern Thought 1, part 4 (February 1941): 13–14.

———. "Dr. Reiser's Humanism." Main Currents in Modern Thought 1, part 5 (March 1941): 12–14.

———. "Language, Mind, and Reality." In Language, Thought, and Reality: Selected Writings of Benjamin Lee Whorf. Edited by John B. Carroll, 246–70. Cambridge: MIT Press, 1956. Essay originally published in 1942.

———. "Linguistics as an Exact Science." In Language, Thought, and Reality: Selected Writings of

Benjamin Lee Whorf. Edited by John B. Carroll, 220–32. Cambridge: MIT Press, 1956. Essay originally published in 1940.

———. "The Relation of Habitual Thought and Behavior to Language." In Language, Thought, and Reality: Selected Writings of Benjamin Lee Whorf. Edited by John B. Carroll, 134–59. Cambridge: MIT Press, 1956. Essay originally published in 1939.

———. "Science and Linguistics." In Language, Thought, and Reality: Selected Writings of Benjamin Lee Whorf. Edited by John B. Carroll, 207–19. Cambridge: MIT Press, 1956. Essay originally published in 1940.

Wildman, Derek E., Monica Uddin, Guozhen Liu, Lawrence I. Grossman, and Morris Goodman. "Implications of Natural Selection in Shaping 99.4% Nonsynonymous DNA Identity between Humans and Chimpanzees: Enlarging Genus Homo." Proceedings of the National Academy of Sciences 100, no. 12 (June 10, 2003): 7181–88.

Wilkins, John. An Essay toward a Real Character and a Philosophical Language. London: Gellibrand and Martin, 1668.

Wilson, David M. The Bayeux Tapestry. London: Thames and Hudson, 1985.

Wilson, Frank R. The Hand: How Its Use Shapes the Brain, Language, and Human Culture. New York: Vintage, 1998.

Wisdom, John. Paradox and Discovery. Oxford: Blackwell, 1965.

Wittgenstein, Ludwig. The Blue and Brown Books. Oxford: Blackwell, 1958. Originally dictated in 1933–35.

———. Lectures and Conversations on Aesthetics, Psychology, and Religious Belief. Edited by Cyril Barrett. Oxford: Blackwell, 1966. Notes taken between 1938 and 1946.

———. On Certainty. Edited by G. E. M. Anscombe and G. H. von Wright. Translated by Denis Paul and G. E. M. Anscombe. Oxford: Blackwell, 1969. Originally in German.

———. Philosophical Investigations. Translated by G. E. M. Anscombe. Oxford: Blackwell, 1953.

———. Philosophical Remarks. 1929–30. Translated by Raymond Hargreaves and Roger White. Oxford: Blackwell, 1975. Remarks written in German in 1929–30.

Wolfe, Cary. Critical Environments: Postmodern Theory and the Pragmatics of the "Outside." Minneapolis: University of Minnesota Press, 1998.

———. "In the Shadow of Wittgenstein's Lion: Language, Ethics, and the Question of the Animal." In Animal Rites: American Culture, the Discourse of Species, and Posthumanist Theory, 44–94. Chicago: University of Chicago Press, 2003.

Wood, David. "Comment ne pas manger—Deconstruction and Humanism." In Animal Others: On Ethics, Ontology, and Animal Life, edited by H. Peter Steeves, 15–35. New York: State University of New York Press, 1999.

Wood, J. G. Bible Animals: Being a Description of Every Living Creature Mentioned in the Scriptures, from the Ape to the Coral. New ed. London: Longmans, Green, 1884.

Xenophanes. Xenophanes of Colophon: Fragments. Translated by James Lesher. Toronto: University of Toronto Press, 1992.

Publication History and Permissions

Portions of chapter 1 were originally published in a slightly different form in "Like Water in Water," *Journal for Cultural Research* 9, no. 3 (July 2005): 265–79. Reprinted by permission of Routledge / Taylor and Francis.

Portions of chapter 1 were originally published in a slightly different form in "If Horses Had Hands . . . ," *Society and Animals* 11, no. 3 (2003): 267–81. A revised version appears in *Animal Encounters*, ed. Tom Tyler and Manuela Rossini (Leiden: Brill, 2009), 13–26. Used by permission of Brill.

Portions of chapter 1 were originally published in a slightly different form in "The Quiescent Ass and the Dumbstruck Wolf," *Configurations* 14, nos. 1–2 (Winter–Spring 2006): 9–28. Used by permission of The Johns Hopkins University Press.

Portions of chapters 1 and 3 were originally published in a slightly different form in "Quia Ego Nominor Leo: Barthes, Stereotypes, and Aesop's Animals," *Mosaic* 40, no. 1 (March 2007): 45–59. Used by permission of Mosaic.

Portions of chapters 2, 3, and 4 were originally published in a slightly different form in "Snakes, Skins, and the Sphinx: Nietzsche's Ecdysis," *Journal of Visual Culture* 5, no. 3 (December 2006): 365–85. Used by permission of Sage Publications.

Portions of chapter 5 were originally published in a slightly different form in "The Rule of Thumb," *JAC* 30, nos. 3–4 (2010): 711–32.

Portions of chapter 5 were originally published in a slightly different form in "Four Hands Good, Two Hands Bad," *Parallax* 12, no. 1 (January 2006): 69–80. A revised version appears in *Kafka's Creatures: Animals, Hybrids, and Other Fantastic Beings*, edited by Marc Lucht and Donna Yarri, 175–89 (Lanham, Md.: Rowman and Littlefield, 2010). Used by permission of Routledge / Taylor and Francis.

English translation of Xenophanes's Fragment 15 first appeared in *Xenophanes of Colophon: Fragments*, trans. James Lesher (Toronto: University of Toronto Press, 2001), 25. Reprinted with permission of the publisher.

Figure 78 (Galápagos Tortoise). Photo by Rob Kroenert.

Figure 83 (Tit). Photograph by Daniel Powderhill, 2009.

Figure 88 (Black Bear). Photograph copyright 2010 by Darren Darbyshire.

Figures 89 (Australopithecus) and 90 (Handy Man). Copyright by Viktor Deak.

Figures 93 (Acanthostega) and 94 (Ichthyostega). Images courtesy of Mike Coates.

Figure 95 (Gorilla). Used by permission of The Dian Fossey Gorilla Fund International, www.gorillafund .org.

Lyrics in the caption for Figure 96 (Orangutan) "I Wan'na Be Like You" ("The Monkey Song"). From Walt Disney's *The Jungle Book*. Words and music by Richard M. Sherman and Robert B. Sherman. Copyright 1966 Wonderland Music Company, Inc. Copyright renewed. All rights reserved. Used by permission. Reprinted by permission of Hal Leonard Corporation.

Figure 99 (Bonobo). Photograph of Kanzi used by permission of the Great Ape Trust.

Index

Bold page numbers indicate one of the CI FERAE.

Dedicated to the countless wild animals who,
though accustomed to freedom by nature,
have been MANSUEFACTA, and are therefore
no longer driven by their own wishes,
nor are able to wander hither and thither,
wherever the spirit will lead them

TOM TYLER is senior lecturer in philosophy
and culture at Oxford Brookes University in Oxford, U.K.
He is coeditor of *Animal Encounters*.

Ciferae was designed and typeset by Judy Gilats in St. Paul, Minnesota.
The text type is Seria and the display face is Eureka Sans.

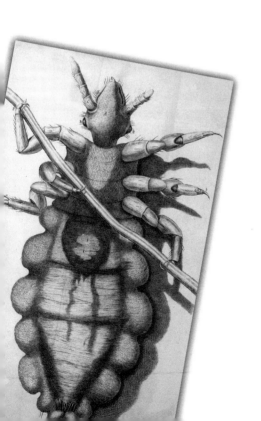